THE APOSTOLIC AROUND-THE-WORLD JOURNEY OF DAVID O. McKAY, 1920–1921

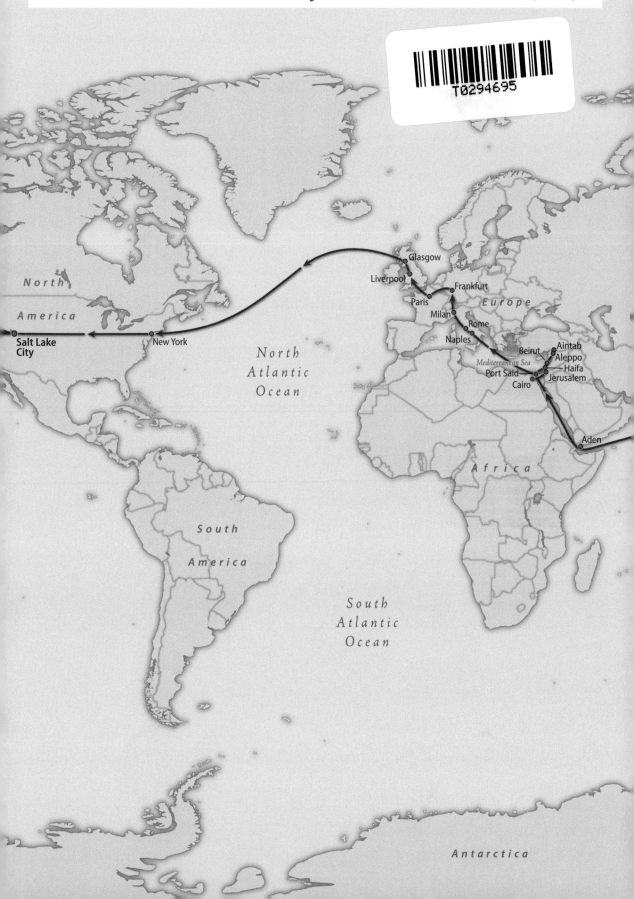

T0294695

To the Peripheries of Mormondom

To the Peripheries of Mormondom

The Apostolic Around-the-World Journey of David O. McKay, 1920–1921

Hugh J. Cannon

EDITED BY

Reid L. Neilson

The University of Utah Press | Salt Lake City

The Defiance House Man colophon is a registered trademark
of The University of Utah Press. It is based upon a four-foot-
tall, Ancient Puebloan pictograph (late PIII) near Glen Canyon,
Utah.

15 14 13 12 11   1 2 3 4 5

Library of Congress Cataloging-in-Publication Data

Cannon, Hugh J. (Hugh Jenne), 1870–1931, author.
To the peripheries of Mormondom : the apostolic around-the-world jour-
ney of David O. McKay, 1920–1921 / Hugh J. Cannon ; edited by Reid L.
Neilson.
        pages   cm
Includes bibliographical references and index.
ISBN 978-1-60781-010-0 (cloth : alk. paper)
1. Church of Jesus Christ of Latter-day Saints—Missions.
2. McKay, David O. (David Oman), 1873–1970—Travel.
3. Cannon, Hugh J. (Hugh Jenne), 1870–1931—Travel.
I. Neilson, Reid Larkin, 1972–   editor.
II. Title.
BX8661.C36 2011
266′.93—dc22
2011010295

All photographs are from the LDS Church History Library collection.
Used by permission.

Printed and bound by Sheridan Books, Inc., Ann Arbor, Michigan.

to

Sarah Richards Cannon

and

Emma Ray McKay

contents

Editor's Preface   ix
Introduction: Around the World with Elder
    David O. McKay and Hugh J. Cannon,
    by Reid L. Neilson   xix
Photographic Essay   xxxiii

chapter 1   Accepting the Apostolic Call   1

chapter 2   Crossing the Pacific Ocean   6

chapter 3   Arriving in the Islands of Japan   13

chapter 4   Touring the Japan Mission   19

chapter 5   Dedicating the Chinese Realm   25

chapter 6   Exploring the Interior of China   32

chapter 7   Visiting Oahu and Maui   39

chapter 8   Calling on Hawaii and Kauai   46

chapter 9   Steaming the South Pacific   53

chapter 10   Staying in the Society Islands   59

chapter 11   Sightseeing in Rarotonga   64

chapter 12   Discovering New Zealand   68

chapter 13   Meandering through Melanesia   76

chapter 14   Stopping over in Western Samoa   82

chapter 15   Resting in American Samoa   88

chapter 16   Surveying Sauniatu   95

chapter 17   Observing in Tonga   101

chapter 18   Returning to New Zealand   107

chapter 19   Inspecting Australia   112

chapter 20   Traveling up the Malay Peninsula   120

chapter 21   Investigating India   126

chapter 22   Wandering in Egypt   132

chapter 23   Worshiping in the Holy Land   139

chapter 24   Returning Home to Utah   147

chapter 25   Coming Full Circle   155

appendix 1   Chronology of LDS Missions Visited
                by Elder David O. McKay and Hugh J.
                Cannon, 1920–1921   159

appendix 2   List of Hugh J. Cannon's *Deseret News*
                "Around the World" Articles, 1920–1922   164

appendix 3   List of Elder David O. McKay's Diaries,
                Conference Notebooks, and Family
                Correspondence, 1920–1921   166

                Notes   169
                Bibliography   233
                Index   239

The year-long fact-finding mission (1920–1921) of Elder David O. McKay of the Quorum of the Twelve Apostles to the Pacific basin frontier[1] was one of the most important twentieth-century moments for The Church of Jesus Christ of Latter-day Saints. Prior to 1920, LDS apostles had only visited the Hawaiian and Japan missions, despite a Mormon presence throughout the Pacific region since the 1840s.[2] Now the First Presidency had charged McKay to visit the church's non–North American missions and congregations "to study their spiritual and, as far as possible, temporal needs, and to ascertain the effect of 'Mormonism' upon their lives."[3] As his biographers describe, McKay's apostolic tour "was a major first step toward comprehending that a worldwide church would consist of more than a series of copies of the Great Basin church."[4] The globalization of the church, not merely its international diaspora, traces its roots to his around-the-world journey in the early 1920s. Accordingly, McKay's traveling companion Hugh J. Cannon's account, showcased in this volume, is one of the more significant texts in the historical cannon of global Mormon studies.

Few Mormon historical figures have captured the attention, and commanded the respect, of church laity as David O. McKay (1873–1970), ninth president of the LDS Church. Born to European immigrant parents on September 8, 1873, in Huntsville, Utah, David was active in church and educational activities throughout his childhood and adolescence. He graduated as valedictorian from the University of Utah in 1897 and then served as a missionary in Scotland. Years later David married Emma Ray Riggs and began his career as an educator. In 1906 he was called to the apostleship and subsequently oversaw the church's entire educational enterprise. McKay was serving as church commissioner of education when the First Presidency instructed him to tour the non-American missions of the church. A General Authority for forty-five years, McKay eventually served as the president and public face of the church for nearly an additional two decades. During his administration, church membership exploded, the number of missionaries increased sixfold, and temples were built in the Pacific basin and Europe. In fact, President McKay regarded his efforts in transforming the LDS Church into a truly global religious organization one of his greatest presidential achievements.[5]

While a general awareness of President McKay and his global contributions continues to grow within the Mormon historical community, the same cannot be said of Hugh Jenne Cannon (1870–1931). Cannon was born on January 19, 1870, in Salt Lake City, to George Q. and Sarah Jane Jenne Cannon. Like his publisher father, Cannon worked in the printing business for much of his life: he served as editor of the Sunday School magazine as well as the church's *Improvement Era* periodical. His notable church service included a call to the German Mission as a young man, as well as twenty-seven years of service on the church's Sunday School board. From 1905 until 1923 he presided over the Liberty Stake, the largest stake (diocese) in the Salt Lake Valley. Cannon also accepted the awesome responsibility of accompanying McKay on a year-long fact-finding journey to the church's congregations, missions, and schools scattered throughout the Pacific world.[6]

Hugh J. Cannon's Manuscript

When the duo returned to Utah in December 1921, after traveling 61,646 miles (23,777 by land and 37,869 by water) around the globe, Cannon began crafting a book-length manuscript detailing their adventures based on his personal writings and reminiscences, as well as those of Elder McKay. Both men, however, were quickly subsumed into their former lives of church service. Cannon resumed his stake presidency responsibilities while McKay returned to his apostolic duties and church commissioner of education assignments. In 1925, LDS leaders called Cannon for a second term as president of the Swiss and German Mission. Following his honorable release in 1928, Cannon returned to Salt Lake City, where he served as associate and later managing editor of *The Improvement Era*. His writing project limped along in the meantime.

Nevertheless, McKay spurred his former traveling companion to complete his book manuscript.[7] While presiding over the European Mission, he wrote Cannon about the future publication of the volume: "I am sufficiently convinced of its importance to suggest that you and I assume jointly the responsibility of publishing that book."[8] But Cannon passed away without warning in 1931 at the age of sixty-one. McKay mourned his dear friend's passing and lamented that "the spiritual side of it [their journey] now may never be told because Brother Cannon was the one who could best tell it." He continued: "That is one of the many reasons why I say I wish that death had postponed this for many years, for he and I have sat together since coming home and have planned ways and means of getting some of these memorable experiences in which God's power was manifest beyond the question of a doubt." The apostle had hoped that their story's publication would increase the faith of the church's youth.[9] Now it seemed that their international adventure might never see the printed page.

Had it not been for the determination of Cannon's widow and children, his book would have died with him. Given his heavy church, family, and professional responsibilities, it is impressive that Cannon completed a relatively polished typescript draft—clearly intended for publication—during the decade between his return to Utah and his sudden death.[10] After her husband's passing, Sarah Richards Cannon, a former LDS magazine editor herself, lightly copyedited his manuscript. In 1951, three decades after McKay and Cannon completed their circumnavigation, and twenty years following Cannon's death, Sarah and her children set out to posthumously publish his manuscript as a book. Months earlier McKay had become the ninth president of the church, following the passing of George Albert Smith. Perhaps Cannon's family felt the timing was now right.

Sarah and her son, George, met with A. Hamer Reiser, longtime general manager of the Deseret Book Company, in hopes of securing a book publication contract that fall. Their meeting, however, took place during a time of transition at the church's publishing arm; several months earlier, Reiser had tendered his resignation so that he could enter into an auto business partnership with his son-in-law in Idaho. Reiser continued his managerial duties, including manuscript acquisitions, until the board of directors selected Alvary H. Parry, a Zions Cooperative Mercantile Institution employee, as his successor on November 12, 1951.[11] It is easy to imagine that the Cannon family's proposal suffered due to its ill timing. To his credit, Reiser agreed to read the 218-page typescript manuscript, despite the pressing demands of relocating his family and professional life to a new state that same month. He was also sensitive to the fact that the submission was a pet project of his church's new president, and he was aware of the longtime family connections of both the Cannons and Richardses in Salt Lake religious, social, and professional circles.

Finding himself between a rock and a hard place—Reiser did not feel that the manuscript warranted a book, but he did not want to upset his religious leader or disappoint the Cannon family—he judiciously deferred to the judgment of President McKay. In a letter dated November 6, 1951, Reiser offered his appraisal of the Cannon manuscript. After reviewing its provenance he noted to President McKay: "I have read this manuscript with very great interest. . . . There is a new timeliness in much of this material especially that which relates to China, Korea and Japan," now that the church once again had members and missionaries in East Asia following World War II.[12] While Reiser acknowledged that the document offered "much valuable faith-promoting inspiration"[13] and that "Cannon had a choice gift of language," he was concerned that the narrative was "written in such a way as to 'date it.'" He recommended that Deseret Book pass on the proposed book. Reiser instead suggested serially publishing various chapters of the narrative in the *Instructor* periodical, also printed by the LDS press. If readers clamored for Cannon's entire story, then his successor could revisit publication options.

Reiser sent a copy of his letter to the Cannon family. While the manuscript's timing may have played a minor role, content and style ultimately thwarted its publication by Deseret Book. One week later, a disappointed George Cannon, on behalf of his mother and siblings, responded to Reiser's proposal: "We feel as you do that the final decision as to what should be done with this manuscript should be left completely up to President McKay."[14] He also sent a copy of his response to President McKay, reiterating his family's stance that he, as the church's president, should determine the proposed book's future. While they were agreeable to having some of the chapters serialized in the *Instructor*, the Cannons expressed their feelings that perhaps the church-owned *Era* or *Church News* periodicals, given their larger readership, might be more suitable publication venues.[15]

During the first week of December 1951, President McKay wrote to George Cannon about Reiser's recommendations stating: "I believe Brother Reiser's suggestion to publish it first in serial form in the *Instructor* is worthy of careful consideration."[16] McKay graciously offered to write a foreword if the typescript ever evolved into a book after its serial publication. Resigned to the fact that neither Reiser nor President McKay were championing the project as anticipated, the Cannons told Reiser that they would be agreeable to having various chapters published in the *Instructor* as Reiser had originally proposed, "as a means of checking its value for publication in book form," and amiably offered to help throughout the editorial and printing stages.[17] No doubt saddened, the Cannons graciously determined to make the best of the situation.

Hugh J. Cannon's widow and children were patient and cordial through the entire process, despite the fact that they were likely frustrated that a book was not forthcoming. The following February, George Cannon again wrote to Reiser, now living in Buhl, Idaho, to ensure that his late father's manuscript survived the management change at Deseret Book. He and his family were understandably concerned that it might fall through the cracks. Moreover, the Cannons were still curious as to how the editors of the *Instructor* were planning to proceed with the serial publication of the individual chapters, as they had still not heard from anyone on the matter.[18] Reiser, still on the company's board of directors, patiently responded to the letter, assuring the family that his successor would be in contact to discuss the project and that the two copies the family had submitted to Deseret Book were in good hands. He had personally passed along one copy of the manuscript to Elder Richard E. Folland, managing editor of the *Instructor*, before Reiser moved to Idaho. Folland would be in touch about it being published serially in the coming months, Reiser promised.[19]

It is unclear what happened to the manuscript after it was passed over for publication by Deseret Book. Three facts are plain, however. First, someone deposited a photocopy of the complete typescript at the Historian's Office, known today as the Church History Library of The Church of Jesus Christ of Latter-day Saints in Salt Lake City. It has been available to researchers for decades on microfilm.[20] Second, chapters of the manuscript were never serialized in the *Instructor* or any other church periodical.[21] Third, the Cannon family never lost hope. Five decades later, Hugh's children again determined to publish their father's long-awaited book. Just months before LDS Church members concluded their year-long study (2005) of President McKay's life and teachings, George, Alice, Max, and Dean, then in their eighties, finally saw their father's book come off a commercial press.[22] They subsequently donated the original typescript to the Church History Library. And so the story continues.

Editorial Procedures

Knowing of the richness and historical importance of Hugh J. Cannon's account, I met with the Cannon family and received their blessing to produce this scholarly edition of their father's typescript account. Given the University of Utah Press's recent scholarly contributions and commercial successes with Gregory A. Prince and William Robert Wright's *David O. McKay and the Rise of Modern Mormonism* and Mary Jane Woodger's *Heart Petals:*

The Personal Correspondence of David Oman McKay to Emma Ray McKay,[23] I was hopeful that it might also publish this President McKay–related gem. When I approached Peter DeLafosse, Utah's acquisitions editor, about the possibility of reproducing Cannon's account, he encouraged me to seek ways to add value to the type-script. How could I make the text more accessible to scholars and laypersons alike? What could I do that would be different from what the Cannon family had already done? With the backing of his press I rolled up my sleeves and got to work.

As I suggested at the beginning of this preface, histories have their own histories. Therefore, it is important for me as the editor and you as the reader to be aware of the "rest of the story" for reasons beyond historical curiosity. Understanding the provenance of Cannon's typescript helped me as editor best determine how to edit, annotate, and lay out the original text; the typescript's history aids me in the retelling of the two men's experiences. Fortunately, I am in possession of a relatively clean draft, with few notations beyond standard editorial marks. The extant draft is a two-volume, 218-page double-spaced typescript divided into twenty-five unnamed chapters. Knowing that Cannon, before he unexpectedly died, was in the final stages of preparing his manuscript for publication encouraged me to edit his text differently than if it were a holographic manuscript still in the formative stage with extensive notes and revisions. Cannon was an editor and therefore a stickler for good prose and grammar.[24]

Accordingly, I have silently fixed general typographical errors, corrected spelling, made minor grammatical changes, modernized punctuation, and standardized capitalization. This editorial work was done in accordance with *Merriam-Webster's Collegiate Dictionary* (10th edition), *Merriam-Webster's Geographical Dictionary* (3rd edition), *The Chicago Manual of Style* (15th edition), and the *Style Guide for Publications of The Church of Jesus Christ of Latter-day Saints* (3rd edition). I have made no material changes to the text, except for adding descriptive chapter titles (Cannon selected the chapter epigraphs). I have consciously not employed the typical editing apparatus. But I have used the following editorial devices to make the narrative more accessible to readers. Whenever a measurement appears in the text, I have provided the metric equivalent in Arabic numerals, up to two decimal points, and abbreviated metric measurements in brackets. For ease of identification, I have supplied or completed personal names in brackets the first time each appears in a chapter.[25] Scholars desiring to view Cannon's final typescript, including his and his wife's handwritten notations, can access a microfilm copy at the Church History Library.

McKay and Cannon met countless persons during their year-long journey. They encountered Americans, Australians, Chinese,

Egyptians, Europeans, Fijians, Hawaiians, Indians, Japanese, Malaysians, Maoris, Palestinians, Samoans, Syrians, Tahitians, and Tongans as they crossed national and cultural boundaries. I attempted, and nearly succeeded, in identifying all of the men and women Cannon specifically referenced in his manuscript. But I only include those individuals whose names are in the text; if someone is merely referred to, such as the son or daughter of so-and-so, I simply provide his or her full name in a note. I identify both men and women by their complete married names.[26]

The traveling duo also traversed national and cartographic boundaries on numerous occasions. I have therefore tried to identify all of the places and geographical features Cannon expressly mentions in his narrative. As some of the place names have changed since the 1920s, I have added the modern equivalents in brackets. For example, Peking is now Beijing, Aintab is now Gaziantep, and Van Diemen's Land is now Tasmania. The world map found on the endpapers, showing East Asia, Australasia, South Asia, the Hawaiian Islands, South Pacific, Middle East, and Europe, should help readers orient themselves as they travel along with McKay and Cannon.

Unlike some historical projects in which the historian laments the paucity of sources, I faced the opposite problem in documenting the McKay-Cannon journey; there is an abundance of material, various versions of the same events, and a mixture of voices in scattered documents, in addition to the book typescript featured in this volume. To begin with, Cannon wrote several dozen letters for the church's *Deseret News*, detailing events as they happened. He then mailed these missives back to Utah, where they were serially published to the delight of church members, most of whom would never venture beyond the borders of the United States in their lifetimes. I have included a complete list of these letters and their publication dates for interested researchers (see appendix 2).

McKay's diaries, available in typescript at the University of Utah, number hundreds of single-spaced pages for this period alone. He wrote several paragraphs and even pages on a nearly daily basis for the entire year (see appendix 3).[27] In addition to McKay's journal travelogue, I also have access to some of the letters the apostle wrote and received during this time period. Perhaps the most important and revealing epistles are the nineteen extant letters he mailed to his wife, Emma Ray, and his children (see appendix 3).[28] I also have culled the miscellaneous articles that McKay wrote for church periodicals, newspapers, etc.[29] Finally, I have McKay's after-the-fact published reminiscences in several volumes, collected and published by his children, church associates, and scholars.[30] The sheer volume of these contemporary accounts prevented me from constantly cross-referencing them to the Cannon manuscript, with important exceptions found in the chapter endnotes. My focus in this volume is the Cannon account.

In my effort to create a rich and complete representation of the McKay-Cannon world journey, I became convinced that I must include dozens of images from their travels. So I was delighted when I happened upon an uncataloged box in the bowels of the Church History Library of hundreds of photographs, photo albums, post cards, and lantern slides chronicling their journey. Much like the photographers who captured on film the frontier of an expanding America, McKay and Cannon sought to document their church's effort to understand the world beyond the Great Basin. The traveling partners, along with the many isolated Latter-day Saints they met as they circumnavigated the globe, sought to record their experiences abroad on behalf of the First Presidency, by writing daily in their journals, drafting and mailing letters to their friends and families back in Utah, and collecting hundreds of snapshots. The traveling duo desperately wanted to help those at home vicariously experience their high adventure abroad. When McKay returned to Utah he transferred hundreds of photographs and postcards from his adventure onto 3¼ × 4¼ inch glass "magic lantern" slides, which he then used to illustrate his globetrotting stories to family, friends, and church members, much like we use PowerPoint presentations to showcase our travels in the twenty-first century.[31] With the help of Church History Library photo archivist William G. Slaughter, I carefully selected dozens of photographs and created numerous illustrations to better entice readers to "come along with us travelers to foreign lands," as Cannon earlier beckoned.

Acknowledgments

The children of the late Hugh J. and Sarah Cannon—George, Alice, Max, and Dean—are to be commended for their diligence in persevering to publish their father's remarkable account. They have done great honor to their family legacy. They are also to be thanked for their willingness to share with me a photocopy of the typescript as well as an electronic version, typed by Katrina Cannon, of the entire work. While they are not responsible for my interpretation of this significant chapter in the budding globalization of the church, they generously gave their blessing to this project, desirous of sharing their father's story with multiple audiences. Max and Dean were especially helpful during the early stages of my work.

I also wish to thank the librarians and staff of the following repositories: the L. Tom Perry Special Collections, the BYU Family History Library, and the Harold B. Lee Library at Brigham Young University; the Church History Library and Family History Library of The Church of Jesus Christ of Latter-day Saints; the Special Collections and the J. Willard Marriott Library at the University of Utah; the Special Collections and Archives at Utah State University; and the Research Library and Collections at the Utah State Historical Society. All of these facilities and their personnel provided valuable assistance. I would also like to thank my editorial assistant Elizabeth Pinborough for her work.

Many thanks to the officers of the Mormon History Association and its 2007 meeting committee for providing me, along with William G. Slaughter, Peter DeLafosse, and Gregory A. Prince, the opportunity to share our prepublication findings with the larger historical community. In a session titled "Chronicling the Peoples and Places of the Pacific: Telling the Travel Story of David O. McKay through Print, Photographs, and Papers," the four of us discussed and debated the importance and legacy of the McKay-Cannon journey with our Salt Lake City audience.

I am grateful to Peter DeLafosse, my acquisitions editor at the University of Utah Press, who has breathed new life into Utah's Mormon Studies booklist and championed works beyond the traditional LDS narrative, including those that detail the international expansion of the church. And the Religious Studies Center at Brigham Young University provided a generous subvention to help defray publication costs. Lastly, I express gratitude to my wife, Shelly, for her support and encouragement while I retraced and chronicled the experiences of McKay and Cannon, some eighty-five years after the fact. She makes our own global adventures worthwhile.

Reid L. Neilson
Bountiful, Utah

Around the World with Elder David O. McKay and Hugh J. Cannon

Reid L. Neilson

The two church officials will study not only conditions in the L.D.S. colonies in each of the islands groups, with regard to physical needs, missionary meeting places and spiritual affairs, but will also make a study of the customs and needs of the people in general at each place visited.

—*Deseret News*, 1920[1]

During this trip which required 366 days, the missionaries traveled on 24 ocean-going vessels. They spent the equal of 153 days on the water, traveled a total of 61,646 miles not counting trips made by auto, streetcars, tugs, ferry boats, horseback, camels, etc. Of the miles traveled, 23,777 were by land and 37,869 were by water.

—Hugh J. Cannon, 1921[2]

"No pen can portray the joy of isolated church members upon learning that a visit from one of the Twelve might be anticipated," stake president Hugh J. Cannon reminisced of his ecclesiastical expedition with Elder David O. McKay of the Quorum of the Twelve Apostles. "Should a prophet in one of our communities today announce that Peter, senior Apostle of our Lord, would appear in person on the following Sunday and address and greet the people, their anticipation could not exceed that of Latter-day Saints residing in remote missions upon learning of Brother McKay's appointment."[3] Cannon was speaking from personal experience; for an entire year he accompanied McKay over sea and land, riding nearly every form of transportation then known to man, to the edges of Mormondom, on behalf of The Church of Jesus Christ of Latter-day Saints. It is clear from the extensive personal writings of McKay and Cannon—as well as records of visited church members scattered on the Mormon periphery—that the traveling duo viewed themselves as latter-day counterparts to early Christian evangelists, like the Apostle Paul and his traveling companion Timothy. McKay and Cannon sought to recapitulate the Acts of their New Testament brethren in the modern age.[4]

Historians, as well as McKay and Cannon family members, have told the basic story of the duo's year-long global circumnavigation, so there is little need to rehearse it here.[5] Instead, the first purpose of this introductory essay is to shed new light on the genesis of their 1921 fact-finding mission. According to the traditional narrative, church president Heber J. Grant called McKay out of the blue to survey the church's Pacific missions and schools, as well as to potentially dedicate China for LDS evangelization. In other words, the fact-finding mission originated in the center of Mormondom and eventually encompassed the borderlands of the church's congregants and colonies. Drawing upon missionary letters, journals, and papers that criss-crossed the Pacific Ocean between America and Asia, however, I will make the case that Joseph H. Stimpson, president of the Japan Mission, acted as an important catalyst in the initiation of McKay and Cannon's circumnavigation of the globe to visit the church's far-flung congregations in 1921. Stimpson's continual pleadings for a general authority to visit his mission helped spur Utah church leaders into action. No historian has explored Stimpson's connection to this historical moment in global church history.

November 1918 marked both the end of World War I and the death of church president Joseph F. Smith. Following precedent, Heber J. Grant, the senior member of the Quorum of the Twelve Apostles, assumed the office of church president. LDS mission presidents stationed around the world began to anticipate a resurgence in evangelization activity and an increased need for personnel. Joseph H. Stimpson, then president of the Japan Mission, was hopeful that more missionaries would be sent his way now that mission-aged men were no longer being drafted into the military following World War I. "We have hopes for some new missionaries but that is all," he wrote to missionary Lafayette C. Lee serving in Sapporo, Japan in 1919. "As yet we have heard nothing that will indicate how soon they will be fulfilled. I hope they will transfer one of the Mormon regiments from France over here in a body. I do not suppose they will need their arms though. We need the numbers however."[6] He likewise pleaded to administrator Harold G. Reynolds at church headquarters: "What we need worst of all is a few more missionaries. . . . [W]e have not had any for over a year now." Laboring under the false assumption that the number of available missionaries had declined far below actual numbers, Stimpson continued: "I realize the unsettled condition of the world has made it impossible to send missionaries out but now peace is restored I hope you will do what you can to get our mission fitted up."[7] But Stimpson's plea for reinforcements went unheeded; authorities did not allocate a single missionary to Japan in 1919. What is more, between 1915 and 1919 the Japan Mission was assigned only fourteen new missionaries out of a total of 3,432 allocated worldwide. While it was certainly possible for church leaders to send more missionaries to Japan, they continued to choose a different course before, during, and after World War I.[8]

By 1920, Stimpson felt isolated and forgotten as the only Mormon mission president in Asia. But he reasoned that if he could convince a general authority to visit Japan and tour his mission that other church leaders would start paying attention and send more elders and sisters.[9] As his entreaties continued to fall on deaf ears, he became more assertive. "Just at the present time there is nothing that we would like more than a visit from some of the general authorities of the Church to see the work being done in Japan and to look over our books and give us some suggestions as to better methods in keeping them," he wrote to the presiding bishopric in January 1920.[10] Stimpson's request seems reasonable, given that no general authority had visited Japan in seventeen years, the first and only being Elder Heber J. Grant. Moreover, no LDS leader had ever visited any of the church's Pacific missions, except for Hawaii. In contrast, many of the North American and European missions were presided over by, or at least visited by, general authorities on a regular basis. Stimpson's counterparts in North America were also able to return to Salt Lake City each spring and fall for the church's general conferences, whereas he could only communicate with church leaders through letters or cablegrams. By 1920 the president of the Japan Mission had not spoken with a general authority in almost five years.

Out of desperation, Stimpson finally sent a pleading missive to one of his former teachers at the Weber Academy in Ogden, Utah, Elder David O. McKay.[11] He informed McKay, who was then serving as the general superintendent of the LDS Deseret Sunday School Union, that the World's Eighth Sunday School Convention, an annual Protestant gathering, was scheduled to be held in Tokyo that October. Would the apostle want to represent the church and tour the mission at the same time? Stimpson suggested that a personal visit by a presiding church officer would pay two major dividends. First, a well-respected firsthand observer could report back "the true condition of the mission to the people in Zion in general and the Authorities in particular and result in a closer co-operation." Second, a general authority could "give an added testimony" and important instructions to the Japanese saints, which would act as a "great incentive for more diligent effort on their part." Then he shed all pretenses: "If we could use the Sunday

School Convention as sort of an excuse for getting some member of the General Board even, if not a member of the Council of the Twelve to come to Japan and see our conditions, . . . it would be of untold value to the work we are doing here in the Orient." To underscore the gravity of the situation in Japan he added: "We have so few missionaries here in the mission at the present time that the devil has to look elsewhere for a workshop."[12] Nevertheless, McKay informed Stimpson that he would be unable to attend the Tokyo convention due to other pressing duties.

Rebuffed by McKay, Stimpson made an even bolder attempt on behalf of his mission that same summer. He invited President Heber J. Grant to return and tour his former Japanese mission field. The mission president also vented his frustrations, specifically the disheartening gossip about his mission that was swirling on both sides of the Pacific. He confided that he was heartsick to hear rumors that church leaders were ready to close down the Japan Mission and that no more missionaries would be sent. While he claimed he did not believe the gossip, he still wondered why his mission seemed to be the First Presidency's lowest priority.[13] President Grant and his counselors responded to Stimpson's letter and attempted to quash the reports in late July 1920. "We were amused to read of the fact that there were no more missionaries to be sent to Japan and that the Mission was to be closed, etc., all of which is news to us," the First Presidency clarified. "There is an old saying that you have to go away from home to learn news. The very fact that you have recently received new missionaries ought to be a complete refutation of the suggestion that we desire to close up the Japan Mission. You were correct in thinking that these statements were nothing more than the imagination of some people who were uninformed." They added that Stimpson's suggestion, that general authorities tour the Japan mission, had their thoughtful consideration. "We believe that such a visit would do an immense amount of good, but the Apostles of course are engaged all the time."[14] Over the next several months President Grant and his advisors seemingly debated Stimpson's proposal.

In addition to Stimpson's constant cajoling, there were historical precedents for church leaders to call someone on an international intelligence-gathering mission in 1920.[15] In early May 1895—twenty-five years earlier—the First Presidency set apart Assistant Church Historian Andrew Jenson for a special mission to visit all of the church's missions around the world to gather historical materials, just as he had done for all of the church's stakes in the United States and Canada. Jenson departed from Salt Lake City days later and did not return until June 1897, two years and one month later. He toured the following countries, groups of islands, and states (in chronological order): the Hawaiian Islands, Fiji, Tonga, Samoa, New Zealand, The Cook Islands, The Society Islands, The Tuamotu Islands, Australia, Ceylon (Sri Lanka), Egypt, Syria, Palestine, Italy, France, Denmark, Norway, Sweden, Prussia, Hannover, Saxony, Bavaria, Switzerland, the Netherlands, England, Wales, Ireland, and Scotland. Jenson traveled 53,820 miles by a variety of steamships, sailing vessels, and small boats; trains; carriages and other animal-drawn vehicles; jinrikshas pulled by humans; and horses, donkeys, and camels. He became the first church member to visit all of the existing international missionary fields.[16]

Moreover, in an April 1896 meeting of the Quorum of the Twelve Apostles, Elder Francis M. Lyman proposed that at least one apostle should annually visit each of the church's non–North American missions. "He favored a trip around the world at least once a year by one of the Apostles. He felt the Apostles should be in a position from personal knowledge through visiting our missions to be able to report their condition correctly to the Presidency of the Church," one attendee noted.[17] Five years later junior apostle Heber J. Grant contemplated touring the missions of the Pacific on several occasions, including while serving in Japan as mission president between 1901 and 1903.[18] The First Presidency also encouraged and financed an exploratory tour of China by two enterprising missionaries—Alma O. Taylor and Frederick Caine—on their way home from Japan in 1910 to determine whether or not they should resume the evangelization of the Chinese, which they later advised against.[19]

Seemingly wearied and intrigued by Stimpson's incessant inquiries, the First Presidency determined in 1920 to send a general authority around the world to observe postwar church conditions, especially in Japan. President Grant and his counselors realized that it was critical that church leaders have a clear understanding of where they should allocate their rebounding evangelistic resources as missionaries were again able to procure foreign visas throughout most of the world. It was at this juncture that President Grant assigned McKay to tour the church's evangelical outposts in Japan, Hawaii, New Zealand, Australia, Samoa, Tonga, Tahiti, and possibly South Africa, the British Isles, the Netherlands, Scandinavia, and Germany. The junior apostle was caught by surprise; he was in the process of moving from Ogden to Salt Lake City. Still, McKay agreed to go and spent that evening with William C. Spence, the church's travel agent, planning his route. The headline "Two Church Workers Will Tour Missions of Pacific Islands" ran the following day in the *Deseret News*. In the accompanying article President Grant announced the forthcoming mission of McKay and Hugh J. Cannon, president of the Liberty Stake. "He [McKay] will make a general survey of the missions, study conditions there, gather data concerning them, and in short, obtain general information in order that there may be some one in the deliberations of the First Presidency and the Council of the Twelve thoroughly familiar with actual conditions."[20] The First Presidency immediately wrote to Stimpson that McKay would soon be on his way to tour the Japan Mission, as well as the other LDS outposts in the Pacific.[21] Stimpson was understandably delighted by the pending apostolic tour.[22]

The second purpose of this essay is to explore how McKay and Cannon's journey was impacted by uneven technologies, especially transportation and communication options, and how these two factors helped enlarge McKay's heretofore provincial worldview into a more cosmopolitan outlook. Just days before Christmas 1920, McKay and Cannon said tender goodbyes to their families, especially to their wives—Emma Ray and Sarah—who were both recovering from recent childbirth. Over the next 366 days, these two husbands and fathers visited the isles of the Pacific, the capitals of Asia, the nations down under, the cities of India, the sacred sites of the Holy Land, and the metropolises of Europe. In his colorful memoir of the journey, Cannon encouraged his readers to imagine themselves as traveling companions. "Come with us, therefore, on our trip around the world," he invited. "If you join us in our experiences, you will sail tempestuous, also placid seas, many of them terrifying, others dreamy and restful. You will go into strange lands, some, comparatively, not yet out of their swaddling clothes, others falling into senility."[23] Not surprisingly, McKay and Cannon both returned to Utah changed men in terms of how they saw the world and the Utah-based church. From an LDS perspective, McKay and Cannon's travelogues demonstrate how extensive international travel impacted church leaders and their administrations in the twentieth century. Just as mission president Stimpson's realities in Japan acted as a catalyst for the commissioning of an around-the-world apostolic tour, the resulting fact-finding mission by McKay and Cannon was one of the mechanisms that helped the church begin to move beyond its American birthplace and traditional borders to an international setting.

As one reads McKay and Cannon's memoirs, one's memory is taxed trying to keep track of the hundreds of social, religious, political, geographical, temporal, and linguistic borders they crossed on an almost daily basis on behalf of the LDS Church over a single year. One is struck by the way their global travels were impacted by the unevenness of the age's transportation and communication technologies. McKay and Cannon did not enjoy the comfort of jumbo-jet transport, a luxury taken for granted in the twenty-first century. While primitive automobiles were available in several of the missions they toured, they more often moved about on trains, streetcars, jinriksha, wagons, horseback, and camels, and even on foot. Perhaps even more jarring to present-day readers of their experiences is their lack of communication connectivity with their families, friends, and ecclesiastical sponsors in Utah. Modern conveniences like email, the Internet, instant messaging, and BlackBerry technology were still eight decades away from development. An occasional cable or telegraph line was all they had as they traversed a multitude of boundaries on the borderlands of the LDS Church.

Religious studies scholar Thomas A. Tweed argues that "terrestrial crossings vary according to the shifts in travel and communication technology."[24] There is no question that technology mediated the duo's international movements. A variety of modes of transportation and communication, as well as their own travel goals, affected the men's journey. Like many LDS leaders and laity, Cannon viewed technological progress as providential: God's hand was in the ongoing development of transportation and communication advances.[25] "How changed are world conditions since Joseph Smith's memorable prayer!" Cannon exclaimed, pointing out the many advances between 1830 (LDS Church's organization) and 1920 (fact-finding mission) that made such a journey feasible. "Inventions which have brought nations so close together, steamships, steam and electric railways, telegraph and telephone, flying machines, and radio were either wholly unknown or in their infancy. Did the effulgent light which accompanied Father and Son to this earth spread beyond the sacred grove in New York and inspire man to turn nature's laws to practical use?" Cannon queried. "Present day knowledge has not only stimulated desire to travel, but modern inventions have provided ways of gratifying that desire. The time had come to preach the Gospel in all the world, and necessity demanded improved means of communication."[26] Cannon and his peers believed that technology was advancing because of, and on behalf of, the restoration of the gospel. While outsiders might challenge the validity of Cannon's sentiments, few would question that mankind's ability to move about, and communicate across, the globe had improved by the early decades of the twentieth century.

There is no question that advances in transportation increased the mobility of the First Presidency's representatives. "Each technological change prompted increased, and transformed, contacts," Tweed notes of the impact of transit on transnational faiths.[27]

McKay and Cannon made their journey during a time of over-lapping and emerging technological advances. As such, the two men's travels were marked by technological steps forward and backward, depending on where they were. Cannon described the various modes of transportation they enjoyed—or endured—on the journey: "The missionaries traveled on 24 ocean-going vessels. They spent the equal of 153 days on the water, traveled a total of 61,646 miles not counting trips made by auto, streetcars, tugs, ferry boats, horseback, camels, etc. Of the miles traveled, 23,777 were by land and 37,869 were by water."[28] As Tweed rightly observes, "There is no simple linear progression in transportation technology in any region or across the globe, since multiple technologies co-exist at the same time."[29] McKay and Cannon experienced jarring shifts in transportation, transferring between cars and camels and from steamers to schooners.

Decades earlier, when the first LDS representatives crossed the globe's major oceans as emissaries, they relied on mercurial trade winds to whisk them to their destinations. In contrast, McKay and Cannon enjoyed the convenience and regularity of steam propulsion, for the most part, as they plied the seas. For the longer legs of the journey they traveled by large ocean steamers, the preferred mode of passenger travel in the early 1920s. But even the finest steamers still subjected passengers to debilitating seasickness. "Have you ever been aboard a vessel on an extremely rough sea?" Cannon asked his readers. "Have you felt it roll and toss and plunge, then when struck full force by a mighty wave which washes its decks, felt it shudder and tremble as though it had received a death blow and must assuredly sink? And all the while the stomachs of the sensitive passengers are performing similar evolutions and are dancing about as wildly as the ship itself."[30] On one occasion, while traveling by steamer up the eastern coast of Honshu, Japan, the two men were caught in a violent storm and the ship itself "began bucking after the fashion of a western bronco." Several of their party began throwing up violently. "President Stimpson's attention was called to the fact that he was losing his luggage," Cannon recalled. "He turned, and his face, a pitiful mixture of ashy gray and yellowish green, confirmed his words: 'My luggage isn't the only thing I'm losing.'"[31] While steamers had taken away the uncertainty of the winds, they were unable to inoculate passengers against the rolling of waves.

When McKay and Cannon arrived in Japan, their first mission visit, they experienced culture shock. By 1920, Japan had emerged on the international stage as a hybrid of traditional Asian and progressive European cultures through its efforts to adapt to, and take advantage of, the world's best technologies. "Here, too, one enters a new world. The people, themselves so different in features and dress from the Europeans, the buildings, temples, pagodas and shrines, rikishas drawn by fleet-footed youths, heavy wagons drawn by men or oxen or small horses or by a combination of all three, all were as unusual as if the stranger were indeed arriving on a heretofore unknown planet," Cannon wrote of their Asian advent. "But no! After running the gauntlet of custom officials he attempts to cross the street and is in grave danger of colliding with an intimate acquaintance—one might say a rattling good friend— a Ford automobile. One feels inclined to pick it up and hug it, such is the delight at seeing something so familiar."[32] McKay and Cannon continued to be fascinated by Japan's mixture of Occidental and Oriental cultures, including its transportation system. While both regarded Tokyo's trains, streetcars, automobiles, and water-craft to be excellent by Euro-American standards, they smiled at the novelty of the antiquated jinrikshas that transported them from the docks to the mission home.

But as McKay and Cannon continued their journey west from Tokyo to Peking [Beijing], via the Korean peninsula, they lamented the more primitive Korean transportation system. "Roads appear to consist mainly of foot paths and the transpor-tation of the country seems to be carried on the backs of cows and oxen," Cannon remembered. "Yonder an immense load of straw moved along the path without any visible means of loco-motion, but somewhere under the mass was a patient cow. At the same time the driver, trudging along on foot, had a huge load on his own back."[33] McKay and Cannon were even more under-whelmed with transit options in interior China. "Think of a city of a million inhabitants without a street car or omnibus line!" a disappointed Cannon noted of Peking. "The principal means of transportation—indeed the only means except for one's legs and an occasional auto or a small horse-drawn carriage at the time of this visit were the innumerable rikishas. These flit rapidly and silently through crowded streets, dexterously avoiding collisions which to the traveler appear wholly unavoidable and furnish an excellent opportunity of seeing Chinese life."[34] The same chaotic scene was repeated in Tianjin, a principal Chinese seaport and city with a population that exceeded one million at the time, which mainly relied on manual labor for transit.[35] The modernized port city of Shanghai, especially its transportation system, in contrast, was a welcomed treat. "There is an incongruous mixture of Occi-dental civilization and Oriental primitiveness in Shanghai," Can-non described. "Unlike Peking, the city has a street car system and other modern means of transportation. On some of the streets the visitor would think he was in Europe; on others not ten minutes distant he might easily imagine himself in the innermost heart of China."[36]

While in Samoa, McKay and Cannon enjoyed the luxury of traveling by horseback during their mission tour. "The trail over which they traveled skirted the seacoast, sometimes along sandy beaches, and occasionally over precipitous cliffs," one of them observed.[37] Still, they had it better than most of the native saints who customarily walked the twenty miles between Apia and Sauniatu.[38] Nevertheless, the two men were delighted to once again find Western transportation comforts in British-colonized Australia. Cars and trains were to be had everywhere; they typically traveled long distances by train, as the combined area of Australia measured about three million square miles. They did observe, however, that the Australian railroads were not entirely up to U.S. standards. "One of the incomprehensible blunders of this enterprising nation is the condition of the railroads. Each state is the owner of its own system, and almost without exception it has a different gauge from all others," Cannon noted in his travelogue. "The result is that the traveler is compelled to change cars frequently when traveling from place to place. This is inconvenient. But when one remembers that freight must also be transferred, one realizes what a needless cost is involved. It is said that freight from Perth in the extreme west to Sydney has to be transferred four times before finally reaching its destination."[39]

From Australia, McKay and Cannon traveled by train up the Malay Peninsula and then across the breadth of India. After riding a steamer from Bombay to the top of the Red Sea and the Egyptian coastline, they were struck and amused by the primitive transportation system of Cairo. In their minds, not much had improved since pharaohs walked the earth thousands of years earlier. As in Korea, where the locals transported goods on the backs of beasts of burden, the Egyptians likewise relied on camel labor. Cannon recalled that he and McKay "passed hundreds of donkeys and camels loaded with vegetables, fruits and other supplies for the city's markets. Indeed, almost everything—coal, brick, building stone and lumber—is carried on the backs of these patient beasts."[40] In keeping with tourist custom, both men hired a camel for a sightseeing trot around the pyramids of Giza. "To ride a camel is in itself a novel experience," one of them observed. "At a word of command from their driver they lie down while the riders mount; at another word they arise, cow-like, on their hind legs first, and unless the rider exercises care he will be precipitated over the animal's head."[41] The duo sitting atop camels in front of the famed Sphinx made for quite a photograph. For better or worse, transportation options fluctuated dramatically as they crossed cultural and national boundaries.

As fact-finding missionaries, McKay and Cannon noted what was needed in the various Pacific Mormon outposts. In several of the missions, unreliable and expensive transportation was a major issue. When they arrived in Tahiti, for example, the brethren saw the great need for the church to own its own ship to help transport missionaries and church members. Cannon noted that the purchase of a large schooner "would enable the elders to go to their fields without such extravagant waste of time and which with wise management might also enable the Church members to escape the traders, some of them unscrupulous, who call for their pearl shell and other products and pay just what they please for it."[42] Away from the comforts of Utah, both men became deeply empathetic to the transportation realities of LDS leaders and members scattered throughout the Pacific world. This crucial paradigm shift would not have occurred if the men had remained in the Intermountain West.

Advances in communication technologies likewise mediated the traveling experiences of the Mormon apostle and his traveling companion. "As with travel technology, multiple media forms have co-existed at the same time," Tweed suggests.[43] Mirroring their uneven transportation experiences, the two men endured various nations' uneven communications platforms as they circumnavigated the globe. For the most part they were only able to contact their families and church colleagues by letters, which often took weeks to reach their destinations. On several occasions they had access to telegraphs and cablegrams, but more often they lacked means of immediate communication with Utah for weeks at a time. Fast, reliable, and inexpensive communication to church headquarters and other Mormon outposts in the region had long been a problem for church leaders and members isolated on the Pacific Rim and in the scattered isles of the South Pacific. McKay and Cannon learned firsthand how difficult and frustrating communication could be under these circumstances.

When they arrived in French Polynesia, for example, the First Presidency's representatives expected to tour the Tahitian Mission with its president, L. H. Kennard. But they were shocked to learn that Kennard, who had not received word of the pending apostolic visit, had departed from mission headquarters three months previously to hold a conference on a distant island and had not been heard from since. McKay, who felt that he had been personally slighted on such an important visit, was worried and upset until the locals explained that this was how things worked in the islands, as there was no means of communication or transportation other than by ship. "There is no regular communication between the islands. The missionaries must travel on trading schooners which ply from one island to another at irregular intervals and must await their chance of finding a vessel which will bring them back to the starting place," Cannon explained to his North American readers, who likely struggled to appreciate how different life was in the South Pacific. "Not infrequently an elder after receiving his release is compelled to nurse his patience in a remote and isolated field for several months before he is able to find means of leaving for Mission headquarters, and the place of embarkation for home."[44] Two of the missionaries McKay and Cannon met at the Papeete docks had been waiting four months for a ship to transport them to their fields of labor. Another elder had already been released but could not find passage back to the ports of California.[45] There was nothing to do but wait. In subsequent years McKay was more empathetic to trials of mission presidents, missionaries, and church members scattered across the Pacific who were hamstrung by these communication and transportation limitations.

McKay and Cannon rejoiced when they were able to sporadically communicate with family and friends by cablegram and telegraph. While steaming across the Indian Ocean, McKay encouraged Cannon to send his eighty-two-year-old mother a "wireless message of love and congratulation" for her birthday, which he happily did. "This was done, and as the good woman was eating her breakfast on the morning of her birthday the words which had traversed thousands of miles of land and water, were delivered to her." He viewed this technology as miraculous saying, "In face of such wonders who will say the Almighty cannot hear the appeals of his children or even read the thoughts of their hearts?"[46] When McKay and Cannon arrived in New York, after crossing the Atlantic, they were thrilled to telegraph their loved ones in Utah. "During a large part of this tour, the men had been completely out of reach of their families. Any of their loved ones might have been dead for several weeks before word could have reached them. This in itself was sufficient cause for gratitude that they were again within telegraphic reach of home," Cannon reminisced.[47] Years into the twenty-first century, it is difficult to grasp and appreciate how asymmetrical international communication networks were in the early 1920s, and the stresses inherent in ecclesiastical administration in the borderlands of the LDS Church.

When McKay and Cannon returned to Utah in December 1921, both men were subsumed into their former lives. McKay returned to his apostolic duties and assignments as church commissioner of education, while Cannon resumed his stake presidency responsibilities. The duo was subsequently called to preside over separate foreign missionary operations during the 1920s: McKay over the European Mission and Cannon over the Swiss and German Mission. Sadly, Cannon passed away unexpectedly in 1931. McKay eventually served as the president and public face of Mormonism for nearly two decades. So what was the legacy of McKay and Cannon's journey to the Mormon peripheries?[48] How did their circumnavigation of the globe reshape their worldviews? Did their year-long journey impact how the church was later administered worldwide?

To begin with, the two church leaders accomplished a number of specific tasks requested by the First Presidency. McKay, for example, dedicated the Chinese realm for the preaching of the gospel in January 1921. Months later, the duo met up with Joseph Booth of the Armenian Mission to distribute church funds earmarked for humanitarian aid in the struggling region. Moreover, the church's governing body had also charged McKay with the "duty to study their spiritual and, as far as possible, temporal needs, and to ascertain the effect of 'Mormonism' upon the lives of the international Saints."[49] As they did so, both men gained a better understanding of the challenges facing the Pacific saints, especially the challenges of uneven transportation and communication technologies in scattered lands. McKay and Cannon came to appreciate that the needs of church members were different in various parts of the world.

Since the end of the nineteenth century, McKay's fellow church leaders had encouraged non–North American converts to remain in their native lands where they could build up the church. While traveling, McKay came to appreciate that if church members on the periphery were no longer expected to gather to "Zion" in Utah—where all of the church's services and programs were offered—then the church needed to provide these opportunities abroad. For example, while in Hawaii McKay was impressed to someday build a church school where the LDS youth of the Pacific could be spiritually and intellectually strengthened, like their counterparts in the Intermountain West. As church commissioner of education, McKay also returned to Utah with a laundry list of ways the church could and would improve its educational offerings in the Pacific basin. One of his early acts as church president was to institute the construction of the Church College of Hawaii, known today as Brigham Young University–Hawaii.

Not only did the Pacific Island and Australasian saints deserve better schools, they also required an increase in the quantity and quality of permanent church infrastructure, McKay concluded on his journey. While church members in North America enjoyed comfortable and substantial meetinghouses, the same could not be said of the international membership. Decades later, McKay instituted a building program unparalleled in Mormon history to rectify this situation. Even more importantly, McKay promised the New Zealand saints that there would someday be a temple in their midst, a pledge he fulfilled during his presidency. He also oversaw the construction of temples in England and Switzerland. As prophet of the church, President McKay put teeth in the church's policy of building up Zion abroad by signaling its permanence through construction projects. The church was no longer going to offer a two-tiered ecclesiastical experience to its membership.

After a year of international travel, McKay came to appreciate that a mere cloning of the church and its programs would not always work abroad, as heretofore believed church headquarters. At the same time, however, McKay grasped that the church must provide a comparable religious experience for its members around the world. It was not until 1921 that an LDS general authority could honestly say that he personally knew what was going on around the world in the church because McKay had been abroad himself.

Photographic Essay

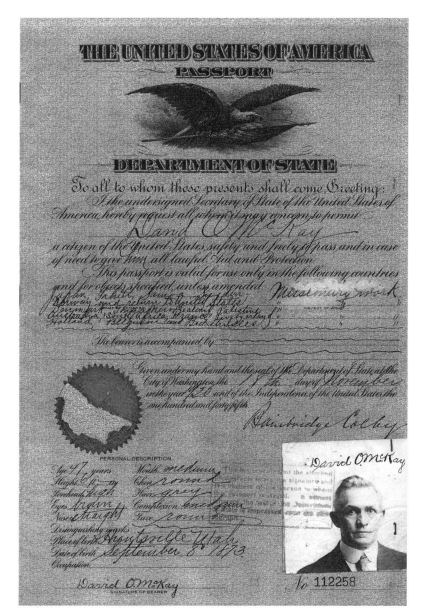

1 David O. McKay's United States passport, issued at Washington, D.C., on November 18, 1920.

" The press of packing and attending to a hundred eleventh-hour duties proved to be a good channel into which my thoughts and feelings were diverted. However, it was not so with Ray. It was placidly evident that she, bless her heroic soul, was making a brave struggle to keep back the tears. She reminded me of one of the pretty little geysers in Yellowstone, it would remain placid and peaceful for a while, but soon the forces, hidden and turbulent, would stir the surface of the water until it swelled, bubbled, and boiled over the rim until the pent up forces were set free. I hope the tears that bedimmed Ray's eyes so frequently during the day proved a relief to the rising emotion she so heroically tried to subdue." (David O. McKay, Diary, December 4, 1920, David O. McKay Papers, Manuscripts Division, J. Willard Marriott Library, University of Utah, Salt Lake City, Utah)

2 Hugh J. Cannon and McKay in light-colored travel suits, 1921.

❝ No pen can portray the joy of isolated church members upon learning that a visit from one of the Twelve might be anticipated. Should a prophet in one of our communities today announce that Peter, senior apostle of our Lord, would appear in person on the following Sunday and address and greet the people, their anticipation could not exceed that of Latter-day Saints residing in remote missions upon learning of Brother McKay's appointment. Keeping that thought in mind one can to an extent imagine the receptions accorded him." (Hugh J. Cannon, "Around-the-World Travels of David O. McKay and Hugh J. Cannon," ca. 1925, typescript, 4, microfilm, Church History Library, The Church of Jesus Christ of Latter-day Saints, Salt Lake City, Utah)

3 Cannon, McKay, and another passenger onboard the *Empress of Japan*, a Canadian Pacific Ocean steamer, while en route to Yokohama, Japan, December 1920.

"In the tossing and heaving of the ship, as well as of internal conditions, there was no respite. She would mount the crest of a huge wave and then plunge head-on; but before hitting the bottom of the trough, she would take a plunge to 'port,' then instantly veer to 'starboard'; hesitating a moment, she would give a 'shimmy'-like shiver and plunge again—turning, veering, 'shimmying' in endless repetition, until it seemed that life was made of nothing else. And all this rough sea was on the placid Pacific! Truly, Balboa was not in a ship but on the sunny side of a California hill when he named these waters the Pacific Ocean. Heaven be merciful to me if we sail a tempestuous sea!" (McKay, Diary, December 16, 1920)

4 LDS Primary Christmas
   celebration with Japanese
   children and American
   missionaries in Kofu, Japan,
   December 1920.

“Even in so-called heathen Japan, elaborate decorations were made in honor
of the Christmas holidays. On each side of the door in front of many buildings, a bunch of pine branches and bamboo canes were to be seen. It is said
the pine indicates a desire for long life, and the bamboo expresses other good
wishes. Under President Stimpson's direction an interesting Christmas program was given at the home. The natives sat on mats on the floor with feet
doubled up under them for nearly three hours and apparently enjoyed it.”
(Cannon, "Around-the-World Travels," 25)

5 McKay and Cannon
   being pulled by jinriksha
   runners in Tokyo, Japan,
   December 1920.

"Among the laboring class, men work like animals. They pull jinrikishas and run for several miles, some even running forty miles a day. They are sturdy, husky fellows, inured to exposure and capable of great endurance." (McKay, Diary, January 5, 1921)

6 Snowy conditions
in Aomori, Japan,
January 1921.

❝ The [Japanese] babies! What they can endure! Cuddled on their mother's
backs, they seem comfortable enough, but when they begin to run around,
they are barelegged and barefooted in the coldest weather. Indeed, they
object to having their feet covered. I have heard a two-year-old youngster
yell until his mother removed his slipper-like stockings and let him down
barefooted on the cold oilcloth covering the floor, and I was none too warm
with my overcoat on! I saw one baby's bare feet sticking out behind his
mother's back during a winter blizzard in Aomori! Kiddies were barefooted,
excepting the sandal, when snow covered the ground!" (McKay, Diary,
January 5, 1921)

Nihonbashi Street, Looking South, Tokyo
(東京) り 通 橋 本 日

142

7 Postcard of Nihonbashi
Street, Tokyo, Japan,
showing how the modern
streetcar system coexisted
with horses, jinrikshas, and
automobiles, 1921.

"Imagine, if you can, being aboard a great airplane which had conveyed you
to some distant inhabited planet. Think what your feelings would be as the
craft settled gently to its landing place and you looked eagerly over the vessel's side at the expectant groups awaiting your arrival. Your emotions, as
you viewed their strange features and attire and listened to their incomprehensible chatter, would probably not be greatly unlike those of the traveler
just emerging from well known Occidental scenes to the unfamiliar ones of
the Orient. Here, too, one enters a new world. The people, themselves so
different in features and dress from the Europeans, the buildings, temples,
pagodas and shrines, rikishas drawn by fleet-footed youths, heavy wagons
drawn by men or oxen or small horses or by a combination of all three,
all were as unusual as if the stranger were indeed arriving on a heretofore
unknown planet. But no! After running the gauntlet of custom officials he
attempts to cross the street and is in grave danger of colliding with an intimate acquaintance—one might say a rattling good friend—a Ford automobile. One feels inclined to pick it up and hug it, such is the delight at seeing
something so familiar." (Cannon, "Around-the-World Travels," 20–21)

8 Japanese laborers and their horses burdened with wood goods, Japan, January 1921.

" Then there are the laborers who pull heavily loaded carts, exerting sometimes a strength that seems entirely beyond them. But on they toil, either
pulling or pushing hour after hour, and day after day; and through it all keeping up a vigor that attests a strong vitality. Among this class, too, the women
work side by side with the men and bear their babies meanwhile." (McKay,
Scrapbook)

(イ447)　SANDALS SELLER　賣靴藁　（俗風鮮朝）

9 Postcard of Japanese
sandal sellers and their
wares, 1920.

10 McKay and Cannon
standing in front of the
bell of the Todaiji Buddhist
temple, Nara, Japan,
January 1921.

" From 9:00 a.m. until noon we lived in the mystic world of ancient Shintoism
and Buddhism. Though the weather was cold and raw, we obeyed all regulations by removing our shoes before entering either a temple, or hall of relics,
and in the sanctum sanctorum, we took off our overcoats." (McKay, Diary,
December 28, 1920)

11 McKay and Cannon feeding
the sacred, domesticated
deer of Nara, Japan,
January 4, 1921.

"Nara, former capital of the empire, is not far behind Nikko as a show place.
Its artistic park is full of deer, believed by the Japanese to be sacred. They
will eat from a stranger's hand. There was a sacred horse, which, probably
due to ignorance on the subject, looked like a common glass-eyed cayuse.
There were sacred pigeons, temples and bells. It would appear that nearly
everything is sacred to a Japanese except his promise, but unless he is outrageously maligned he esteems a promise as the least sacred thing in the
world." (Cannon, "Around-the-World Travels," 30–31)

12 American LDS
missionaries with
Japanese church members
and investigators,
January 1921.

❝ Trained as he is in Sunday school procedure and loving the work as he does,
one cannot imagine Brother McKay being embarrassed by a crowd of Sunday school children; and still he was visibly so at the first School he attended
in Tokyo. A number of children came to the mission house. Except for the
fact that the boys wore plain kimonos and the girls gaily colored ones, there
was little difference in their dress. Brother McKay wanted to greet them
properly and held out his hand for that purpose, but their surprised glances
traveled from his hand to his face, to ascertain if possible what they were
expected to do. Later he learned that shaking hands is an unknown custom with them. One might go on almost indefinitely describing Japanese
peculiarities, but time and space forbid. Suffice it to say that they are an
extremely courteous and delightfully interesting people and one sails regretfully away from their land." (Cannon, "Around-the-World Travels," 23–24)

13 Cannon talking with Chinese beggars while en route to Peking [Beijing], China, January 1921.

❝China is a land of beggars and parasites. If there are more hideous, loath-some creatures to be found on the globe than we have seen in Peking, in Tien Tsin, or even in Shanghai, I hope I may avoid the sight of them.❞
(McKay, Diary, January 16, 1921)

14 McKay climbing the steps of a Chinese temple in the Forbidden City while in Peking [Beijing], China, to dedicate the Chinese Realm for the preaching of the LDS gospel, January 1921.

" China appears to be made up of not a religious but a superstitious people. Their so-called religion is a mixture of Taoism, Confucianism and Buddhism. This will not be an insurmountable obstacle in their way of accepting the gospel, once their superstition regarding evil spirits can be overcome."
(McKay, Diary, January 16, 1921)

15 Cannon on the Great Wall of China, Ching-lung-Chiao, China, January 11, 1921.

"China is a disintegrating nation. Faded is the glory of her past, impotent the power of her once mighty government. The art and splendor of her picturesque temples, like the Great Wall, are permitted to go to decay; so are the manhood and the womanhood of the nation. China needs another Confucius, another Kubla Khan, to lead and inspire the young Chinese who are glimpsing the light." (McKay, Diary, January 16, 1921)

T. K, K Tenyo-Maru,　　　丸洋天　　船漁洋東

16 Postcard of the *Tenyo Maru*
which McKay and Cannon
sailed from Shanghai,
China, back to Yokohama,
Japan, January 1921.

❝The water was as pacific as one could expect it to be from its name. One
wonders how a comparatively few miles can make such a vast difference as
is to be seen between Japan and China. One country is fertile and green and
the other is most desolate. Naturally southern China is less austere, but there
is little difference in latitude between Japan and that part of China which
Brother McKay visited." (Cannon, "Around-the-World Travels," 47–48)

17 McKay and Cannon
with American LDS
missionaries and Japanese
church members, Japan,
January 1921.

❝ These people are certainly winning my admiration and true esteem. The
refinement and courtesy so manifest at nearly every turn, the taste in dress,
and the beauty of many of the better class of women, the charm and beauty
of young maidenhood and sweet young girlhood, the luxuriance of foliage
and the graceful, well-preserved trees in the groves and forests that abound
everywhere, the splendor of Nature in gorges and waterfalls, and everything
else, all combine to attune a man's sense of appreciation to the highest pitch.
Certain it is that thirty days in Japan and China have completely changed
my views hitherto entertained of the Orient and Oriental people.❞ (McKay,
Diary, January 24, 1921)

18 Honolulu Harbor, Oahu,
    Hawaii, 1921.

      "It seemed hardly possible that the new world which our travelers entered
at the harbor of Honolulu is on the same globe as the cheerless one seen at
China. This was truly a fairyland. Palms, ferns, flowers, and luxuriant tropical foliage, all contribute their part toward making this a terrestrial paradise.
But before driving along the beach, which was lined with coconut palms,
always leaning toward the sea, and with the stately royal palms, as straight
as any arrow ever made, visitors must steam into the harbor at the entrance
to which they are met by a crowd of boys and young men in the water who
swim about the vessel and dive for coins thrown overboard by prodigal passengers." (Cannon, "Around-the-World Travels," 51)

19 Hawaiian LDS Church members preparing a feast for McKay and Cannon, Hawaiian Islands, February 1921.

"No visitor among the Polynesians is likely ever to forget the feasts which are prepared and set before him. As the Hawaiians do not often have the opportunity of entertaining one of the General Authorities of the church, they were anxious to make Brother McKay's stay among them pleasant. The tables were usually covered with a cloth of ferns and at the outset literally groaned with the loads they bore. The aim of the natives is to transfer the load and consequent groaning to the visitor." (Cannon, "Around-the-World Travels," 54)

20 McKay and Cannon
with American LDS
missionaries and
Hawaiian church members
in front of chapel,
February 1921.

❝ More than three hundred eager people awaited the arrival of the visitors in the comfortable chapel. As is customary they all arose as the brethren entered and remained standing until the visitors had taken their seats. The joy of these people in meeting one of the General Church Authorities was thoroughly genuine and was akin to that which redeemed souls will have when they gaze upon the face and hear the voice of the Redeemer." (Cannon, "Around-the-World Travels," 61)

21 Treacherous Pali highway that connects the windward and leeward sides of Oahu, Hawaii, February 7, 1921.

" In traveling by auto from Honolulu to Laie the usual course passes over the Pali, one of the real scenic spots of the world. From this elevated point one can look into a valley where many thousands of acres are producing bounteous crops of pineapples and sugarcane. And beyond is the sea. A paved road zigzags like a great serpent from this spot down the steep mountainside and into the valley. A majestic mountain towers above the Pali on one side and a precipice yawns on the other." (Cannon, "Around-the-World Travels," 54)

22 Sugarcane fields near
    Laie, Oahu, Hawaii,
    February 1921.

“ At Laie, about thirty-five miles from Honolulu, the church owns a rather
large and productive plantation, a considerable part of which is devoted to
sugarcane and pineapple culture. The temple is located here, and a school is
also maintained by the church. One of Brother McKay's especial duties was
to visit our schools, and some little time was spent in this beautiful place.”
(Cannon, “Around-the-World Travels,” 52)

23 Hawaiians in traditional
female dress with ukulele,
Hawaii, February 1921.

24 Waikiki Beach and
beachfront hotels with
Diamond Head in the
distance, Oahu, Hawaii,
February 1921.

25 McKay naming the local
flora, Maui, Hawaii,
February 9, 1921.

" Hawaii is called the 'Come Back Land.' Even if there were no contributing
causes, the country itself would justify the designation. But when to the
physical beauty of the place is added the music, the deep and touching love
of the people, the joy they manifest at meeting, and the sincere sorrow at
parting it is easy to understand how appropriately it could be thus named."
(Cannon, "Around-the-World Travels," 69)

26 Unidentified church member, McKay, and Cannon feted with leis at Lahaina Harbor, Maui, Hawaii, February 9, 1921.

27 McKay with schoolchildren in Rarotonga, Cook Islands, April 1921.

❝ The tropical island, some of whose mountains reach a height of three thousand feet, the intensely blue sea and the comparatively faded blue of the eastern sky, brilliant red, yellow and green shades of the departed sun and the purple reflection from adjacent hills all combined to furnish every imaginable gradation of color. It was truly a picturesque scene. When entering harbors of the South Seas, the traveler inclines to the belief that the last one visited excels all others in beauty. Raratonga is one of the most fertile and valuable of the Cook group, and though considered an unusually good specimen of the volcanic order, it is surrounded by a coral reef. . . . In the waning light these crumbling hulks added to the romance of the place." (Cannon, "Around-the-World Travels," 87)

28 McKay and Cannon at
    the Hui Tau, Huntly, New
    Zealand, April 22, 1921.

" The great annual event among church members in New Zealand is the 'Hui Tau,' or mission conference, which is usually held during the autumn month of April. Followers of this narrative will understand that they are now in the southern hemisphere where there is a complete reversal of seasons. Christmas comes almost in midsummer. Many of the Maoris are comparatively wealthy, and they have purchased a number of immense tents, comparable in size to those used by a three-ringed circus in the United States. One of the largest of these is used for meetings and at night as an immense bedroom, the beds being made upon the ground." (Cannon, "Around-the-World Travels," 93–94)

29 Group of Maori
waitresses at the Hui Tau,
Huntly, New Zealand,
April 22, 1921.

"Following the service, as many as could be seated at the first tables, answered the call to 'Kai.' Under a canopy fully as large as that in which services were held, were arranged eight long tables each with a seating capacity of forty persons. Four girls furnished these tables and served the guests, each group taking charge of eighty persons at every sitting. Each group, too, had its own boiler for cooking, its own tanks for dish-washing and its own cupboards for the dishes, and every plate, cup and saucer, knife, fork, and spoon was accounted for. Boiled meat, potatoes, spinach, bread, butter, jam, and cheese made the principal eatables; but cake, watermelons, and other fruits and delicacies were also served. Some of the meat and potatoes were prepared in the 'Hangi,' that is, cooked in a pit in the good old Maori fashion, except that chains were heated instead of rocks. And we must admit that meat thus cooked is far more tender and delicious than that boiled in the more modern manner. As the women peeled the potatoes, it seemed by the ton, or washed dishes, literally by the hundred, they worked in unison to the rhythm of some song, hummed as gleefully as though they were having a Jubilee. Sometimes the young girls having 'finished the dishes' would wind up with a touch of the 'Kopi Kopi' or 'Hula Hula.' How efficient this organization and how effectively it worked may be partly realized when I tell you that during the four and one half days of the 'Hui Tau' approximately 10,000 meals were served! And that, too, without any apparent extraordinary effort!" (Cannon, "Around-the-World Travels," 98–99)

30 Cannon and McKay with
the Ruruku and Elkington
families at the Hui Tau,
Huntly, New Zealand,
April 22, 1921.

31 New Zealand Latter-day
Saints performing the
"haka" dance for McKay
and Cannon at the Hui
Tau, Huntly, New Zealand,
April 22, 1921.

"'Haire Mai! Haire Mai!' rings out shrill from a hundred voices above which
are those of the feminine variety. Then begins a dance in which the men lead
in a rhythmic chant, and yelling a challenge which is answered in harmony
with the swaying movement of body and the uniform swinging and beating
of arms. Their eyes roll until one can see nothing but the whites; they roll
their tongues and make horrible grimaces." (McKay, Diary, April 22, 1921)

32 Sidney Christy, David O.
McKay, Rawhate Parata,
and Hugh J. Cannon at
the Hui Tau, Huntly, New
Zealand, April 23, 1921.

" A prominent figure of the gathering was Sid Christy, who now holds the title
of chief among his people. For some years he was in Salt Lake, a student of
the Latter-day Saints High School and a star on the basketball team. He is
now married and has a large family. Speaking of the *hongi* and comparing it
with the white people's habit of kissing, he thought the advantages were all
in favor of the native custom. He said, 'If you kiss a man's wife, he is likely
to beat you up, but the *hongi* which means the same thing to us, can be
indulged in with impunity.'" (Cannon, "Around-the-World Travels," 94–95)

33 One of the decorated
boats that escorted
McKay and Cannon into
Apia Harbor, Samoa,
May 11, 1921.

" The welcome accorded the visitors is quite as indescribable as a tropical landscape or sunset. President Adams and his wife, Thurza T. Adams, and Elder Frank D. Griffiths and his wife, Retta M. Griffiths, were early alongside the *Tofua,* each couple being in a long rowboat decorated with garlands of vines and flowers. Brother McKay was taken in one of these boats with twenty-two muscular and highly elated natives handling the usual long oars. Brother Cannon and President Coombs were taken in the other with Brother and Sister Griffiths and eighteen sturdy rowers who used short paddles instead of oars; and when they applied their strength in perfect unison to these paddles the boat almost jumped out from under its occupants. The boys had to be held in check as they were much inclined to beat the boat with the chief visitor to the pier." (Cannon, "Around-the-World Travels," 114)

34 McKay arriving in
    Apia Harbor, Samoa,
    May 11, 1921.

35 The Sauniatu Latter-day
Saint Band marching in
honor of the arrival of
McKay and Cannon, Apia,
Samoa, May 11, 1921.

"Upon landing, the custom officials threw open the gates and courteously
declined to make any examination of luggage. The streets were packed with
people, and the church school band from Sauniatu, composed of native boys
with the exception of Elder Ray W. Berrett, played stirring strains. After the
greetings were over, a procession was formed headed by the band, and the
visitors were taken to mission headquarters. Business in the town was at
a standstill. Stores, banks, and offices were closed and everybody was on
the streets. All had heard of apostles, but this was the first opportunity ever
given most of these people to see one. Be it said to the credit of practically
all the natives and a large percentage of whites, that regardless of their own
religious beliefs they looked upon Brother McKay as a divinely called servant
of the Lord." (Cannon, "Around-the-World Travels," 114)

36 Cannon and McKay on
    land in Apia Harbor,
    Samoa, May 1921.

37 McKay and Cannon
witnessing a baptism in
Samoa, May 1921.

"During this conference an unusually impressive baptism service was held in a limpid stream near the mission home. Amid tropical foliage and surrounded by the white-clad figures, those present felt they were standing almost in the visible presence of angels. Elder Ralph A. Thacker led twenty-one humble converts into the water; among them was Robert Reid, said to be the most influential half-caste in British Samoa." (Cannon, "Around-the-World Travels," 119)

38 Samoan local climbing coconut tree, Upolu, Samoa, May 1921.

❝ Everywhere natives were gathering and breaking coconuts for the market. It would surprise a European to see how completely these nuts cover the ground. There were literally millions and millions of them, and preparing them for shipment is one of the chief occupations of the people. Reference has heretofore been made to the thirst-quenching liquid which these nuts contain. The natives are very proficient in selecting those of proper ripeness and are always ready to climb a tree to obtain for a stranger the very best drink which can be had. On a hot day, and there are no days in Samoa which are not hot, this beverage is very refreshing.” (Cannon, “Around-the-World Travels,” 133)

39 Samoan LDS sisters
teaching McKay how
to extract milk from a
coconut, Samoa, May 1921.

40 Unidentified American
   missionary, McKay,
   and Cannon dressed in
   traditional Samoan attire,
   Samoa, May 1921.

41 McKay, Cannon, and
unidentified American
elder and sister
missionaries on horseback
to ride the twenty miles
from Apia, the capital city,
to Sauniatu, the valley of
the LDS gathering, Samoa,
May 28, 1921.

" Sauniatu is the principal branch of the church in Samoa. Here the best school
on the islands is located, and the church owns a large plantation of coconut
trees. Brothers McKay and Cannon and President and Sister Adams rode
on horseback to this place. The trail over which they traveled skirted the
seacoast, sometimes along sandy beaches, and occasionally over precipitous
cliffs. The intense blueness of the sky, the still deeper blue of the water, the
thundering surf on the coral reef, magnificent trees of every tropical variety, among which the stately coconut palms predominated, will never be
forgotten by those who have the good fortune to pass that way." (Cannon,
"Around-the-World Travels," 132–33)

42 The Sauniatu Latter-day
Saint Band, Apia, Samoa,
May 28, 1921.

"As we walked slowly toward the conference house, the band struck up 'The Star Spangled Banner.' To hear that old air away off here in Samoa, played so impressively by Samoan boys, to see the women of the village, all dressed in white and men well dressed standing in line opposite the women; to walk along a well-cleaned roadway strewn on each side with palm branches; to realize that every heart was beating a welcome, even though it was accompanied by a feeling of curiosity, made me feel that this simple unostentatious greeting from the little village of Sauniatu was one of the most impressive of our entire trip. My feelings were stirred and found expression in a tear or two that trickled over the eyelids." (McKay, Diary, May 28, 1921)

43 Latter-day Saints in front
of a monument erected in
Sauniatu to commemorate
McKay's visit and apostolic
blessing given on May 31,
1921, Sauniatu, Samoa,
May 1922.

" Their own feelings deeply stirred and with bedimmed eyes the visitors
pressed through the crowds and mounted the horses which were in waiting. The people followed them across the bridge which spans the beautiful
stream and the band played 'Tofa mai Feleni' (Goodbye, my Friend). As
Brother McKay looked back through the avenue of trees and saw the band
and crowd following, he felt impressed to return and offer a prayer with
them, and this inspiration was immediately followed. As he prayed for and
blessed the multitude, one was unconsciously reminded of that touching
farewell which the Savior took of the people, as recorded in the Book of
Mormon, Third Nephi, Chapters 17 and 18. Though the Christ was not present in person, he was represented by a divinely chosen servant and his comforting spirit was felt by all. Later it was learned that the prayer had been
written, as nearly as it could be remembered by Brother Sua Kippen and others, and was placed in the corner stone of an impressive monument which
was erected on the place." (Cannon, "Around-the-World Travels," 137)

44 McKay, Cannon, and a
   crowd of church members
   and friends witnessing
   a baptism in a brick and
   concrete font in Samoa,
   May 1921.

45 McKay next to author Robert Louis Stevenson's grave, Apia, Samoa, July 7, 1921.

❝ At six o'clock, we were all astir, preparing to climb to the top of the hill, where rests the body of the Scotch poet, Robert Louis Stevenson. When we reached the lodge gate, at about 7:30 a.m., it began to pour; but we sought shelter in the lodge, so escaped getting wet. We continued in the cart as far as the stream that runs at the foot of the hill. From there, only 'Shanks' ponies' served to carry us. The ascent is not precipitous now, but the trail cut by the natives who carried or dragged the casket to the top was almost perpendicular. They truly had to climb on their hands and knees. The higher we climbed, the more beautiful became the view of the surrounding country. How typical of intellectual and spiritual experiences as well!" (McKay, Diary, July 7, 1921)

46 The home of author
    Robert Louis Stevenson,
    Apia, Samoa, July 7, 1921.

47 McKay and Cannon
"meet" McKay and
Cannon through a double
exposure photographic
trick in Brisbane,
Australia, 1921.

48 Water buffalo–powered
well, likely in India,
October 1921.

❝ For ages the cow was looked upon in India as being sacred, and to this day more or less sanctity is attached to her. But with the ox it is different. His lot and that of the Asiatic buffalo is so hard, all the heavy work being assigned to them, that were they capable of thought they might anticipate the butcher's block as a paradise." (Cannon, "Around-the-World Travels," 177–78)

49 Taj Mahal, Agra, India,
October 10, 1921.

" Comparatively few people in Utah know anything about Agra, but all have
heard of the renowned Taj Mahal, 'A Dream in Marble.' This structure is
considered by travelers the most beautiful building in the world. Artists and
poets have attempted to describe it, but these efforts fall so far short that no
attempt will be made here, for the beauty of its architecture and the material
of which it is composed, consisting of white marble adorned with precious
stones, is indescribable. The mature person who has not stood before things
so beautiful that he has not known whether to kneel down and pray or sit
down and cry, is deserving of pity. Such feelings come over the visitor to
the Taj Mahal. With uncovered head, one stands in awe before it. If a word
passed between Brothers McKay and Cannon during this visit, it was spoken
in a whisper." (Cannon, "Around-the-World Travels," 180)

50 Arab woman with camel,
Suez, Egypt, October 1921.

❝On our right through the glasses we can see camels lying lazily in the sun, some of them still carrying their loads on their backs. It may be that they are just getting ready to start out as a caravan because in the distance I can see three camels and a man starting across the sandy waste. During the forenoon, we passed hundreds of men, mules, and camels working along the bank, evidently with the purpose of widening the canal. It was an interesting sight to see the camels, the faithful old beasts, lie down while the men shoveled the sand into the boxes attached to the backs of these ships of the desert, and then rise and wobble out of the pit, climb the hill, and go deposit their burden by again lying down.❞ (McKay, Diary, October 24, 1921)

51 Tree-lined road leading to
the famed pyramids, Cairo,
Egypt, October 26, 1921.

"As we approached nearer, and saw half-covered in mist the pyramid of
Cheops standing near, I felt much the same sensation that I had when I
first glimpsed the Grand Canyon of the Colorado—a realization that I was
not comprehending its magnitude. But as we climbed up the sandy incline
and listened to Abdul and stood beside the massive stone in this wonder of
wonderful tombs, its massiveness began to dawn upon me." (McKay, Diary,
October 26, 1921)

52 Cannon and McKay on
    camelback in front of
    the Sphinx, Cairo, Egypt,
    October 26, 1921.

" We visited the Sphinx. It is in a depression and cannot be seen from a distance. The feelings which overpower the visitor when looking at this silent
face and figure with the pyramids in the background and the historic valley below, all of which were ancient when Joseph and Mary brought the
infant Savior from Palestine for safety, cannot be described." (McKay, Diary,
October 26, 1921)

53 British tank and Jerusalem
resident, November 1921.

"The special missionaries were in Jerusalem on November 2, 1921. On that
date every shop in the city was closed and the people indulged in such serious rioting that British soldiers were called into action and armored trucks
carrying machine guns were stationed about the city. The trouble started as
a protest against the declaration of Lord Balfour of England, that Palestine
should be set apart for the Jews. By this declaration, the British statesman set
in motion, to a far greater extent than he imagined, the fulfillment of prophecy, for not only do the Bible and the Book of Mormon foretell such a gathering of the Jews, but a modern prophet, Orson Hyde, one of the Twelve,
predicted that England would play a leading part in this gathering." (Cannon,
"Around-the-World Travels," 196)

54 Celebrated birthplace
of Jesus Christ in the
Church of the Nativity,
Bethlehem, Palestine,
November 1, 1921.

"I have not been disappointed in my visit to old Jerusalem. The picturesque site on the four historic and frequently-mentioned mounts, and its relative position to other Biblical centers have been so clearly impressed upon my mind that this geographical significance itself is quite sufficient reward for the journey. Besides this, the trip from Jerusalem to Jericho and the Valley of the Jordan, with all their Biblical associations, was so full of interest and instruction that, were there nothing else, I should feel gratified. No, I'm not *disappointed* but *grieved*—grieved to see the Manger, the sacred cradle, profaned by the contentious spirit of the jarring, selfish creeds—grieved to see the spot desecrated by lavished wealth—grieved to learn of the feuds and fatal quarrels that have occurred upon the very spot where the Son of God was born—grieved to see the keys of the Holy Sepulchre kept by a follower of Mohammed because the professed Christians cannot trust one of their number with them! Grieved to witness these same so-called Christians uniting with Mohammedans in opposing the return of the Jews to the Holy Land! How far, oh how far from the simple principles of the Gospel have they wandered who now profess to be the direct descendants of the primitive Church! Greeks and Romans both have completely apostatized; and the various sects of Protestantism, of course, are over wandering in darkness because they have no authority to officiate in his name!" (McKay, Diary, November 4, 1921)

It is the man who is the missionary. It is not his words. His character is his message.
—Drummond[1]

We need your company, friends. Coleridge[2] voiced a universal truth when he said, "What no one with us shares, seems scarce our own—we need another to reflect our thoughts."[3] That conception followed to its conclusion is one of the great reasons for missionary work.

Come with us, therefore, on our trip around the world. If you join us in our experiences, you will sail tempestuous, also placid seas, many of them terrifying, others dreamy and restful. You will go into strange lands, some, comparatively, not yet out of their swaddling clothes, others falling into senility. You will be delighted with colorful Japan; awed by somber China; captivated by the "Come Back Land" of Hawaii; brought to tears by other hospitable South Sea Islands, including New Zealand and the continent of Australia; interested by over-populated Java;[4] entranced by mystic India; inspired by historic Egypt; subdued, and unfortunately incensed, by holy Palestine. Naturally the temptation to linger unreasonably long in some of these lands must be resisted.

You will be strictly an "uncommercial traveler," seeking neither sales nor business opportunities, and yet it is not to be a pleasure trip. You are to meet new peoples—not in a mere casual sense; but a feeling of intimacy so strong will be engendered that those of other races, other language, color, and customs will come to you and lay bare their hearts with the confident freedom of lifelong friends. It will be your duty to study their spiritual and, as far as possible, temporal needs, and to ascertain the effect of "Mormonism" upon their lives. Though your journey is westward, in due time eastern lands will be reached, whence all that is mystical as well as much that is true in religion has come.

Utah has an "Around the World Club" with a remarkably large membership, many of her citizens having encircled the globe. Still, the journey you are invited to make is the first of its kind ever undertaken. A man holding the holy Apostleship,[5] a "special witness" for Christ, is going in the authority of his calling to visit fields heretofore unvisited by any such authority—Tahiti, Samoa, Tonga, New Zealand, Australia, and India.

Seemingly the party will have an attentive and all-powerful advance agent, so that no concern need be felt regarding accommodations. The steamship company may tell you their lists are already filled and no more passengers can be accepted. Pay no attention to them, for your agent has a way of securing just what you need at the last moment and in the face of difficulties which apparently are insurmountable. One inclined toward skepticism may say this agent's name is Chance; but among those who believe in the authority which sent the party out and in the promises which were made, there will be no disposition to give chance the credit for the remarkable things which transpired. You will become acquainted with the leader of the expedition. Perhaps many will say, "We already know him," but accompany us and you will later confess that you knew him merely by sight. Upon returning you will really *know* him—not a mere bowing acquaintance, but actually having become the friend of his bosom.

And thereby a study in psychology will be presented, the like of which cannot be found elsewhere. The man who leads you believes, even claims he knows, he is a personal representative of Christ the Lord. He feels keenly his authority, the dignity and greatness of his appointment which would not be exchanged for the wealth of kingdoms. It will be interesting to note how the high calling affects the individual and how you will react toward the apostle and toward the man after a year of almost hourly association.

People on their knees will kiss his hand, bathing it meanwhile with sincere tears, and he will graciously submit; others likewise will be seen kissing the hands of other church potentates. These two experiences may awaken widely divergent impulses in your heart. The thoughtful observer will demand of himself adequate reasons for the difference, and these may perhaps be found.

Of course it is understood that you are not to go in person. In The Church of Jesus Christ of Latter-day Saints, men are called and set apart,[6] instructed and given authority to do certain things, and "no man taketh this honor unto himself."[7] Therefore no duty is to be assigned you, and you will not only be an "uncommercial traveler," but an invisible and silent one as well.

How changed are world conditions since Joseph Smith's memorable prayer![8] Then, this trip would have aroused universal comment. Inventions which have brought nations so close together, steamships, steam and electric railways, telegraph and telephone, flying machines, and radio were either wholly unknown or in their infancy. Did the effulgent light which accompanied Father and Son to this earth spread beyond the sacred grove in New York and inspire man to turn nature's laws to practical use? Present-day knowledge has not only stimulated desire to travel, but modern inventions have provided ways of gratifying that desire. The time had come to preach the gospel in all the world, and necessity demanded improved means of communication.

While still the junior member of the Quorum,[9] President Heber J. Grant[10] urged that one of the Twelve be sent to the South Sea Islands to visit missionaries and church members and stabilize their spiritual values. But, notwithstanding its acknowledged merit, the idea seemed impossible of accomplishment, and no step was taken in this direction until two years after the leadership of the church fell upon him who had first suggested it.

At a meeting of the Presidency[11] and Apostles held October 14, 1920, Elder David O. McKay[12] was formally called to visit the missions of the Pacific and probably to go around the world. The following day Hugh J. Cannon[13] was asked to accompany him.

No pen can portray the joy of isolated church members upon learning that a visit from one of the Twelve might be anticipated. Should a prophet in one of our communities today announce that Peter,[14] senior apostle of our Lord, would appear in person on the following Sunday and address and greet the people, their anticipation could not exceed that of Latter-day Saints residing in remote missions upon learning of Brother McKay's appointment. Keeping that thought in mind one can to an extent imagine the receptions accorded him.

His selection was a happy one. He was admirably suited for the important work, and it may be stated at the outset that he measured up to every expectation. His striking personality and genial disposition captivated church members, and even among strangers won numberless friends for him, and even of greater importance, for the cause he represented. Even while preparations for the trip were in progress, it was discovered that his personality is built largely upon the fact that he is so tremendously and righteously human. Anything other than perfect frankness is abhorrent to his honest soul, and fellow travelers soon learned that he was a "Mormon." Sometimes the news was imparted rather abruptly as in the following instance.

It was a beautiful autumn evening in April (the reader will note this was in the Antipodes where the seasons are reversed) when the special missionaries embarked on the *Tofua* at Auckland,[15] New Zealand, for Samoa. The best available accommodations were in a cabin with two other gentlemen. Brother Cannon retired early and did not see the unknown roommates that night. Next morning while standing before the glass, shaving, he noticed that Brother McKay and the strangers were awake. Suddenly Brother McKay said: "The company must think highly of this cabin to put into it two ministers and two 'Mormon' missionaries."

The look of horrified astonishment on the strangers' faces, as revealed by the mirror, was almost more than the man before the glass could endure without an explosion. There was a long, and, except for the humor of it, painful silence. The ministers had nothing to say, and Brother McKay evidently felt nothing more was necessary at that time. One of these men was seasick during the entire voyage to Fiji, where he disembarked. With the others, the missionaries subsequently became excellent friends and had many interesting interviews.

Another incident illustrative of Brother McKay's character may be related here. He and his companions, including the late Joseph Wilford Booth,[16] had traveled from Beirut[17] on the Mediterranean to Baalbek,[18] "city of the sun," in Syria, a journey over the famed mountains of Lebanon, to which detailed reference will be made in proper order. Darkness was upon them before Baalbek was reached, and as they were to take a train the next morning for Aleppo,[19] their only opportunity to see the noted ruins of the Temple of Baal[20] was to do so as day was breaking. A guide proffered to show the place for a trifling sum and a bargain was made.

To gain access to the grounds, on the following morning, the visitors were obliged to go through a deep, dry moat, then climb over the gate. This fact and something said later at the hotel prompted Brother McKay to make inquiries, from which he learned that visitors to these ruins are expected to pay for admission. Though his train was due to leave shortly, he hastily dispatched a messenger with the entrance fees, and the gratified keeper of the grounds ran breathlessly to the station just in time to thank Brother McKay, who was well known at least to the hotel people as a "Mormon," for his honesty.

To increase the numberless accounts of world trips, viewed from one standpoint, is quite inexcusable. But because of its nature this tour made history for the church, and it seems proper that the important incidents be recorded. Then, too, it was so filled with faith-promoting experiences, the nearness of the Almighty was so unmistakably evident, that to preserve an account of it in book form seems justifiable.

The task of preparing the work is a formidable one, but if an account sufficiently graphic could be prepared to make the reader, even in a slight degree, participate with the travelers in experiences had in China, in Hawaii, the Holy Land,[21] indeed in every country they visited, the time devoted to its preparation would be well spent. Attention has been given to a natural human tendency to indulge in exaggeration as the incidents fall into perspective. Occurrences of minor importance are often made to appear epochal. A sincere effort to guard against such danger has been made, by constant reference to the two daily journals kept during the trip.

There is one consoling thought connected with this effort: being a description of a journey around the world it should be easy to keep on the subject.

It may not be amiss to state this early in the narrative that reference to a duty satisfactorily accomplished by the author is made with no boastful spirit. The reader may recall the experience of Philemon C. Merrill[22] when the prophet Joseph [Smith][23] commanded him to throw an offensive braggart in a wrestling bout. He suddenly became endowed with superhuman strength and easily succeeded in a task ordinarily quite beyond his power.[24] So it was when Brother McKay asked the writer to do certain things; in no single instance were they impossible, notwithstanding they often appeared so, but on the contrary were usually accomplished with singular ease.

In this church frequent reference is made to Nephi's[25] statement, "The Lord giveth no commandment unto the children of men, save he shall prepare a way for them that they may accomplish the thing which he commandeth them."[26] Another truth is that the Lord also prepares the way for his people to obey ordinary instructions given by church leaders. Perhaps this deserves a word of amplification. One can understand the natural reluctance of the authorities to say, "Do as we advise and you will be blessed," but a century of church history proves that the safe course is to follow counsel. "And the day cometh that they who will not hear the voice of the Lord, neither the voice of his servants, neither give heed to the words of the prophets and apostles, shall be cut off from among his people."[27] Whether the instruction is to secure accommodations on a crowded steamship, or to plant certain crops, to build canals, or fill foreign missions, the faithful Latter-day Saint feels he can do not only the thing which the Lord commands, but also that which is simply asked of him by those who are sustained as prophets, seers, and revelators.[28]

The courage we desire and prize is not the courage to die decently but to live manfully.

—Carlyle[1]

In the Salt Lake Temple,[2] on December 2, 1920, the special missionaries were set apart for their work by the Presidency and the Twelve. This occasion merits attention because of the inspired promises which were made and their subsequent miraculous fulfillment. Had the travelers expressed the innermost desires of their hearts, the result could hardly have been more satisfactory. No prophet of old ever spoke with more certainty than did President Grant, as he pronounced a blessing upon Brother McKay, stating, among other things, that he should have power to avoid dangers both seen and unseen and that his course should be directed by the whisperings of the divine spirit.

To men going into strange lands, meeting tempests, tropical heat, possibly wrecks on vessels or trains, or contagious diseases, what more desirable promise could be made?

The late President Anthon H. Lund[3] was called to lead in blessing Brother Cannon. Some apprehension had been felt as to what might happen—what inconvenient delays—should serious sickness overtake either one of the party. Brother Cannon was particularly concerned for shortly before, he had suffered from a painful illness. But anxiety vanished with the words: "We bless you that you may have health and strength on your journey, that sickness may have no power over you; but if seasickness or anything like that comes, it will be of short duration."

Attentive readers will see how literally these promises were fulfilled. Little did the travelers think then that never again in mortal life would they hear the voice of that kindly saint, President Anthon H. Lund, the man whom everybody loved.

Missionary work has developed courage of a high and unusual order. And this quality in its perfection is not shown by the men who go. They are crusaders, so to speak, marching to martial music, and inspired also at the thought of the new experiences which await them. But the valorous wives who remain behind have no such stimulant. They face a colorless and difficult period, with loneliness playing the chief role. Saying good-bye is never easy. In this instance it was doubly hard because shortly before, Sister [Emma Ray] McKay[4] had presented her husband with a sturdy son[5] and Sister [Sarah R.] Cannon[6] had given to hers a beautiful daughter,[7] and neither of these good women had fully regained her strength.

On December 4, 1920, the train was boarded for Portland.[8] Pleasant and profitable was the two-hour interview, as the travelers neared Pocatello,[9] with Elder Frederick A. Caine,[10] now president of the Idaho Falls Stake,[11] who for eight years was a missionary among the Nipponese. This observant man gave information about Japan, the first objective after leaving America, which was very helpful.

To lovers of scenic beauty, the ride from Utah to Oregon is a delightful one. For many miles the pine-clad hills were covered with snow, blending white with green into a beautiful picture.

A brief stay in Portland—three and a half hours—permitted the missionaries to attend Sunday evening service in a church-owned chapel, which would be a credit to any ward[12] in Utah. They met a number of friends, made new acquaintances, were entertained in the mission home by President Heber C. Iverson[13] and his good wife[14] and family, and had a short drive about the city.

The stopover in Seattle[15] was of even shorter duration—one and a half hours, but long enough to have a little visit with Elders Reed Michelsen and William S. Maxwell[16] who, on a raw winter morning long before daylight, were awaiting the belated train.

A conference had just been held in Bellingham[17] and the missionaries in attendance were at the station to wish the brethren a pleasant journey as the train passed through.

The depression incident to leaving the land of the Stars and Stripes was somewhat allayed in Vancouver[18] by the hearty welcome received from missionaries and others. Brother Stephen Markham Dudley,[19] grandson of that loyal man, Stephen Markham,[20] who was often with the prophet in the troublous days of Nauvoo,[21] and by whose side Brother Joseph [Smith] slept in Carthage[22] the night prior to his martyrdom,[23] placed himself and his auto at the disposal of the visitors, and after visas for passports and arrangements for transportation were completed, a question

[7]

Crossing the Pacific Ocean

arose in their minds as to how this could have been accomplished without his aid. His jolly little wife,[24] eager to visit with one of the general church authorities,[25] not only rode with the party, but to their wonderment found time to prepare an excellent dinner for fifteen people.

The predominant thought after meeting the missionaries in and about Vancouver, and indeed in every field, is one of surprise that they are so misunderstood. More than a score of them were present, several lady missionaries among the number, all conscientiously devoting their time, meanwhile paying their own expenses, to broadcast the message of "Mormonism." Let us pause to look into their faces, indicative of lofty ideals. One sees no fanaticism, only a sublime and cheerful confidence; no egotism, only trustfulness in the Almighty; no smugness, only humility. Had a prophet arisen and foretold that all were destined to die as martyrs, hardly a cheek would have blanched. But had he declared that one among them would lose his most priceless possession, virtue, it would have caused most poignant grief. They were ready, to the last man, to die for the gospel, and were also determined to do the more heroic thing—live for it.

This tour took the travelers into fifteen mission fields and brought them into close contact with fully three hundred missionaries. What is said of church representatives in Vancouver is true of all; not that the missionaries are precisely what the church would have them be. Many are inexperienced and a few are ignorant, some inexcusably and embarrassingly so, but with surprisingly few exceptions their personal lives are above reproach. Furthermore, they are almost always dignified ladies and gentlemen, a credit to the cause they represent.

The statement regarding the moral character of missionaries is received with surprise or incredulity by strangers. When they learn that young men, often of tender years, are sent from farm or shop or school to face the temptations met in great cities, they are more than ever disinclined to believe the statement. And if partially convinced, they ask whence comes the power which enables those boys to remain clean.

What is the answer? It cannot be given in a sentence. First, they are called, ordained, and assigned to their fields by men who are themselves strictly virtuous. A statement attributed to Confucius[26] illustrates the importance of this point. The noted philosopher held a position of trust in one of the Chinese provinces, and all associated with him were renowned for their impeccable honesty. A neighboring ruler, whose district had exactly the opposite reputation, called on Confucius and asked: "What can I do to end the vicious dishonesty which exists in my department?"

"Return home and be honest yourself," was Confucius's simple answer.

In their homes these missionaries are taught that it is better to lose life than virtue. The Book of Mormon[27] tells them that sexual sin, murder excepted, is the most grievous in the eyes of the Almighty.[28] At the meeting of missionaries in Vancouver, one elder read from the Doctrine and Covenants:[29] "Let virtue garnish thy thoughts unceasingly; then shall thy confidence wax strong in the presence of God. . . . The Holy Ghost shall be thy constant companion."[30]

The writer of this account recalls two solemn occasions to which he was an unhappy witness. One, missionaries, almost broken-hearted, were called together to excommunicate[31] from the church an associate who had forgotten his covenants and fallen into transgression. Bitter tears were shed by the accused and by those sitting in judgment on the case.

The other occasion was when a white-haired father and his family surrounded the casket in which a son had been brought home from the mission field. With tears streaming down his cheeks and with broken voice the father spoke: "Our boy has come home, has returned to us in a coffin, but thank God he has come home clean."

This, perhaps, answers the strangers' questions. It is the great vitalizing power with the missionaries which keeps their moral fiber from decay.

Thus far the trip was filled with delightful incidents, every moment pleasantly spent, but evidently it was to be a working not a pleasure trip, for diligence is one of Brother McKay's outstanding characteristics.

Yokohama,[32] principal seaport of Japan, lies almost directly west of San Francisco.[33] Our younger readers, and perhaps some older ones, may wonder why the nearest way to Yokohama is to travel north until the snowy mountains of the Aleutian Islands[34] are visible. This is due to the fact that the earth, being nearly round, is more narrow as one goes north.

Numerous invitations to dinners and other social affairs where refreshments were served were extended to the special missionaries during the weeks immediately preceding their departure. Such acts, intended as kindness and greatly appreciated, were poor preparation for a rough ocean voyage. Some of these delightful dinners were destined to come up later in a most distressing manner.

Have you ever been aboard a vessel on an extremely rough sea? Have you felt it roll and toss and plunge, then when struck full force by a mighty wave which washes its decks, felt it shudder and tremble as though it had received a death blow and must assuredly sink, and all the while the stomachs of the sensitive passengers are performing similar evolutions and are dancing about as wildly as the ship itself? Frequently not more than a dozen people out of several hundred passengers were at meals.

Here was seen the first evidence of the prophetic power of those who set the special missionaries apart. Brother Cannon had never been a good sailor. On previous journeys he had invariably been seasick if the water was rough, but here the words of President Lund were literally fulfilled. Brother McKay, being the leader of this tour, maintained his supremacy in the matter of seasickness as in all other things. He does nothing by halves, but treats every subject exhaustively, going to the very bottom of it, and this occasion was no exception. Seasickness is undertaken with the same vigorous energy which he displays in running for a train. In either case, those in front should dodge.

The following excerpts from a letter, written by him to friends at home, will prove interesting:

> You remember what Oliver Wendell Holmes says about an "outer" door and an "inner" door to every person's feelings? Well, since you are dear friends to whom the inner door of my feelings has always been hope, I think I will give you some of my *inside* history of this never-to-be-forgotten voyage.
>
> Brother Hugh J. and I were in prime condition, I thought, when we boarded the *Empress of Japan* on the evening of December 7, 1920. Kind friends had showered us with good wishes and blessings, had feted and dined us for weeks previous, and had sent along with us boxes of the choicest cream chocolates to make our journey sweet and delightsome. Even as we walked up the gang plank at Vancouver, we were accompanied by a score of elders and saints, who, with President Iverson bade us a heartfelt *Bon Voyage*.
>
> It was storming when we left port, and the movement of the boat was keenly perceptible even before we went to sleep. The pitching of the vessel in the night awoke me and every nerve and muscle of my body responded to every movement of the boat. As this movement became more pronounced and intense, the contents of my digestive organs joined in unison with nerves and muscles. Twenty-one years ago, one morning on the Atlantic, I had experienced a similar feeling, so I knew I had better dress carefully, and get on deck.
>
> At that moment Bro. Cannon jumped out of bed as bright and pert as a ten-year-old boy. He could steady himself as

though he were anchored. With no apparent difficulty, he dressed himself, and even shaved—an operation, which, though ordinarily simple enough, seemed to me under the circumstances, almost marvelous. I concluded to take his advice when he said, "If you aren't feeling well, I suggest you don't look in this mirror."

No, I wouldn't eat breakfast, probably would feel better if I fasted. It was a dismal sounding gong that called us to breakfast anyhow—a fitting accompaniment to the gloom of the weather. However, before attempting to dress I ate an apple which Hugh J. handed me. Without hurry I put on my clothes, and started for the deck; but the swaying staircase and the madly moving world of water stirred my feelings with a desire for solitude. Yielding, I hurried to my room, where in less time than it takes to tell you, the apple and I parted company forever. I wondered what there was in common between a Jonathan apple and a Jonah that could produce such like effects.[35] Though I arrived at no definite conclusion, one thing was most certain: My sympathy was wholly with the whale. I understood, too, how Jonah escaped being thrown into the sea. If I could have entirely followed the whale's example, I, too, would have swum for land.

Hugh J. returned from breakfast looking as robust and rosy as an athlete. . . . Limp and dejected, I looked at him, healthy and happy, and began, right then and there, to doubt the wisdom of the Revolutionary statesman[36] who declared that "all men are created equal."

Feeling somewhat better, I started again for the deck, and was not a little consoled when I passed a poor Chinaman with perspiration standing in beads on his jaundiced-looking face, and sitting holding his knees looking, as I'm sure he felt, the most forsaken, limpy lump of humanity in existence.

At any rate, I had company in furnishing amusement for the chosen few. This time I reached only the top of the stairs, when that intense yearning to be alone drove me back to my cabin. Good-bye last night's dinner! Good-bye yesterday's luncheon! And during the next sixty hours, good-bye everything I had ever eaten since I was a babe on Mother's knee! I'm not sure I didn't cross the threshold into the pre-existent state.

In the tossing and heaving of the ship, as well as of internal conditions, there was no respite. She would mount the crest of a huge wave then plunge head-on; but before

Crossing the Pacific Ocean

hitting the bottom of the trough, she would plunge to "port,"[37] then instantly veer to "starboard;"[38] hesitating a moment, she would give a shimmy-like shiver and plunge again—turning, veering, "shimmying" in endless repetition, until it seemed that life was made up of nothing else. The dance floor is not the only place where disgraceful, degenerate movements may lead to ill.

And all this was on the placid Pacific! Heaven be merciful to me if we sail a tempestuous sea!

Thursday, I managed to eat a little soup and retain it. Friday, though the sea began heaving with renewed vigor, I continued to gain. One incident that day proved a very great impetus to my speedy convalescence. Brother Hugh hadn't been quite so brisk as usual, and I noticed that his rosy cheek had assumed a somewhat faded hue; but he went to breakfast as usual, thus maintaining his excellent record of not having missed a meal. I was still holding pretty close to the old berth. About 10:30 he came in somewhat flushed about the face, but pale about the mouth and eyes. For a moment, neither of us said anything; then the humor of the situation getting the mastery, he said: "I guess I might as well confess to you that I've just had my turn." In the interim of laughter, he explained that after breakfast he went to the library to write some letters, when all at once he became aware of an unpleasant feeling creeping over him. With the instinct of his sea-faring ancestors, he started for the pure sea breezes that were blowing on deck; but suddenly the company of fellow-passengers became most objectionable and turning his back upon them, he started downstairs most unceremoniously. Fortunately, he managed to reach the passageway leading to our room, when, presto! he reached seclusion, but the deck behind him looked like the "Milky Way." The incomprehensible thing to me is that this spontaneous outburst ended his sea-sickness.

We had a pretty rough voyage, and a cold one, having sailed so far north that we could glimpse the snowcapped mountains of the Aleutian Islands. However, messages received disclosed the fact that the *Monteagle,* a sister ship to ours, though she left eight days before we did is only a comparatively short distance ahead of us with most of her life boats washed overboard. Undoubtedly, she was in the center of the sweeping gale.[39]

He drew a circle that shut me out—
Heretic, rebel, a thing to flout.
But love and I had the wit to win!
We drew a circle that took him in.
        —Edwin Markham[1]

A mortal! His life like a torrential mountain stream dashing against jagged rocks, foaming, roaring, then finding quiet places of depth and restfulness, places of meditation and with opportunity to pray that it may not dissipate itself in purposeless spray! What a study he is for his fellowmen. This is particularly true aboard ship where one has time for contemplation. What secrets, hopes, ambitions are locked in the breast of the gentleman sitting opposite? On deck a woman makes a heroic effort to smile, but one suspects her heart is leaden, for there was something akin to tragedy on her face as the vessel left port. It would make a pungent picture if the story of these lives were thrown upon a screen. And how startling it would be if such a picture were embellished by the thoughts of the actors! There would be pathos and comedy, tragedy, despair, romance, with all their variations.

Here is unmistakable culture making the society of this passenger very delightful, but unfortunately others are of quite a different class. However, the observant person learns that it is unwise arbitrarily to classify fellow travelers. Not infrequently some, at first highly rated, prove disappointing in one particular or another; and often those looked upon with less favor show admirable qualities.

A case in point was a lady aboard the *Empress of Japan*, who was traveling with her husband. A handsome, though rather coarse-appearing and loud-speaking woman, her conduct was offensive to many of the passengers. But the maternal tenderness she exhibited toward the children of a lady who was ill touched the hearts of all who saw it. As she cuddled one curly little head to her breast, tears came into her eyes; her hoydenish spirit was subdued and chastened, another instance of a helpless child calling forth the angelic instincts of true womanhood. A man, who had often been heard to flatter her, remarked that she was a beautiful flower. She retorted, "A flower! Bah! I'm nothing but a weed." Then as she pressed the little head closer to her bosom, she wistfully added, "But I'm a better weed for having held this little one in my arms."

Crossing the 180th meridian,[2] that mythical line running from the North to the South Pole, is a time of interest aboard ship. The westbound traveler who crosses this line loses a day, when eastbound he gains one. For instance, our travelers retired Tuesday night, December 14th, and arose the following morning on Thursday, the 16th. Had they been sailing eastward and reached this line Tuesday evening, they would have retired as usual, and next morning it would still be Tuesday. This arrangement was made by mutual consent of all civilized nations, and the 180th meridian was chosen because it traverses the Pacific Ocean, touching practically none of the islands, and consequently this arbitrary change of days does not disrupt social, religious, or business affairs.

The necessity for such an adjustment is obvious. Suppose the reader enters upon a trip around the world. Going west, he of course travels with the sun and is obliged daily to turn his watch back to keep the correct time. Upon returning to the starting point he would have turned his watch back twenty-four hours, thereby losing an entire day. He would think it was Saturday when in reality it would be Sunday. Conversely, when encircling the globe traveling east, the watch is set forward each day. Of course the days are shorter than normal, and upon returning the traveler has gained twenty-four hours. He would think it was Sunday when it was Saturday. The change made at the 180th meridian equalizes this difference, whatever the direction of one's travels, and keeps the days of the week straight for the whole world.

Incidentally it furnishes our missionaries with an unanswerable argument against those who, notwithstanding the importance they attach to their day of worship, are still influenced by an imaginary and man-made line. It is an actual fact that people living in the South Sea Islands, and but a few miles apart, worship on different days.

During the night of December 22nd, the missionaries emerged from an extremely gloomy and tempestuous winter into what seemed a balmy spring. What difference sunshine makes in our lives! Nature had changed moods and even morose passengers followed her example.

The *Empress* was anchored just outside the breakwater of Yoko-hama harbor. Rosy tints of the rising sun spread over serene sea and landscape, and a fleet of white-sailed smacks making for their fishing fields added brilliancy to the scene. Off in the distance the sacred mountain of Japan, Fujiyama,[3] majestic in its covering of snow, but its natural austerity lessened by the mellow morning light, presented an inspiring picture. The justly famous "glow" of early morning in the Swiss Alps,[4] about which one often reads and too seldom sees, was visible in all its glory on Fujiyama, though it was one hundred miles [160.93 km] away.

Imagine, if you can, being aboard a great airplane which had conveyed you to some distant inhabited planet. Think what your feelings would be as the craft settled gently to its landing place and you looked eagerly over the vessel's side at the expectant groups awaiting your arrival. Your emotions, as you viewed their strange features and attire and listened to their incomprehensible chatter, would probably not be greatly unlike those of the traveler just emerging from well-known Occidental scenes to the unfamiliar ones of the Orient.[5] Here, too, one enters a new world. The people, themselves so different in features and dress from the Europeans, the buildings, temples, pagodas and shrines, rikishas[6] drawn by fleet-footed youths, heavy wagons drawn by men or oxen or small horses or by a combination of all three, all were as unusual as if the stranger were indeed arriving on a heretofore unknown planet.

But no! After running the gauntlet of custom officials he attempts to cross the street and is in grave danger of colliding with an intimate acquaintance—one might say a rattling good friend—a Ford automobile. One feels inclined to pick it up and hug it, such is the delight at seeing something so familiar.

Without counting small isles whose coast line is less than two and a half miles [4.02 km], Japan is composed of nearly five hundred islands, 162,000 square miles [419,578 sq. km], approximately but twice the size of Utah. When it is remembered that but one twelfth of the land is arable and that it supports approximately sixty million people, one can understand the phenomenal economy which is a potent cause of the country's greatness. Every child has thought of the Chinese and Japanese as standing with their feet up and heads hanging down. We adults view their habits in a similar light. It is a land of incongruities. On every hand, the European meets with, to him, highly interesting and even astonishing sights and experiences. In passing, it might be noted that in Japan all who are not Oriental are European. The ladies have their hair dressed in a quaint but artistic fashion and, even on the streets, wear kimonos[7] whose color and design might well arouse

Arriving in the Islands of Japan

the envy of their foreign sisters; but the clumsy wooden sandals[8] detract much from their appearance. A few Japanese maidens, shod thus, tripping daintily along the paved streets make almost as much noise as a band of wild horses would do.

During most of the year the profusion of flowers gives off a delicate perfume, but with this are mingled many offensive odors. One is delayed on the street by a cumbersome ox-cart or must wait while a swarm of rikishas flit by, and sees flying overhead a strictly modern airplane. The people remove their shoes, or the strips of wood which answer therefore, upon entering a house or church, or even a store, but hats need not necessarily be removed. They eat with chopsticks which are hardly as thick as, though slightly longer than, a lead pencil, and the dexterity displayed in taking two of these sticks in one hand and with them picking up all kinds of food is indeed surprising.

The Japanese are said to bathe more often than any other people in the world, and no home is complete without a bathroom. Often these are exposed to the weather and gaze of the curious pass-erby in summertime and are only partially protected from wintry blasts by bamboo screens which can be raised or lowered at will. President Grant, who was the first missionary from our church to Japan and who is well acquainted with Nipponese customs, says when one has visitors in that land it is regarded as a compliment to ask them to bathe.

For generations these people have had the habit of sitting on their feet, not cross-legged as the Pacific Islanders do, but with the feet bent back under them. They tire when they sit on chairs; and in trains and even in the meetings which were held, they often climbed on benches or chairs and doubled their feet under them. Some writers attribute the universal shortness of Japanese legs to this habit.

Babies are carried on their mothers' backs, as the American Indians do, and women frequently engage in very hard labor while thus burdened. And speaking of babies, one is reminded of the curious Japanese method of reckoning age. A child born December 31st is considered two years old on January 1st, because it has lived in two different years.

In most countries the purchaser who buys in quantities obtains a better price, but the reverse is true in Japan. For example, Brother McKay wanted a pencil, the price of which was two sen.[9] It was learned that twelve would cost twenty-five sen. A single collar cost fifty sen; half a dozen would cost seventy sen each. The underlying thought is based on justice. A person wealthy enough to buy in quantities should pay a higher price. For this reason they have a price for the man who walks to the store, a higher one for him who rides in a rikisha, and he who rides in an auto must pay the maximum.

The politeness of the Japanese is proverbial. A stranger could not easily lose himself. He inquires the way to a certain place. Perhaps the person addressed does not understand him, but usually he will stop every passerby until one is found who does understand, and will often accompany the stranger and point out the way or even go with him to his destination. The man or woman whose hair is beginning to turn gray is never permitted to stand in a street car, and the conductors on cars and trains lift their caps and ask for fares or tickets most apologetically.

The story is told of two travelers who inquired the way to a certain street. The man accosted did not possess the desired information, and stood in embarrassment while they walked on. A moment later they heard him calling and waited while he ran breathlessly to them. He fairly exuded apologies: "Will you kindly pardon my inexcusable ignorance in not being able to give you the information you asked for? My brother came along, just after you left me, and I asked him, and to my shame he did not know either."

Trained as he is in Sunday school[10] procedure and loving the work as he does, one cannot imagine Brother McKay being embarrassed by a crowd of Sunday school children; and still he was visibly so at the first school he attended in Tokyo.[11] A number of children came to the mission house. Except for the fact that the boys wore plain kimonos and the girls gaily colored ones, there was little difference in their dress. Brother McKay wanted to greet them properly and held out his hand for that purpose, but their surprised glances traveled from his hand to his face, to ascertain if possible what they were expected to do. Later he learned that shaking hands is an unknown custom with them. One might go on almost indefinitely describing Japanese peculiarities, but time and space forbid. Suffice it to say that they are an extremely courteous and delightfully interesting people, and one sails regretfully away from their land.

The gospel has not made great headway in Japan. Comparatively few hearts have been touched by the divine power. The people through curiosity will investigate, but they do so as they might study a scientific theory, and while recognizing its worth as a splendid moral and social system, they fail to discover its divinity. One could not find a better exemplification of the statement that the things of God cannot be understood except through his spirit. The devotion of the few into whose hearts the convincing

Arriving in the Islands of Japan

testimony had really entered, resembled that of faithful church members the world over. But some have accepted the gospel merely as an experiment and in much the same spirit which they manifest in adopting European clothing that can be laid aside at will.

CHAPTER 3

The first and best victory is to conquer self; to be conquered by self is, of all things, the most shameful and vile.

—Plato[1]

The Japanese mission,[2] at the time of the visit herein described, was in charge of President Joseph H. Stimpson,[3] then nearing the end of his second term of service there, he having spent a total of eleven years in that field. His wife accompanied him as a bride on the last mission and at the time of this visit they had three beautiful children,[4] the oldest of which talked Japanese as fluently as he did English. Perhaps no better opportunity will present itself to say that Sister [Mary E.] Stimpson[5] is one of the gems of the church, hospitable, industrious, and willing to expatriate herself because of her deep and abiding love for missionary work.

The mission home was a comfortable one. Conforming to usual Japanese custom, the visitors were immediately invited to bathe, and having heard of the novel methods, they were glad to accept. A fire is built in the iron box in one end of the tub, which in this instance was a wooden affair about four feet [1.22 m] deep and nearly as wide. This oven heats the water almost to the boiling point. The bather is supposed to wash himself thoroughly, for which purpose there is a basin, soap, and hose with running water; then he climbs into the tub and soaks in water as hot as it is humanly possible to have it and live. Thus the entire family bathes in the same water without having it become very dirty.

Even in so-called heathen Japan, elaborate decorations were made in honor of the Christmas holidays. On each side of the door in front of many buildings, a bunch of pine branches and bamboo canes were to be seen. It is said the pine indicates a desire for long life, and the bamboo expresses other good wishes. Under President Stimpson's direction an interesting Christmas program was given at the home. The natives sat on mats on the floor with feet doubled up under them for nearly three hours and apparently enjoyed it.[6]

Meetings were attended by the special missionaries in Tokyo, Kofu,[7] and Osaka.[8] The people listen attentively, but it is rather discouraging to think that after almost twenty years of earnest work there were but 125 church members in Japan. Brother McKay intended going to Hokkaido[9] on the north island where there was a branch[10] of the church. A start was made with Brother and Sister Stimpson and their baby in the party. The steamer, plying between the islands, was anchored in the open sea and a tug conveyed the passengers to it. A violent storm was raging, and even before the tug left its pier it began bucking after the fashion of a western bronco. Passengers resembled animated shuttlecocks. Sister Stimpson literally tossed her baby to Brother Cannon while she threw sundry other things to the fishes. This was her first experience with the malady. As the tug came alongside the steamer, the danger of attempting to jump from one vessel to the other became evident. One moment they would crash violently together and the next would be so far apart that even a trained broad jumper could not make the spring. A strong impression to turn back came to Brother McKay, and though greatly disappointed all agreed it would be unwise to proceed in the face of this feeling.

The suitcases, etc., were being shifted to the steamer when President Stimpson's attention was called to the fact that he was losing his luggage. He turned, and his face, a pitiful mixture of ashy gray and yellowish green, confirmed his words: "My luggage isn't the only thing I'm losing." It should be recorded to Brother McKay's credit that in this case he escaped seasickness—by an extremely narrow margin. It will never be known what would have occurred had they gone on, but having in mind the prophetic words, that the head of this tour should be inspired to avoid dangers seen and unseen, no one would have dared disregard the impression.

The Japanese are as modest as the Yankees, and not a whit more so, when talking of their own land. One is not justified in speaking of the beautiful, they say, until Nikko[11] has been seen. It is truly a delightful place and a visit there vindicates in large measure the pride which the natives have in it. The ornate temples and "sacred" places are bewildering in number and beauty, though some of the beauty borders on the grotesque. Indeed, throughout Japan there is a mixture of the sublime and what to the European is the ridiculous, how sublime and ridiculous only those know who have visited the land.[12]

At all "sacred" places the visitors had to remove their shoes, and at the "sanctum sanctorum" they were obliged to discard overcoats as well, despite extremely cold weather.

President Stimpson tells of three elders who visited this place and were told at the door that no one without faith could enter.

"We have faith," was the missionary's reply.

"If you have faith, you may come in for one yen each."

"But we have more faith than that," replied the elder. "We have faith that we can all come in for one yen." Their faith was effective.

One's stock of adjectives is exhausted in attempting to describe the carvings and decorations on the buildings. Here are the originals of the three monkeys, one of which holds his hand over eyes, one over mouth, and one over ears, indicating that man should see no evil, speak no evil, and hear no evil. The cryptomeria trees[13] are as indescribable as the temples. They are extremely tall and stately evergreens, many of them six or seven feet [1.83 m or 2.13 m] in diameter and some of them much more than that.

At one place many stone lanterns about six feet [1.83 m] high were seen, and among them was one which, according to tradition, had formed the intolerable habit of turning into a ghost and frightening everybody away, so a wire cage was placed around it. Since then it has behaved properly.

After viewing the river, the waterfalls, forests, temples, and shrines, one leaves the place with the feeling that the Japanese are not far wrong in their boastful statement regarding its beauty.

In the car with Brother McKay and his party between Nikko and Tokyo were a number of natives. In one corner was a dainty young lady attired in the usual attractive Japanese style, with elaborate hair dressing, highly colored and beautiful kimono, stockings which reached to her ankles and the inevitable wooden sandals. She was accompanied by a young man and an older lady, and in due time they opened a package of lunch. Chopsticks, kept in sealed wax paper as a sanitary measure, were used to pick up the food, not a particle of which was touched by the hands. The skill displayed in using these sticks attracted the attention of our curious Americans and perhaps they watched the diners more intently than good breeding would permit. The lunch reminded them that thoughtful Sister Stimpson had brought along a box of sandwiches, and they, too, began their meal.

Think how an American eats a sandwich! He takes it in one hand, or perhaps in two, and tears away at it very much as a bear would do. It was not long until, instead of being observers, the Americans became the observed. A little girl sitting opposite tried vainly not to smile. Too polite to laugh openly, she turned her head and looked out of the window to conceal her amusement.[14]

The missionaries believed their hands were clean at the commencement of the meal, but at its conclusion Brother McKay went to the washroom, and when he rejoined his party, remarked: "Do you know what those people said as I came by them? If they did not actually say it they thought, 'Now that he has eaten with his dirty hands he has washed them.'" After all, many habits which seem peculiar or even ridiculous to us might be imitated with profit.

On a part of this trip, it was not possible to secure accommodations in anything but the first-class sleeper, and in the mission field to travel first class is not usually deemed compatible with the proper spirit of humility. Brother McKay, however, consoled his associates by telling of Brother [Christian D.] Fjeldsted's[15] prayer, "Give us de best dere is, Lord, for you know, Lord, de best is none too good for us." Some of our readers will remember Brother Fjeldsted as a good old Danish brother, now gone to a splendid reward, who was one of the First Council of Seventy.[16]

Having letters of introduction to Dr. [Eikichi] Kamata, president of the Keio University[17] at Tokyo, and Mr. Konoto, immigration commissioner of Japan, Brother McKay and his party called on them. Both of these gentlemen had been in America and spoke English fluently. The university president was surrounded by professors and other guests who were eating, drinking, and smoking in his office. The other gentleman was visited at his home. When the maid opened the door at the last named place, she dropped on her knees and bowed until her head touched the floor. Visitors must remove their shoes before entering a Japanese home and as the weather was cold our travelers had taken their slippers with them. This gentleman was the embodiment of courtesy and expressed a desire to aid Brother McKay or the missionaries in every way. The maid brought cups of coffee and presented them to the visitors, first dropping on her knees. When it was explained that they would prefer hot water instead of coffee, that was brought with equal courtesy.[18] These visits were made on January 1st, there, as at home, a great holiday. Bands were out in gorgeous uniforms. Gaily dressed men, women, and children thronged the streets, and the colors were remarkable and in some cases startling. Street cars were crowded; almost every rikisha was in use, a large number of them having two men, tandem fashion, so that greater speed could be attained and a more elaborate display made. Many of the rikisha men were barelegged, but President Stimpson said one must be here in the summer to see bare legs at their best—or worst.[19]

Few experiences come to church members which are more inspirational than to attend a missionary meeting in the field. The courage, faith, and devotion of our young men, their exemplary and self-sacrificing lives, bear a most eloquent testimony of the divinity of this work. No sermon, howsoever gifted the speaker, is comparable to this practical demonstration of desire to serve one's fellowmen.

The meeting held in Tokyo was as a rich feast to a hungry man. Elders Myrl L. Bodily[20] and [Louring A.] Whittaker[21] had come in from Hokkaido, where they were laboring with energy and ability. The same spirit was manifested by Elders Owen McGary[22] and Irwin T. Hicken,[23] laboring in Osaka, Elder [Joseph S.] Pyne[24] and [Deloss W.] Holley[25] from Kofu and Elder [Alma] Howard Jensen[26] who, with President and Sister Stimpson, was working in Tokyo. To think of these young and inexperienced missionaries and their earnest efforts to redeem a benighted people is to praise the Lord. One is reminded of other modest characters, now acknowledged heroes, the ancient prophets and apostles of the Bible and the early leaders of the church.

If further evidence of the divinity of this work were needed, it could be found in the love which characterizes the missionary. With possibly one exception, the visitors had met none of these brethren before; but still they seemed to be life-long acquaintances—nay, more than that, of one family, brothers in the flesh instead of merely in belief. As the visiting party boarded the train for Osaka, the elders remaining in Tokyo ran along the platform to again press Brother McKay's hand and hear his words, "The Lord bless you, my brother."

Nara,[27] former capital of the empire, is not far behind Nikko as a showplace. Its artistic park is full of deer, believed by the Japanese to be sacred. They will eat from a stranger's hand. There was a sacred horse, which, probably due to ignorance on the subject, looked like a common glass-eyed cayuse.[28] There were sacred pigeons, temples, and bells. It would appear that nearly everything is sacred to a Japanese except his promise, but unless he is outrageously maligned he esteems a promise as the least sacred thing in the world.

Fourteen hours with an express train carried the travelers from Osaka to Shimonoseki,[29] the point of embarkation for Fusan,[30] in Korea. As they proceeded southward the climate became milder and before the sea was reached many heavily laden orange trees were seen. Men and women were plowing their rice fields, if drawing a pointed stick to which a cow is hitched, through mud almost knee deep can be called plowing.

Comfortable quarters were obtained aboard the *Komo Maru* which plies between this Japanese island and the mainland of Asia. As the vessel left the busy and lighted harbor and entered the inky blackness which prevailed outside and the brethren thought of the strange country and people to which they were going, their own ignorance of the customs and language, they thought of another journey taken by a man oppressed with serious sickness and the exalted words which he wrote:

"Lead, kindly Light, amid the encircling gloom,
Lead Thou me on!
The night is dark and I am far from home;
Lead Thou me on!
Keep Thou my feet; I do not ask to see
The distant scene; one step enough for me."[31]

CHAPTER 4

And this gospel of the kingdom shall be preached in all the world for a witness unto all nations; and then shall the end come.

—Matthew 24:14

An important part of Brother McKay's special mission was to visit China, and, if he felt so impressed, to dedicate[1] that vast realm for the preaching of the gospel. China had a well-developed civilization twenty-five centuries before Great Britain came into existence, and her age, if nothing else, should command respect. The thoughtful reader will appreciate some of the difficulties which our missionaries will encounter should they be called to that land, and the duty confronting this missionary party was approached with a sincere prayer for guidance to do what the Almighty desired, and nothing more.

These brethren were not the first from our church to set foot in China. Shortly after the people arrived in Utah, Elders Hosea Stout, James Lewis, and Chapman Duncan were sent to this benighted land. It seemed, however, that the time for preaching the gospel to the heathens had not arrived, and little was accomplished.[2]

The transition from bright and colorful Japan, an aggressive and virile world power in the making, to somber and gloomy China, a nation of decay and senility, is less abrupt because the traveler passes en route through Korea, an intermediate country less cheerful than the one and less funereal than the other.

Landing in Fusan, Korea, the visitors felt they were in another world, and their hasty journey through that land to Mukden [Shenyang], Manchuria,[3] accentuated the feeling.[4] The bearing and dress of the people, especially their strange and varied headgear, the clusters of homes whose color and shape make a village in the distance look like a group of toadstools, all awaken a desire within the traveler to tarry and become better acquainted. Nor are the sterile, rocky stretches of land and the bleak mountains without interest, though not approaching Japan in point of beauty. Roads appear to consist mainly of footpaths and the transportation of the country seems to be carried on the backs of cows and oxen. Yonder an immense load of straw moved along the path without any visible means of locomotion, but somewhere under the mass was a patient cow. At the same time the driver, trudging along on foot, had a huge load on his own back.

Straw appears to be the country's chief building material, as from it practically all the roofs and many of the sides of the houses in the country districts are constructed.

At Mukden it was necessary to change money into Chinese, a task approached with considerable trepidation, as travelers are warned against counterfeit money with which China is flooded. Not only was the bogus article a serious menace to the uninitiated, but bills issued by supposedly reputable banks had little or no value outside of the bank's particular district.

Brother McKay undertook to attend to this business while his companion secured railroad accommodations. The latter task was completed first and Brother Cannon found his chief standing somewhat uncertainly before a stoical Chinese money changer who had a "take it or leave it" look on his face. Brother McKay justly felt that the man was robbing him, and his Scotch blood rose in an instant and in vigorous rebellion at such thought. At that moment an American, who was leaving China and who had been making desperate efforts to exchange Chinese money for good American dollars, came up. The money changer's face lost some of its placidity as he saw his profits vanish while the fellow countrymen carried on their own negotiations. Not only was considerable money saved in the exchange but this gentleman gave information which subsequently was of great value to the travelers.

A glance at his map will show the reader that Mukden is far to the north and naturally, in midwinter, is extremely cold. From here the brethren entered China proper, another new world. And a ragged, dirty, starving, benighted, and altogether forbidding world it was. On that part of the country through which they traveled, practically no rain had fallen for two years, and at the stations they were besieged by beggars whose pinched features and half-clothed bodies bore pitiful evidence of intense suffering.

A stop was made at Shanghaiguan,[5] where so much fighting has been done during the present revolution. Here the missionaries caught their first glimpse of the Great Wall of China,[6] one of the marvels of all time. A British engineer has figured that it contains enough material to build a wall six feet high [1.83 m] and two feet [0.61 m] thick which would reach around the world at the equator. As the train was to remain there for a short time the missionaries started out to obtain a nearer view of the wall and perhaps a picture, when they were so beset by hordes of beggars that further progress was impossible. Though the weather was but little if any above zero, these pitiable creatures were nearly naked. It would be a compliment to call them ragged, and if some of them were not really starving they were past masters in the art of deceiving.

En route from Mukden to Peking [Beijing][7] many Japanese soldiers were seen along the railway line, and in their hearts, the travelers rather resented what seemed to be an unwarranted intrusion. But at one station, and much to their surprise, they saw an American flag and a group of real U.S. soldier boys. Their surprise hardly equaled that of one young chap as Brother McKay gave him a bear hug, which pleased him greatly after his astonishment had subsided. Though China at that time was comparatively peaceful, foreign powers were guarding the railway lines. This reconciled the visitors somewhat to the sight of the Japanese soldiers.

Think of a city of a million inhabitants without a street car or omnibus line! The principal means of transportation—indeed the only means except for one's legs and an occasional auto or a small horse-drawn carriage—were the innumerable rikishas. These flit rapidly and silently through crowded streets, dexterously avoiding collisions which to the traveler appear wholly unavoidable, and furnish an excellent opportunity of seeing Chinese life. A facetious American has dubbed these conveyances "pull-man" cars. This was Peking.

The missionaries had some little difficulty in finding a suitable hotel through the unjustifiable interference of a man who pretended to be able to understand English, but who did not really understand it or else willfully misled them.[8]

These brethren can never think of January 9, 1921, without a feeling of deep solemnity. As they approached the city on the previous evening they had looked in vain for a suitable spot away from the turmoil of the place where the dedicatory prayer could be offered should Brother McKay feel so impressed. Nothing but barren fields was to be seen. As the following day was Sunday, it was deemed the fitting time to attend to this duty, if it were to be done at all, and Peking seemed the proper place. The hordes of insistent and repulsive beggars made anything but a favorable impression. One could hardly restrain the thought that preaching the gospel to them was in reality "casting pearls before swine."[9]

However, with morning came a strong impression that the land should be dedicated for this purpose. But where to find a suitable place for the fulfillment of this duty was a serious question. It was felt that such a prayer should be offered under the blue heavens and in quiet, and from what they had seen of the city, no such spot existed. Naturally this duty might have been performed in a room of the hotel, but who could tell what gross sins might have been committed there?

It was an intensely cold though bright and clear winter morning as the missionaries went out into the narrow, crooked streets crowded with chattering and for the most part squalid Chinese. Placing themselves in the hands of the Lord to lead them as He saw fit, they walked almost directly to the walls of the "Forbidden City,"[10] the former home of emperors and nobility. Entering the gate they walked past shrines, pagodas, and temples fast falling to decay, as all else in China is, and came to a grove of what they took to be cypress trees. A hallowed and reverential feeling was upon them. It was one of those occasions which at rare intervals come to mortals when they are surrounded by a presence so sacred that human words would be disturbing. The brethren were very sure unseen holy beings were directing their footsteps.

On the way to this grove many people were passed, but the number gradually diminished as they reached its borders. In it only two men were to be seen, and these left almost immediately. There, in the heart of the capital of the most populous nation in the world, unnoticed and undisturbed by the multitudes who were almost within a stone's throw of them, they supplicated the Lord for his blessing, after which Brother McKay offered the dedicatory prayer which in substance was as follows:

> Our Heavenly Father: In deep humility and gratitude, we thy servants approach thee in prayer and supplication on this most solemn and momentous occasion. We pray thee to draw near unto us, to grant us the peace asked for in the opening prayer by Brother Cannon; and to let the channel of communication between thee and us be open, that thy word may be spoken, and thy will be done. We pray for forgiveness of any folly, weakness, or light mindedness that it may not stand between us and the rich outpouring of thy Holy Spirit. Holy Father, grant us thy peace and thy inspiration, and may we not be disturbed during this solemn service.
>
> For thy kind protection and watchful care over us in our travels by land and by sea, we render our sincere gratitude. We are grateful, too, for the fellowship and brotherly love we have one for the other, that our hearts beat as one, and that we stand before thee this holy Sabbath day with clean hands, pure hearts, and with our minds free from all worldly cares.

Though keenly aware of the great responsibility this special mission entails, yet we are thankful that thou hast called us to perform it. Heavenly Father, make us equal, we beseech thee, to every duty and task. As we visit thy Missions in the various parts of the world, give us keen insight into the conditions and needs of each, and bestow upon us in rich abundance the gift of discernment.

With grateful hearts, we acknowledge thy guiding influence in our travels to this great land of China, and particularly to this quiet, and secluded spot in the heart of this ancient and crowded city. We pray that the petition setting this spot apart as a place of prayer and dedication may be granted by thee and that it may be held sacred in thy sight.

Holy Father, we rejoice in the knowledge of the Truth, and in the restoration of the Gospel of the Redeemer. We praise thy name for having revealed thyself and thine Only Begotten Son to thy servant, Joseph the Prophet, and that through thy revelations the Church, in its purity and perfection, was established in these last days, for the happiness and eternal salvation of the human family. We thank thee for the Priesthood, which gives men authority to officiate in thy holy name.

In this land there are millions who know not thee nor thy work, who are bound by the fetters of superstition and false doctrine, and who have never been given the opportunity even of hearing the true message of their Redeemer. Countless millions have died in ignorance of thy plan of life and salvation. We feel deeply impressed with the realization that the time has come when the light of the glorious Gospel should begin to shine through the dense darkness that has enshrouded this nation for ages.

To this end, therefore, by the authority of the holy Apostleship, I dedicate and consecrate and set apart the Chinese Realm for the preaching of the Gospel of Jesus Christ as restored in this dispensation through the Prophet Joseph Smith. By this act, shall the key be turned that unlocks the door through which thy chosen servants shall enter with Glad Tidings of Great Joy to this benighted and senile nation. That their message may be given in peace, we beseech thee, O God, to stabilize the Chinese government. Thou knowest how it is torn with dissension at the present time, and how faction contends against faction to the oppression of the people and the strangling of the nation's life. Holy Father, may peace and stability be established throughout this republic, if not by the present government,

Dedicating the Chinese Realm

then through the intervention of the allied powers of the civilized world.

Heavenly Father, manifest thy tender mercy toward thy suffering children throughout this famine-stricken realm! Stay the progress of pestilence, and may starvation and untimely death stalk no more through the land. Break the bands of superstition, and may the young men and young women come out of the darkness of the past into the Glorious Light now shining among the children of men. Grant, our Father, that these young men and women may, through upright, virtuous lives, and prayerful study, be prepared and inclined to declare this message of salvation in their own tongue to their fellowmen. May their hearts, and the hearts of this people, be turned to their fathers that they may accept the opportunity offered them to bring salvation to the millions who have gone before.

May the elders and sisters whom thou shalt call to this land as missionaries have keen insight into the mental and spiritual state of the Chinese mind. Give them special power and ability to approach this people in such a manner as will make the proper appeal to them. We beseech thee, O God, to reveal to thy servants the best methods to adopt and the best plans to follow in establishing thy work among this ancient, tradition-steeped people. May the work prove joyous, and a rich harvest of honest souls bring that peace to the workers' hearts which surpasseth all understanding.

Remember thy servants, whom thou hast chosen to preside in thy Church. We uphold and sustain before thee President Heber J. Grant who stands at the head at this time, and his counselors, President Anthon H. Lund and President Charles W. Penrose.[11] Bless them, we pray thee, with every needful blessing, and keep them one in all things pertaining to thy work. Likewise bless the Council of the Twelve. May they continue to be one with the First Presidency. Remember the Presiding Patriarch,[12] the First Council of Seventy, the Presiding Bishopric,[13] and all who preside in stakes, wards, quorums, organizations, temples, Church schools, and missions. May the spirit of purity, peace, and energy characterize all thy organizations.

Heavenly Father, be kind to our loved ones from whom we are now separated. Let thy Holy Spirit abide in our homes, that sickness, disease and death may not enter therein.

Hear us, O kind and Heavenly Father, we implore thee, and open the door for the preaching of thy Gospel from one end of this realm to the other, and may thy servants who declare this message be especially blest and directed by thee. May thy kingdom come, and thy will be done speedily here on earth among all peoples, kindreds and tongues preparatory to the winding up scenes of these latter days!

And while we behold thy guiding hand through it all, we shall ascribe unto thee the praise, the glory and the honor, through Jesus Christ our Lord and Redeemer, Amen.

The brethren felt that this prayer was acceptable to the Almighty.[14] His spirit gave approving testimony and at the same time revealed for their comfort and blessing some things which should transpire in the future.

Poor old China, the victim of intrigues among nations who covet her coal and iron deposits, the victim of floods and droughts, of famines and pestilence, and worst of all, the victim of her own inefficiency and helplessness! Assuredly she needs someone to plead her cause before the throne of grace. China is living in the dead past of two thousand years and has hardly begun to realize it.[15]

And still her condition is not hopeless. She is as one passing through travail. A new nation, let us hope, is being born, a nation of great potential power, with leaders sufficiently wise to develop and properly exploit her natural resources. Among this people are hosts of splendid individuals, men and women of stable character, of refinement and intelligence. That many of them will accept the truth when it is presented to them cannot be doubted, if one may judge from the faithful Latter-day Saints of that race who have joined the church in Hawaii and Samoa.[16]

This chapter should not be closed without expressing the hope that should any reader of these lines be called to labor as a missionary in that land he will not feel he is going among a people who are unworthy of his efforts. He will find there castes and outcasts, but among both will be found men and women who will prove a credit to the church.

Exploring the Interior of China

 The vice of our theology is seen in the claim that the Bible is a closed book, and that the age of inspiration is past.

—Emerson[1]

On the day following the dedication of China for the preaching of the gospel, a visit was made to Charles R. Crane,[2] United States ambassador. Mr. Crane, an affable and intelligent gentleman, proved to be somewhat familiar with the history of the "Mormon" people. He made the statement that they could make a distinct and valuable contribution to China's advancement because of their successful experience in redeeming arid regions.[3]

Mr. Crane spoke feelingly of conditions prevailing in that distressed land where fifteen million people were facing starvation and must inevitably meet this fate, he said, unless help came from the outside. It was reported that in some districts men were killing their wives and, what is infinitely more horrible, selling their daughters into shameful slavery to avoid seeing them tortured by hunger.

Think of what the perfectly organized Church of Jesus Christ could do for this people! Presumably more than four hundred million had enough to eat, while fifteen million were starving. Had those with sufficient food accepted and obeyed the simple practice of fasting one day each month and given the food thus saved to the poor, and this had been distributed without cost, as the Lord wills it should be through his organization, the fifteen million sufferers would have had two meals a day for a month, by which time another fast day would have rolled around and furnished them with an additional thirty days' supply. Well might the Lord say, "For as the heavens are higher than the earth, so are my ways higher than your ways, and my thoughts than your thoughts."[4]

Pride in the ability to speak a foreign language is rather universal. Often this ability resembles the 180th meridian—purely imaginary. In Japan a milk cart bore the illuminating inscription "Virtuous Milk." Well, why shouldn't it? Virtue denotes purity. Another sign read, "Photographer executed." Upon approaching the elevator of their hotel in Peking, the special missionaries saw written in bold letters, "No Raisins." For a moment they were nonplussed, then it occurred to them that "raisin" is an elevator's chief occupation. The power was off in the next hotel at which the missionaries stopped and the sign on the elevator there read, "No Currents."

However, it is not to be supposed that these people lack in ability as linguists. In apparent contradiction to what has been said, many Chinese speak excellent English, and on the main lines of travel the stranger may go to a ticket office and state his needs with every assurance of being understood. A visit to the Peking Teachers' College, maintained by the government, aroused wonderment. Those who believe the Chinese are a degraded and ignorant people should have been with this party. Native boys were studying college subjects and in several classes were using English textbooks. The president of this college is a graduate of Columbia University,[5] and the professor who showed the visitors around spoke their language almost faultlessly.

An entire book should be written about the great Chinese wall or it should be dismissed with a line or two. Brother McKay and his companion viewed it from Ching-lung-Chiao[6] and at the expense of some energy climbed to the highest point of the wall anywhere near the village and were richly rewarded for the effort. It would reach farther than from Salt Lake City[7] to Chicago[8] and has stood for more than two thousand years, formerly an insurmountable barrier to the invading hordes of Tartar tribes. It twists and writhes over the desolate and barren mountains like a ponderous serpent.

Leaving Peking by train, the missionaries had a good opportunity of comparing the courtesy of a Chinese gentleman with that of a European traveler, and to the shame of the white race the comparison was altogether in favor of the so-called heathen. This gentleman, evidently wealthy, was accompanied by his son and a host of servants. With charming courtesy, they had the servants bring to each of the missionaries a cup of tea and cigarettes. The visitors endeavored to show appreciation for the thoughtfulness, though declining their offerings.

The route from Peking to Shanghai[9] leads through Tianjin,[10] a city of a million people and the sea port of North China. When our travelers alighted from the train and showed a disposition to take rikishas, the men fought so ferociously for the chance to earn a fare that policemen, with clubs about three feet [0.91 m] long and as thick as a very heavy cane, actually beat them off as they would a pack of yelping wolves, which indeed they resembled more than human beings. Though the insistent attention of these creatures was extremely annoying, one could not suppress a feeling of deep sympathy for them. They appeared willing to work, but the opportunity of earning a few cents was evidently rare.

It is thirty-two hours with a fast train from Tianjin to Shanghai, and the route runs through the edge of the Shandong province,[11] one of the districts most affected by the famine. Even from the railroad many heartrending sights were to be seen. Millions of people live in mud hovels, less habitable than the Indian tepee.

But the zenith of primitive living was seen on the boats at Pukou,[12] where the famed Yangtze River[13] was crossed on a ferry plying between that city and Nanking [Nanjing].[14] On these boats or rafts children are born, reared, married, raise their own families, and die. Almost their first visit ashore, and certainly their last, is when they are carried out and buried in some mound in a barren field.

As has been stated, the impelling motive in writing an account of this tour is to bear witness of the goodness of the Lord to those who depend upon him. On one occasion President Wilford Woodruff[15] was heard to say to a departing missionary, "When you need clothes, or food, or a bed just tell the Lord and he will supply it." Of course these words are true, for they merely state in slightly different form a positive promise of the Master himself, a promise often put to the test by members of this church.

This special missionary party had reason to know that the Almighty always does his full part. Their train arrived in Shanghai at eleven p.m. and though reservations had been made in advance through the hotel in Peking, no accommodations were available. People were occupying chairs in the lobbies of every respectable hotel in the city. But the Lord had been asked to open the way for his servants, and after some delay the clerk concluded it would be possible to put cots in the ladies' drawing room; and this he did upon being assured that the missionaries would be up and dressed early on the following morning.

They learned the next day from an American doctor that he had been obliged to sleep on a billiard table with his overcoat as a pillow and with no bedding, though he was a frequent patron of this hotel and felt he had a "pull" there. It is a significant fact, too, that he arrived at the hotel before they did. The following evening the brethren had a comfortable room to themselves.

There is an incongruous mixture of Occidental civilization and Oriental primitiveness in Shanghai. Unlike Peking, the city has a street car system and other modern means of transportation. On some of the streets the visitor would think he was in Europe;

on others not ten minutes distant he might easily imagine himself in the innermost heart of China.

A most delightful voyage is that from Shanghai to Kobe,[16] Japan. For many miles the sea is discolored by the muddy waters of the Yellow [Huang][17] and the Yangtze Rivers. The first Japanese point to be reached was Nagasaki,[18] famous as the chief coal-loading station of the Far East.[19] Here, man power seems to be the cheapest thing on the market, and the largest steamers are loaded by hand. This operation furnishes one of the sights for which Nagasaki is famous. A number of barges come alongside the vessel and from these a series of platforms are built to the deck. Workers are stationed on each platform and the coal is passed from one to the other in baskets which contain about twenty-five pounds of coal. Men and women, boys and girls are engaged in this work. And how they do work! These baskets are passed from one person to the next with surprising rapidity, each line of people sending up about fifty baskets per minute, and there were enough lines working to put on about 500 tons per hour. They worked loading the *Tenyo Maru* from five o'clock in the morning until late that afternoon, though they had put three thousand tons into another ship during the night. In spite of this they were a merry and apparently lighthearted crowd, but signs of fatigue were evident before their task was completed. On one occasion when rushed for time, 5,500 tons of coal was loaded into one vessel in seven hours.

It would be worth a trip across the Pacific to see this beautiful landlocked harbor, with the green terraced slopes, the unique and picturesque houses lining the water and extending to the tops of the surrounding hills, the quaint water craft of every description including gondolas much resembling, though not so beautiful as, the Venetians.

The missionaries went ashore for a few hours and walked to the summit of one of the scenic hills. The houses, as is customary in Japan, are crowded close together, and inasmuch as they are all open, the visitor feels he is intruding into the privacy of the family; but there was evidence that no privacy exists, nor do the people desire it. The Europeans, with their strange clothes and manners, were a source of interest and amusement to the native children who had quite as much enjoyment out of it as the strangers did.

From Nagasaki to Kobe the vessel steams through the Inland Sea.[20] The mainland is visible on one side, and on the other are numerous mountainous islands, making the scene most picturesque and delightful. The water was as pacific as one could expect it to be from its name. One wonders how a comparatively few miles can make such a vast difference as is to be seen between Japan and China. One country is fertile and green and the other is most desolate. Naturally, southern China is less austere but there is little difference in latitude between Japan and that part of China which Brother McKay visited.

When pulling up to the wharf at Kobe, the vessel bumped into the concrete wall. Apparently this was not serious, but nevertheless it was destined to play a part in the brethren's plans.

The trip from Kobe to Tokyo was made by rail, as the passengers have the option of continuing with the boat or going overland and rejoining it at Yokohama. The missionaries again stopped off in Osaka and with the elders laboring there went to Kyoto[21] which is one of the most beautiful of all Japanese cities.

The sleeping cars in China and Japan are arranged on much the same order as are European day coaches—in compartments. These are very convenient when one is fortunate enough to secure a compartment alone or when the other occupants are of an agreeable sort; but when one has an upper berth and the man underneath smokes at least three times during the night, as was the case on this trip, it is far from pleasant.

This same smoker jumped simultaneously out of his bed and his kimono, which answered for pajamas, and wholly unadorned went through certain setting-up exercises, paying no more attention to fellow travelers or to the men and women who passed the open door than they paid to him. Indeed, a very fine looking young woman stepped into the doorway in order to permit a gentleman to pass her in the narrow corridor; but she and the unadorned man were equally unconcerned.

Mention has been made of the crowded condition of the hotels. The ships traveling eastward were likewise unable to care for the traffic at this season, and considerable difficulty was had in securing accommodations at all. While in Shanghai, efforts in this direction had been made, and the travelers finally succeeded in being booked in a cabin for three, the other occupant being a Chinese, who was to come aboard at Yokohama.

En route to Tokyo, Brother McKay asked Brother Cannon to stop off at Yokohama to see if he could not secure a cabin for two. At first the company courteously but positively declared this to be wholly impossible, but before Brother Cannon left the office the desired accommodations had been obtained, and the hand of the Lord was acknowledged in this matter, for the company declined to make any additional charge.

The skeptical reader will see nothing miraculous in this incident and will attribute it to chance, but these things occurred with such frequency during this tour that to give credit to chance or to any earthly power would be ungrateful. Chance does not discriminate between missionaries and other travelers, and on this and many subsequent occasions these brethren secured accommodations which even the steamship companies said could not possibly be had.

While in China and en route back to Japan, Brother McKay was concerned because he felt he should have two days more in which to complete the work in that land. But his plans seemed to demand that he sail with the *Tenyo Maru* as this was the only vessel which would take his party to Hawaii early enough to keep up with the outlined program. Brother Lloyd O. Ivie,[22] the newly appointed president of the Japanese mission, was expected on the next boat and it was desirable that Brother McKay should be present and arrange for the transfer of presidency and give such instructions as he might deem proper.

However, the *Tenyo Maru* was scheduled to sail without giving the opportunity of seeing Brother Ivie, or making other needed arrangements for the transfer. The brethren, though disappointed, prepared to leave at the scheduled time but learned after all their packing had been done that the apparently insignificant bump received by the vessel in Kobe was sufficiently serious to demand two days' delay, exactly the time needed, while the damage was being repaired.

Brother Ivie did not arrive as expected, but this extra time was sufficient for Brother McKay to make proper arrangements for the care of the mission after President [Joseph H.] Stimpson left, he having already been released and his passage to the United States engaged and paid for; so that while the accident was an inconvenient one for the steamship company and most of the passengers and resulted in the discharge of the captain, it was a fortunate one for the missionaries.

The visit to these lands was delightfully interesting.[23] The Japanese are looking for the best in everything, in science, in inventions, in government, in ships, in machinery; and it seems reasonable to expect that someday they will begin looking for the best in religion. But the sham and sophistry, the mass of error put forth under the label of Christ's holy church will not satisfy their critical minds, and has added to the suspicion with which they view foreign beliefs.

Most of the nations of the earth were represented at the wharf when the time finally came for the *Tenyo Maru* to leave for San Francisco via Hawaii.[24] It was a perfect bedlam. The band was playing, porters were hurrying aboard with luggage, mail wagons were forcing their way through crowds, bringing the last mail to the vessel.

As the boat moved slowly from the pier, most of those onboard threw rolls of colored paper to friends on shore, retaining one end themselves until there was a gorgeous mass of streamers connecting vessel with land. As the ship pulled out, the papers were unrolled and were so long that they extended some distance into the harbor, their own weight finally breaking them. It was a beautiful symbol of the ties which bind those departing to loved ones, and of the heart strings which are broken when the parting hour arrives.[25]

CHAPTER 6

In my labors as a missionary, it was much easier for me to ask the Lord for what I
needed than to ask of man; and the Almighty never failed to hear.

—George Q. Cannon[1]

It seemed hardly possible that the new world which our travelers entered at the harbor of Honolulu[2] is on the same globe as the cheerless one seen at China. This was truly a fairyland. Palms, ferns, flowers, and luxuriant tropical foliage, all contribute their part toward making this a terrestrial paradise. But before driving along the beach, which was lined with coconut palms, always leaning toward the sea, and with the stately royal palms, as straight as any arrow ever made, visitors must steam into the harbor at the entrance to which they are met by a crowd of boys and young men in the water who swim about the vessel and dive for coins thrown overboard by prodigal passengers.

President E. Wesley Smith[3] met Brother McKay's party at the pier and after Sister Kamohalii, a native member, had placed *leis* about their necks in behalf of the sisters of the branch, he took them to the very beautiful mission home where Sister [Mary H.] Smith,[4] the children, and Elders Lee Van Wagoner and Roland Browning[5] and Sisters Wealthy Clark[6] and Ivy May Frazier[7] extended hospitable welcome.

Hawaii furnishes a page of important missionary history. Among the first company sent to this land was George Q. Cannon. A few years later Joseph F. Smith,[8] at the time only fifteen years old, also went to this field. Though not on the islands at the same time, it was largely due to mutual interest in the natives that they first became well acquainted. Subsequently they labored together in the Quorum of Twelve and for more than a score of years were associated as counselors in the First Presidency and loved each other with all their intense natures.

It seemed fitting that a son of each of these men should be present during the meetings held in Hawaii by Brother McKay. More than once during the visit it was felt that the spirits of these departed leaders were present, and some experiences were had which are too sacred to publish to the world.[9]

The Hawaiian Islands offer almost as good a demonstration of Japanese life as does Japan itself, and there are so many Chinese residing there that, except for the beautiful surroundings, the visitor might easily think he was in China. At the time of this visit the Hawaiian Territorial Board of Health gave out figures which indicated that the pure native blood was being replaced by that of more vigorous nations. Of the 263,666 inhabitants, 159,900 were listed as Asiatics, divided as follows: 110,000 Japanese, 22,800 Chinese, 5,100 Koreans, and 22,000 Filipinos. There are also many Portuguese on the islands as well as representatives from almost every nation under the sun.

At Laie,[10] about thirty-five miles [56.33 km] from Honolulu, the church owns a rather large and productive plantation, a considerable part of which is devoted to sugarcane and pineapple culture. The temple is located here, and a school is also maintained by the church. One of Brother McKay's especial duties was to visit our schools, and some little time was spent in this beautiful place.

The children in attendance at this institution ranged in age from seven to fourteen years. They were under the direction of William T. Cannon, Jr., who was acting as principal, assisted by Mary S. Christensen,[11] Evelyn Olson,[12] Edith L. Bell,[13] Jane Jenkins,[14] Genevieve Hammond[15] and Elizabeth Hyde,[16] all missionaries giving their time gratuitously to this work.

Children and teachers formed in line and participated in the flag-raising ceremonies. When all was in readiness, little William Kaaa, a full-blooded Hawaiian, stepped from the ranks and said:

> Hats off!
> Along the street there comes
> A blare of bugles,
> A ruffle of drums,
> A flash of color beneath the sky,
> Hats off!
> The flag is passing by.

Then Master [Thomas] Marr Waddoups,[17] a young American, repeated:

> Now raise the starry banner up,
> Emblem of our country's glory,

And teach the children of this land
Its grave and wondrous story;
Of how in early times it waved
High o'er the Continentals,
Who fought and made our country free,
The one true home of liberty.

Next came a Japanese boy, Otockochi Matsumoto:

Salute the flag, oh children,
With grave and reverent hand,
For it means far more than the eye can see,
Your home and your native land.
And many have died for its crimson bars,
Its field of blue with the spangled stars.

At the conclusion of this verse, the entire school, including teachers and visitors, saluted the flag: "I pledge allegiance to my flag and to the republic for which it stands; one nation indivisible, with liberty and justice for all."

This done, William Kaaa again stepped forward, and the ceremony was concluded with the following:

This flag that now waves o'er our school,
Protecting weak and strong,
Is the flag that vindicates the right
And punishes the wrong.

In the group participating in these exercises were Hawaiians, Americans, Chinese, Japanese, Portuguese, and Filipinos, and possibly some other nationalities.

America is indeed a "Melting Pot" and, aided by the gospel, it can make one people of all nations.[18]

A pleasant duty of the special missionaries was to visit the temple, at that time presided over by Brother William M. Waddoups,[19] who has since been made president of the mission. Before doing so, however, they had breakfast with the family, and Sister [Olevia S.] Waddoups[20] proved herself not only a devoted missionary but an excellent cook as well. Though this was on February 7th, the visitors were furnished with all the freshly picked strawberries they could eat, and around this home and on adjoining land banana trees were growing in profusion.

In traveling by auto from Honolulu to Laie the usual course passes over the Pali,[21] one of the real scenic spots of the world. From this elevated point one can look into a valley where many thousands of acres are producing bounteous crops of pineapples and sugarcane. And beyond is the sea. A paved road zigzags like a great serpent from this spot down the steep mountainside and into the valley. A majestic mountain towers above the Pali on one side and a precipice yawns on the other, and around this point a perfect hurricane constantly sweeps. It frequently blows the tops off autos and it is impossible for even a strong man to stand erect. Strangely enough, the wind is felt only at one spot; thirty feet [9.14 m] distant it is perfectly calm.

No visitor among the Polynesians is likely ever to forget the feasts which are prepared and set before him. As the Hawaiians do not often have the opportunity of entertaining one of the General Authorities of the church, they were anxious to make Brother McKay's stay among them pleasant. The tables were usually covered with a cloth of ferns and at the outset literally groaned with the loads they bore. The aim of the natives is to transfer the load and consequent groaning to the visitor.

One breakfast served to the special missionaries consisted of beef, eggs, shrimps, several kinds of fish, various vegetables, fruits of all kinds, chicken, the characteristic Hawaiian poi, bread, French toast, green onions, and pie, and all in almost limitless quantities. If that is a breakfast, the imagination is inclined to balk if asked to conjure up a dinner.

During this visit a Honolulu paper printed a news item of unique interest to people from the semiarid West. L. [Lawrence] H. [Hite] Daingerfield, meteorologist in charge of the U.S. weather bureau at Waialeale,[22] on the island of Kauai, certifies that from January 7, 1920, to February 3, 1921, 590 inches of rain fell. With such an abundance of moisture and a tropical climate one can easily understand why the country is so green and beautiful.

Brother McKay's party, in company with President Wesley Smith, visited the island of Maui where they were welcomed by Elders Byron D. Jones,[23] Samuel H. Hurst, Leslie Dunn, Chester H. Nelson,[24] Lester Williams,[25] and two native elders, David Keola Kailimai[26] and David Kalani.

This island means much to the church, for here missionary work among the dark-skinned people was really started. December 23, 1850, a company of ten missionaries landed in Honolulu from Utah. The youngest member of the party was George Q. Cannon. They had worked their way across the desert from Utah to San Francisco, then in the height of the gold fever, and had earned sufficient money in California to engage passage to the islands. The elder in charge of the party became discouraged and decided to return home, but this suggestion was wholly contrary to Brother Cannon's feelings. He was in a peculiar position. Obedience to those presiding over him was a cardinal part of his nature, but he could not feel that it was right to leave the field because difficulties, howsoever insurmountable they appeared, confronted them. As many months must elapse before an answer could be expected from Salt Lake, he submitted the matter to the Lord, promising that he would do whatever was desired of him if he could but know the wishes of the Almighty.[27]

Fifty years later, and but a few months before his death, he again visited the islands at the great Jubilee which was held in the fall of 1900.[28] After his return to Salt Lake, he met with his family and related some experiences of his life and particularly of his recent trip. His impressive words were those of an honest man who knew his earthly days were numbered and who desired to leave final testimony as a legacy to his posterity. After relating many details of his visit and the memories which it awakened, he said in effect:

> We were riding in a carriage with President Samuel E. Woolley[29] when we came to a spot which to me was very sacred. Leaving the others behind and with the request that I should not be disturbed, I walked into a garden among the banyan and banana trees and stood on the spot where I, as a young and inexperienced man beset by problems which I myself could not solve, had pleaded with the Lord for guidance, promising him I would do his will if he would but reveal it to me. There in that garden, the Lord talked with me as one man talks to another, telling me I should remain, for a great work was to be done among that people.

It was with chastened spirits that Brother McKay and his party went over this ground. All about them were evidences of the fulfillment of the promise that a mighty work was to be done among those lovable and honest hearted souls. This point was emphasized by an interview which Brother McKay, in company with Brothers Smith and Cannon, had with Dr. Louis R. Sullivan,[30] anthropologist in charge of the British [Bishop] Museum[31] in Honolulu and the man who was directing a number of scientists in an endeavor to trace relationship between the various Polynesian races and the American Indians.

During an interview with this courteous and learned gentleman, Brother McKay said, "Dr. Sullivan, you have examined the Hawaiians as a scientist, have been in their homes, have conversed with and questioned them, have made numerous physical examinations and now know your subject. How do the 'Mormons' among these people compare with the others?"

The doctor answered instantly, "You have the cream of the islands." Then he proceeded, "I do not know whether what you have appeals to the best natives, or whether you take them as they come and make the best out of them. But certain it is that you have the best now."

It was in Wailuku,[32] on the island of Maui, that the Book of Mormon was translated and where that faithful man lived, Brother [Jonathan H.] Napela,[33] who rendered such valuable assistance to this work and whose name is so often mentioned in "My First Mission,"[34] written by George Q. Cannon. The visiting brethren had the pleasure of meeting his grandson, Brother Titus Parker.

Elder [David] Kailimai's Ford was at the disposal of the visitors and in it they rode out to visit and have dinner with some members of the church who live far up on the side of Haleakala,[35] the largest extinct volcano in the world. From here they drove to Pulehu[36] where George Q. Cannon and Brother Napela preached with such power that 97 of the 100 people who came to hear them were converted. (The tradition is that Brother Cannon was not standing on the ground on this occasion, but was in the air and that a great light shone about him.)[37]

Under a beautiful tree on the lot where this occurred and where the church now has a neat little chapel, the visiting brethren engaged in prayer. It was an occasion which none of them will ever forget, for they stood almost in the visible presence of celestial beings. In looking back on the trip after the lapse of several years, there are few, if any, experiences which are more impressive than this.[38]

Aboard the *Mauna Kea* which was to convey the party to Hilo,[39] on the island of Hawaii, the missionaries met a wealthy gentleman from Salt Lake who was touring the islands with his wife. Being acquainted with these people, the brethren were soon engaged in conversation with them and Brother Cannon said:

> Through that canyon my father walked seventy years ago. He was young and inexperienced, without food, friends, money or suitable clothing, and without the language. Indeed, almost the only thing he did possess was a sublime faith in the thing he had come to do. While attempting to cross a stream he had fallen into the water and presented a bedraggled and poverty-stricken appearance, but the Almighty gave to some influential people, whose home he passed, the impression to go out and meet him. Among those who thus came was a prominent native judge, a man

noted for his learning and goodness. Through this meeting he and his family came into the Church, and he was of great assistance in translating the Book of Mormon into the Hawaiian language.

The man who met and befriended the forlorn-looking youth was Brother Napela referred to above.

Visiting Oahu and Maui

Calling on Hawaii and Kauai

Thou wilt show me the path of life: in thy presence is the fulness of joy: at thy right hand there are pleasures for evermore.

—Psalm 16:11

The ride from Lahaina,[1] on the island of Maui to Hilo, on the island of Hawaii, is a very beautiful one. The sea and the distant islands were especially attractive between daybreak and sunrise. Overshadowing the boat towered the highest mountain in the Pacific, Mauna Kea,[2] 14,000 feet [4,267.20 m] high, snowcapped and blushing because of the kiss which it, in view of curious spectators, was receiving from the sun. Silvery flying fish were rising from the water and at no great distance several whales could be seen.

As the visiting party approached the conference house in Hilo, several missionaries were busy with grubbing hoes in the yard. They were clearing out the weeds, which in this instance were banana plants, an excellent illustration of the truth that the choicest plants, like human beings, are weeds if they do not remain within their own bounds.

Edwin K. Winder,[3] a grandson of that stalwart church worker, President John R. Winder,[4] was in charge of this district, and his wife, a granddaughter of President George Q. Cannon, was matron of the conference house; and the welcome extended the visitors was a heartfelt one.

Hawaii is the largest island of this group and one of the most productive. Thousands and thousands of acres of sugarcane grow without irrigation. Through many of these plantations there are cemented waterways, and a strong head of water carries the cane to the mills, instead of the usual method being followed which is to lay a portable track through the fields and run a small engine and train of cars direct from field to mill.

Attending the missionary meeting, which was held in Hilo, besides the visiting brethren, were President Winder and his wife,

Alma Cannon Winder,[5] Sister [Edith] Virginia Budd,[6] and Elders Roscoe C. Cox,[7] Ben E. Swan, Boyd C. Davis,[8] Milo F. Kirkham,[9] James W. Miller, Leland N. Goff,[10] Leslie F. Stone,[11] and George M. Bronson.[12] These missionaries, not one of whom was much past his majority and some of whom were not yet out of their teens, were laboring with courage and devotion among this dark-skinned people, and their testimonies indicated that they were finding unspeakable joy in their work.

So interesting was this meeting that a veritable banquet was forgotten, and a good family with their host of assembled friends was kept waiting. Among the company was the most famous string quartet on the islands. And how these boys did sing and play! Their happy faces, sparkling eyes, the skill of their fingers and beauty of their voices are no more to be described than was the meal itself, consisting as it did of every kind of tropical fruit and everything else which a bounteous land produces and which willing and apt hands could prepare.

More than three hundred eager people awaited the arrival of the visitors in the comfortable chapel. As is customary, they all arose as the brethren entered and remained standing until the visitors had taken their seats. The joy of these people in meeting one of the General Church Authorities was thoroughly genuine and was akin to that which redeemed souls will have when they gaze upon the face and hear the voice of the Redeemer.

"Man is that he might have joy."[13] This is not merely a privilege which mortals may accept or reject at will. It is a duty. And the Hawaiians set their white coreligionists a worthy example by finding in their worship the most exquisite joy known to man, and which after all is a foretaste of future heavenly joy.

Space will not permit of reference to every feast, either of a spiritual or mundane nature, given to Brother McKay's party, but those which are briefly mentioned here are typical of all the others.

Thirty-seven miles [59.55 km] from Hilo is Kilauea,[14] the largest active volcano in the world, so colossal that it makes the time-honored and destructive Vesuvius boil and sputter with furious envy. After the meeting referred to above, nine missionaries were taken in Fords owned by local members to this seething inferno. During the remainder of the night and until after sunrise next morning, the visitors walked about the crater and were awed by its greatness. In some places the lava might easily have been reached with a walking stick were it not for the intense heat which forbids too close an approach. There are rivers and lakes of molten material, bubbling, hissing, and performing weird and fantastic tricks. Huge masses of the fiery substance are being constantly thrown into the air in the most grotesque and monstrous forms, as though they had been spewed from the mouth of some Herculean monster. At times the sulphureous fumes are almost overpowering, and there seemed justification for the statement made by one of the party that it was hell itself. He added that as a result of the numerous feasts which had been crowded upon him he felt exactly like the volcano.

No greater contrast can be imagined than that offered by Kilauea and that which meets the gaze as one descends into the valley. Behind, wrathful purgatory; in front, attractive Elysium[15] foliage, the distant picturesque town, and the exquisite blue ocean as a background make a scene so impressively beautiful that the fortunate visitor feels it can never be effaced from memory.

Many tears were shed as good-bye was said when the missionary party embarked for Honolulu. The brethren were almost smothered in leis, and their own eyes were moist as they bade farewell to these affectionate people.

Some months before this tour was planned, Elder George Bowles,[16] now bishop of Belvedere Ward,[17] his wife Christine,[18] and his son George[19] accepted a call to go to the Hawaiian Islands. Before leaving Salt Lake he had a dream in which he saw the special visitors on the islands. So impressive was this manifestation that he told some of his friends he would surely see these particular brethren in Hawaii, though at that time nothing seemed less likely.

The special missionaries had the pleasure, in company with Elder Wilford J. Cole,[20] of riding on horseback over the beautiful plantation at Laie owned by the church and which he was then managing.

A number of missionaries devote a part of their time in assisting President [William] Waddoups with the temple work. Among those thus engaged were John L. Larsen,[21] Arnold B. Crystal,[22] Arnold B. Bangerter[23] and his wife Hazel M. Bangerter,[24] David J. Smith[25] and J. Clair Anderson.[26]

After visiting the islands of Oahu, on which Honolulu is located, and Maui and Hawaii, one can hardly imagine anything more like a garden; and still it is said the island of Kauai is the real garden of the group. A visit was made to this place, and the travelers were inclined to agree that this claim was not without foundation. The landing was made at 3:30 in the morning at Nawiliwili.[27] The steamer anchored outside the breakwater and passengers went ashore in small row boats. The sky was as black as ink and the darkness and uncanny swish of oars through the water made the traveler feel that the silent boatman was taking him on his fateful journey across the river Styx.[28]

Church members on this island have purchased a Ford and given it to the missionaries, as two elders have the entire island to cover. Brother Lloyd D. Davis met the visitors at the wharf with this machine, and the way they traveled over the island visiting friends and members and keeping appointments for meeting was a poor example to set for those who live in a country where speed regulations must be observed.

There were few places visited on this world tour which will withstand the dimming effect of passing years longer than will "Beach House" on this island. It is the home of a Mr. McBryde, a very wealthy man and good friend of our people. Though the house itself is simple, the white sandy beach, the placid bay, lawns, beautiful flowers, coconut and royal palms, evergreens, the purple and pink bougainvilleas, so profuse as to make a perfectly gorgeous sight, all combined to make the place little short of enchanting.

Not far from this attractive home is the "spouting horn." A jutting ledge of lava rock reaches to the ocean. In this rock there was evidently a seam softer than the rest and during past ages waves have bored a long hole which comes to the surface about fifty feet [15.24 m] from the sea. The breakers come in with such irresistible force that the water is driven through this hole and spouts from fifty to a hundred feet [15.24 m to 30.48 m] in the air, resembling Old Faithful[29] in Yellowstone[30] in everything except regularity.

The missionary meeting which convened in Honolulu was, if possible, the most inspirational of any held on these islands. There were in attendance Elders Ora H. Barlow,[31] Kenneth C. Weaver,[32] Ferrin R. Harris,[33] Douglas F. Budd,[34] John Parker,[35] Joseph F. Smith,[36] son of the late Hyrum M. Smith,[37] Leroy E. Carroll, A. Harris Chase,[38] Adelbert Barnett,[39] Wallace H. Penrose,[40] grandson of the late President Charles W. Penrose, Robert Plunkett,[41] and Heber S. Amussen,[42] and some others whose names are recorded elsewhere in this chronicle.

Their names are mentioned for a special reason. It has often been claimed by enemies of the church that, though older Mormons might stubbornly adhere to their belief, young men and women of the second, third, and fourth generations would not be so true. Among the hundreds of representatives of the church whom these special missionaries met during this tour, there were very few who belonged to the first generation. Most of them belonged to the third, fourth, and many to the fifth. All of them had the opportunity of bearing their testimony and did so with a fervor which emphatically belied the claim referred to above. The special missionaries did not ask the elders what generation in the church they represented, but since that time the author of these lines has put the question to 391 missionaries in different fields with the following results: first generation, 16; second, 37; third, 151; fourth, 163; fifth, 24.

Missionary fields as well as the work at home give irrefutable proof that "Mormonism" is "carrying on," and that every prediction made concerning its growth and stability is being fulfilled. The false prophets are those who predicted its disintegration, the true ones those who foresaw and foretold its success.

The last of the meetings in Hawaii was held in that delightful spot, Laie. It was a busy Sabbath day. The Sunday school, presided over by Brother Charles J. Broad,[43] was a very creditable one. For nine years Brother Broad was superintendent of the school in Honolulu and during that period he was never once late, and the only time he was absent was when his son lay dead in his home.

As soon after landing in Honolulu from Japan as it was possible for Brother McKay to decide when he would be ready to leave, efforts were made to secure accommodations on board a vessel for San Francisco, as the steamers here were even more crowded than those farther westward. No hopes were held out that berths could be secured for several weeks, but these missionaries were on the Lord's business. Brother McKay had made appointments ahead which must be filled or serious disappointment would result.

As his work on the islands neared completion, a slight hope was extended that the required accommodations could be had, but the company was far from positive in their statements. However, all preparations were made to leave, even to the farewell which was held in the grounds of the mission home.

This was an unforgettable evening, the most beautiful that the author has ever seen. In the house and gardens were 450 people, among them a number of friends who had not yet joined the church. The Royal Hawaiian Band,[44] led by Major [Mekia] Kealakai,[45] who has achieved distinction as a leader in Europe, as well as in his native land, was in attendance. These musicians had come voluntarily because of the esteem in which our people are held and because several members of the band are our own "Mormon" boys.

In addition to the band there were a number of noted vocalists and instrumentalists present. It is surprising how quickly the Hawaiian music takes hold of one's heart, and it was especially easy for it to do so on this occasion. In an exquisitely beautiful tropical garden under the bluest sky and the brightest of full moons imaginable the touching "Aloha Oe" sung by the natives and accompanied by their sweet and plaintive stringed instruments was irresistible.

At the conclusion of the evening's program, Brother McKay dedicated the mission home.

The good-byes, regretfully and in many cases tearfully said, lasted far into the night. Then the packing had to be done, for late that afternoon the steamship company had said that berths of some kind would be furnished. Scarcely were the travelers safely tucked under the indispensable mosquito netting, a most necessary precaution to take in this and other tropical countries, when strains of sweet music greeted their ears. A quartet of native brethren serenaders sang and played, and one can hardly imagine anything musical which would be more affecting.

The farewells and music were all repeated the following morning as the special missionaries were ready to go aboard their vessel, and in addition *leis* were hung about their necks until they were almost buried. So bedecked were they that when they went aboard several of the passengers asked them to stand while Kodak pictures were taken, and one man said, "Don't you fellows feel lonesome out in the world like this without any friends?"

Through a Mr. Hardeman who was aboard and whom the brethren had met en route to Japan, the passengers soon learned that Brother McKay was a "Mormon" apostle.

In Hawaii there are about eleven thousand church members and they equal in devotion and faith the Latter-day Saints anywhere in the world. Indeed in the matter of faith, one might almost say they are superior to most other church members. In all Polynesian islands[46] one sees that childlike and effective trust which was exhibited by the two thousand young Lamanites of whom we read in the 56th and following chapters of Alma in the Book of Mormon.[47]

It is hardly too much to say that all natives of these islands know the doctrines taught by this church are true, and the sole reason why all, or nearly all, do not accept the truth is that they are not willing, or lack the moral strength, to obey its strict teachings. It frequently happens that a baptized member, who has indulged his appetite for tobacco or liquor, will refuse to open a meeting with prayer because he is oppressed by the consciousness of unworthiness.

In the summer of 1920, a company of New Zealanders came to Hawaii for the purpose of doing temple work. Two of these brethren whose homes were far apart had no opportunity of comparing genealogies until they reached Laie. There, a comparison showed that they both were descended from a Hawaiian chief, Nameal Hema, who lived more than a thousand years ago. Later it was discovered that several Hawaiian families also traced their records back to this same Hema. Dates and names leave no doubt that this chief is the common ancestor of many families in both countries.

Dr. Sullivan, already referred to, was directing an expedition of scientists who were endeavoring to trace the relationship of the different Polynesian peoples and to connect them, if possible, with the American Indians.[48] At the time of Brother McKay's visit this gentleman seemed to be certain of the relationship, though he stated that it was not yet a scientifically demonstrated fact.[49]

Hawaii is called the "Come Back Land." Even if there were no contributing causes, the country itself would justify the designation. But when to the physical beauty of the place is added the music, the deep and touching love of the people, the joy they manifest at meeting and the sincere sorrow at parting, it is easy to understand how appropriately it could be thus named.

A miracle simply means a phenomenon not understood.
—Dr. John A. Widtsoe[1]

As was expected, the *Maui*, on which the special missionaries took passage for San Francisco, was very much crowded. They had been anxious to obtain a cabin to themselves in order better to prepare and consider the reports of their visit to China, Japan, and Hawaii which should be made to the General Authorities. Instead of obtaining the desired accommodations, however, they were in separate cabins, each with two other men as fellow travelers. Upon boarding the vessel, the purser was visited in an effort to change this arrangement, but he said:

> Were it not for the fact that we do so much business with your people, you could not have found a place on board at all, for we are actually leaving travelers behind whose applications for passage were made sixty days before yours. At this moment we have a passenger who was willing to pay six hundred dollars for a stateroom deluxe who is sleeping in the steerage, because that is the best we could do for him.

This official was assured that the brethren did not desire to be alone for selfish reasons, but only because such a thing seemed necessary for the proper completion of their work. Though understanding and appreciating their needs, he was powerless to do anything for them.

Before bedtime came, however, the missionaries were alone in their own cabin. The details of how this was accomplished are unimportant and would take too long to relate here, but sitting on the side of his berth and discussing the matter, tears came into Brother McKay's eyes as he said: "No one can tell me that things come about in this marvelous manner merely by chance. The skeptic may say the Lord has nothing to do with our arrangements, but I know he is doing for us that which we cannot do for ourselves."

This remark and the spirit which prompted it, a willingness to acknowledge the hand of the Almighty in all things, led the brethren to consider and enumerate some of the things, simple in themselves but nonetheless miraculous in their eyes, which had occurred during their eventful journey.

1. President Grant in setting Brother McKay apart for this work had sealed upon him the power to avoid dangers seen and unseen, together with the necessary wisdom to analyze and understand the needs of the missions which should be visited. An undeniable manifestation of this power had been received.

2. President Lund had promised Brother Cannon that if he were seasick or had any other sickness, it would be of very short duration, and though he had been a poor sailor heretofore, he was sick but five minutes, in spite of the fact that extremely rough seas had been encountered.

3. The brethren were never hindered by unfavorable weather except once, and on that occasion they were convinced the delay was for their own good. Storms which must inevitably have delayed them in their work and in some cases would have prevented their doing it, preceded them by a day or two or followed immediately after.

4. Though total strangers in the city, they were led to the best spot in Peking in which to dedicate the great Chinese realm for the preaching of the gospel. As they became acquainted with the city subsequent to the performance of that sacred duty, they were convinced that no place equally suitable could have been found.

5. In changing money in China, where there is so much counterfeit, they met an American at the right moment who gave them advice which was worth many dollars to them. Judging from the experience of other travelers whom they met, it was nothing short of a miracle for two men to travel as many miles as they did in China and say truthfully that they did not lose a cent in exchange or counterfeit.

6. They arrived in Shanghai at midnight, total strangers to the city and its people, and were given beds when regular customers of the hotel were being turned away. In every hotel in the city travelers were obliged to sit in the lobbies all night.

7. They secured a stateroom to themselves on a ship leaving Shanghai after the company had told them positively it could not be done.

8. This ship ran into the wharf at Kobe, Japan, and although the injury was slight it caused a delay of two days which were sufficient to enable the brethren to complete their work in that land.

9. They obtained exclusive accommodations on the vessel leaving Honolulu when to all human appearances such a thing was impossible.

10. At President [Heber J.] Grant's suggestion, they went first to Japan. Many people thought it a very unwise itinerary, and at that time it seemed so to them. But nothing wiser could have been planned. In Japan and China, the needs of those countries were seen from the missionary point of view, and in Hawaii it was seen how some of the needs could be supplied by natives of those lands.

These and many things of a similar nature could be pointed out which the confirmed skeptic must admit were remarkable, even while denying the intervention of any higher power. But the thing worth noting is this: Such intervention *DID NOT* occur with other travelers. If chance were to be credited, it was showing reprehensible partiality. However, the most comforting blessing which came to these missionaries cannot be described and would not be understood by the unbeliever. That was the sweet spirit of peace and the assurance that the Lord was with them and would protect them, no matter what the outward danger was, that their loved ones would be preserved, and that every promise made them by the servant of the Lord would be fulfilled.

As the *Maui* neared the Golden Gate[2] leading into San Francisco harbor, a fog so dense settled down upon the water that one could hardly see an object two yards [1.83 m] away. Every few moments a bell could be heard in the distance, and guided by those sounds Captain [Peter] Johnson directed the great ship, loaded with hundreds of human beings, safely to its pier. How did he do it? Because he knew the way and understood the signals.

Involuntarily the mind of the thoughtful man reverted to his church. Did his captain know the way? Was he acquainted with the signals? Or was he, amid the darkness and fog, stubbornly ignoring every warning and blindly leading precious souls who trusted him into dangers which must inevitably overwhelm them? These travelers were devoutly thankful for the assurance they had that their captain knew the way.

Among all who are acquainted with him, President Heber J. Grant is known as an unusually bighearted and generous man. These special missionaries had additional occasion to see and appreciate his generosity, for upon arrival in San Francisco they found he had, at his own expense, brought Sisters [Emma Ray]

McKay and [Sarah Richards] Cannon to California to see their husbands for two days before they should sail for the South Seas.³ This meeting was a joyful one, made more so by the fact that it was so entirely unexpected.

Final farewell should not be taken of Hawaii without a further word being said of the very beautiful temple which is built upon an eminence overlooking the sea and valley at Laie. A world traveler aboard the *Maui* told Brother McKay that it was the most beautiful of all the temples built by the church, and indeed, he called it an architectural gem, and many of the passengers spoke in high praise of its artistic beauty.⁴ One man said he had driven past the building but was short of time and consequently did not go through it. He was not so well informed as a young lady, an American, who was met some years ago by Elder Levi Edgar Young⁵ and a party of our missionaries on one of the Swiss lakes. Upon hearing they were from Utah she asked,

"And did you really live among the Mormons? And were you ever able to get into their sanctum sanctorum, the Holy of Holies?"

"Yes, we have been in their temple."

"But I thought they didn't allow anyone but 'Mormons' to go in?"

"They don't," was Brother Young's reply, and the young lady lapsed into embarrassed silence.

For some time after the war it was almost as difficult for an American to obtain permission to leave his own country as it is for a Jap to come into it. One visit after another had to be made to the offices of the various consuls, particularly to the British who had to visé passports before the travelers could sail for New Zealand. The path between this office and that of the steamship company was pretty well worn. During one visit the consul said:

"I suppose you feel that you are between the devil and the deep sea."

"Yes, literally," was the answer, "when we are between the British consulate and the steamship company's office."

His sense of humor was keener than that of most consuls, for he added: "And of course you would not call the British consulate the deep sea."

It seemed necessary that the special missionaries send their passports to Washington⁶ for correction before they could sail, and as word reached President Grant just at this time that President Anthon H. Lund had passed to his glorious reward, it was decided that these brethren should return to Salt Lake, attend the funeral, and have their papers properly prepared while they were waiting.

After a delightful visit in Utah, the missionaries again entered upon their journey, leaving Salt Lake City March 26th, 1921.

A day that is not crowded almost to overflowing with pressing matters is almost unendurable to Brother McKay, so when he learned upon arrival in San Francisco that the *Marama* would sail Tuesday instead of Monday, as had been expected, he decided to run down to Los Angeles[7] to have a final visit with President Grant who was in that city. Brother Cannon promised to have everything in readiness upon his return Tuesday morning.

It was found, however, that application for permission to leave the United States must be made in person by the applicant, and in spite of appeals and explanations to the official in charge he remained obdurate. The British consul could not give the visas until these papers had been obtained, and the steamship company could not issue the tickets without a visa. Brother McKay's train, which should have arrived two hours before the boat sailed, was nearly an hour late, and it required some real hustling to secure the necessary papers and reach the *Marama* in time. Later he explained that it had seemed wholly impossible for him to board the train in Los Angeles at all, as it was made up entirely of Pullman cars and every berth had been sold. Some energetic work, combined with faith, on the part of himself and President Joseph W. McMurrin[8] finally accomplished his purpose.

One of the interesting things met by the traveler going toward the equator for the first time is the number of flying fish which rise from the water as the ship approaches. So numerous are they that they appear like a beautiful silver cloud coming up out of the sea.

There is an old legend that when a vessel crosses the equator, Neptune[9] and his followers come aboard and hold court, passing sentence of more or less severity upon all who are brought before him. In these modern times some enterprising passenger usually takes the old sea god's part. All passengers, both men and women, who are making their debut into the southern hemisphere, are warned that they had better dress in bathing suits or in old clothes, as they are likely to be considerably mussed up. The *Marama* was not slighted, for there was the flaxen-haired Neptune with trident and entire court, including his wife who, under her paint, looked suspiciously like a brawny Scotchman who was constantly trying to borrow matches from someone. Our travelers with scores of others were hauled before him.

Brother McKay, in defiance of the warning, was dressed in his best suit of white, and many of the passengers expected to see some great sport. But Neptune after looking at him doubtfully for a few moments merely ordered that he appear at dinner with his hair parted in the middle.[10]

The usual penalty was to have a thick coat of lather made up of what seemed to be salt water and flour spread on thickly with a stiff whitewash brush and scraped off with a rough wooden razor. A long tunnel had been formed by putting deck benches together so securely fastened that no amount of pressure from within would enlarge the aperture, and through this the novitiate had to crawl, while the hose with a heavy pressure of water behind it was turned on him. The fresh salt water was invigorating and delightful, but for a rotund man[11] to crawl through a tunnel several sizes too small for him was not so agreeable, and the shouts of the crowd, while they may have accelerated his speed, did not add greatly to his enjoyment of the occasion.

There is something intensely fascinating about the tropical ocean. The indescribable blue of the water is only equaled by the blue of the heavens. The splendor of the sunsets will never be forgotten by one who has seen them. The gorgeous colors gradually fade away and are supplanted by the brilliant stars, than which nothing is more inclined to turn one's thoughts heavenward. The north star[12] and the "dipper"[13] have disappeared and the first stars of the southern cross[14] are appearing above the horizon.

In one respect the passengers aboard the *Marama* set a praiseworthy example. The bar was closed and not a game of any kind was played on the Sabbath day. In the evening, most of the passengers congregated in the social hall and sang hymns.

Twelve days after sailing from San Francisco, the special missionaries landed at Papeete,[15] the chief city of the Tahitian[16] or Society Islands,[17] and called the Paris of the Pacific. The group is controlled by France and as a result there is a decidedly French air about the place. Most of the natives speak that language which is taught in the schools.

The low-lying coral islands barely rise above the waterline and are very beautiful. They are covered with a dense growth of coconut and other tropical trees and vegetation, and their inhabitants appear to have the same delightful characteristics as the other Polynesian races.

He that goeth forth and weepeth, bearing precious seed, shall doubtless come
again with rejoicing, bringing his sheaves with him.

—Psalm 126:6

Attractive as they appear to the traveler, the Society Islands offer
many difficulties, some of them of a severely trying nature to the
missionary. The visitors had a good opportunity to see a few of
the unpleasant experiences with which our elders have to con-
tend. President L. [Leonidas] H. Kennard,[1] who was presiding
there at the time of this visit, had gone out three months before to
hold conferences on some of the islands and had not been heard
from since. This situation alarmed Brother McKay greatly until
explanation was made that it was not an unusual one.

There is no regular communication between the islands. The
missionaries must travel on trading schooners which ply from
one island to another at irregular intervals and must await their
chance of finding a vessel which will bring them back to the starting place. Not infrequently an elder, after receiving his release, is
compelled to nurse his patience in a remote and isolated field for
several months before he is able to find means of leaving for mission headquarters, and the place of embarkation for home.

Upon the arrival of the *Marama* in the scenic harbor of Papeete, the special missionaries were met by Elders Melvin Strong,
Grant L. Benson,[2] George C. Nelson,[3] and Wallace Martin.[4] Of
these four, Elders Nelson and Martin had been there four months
awaiting an opportunity to go to their fields of labor, and Elder
Benson, though released some weeks before, had been unable
to arrive in time to take the last boat and was obliged to wait a
month for the next one. Elder [Leonard J.] McCullough,[5] though
released at the same time as Elder Benson, was not yet there and
probably would not be for another two months.

Brother McKay was much perplexed as to the best thing to do. Nothing could be more uncertain than the date of President Kennard's return. He might be home in a few weeks or it might be several months. To visit any of the islands without him seemed a useless procedure and one which would have cost from $750 to $1,500 if a special boat were chartered. To go with a chance trading schooner and perhaps be gone for months was wholly impracticable in view of the program before the brethren.

It was tentatively decided, therefore, that Brother Cannon should remain until the special boat came along, which was scheduled for three weeks later, and with this vessel he should follow to New Zealand. Brother McKay, it was thought, had better go on with the *Marama* which was to proceed south on the following day.

The one thing which made the execution of this plan somewhat doubtful was the fact that the officials had taken up their passports as the brethren left the *Marama* in the evening. The following day was Sunday, and a great celebration was being held in honor of the newly arrived governor of the islands. Amid the confusion and excitement, and with all offices closed for Sunday, the prospect of obtaining passports seemed far from bright. But Brother McKay instructed Brother Cannon to obtain them, and as has already been stated, on this trip at least it was invariably possible to follow instructions.

The first official was awakened at six o'clock in the morning by Brothers Cannon and Benson. This gentleman promised to meet the brethren at the passport office at 8:30, a promise which he failed to keep. Every officer connected even remotely with the passport department was visited. All were helpless or unwilling to do anything.

Meanwhile, the *Marama* was preparing to sail at five in the afternoon. Brother McKay attended Sunday school and afternoon meeting and Brother Cannon spent as much time in these gatherings as could be spared from his apparently fruitless efforts to obtain the necessary papers. Just before the afternoon meeting, their troubles were explained to Brother Timmy, a prominent native church member. He placed himself and his auto at their disposal. Brother Cannon went with him to the passport office. Two policemen were guarding the place, and to them Brother Timmy said:

"Two of my friends are here and must have their passes before the boat sails."

"But we have no right to touch the passes," was the answer.

"You show me where they are, then turn your backs, and I will be responsible to your superior officers."

The policemen pointed to a certain drawer and walked out of the room, and Brother Timmy secured both passes.

After the meeting Brother Cannon hurried to the boat to have his trunk and other belongings taken ashore, but Brother McKay discovered in an apparently accidental way, but in which the brethren acknowledged the hand of the Lord, that the boat on which Brother Cannon was expected to follow to New Zealand had been taken off that route and would not sail as had previously been scheduled. It was therefore hastily decided that the two missionaries should proceed together.

During the hour which intervened before the *Marama* was to weigh anchor the missionaries visited a schooner owned by a company of French traders. The captain[6] of the vessel is a native Tahitian and a devoted member of the church. The missionaries laboring in Papeete told a story, which he modestly confirmed, of a banquet held onboard the ship as he was about to be given the command. The owners, in accordance with the prevailing custom, had provided liquor and tobacco in liberal quantities for the banquet, and some friends of this brother told him he would have to drink when they proposed a toast to the new captain. He replied he would not touch liquor. His friends with the best of intentions urged him to do so, saying the owners would consider it an insult if he refused and would doubtless take the command from him, but despite these appeals he remained obdurate.

When the night of the banquet came, someone proposed a toast to the new commander and all arose to drink it. It was then noticed that the captain himself had a glass of water in his hand. His employers inquired why, and he explained that drinking liquor was against his religious convictions. "Oh, well, take a cigar, and we will excuse you from drinking," was the reply.

"But I do not smoke either," said the brother and proceeded to explain the Word of Wisdom[7] to the surprised and curious crowd.

The governor of the islands was present and congratulated the owners of the vessel on having a man of such character in charge of their ship. He continued: "He will be a far more trustworthy captain if he observes what he calls the Word of Wisdom than he otherwise would be, and a man of that character may be relied upon for his honesty."

There are not many church members in Papeete, but all were at the wharf to say good-bye, and it was evident they have the same sweet spirit which is so apparent among all true members of the Church of Christ. They are generous to a fault and the brethren were loaded with fruit, shells, and beads.

Though it was a relief to be out at sea again after the oppressively hot day on shore, the missionaries watched the land recede from view somewhat regretfully, for they felt that little had been accomplished during the brief visit. Still, their especial mission was to see what the various fields needed and the need of this one seemed apparent—a 75-ton schooner which would enable the elders to go to their fields without such extravagant waste of time and which with wise management might also enable the church members to escape the traders, some of them unscrupulous, who call for their pearl shell and other products and pay just what they please for it.

As the brethren sailed away, this thought came to their minds: Neither one of them had ever met any of the missionaries laboring in Papeete and of course were wholly unacquainted with the members of the church residing there. Suppose some man well-informed as to church doctrines and practices but not a member, learning of this proposed trip, had gone ahead and visited the islands professing to be Brother McKay. How long would it have taken the missionaries and faithful church members to discover the imposition? Certainly not long. The Savior said, "And the sheep follow him: for they know his voice. And a stranger they will not follow, but will flee from him: for they know not the voice of strangers."[8]

The childlike faith of the natives of Tahiti is as nearly perfect, one is inclined to think, as faith can become in this world. An entire volume might be filled with accounts of faith-promoting incidents which have come to the attention of the missionaries. Sister Venus R. Rossiter,[9] wife of President Ernest C. Rossiter[10] who for a number of years was president of the Tahitian Mission and at the time this is being written is in charge of the French Mission,[11] relates the following:

> On one occasion, Mohi, now a faithful native missionary, sailed with a number of his Chinese laborers from one of the islands of the group to Tahiti, the main island. He had onboard a cargo of copra (dried coconut) and after the frail vessel had reached the open sea it was overtaken by a tremendous waterspout which literally picked it up and tossed it into the air. As the boat fell upside down, the passengers and the cargo were cast into the sea. Being excellent swimmers, all were able without difficulty to take care of themselves in the water and one by one succeeded in climbing onto the wrecked vessel. But there, though temporarily safe, they were helpless. For seven days and nights they sat there; alternating between hope and despair, they scanned the horizon with prayers that they might be rescued.

One by one the Chinese laborers, exhausted by watching and overcome by the heat and the want of food and water, slipped off the overturned vessel into the sea. Attracted by the dead bodies, a large number of sharks surrounded the boat and waited hungrily for the next victim. With bodies pitiably swollen from the blistering sun and the salt water, it seemed useless to hope longer. But the undaunted Mohi continued to pray, and promised the Lord that if he and his family were rescued he would devote the remainder of his life to the preaching of the Gospel. On the evening of the seventh day, when hope had well nigh forsaken the stoutest of the gaunt and famished group, they saw a steamer coming directly toward them. Life boats were lowered and the party was saved.

Through a translator, the captain told Mohi that he had been induced, by an influence which to him was incomprehensible, to order the mate to change the usual course, going twenty miles [32.19 km] farther to the right than he had ever done before, and this led the ship straight to the shipwrecked party.

At the present writing, twelve years have passed since this occurred, but true to his promise this dark skinned but worthy man is still declaring the message of salvation to his fellowman. And not he alone, but his two sons who were with him at the time, Viao and Tuhiva [Mohi], are likewise diligent and have ever been ready to explain the truth on every opportune occasion.

It is interesting to note that this same Viao is the captain heretofore mentioned in this chapter who could not be induced to drink liquor or smoke when the circumstances, to a weaker man, would have seemed to make such violation excusable.

Some religious enthusiasts think only of the lilies of the field and forget the parable of the talents.

—Babson[1]

It was evening when the *Marama* cast anchor before the tiny village of Avarua on the island of Rarotonga,[2] six hundred and thirty miles [1,013.89 km] south of Tahiti. The tropical island, some of whose mountains reach a height of 3,000 feet [912 m], the intensely blue sea and the comparatively faded blue of the eastern sky, brilliant red, yellow, and green shades of the departed sun and the purple reflection from adjacent hills all combined to furnish every imaginable gradation of color. It was truly a picturesque scene.

When entering harbors of the South Seas, the traveler inclines to the belief that the last one visited excels all others in beauty. Rarotonga is one of the most fertile and valuable of the Cook group,[3] and though considered an unusually good specimen of the volcanic order, it is surrounded by a coral reef, the dangerous nature of which is attested by remnants of two wrecks standing as grim sentinels at the harbor's entrance. In the waning light these crumbling hulks added to the romance of the place.

Immediately the *Marama* was surrounded by innumerable native canoes, barely large enough to carry one person and each equipped with an outrigger to prevent capsizing. As darkness crept over the enchanting scene, the occupants of the tiny skiffs took advantage of the ship's lights which attract flying fish thus making it much easier to catch these denizens of tropical waters.

All through the night the work of discharging and taking on cargo continued. Naturally, the freight taken aboard consisted principally of fruit, mostly oranges and bananas, and to sleep amid the prevailing noise was quite impossible, for the native laborers keep up a constant chattering and singing.

The next morning it was noticed that a large number of sharks surrounded the *Marama*. The sailors baited an immense iron hook attached to a thin but very strong rope and succeeded in catching a shark. He fought vigorously for liberty, but hook and rope held him though the water was lashed into foam by his desperate efforts to escape; and he was finally hauled onto the lower deck, and there killed by being hit over the nose with an iron bar. After he was supposed to be dead, he gave a last convulsive flop, striking Brother McKay with his tail and almost ruining a pair of white trousers.[4]

A number of passengers welcomed the opportunity of riding around the small island in a Ford truck with seats along the sides. The road which skirts the seashore for the entire distance is about twenty miles [32.19 km] long, and as it leads through a number of native villages, the travelers were able to see something of the people and their customs. Their living is indeed primitive. The "pareu"[5] is the principal, indeed the sole, article of dress in almost every case. It resembles a red and white tablecloth and is tied about the body and hangs to the knees. Of course, no shoes or stockings are worn and as the only use the natives have for a house is to protect them from sun and rain, their buildings are as primitive as their dress. Fish and fruit furnish the principal diet, and nature provides these in abundance.

In referring to the native dress, it is but fair to commend the modesty of the women, for when they heard or saw a party of strangers approaching they invariably disappeared from sight or put something over their shoulders.

It was interesting to learn that cement was used here long before the advent of the white man. Apparently, all graves are of this material. The claim formerly made by opponents of the Book of Mormon that cement is a modern discovery and reference to it in that record[6] proves the book to be a fraud has long since been abandoned. Had it not been, this island would furnish evidence which is irrefutable.

When halfway around the island the driver stopped, climbed a coconut tree, and supplied the party with nuts. These, when picked green, furnish a most refreshing drink, and when ripe, as all know, the coconut is very good. More than that, under some circumstances it is perfectly delicious. The meat of the nut is grated and put through a process of beating and wringing until it looks like the richest of whipped cream and as for taste—well, like the Hawaiian volcano, it is indescribable. A banana of proper ripeness with this as a dressing is a dish not to be found outside the tropics. During this ride, in addition to coconuts and bananas, the travelers saw breadfruit, mangos, guavas, oranges, and many other fruits which were unknown to them.

Two facts regarding the island are worthy of note, and do credit to the New Zealand government under whose protectorate it stands. One is that the use of intoxicants is forbidden; the other is that the land is apportioned among the natives in accordance with their needs and cannot be sold. It may be leased but usually the owners cultivate it. The result is prosperity and apparent peace. Apropos of the people working their own land, the following story comes to mind:

A number of years ago a hardheaded mayor of one of our Utah towns was making a speech at the laying of the cornerstone of a public building. To illustrate his remarks he attempted to quote: "He who by the plow would thrive, / Himself must hold the plow or drive." Not being accustomed to quoting poetry, he got it: "He who by the plow would thrive, / Must either hold the plow or drive himself." The titter which arose reminded him that he had made a mistake. His next effort was: "He who by the plow would thrive, / Must either drive himself or hold the plow." This time the titter developed into a laugh. "He who by the—" Here he floundered helplessly. "Hang it, friends, I can't quote poetry, but I know if you've got plowing to be done you had better do it yourself or watch the hired man pretty close."

As the party alighted from the Ford at the water's edge it was noticed how high the *Marama* stood out of the water, due to her light load. A young lady called attention to the fact and asked the reason. Her escort, with assumed seriousness, said, "Why the tide is out now; at high tide she will be all right." The answer satisfied the damsel until the smiles of the crowd caused her to realize how ridiculously gullible she had been.

Our travelers steamed away from the charming island, under a glorious full moon which shone upon them out of a northern sky as they were now well within the southern hemisphere.[7] The Southern Cross,[8] instead of the North Pole or the "dipper"[9] was now the outstanding group of stars. The brethren appreciated very much the opportunity of visiting this island for one day, but were no less thankful that they were not obliged to remain for a month or two until the next southbound boat came along.

An incident occurred between Rarotonga and New Zealand which may be fitly introduced here. One of the passengers was a handsome, well-educated, widely traveled widow, an excellent musician and a brilliant conversationalist. Evidently her faith in the male sex was at low ebb, and her conception of Mormon morality not less so. In response to something she had said, Brother McKay spoke of our church standards, saying our young men are taught to be as pure as the girls they marry. The lady was incredulous. Such a thing was well nigh unbelievable. Pointing an accusing finger at Brother McKay, she said, "But you cannot tell me you were virtuous when you married your wife!"

"Yes, madam, I was and have been ever since." Had the whole world seen him and listened to his answer, the whole world would have been convinced, as was the lady, that he spoke the truth. She sank back in her chair, astonished, speechless—but convinced.

[67]

Sightseeing in Rarotonga

Give me a rub with thy brown nose,
And I will rub with mine.
Such salutations in this land
May seem to you divine;
But when I see before me now
Three hundred in a line,
'Tis just one rub for your brown nose,
Three hundred rubs for mine.

Prior to Brother McKay's departure to preside over the European Mission in the fall of 1922, a social was given in his honor by the General Sunday School Board at the home of Elder Stephen L. Richards,[1] of the Quorum of the Twelve, and his hospitable wife. Each board member was asked to write a line or two of poetry about the honored guest, and the above verse, the author of which should remain unknown, purported to describe Brother McKay's arrival among the Maoris in New Zealand.

As for the number of brown noses, the writer might have multiplied the three hundred several times without exaggeration. But with the *hongi*, as the New Zealand salutation is called, the noses are not rubbed but pressed against each other. If one attempts to rub, the other nose is likely to describe an arc about one's face. The degree of pressure indicates the esteem in which those participating hold each other, and with the special missionaries the *hongi* was long and severe. At the same time the natives gave a sort of moan, with an inflection of pleasure when the noses met and of sorrow as the moment of parting approached.[2]

Mention should be made, however, of several things which happened before the brethren were asked to greet the natives in the approved Maori fashion.

First of all they landed in Wellington, located on the south end of the north island, and were met by President George S. Taylor,[3] now deceased, and Elders Graham H. Doxey,[4] Julius V. Madsen,[5] and other missionaries.

Here in the steamship company's storeroom, Brother McKay found his trunk, just as he said he would, though it had been unaccountably lost in San Francisco when the travelers arrived from Hawaii. How it came to be sent to this far-off land will ever remain a mystery.[6]

While in Wellington, the capital of New Zealand, a call was made on Dr. [Maui] Pomare,[7] one of the colonial ministers and a highly educated gentleman, who had made a study of the effect of Mormonism upon the Maoris.[8] The doctor himself has some native blood in his veins and is proud of the fact, as well he might be. He made the positive statement in answer to a question by Brother McKay, that he wished all the natives were Mormons, for then, "They would all be decent citizens." Since this visit was made, Dr. Pomare has been knighted by the king of England.

The great annual event among church members in New Zealand is the "Hui Tau," or mission conference which is usually held during the autumn month of April. Followers of this narrative will understand that they are now in the southern hemisphere where there is a complete reversal of seasons. Christmas comes almost in midsummer.

Many of the Maoris are comparatively wealthy, and they have purchased a number of immense tents, comparable in size to those used by a three-ringed circus in the United States. One of the largest of these is used for meetings and at night as an immense bedroom, the beds being made upon the ground. Brother McKay has described it thus:

> Every four feet [1.22 m] around its entire circumference constituted a bedroom, and a similar double tier extended from the speaker's stand down the middle to the opposite end. Thus feet to feet hundreds of heads pointed toward the outside and hundreds of others toward the middle of the tent, a passageway being left open all around this combination bedroom and assembly hall; beds remaining intact, and were sat upon or reclined upon during the services.
>
> For the convenience of those people who like to sleep in church, I recommend this combination scheme most highly.[9]

The "Hui Tau" of 1921, the year of the visit herein described, was held in the outskirts of Huntly,[10] a village of the Waikato district in the "heart of Maoriland." On the train en route to this place the visitors met a number of church members who were going to the conference and were introduced to them and to the *hongi* at the same time; and although the missionaries felt that their noses were pressed quite out of shape, this was but a foretaste of that which was to come.

A prominent figure of the gathering was Sid Christy, who now holds the title of chief among his people. For some years he was in Salt Lake, a student of the Latter-day Saints High School and a star on the basketball team. He is now married and has a large family. Speaking of the *hongi* and comparing it with the white people's habit of kissing, he thought the advantages were all in favor of the native custom. He said, "If you kiss a man's wife, he is likely to beat you up, but the *hongi* which means the same thing to us, can be indulged in with impunity."

The tents were erected in a vacant field about a mile [1.61 km] outside the city limits and all roads seemed to lead to the place, for in every direction one could see crowds on foot and in vehicles of various kinds pressing thither. Again we quote from Brother McKay:

> Hundreds of people were already assembled in the open space between us and the two largest tents; and what we saw and participated in during the next two hours contributed to make that day one of the most unique and interesting of this extensive tour.
>
> Sister [Ida A.] Taylor,[11] Miss Miriam [Taylor],[12] and others from the Mission House had joined us. Brother Sid Christy had come bounding to extend greetings and fortunately for us, put us at our ease by timely suggestions and explanations. As our party began to walk slowly toward the assembled multitude, our ears were greeted by a shrill cry from a score of women's voices, "Haere Mai! Haere Mai!" and other terms of welcome, accompanied by such wild gesticulations, jumping, dancing and grimacing that, had it not been for the assurances of Brother Christy, I should have thought we were about to be attacked instead of welcomed.
>
> This welcome was followed by the "Haka" or war dance by a dozen men or more in front of the crowd, urged enticingly on by the dancing of two women, one at each end of the row of warriors. How they wriggled and writhed, rolling their eyes until only the whites were visible, lolled their tongues and made unsightly grimaces! I was fascinated and yet worried because surely some acknowledgement must be made of this most demonstrative welcome.

However, when within a hundred yards [91.44 m] of the dancing group, we were told to stand still. The representative of the "king" of the district, an uncle, we were informed, stepped forward, flourishing a cane, and walking briskly forward and back, delivered an impassioned address of welcome. He was followed by the next man in rank, and he by several others, each expressing his joy and gratitude for the visit of those who had traveled so far to meet them.

At this point we should have followed in true Maori fashion, but as the crowd was waiting to shake our hands, it was suggested by our host that they would "accept the *hongi* as a gracious reply." And so, beginning with the woman on our left, we clasped hands and pressed noses with the entire assembly!

Again we learned by experience that the *hongi* varies in degree and intensity as does our kiss, though perhaps not with the same significance.

As we took our places in the seats provided for us, we saw entering the grounds a group of visiting Maoris.

"Haere Mai! Haere Mai!" again cried the women, and again the gesticulating, dancing and speech making.

Then we saw the reciprocal performance. At the conclusion of the addresses as mentioned above, both sides remained silent, and all heads were bowed. Soon we heard moans, and we noticed that men and women were crying. It was not make-believe, either, for tears were flowing. This was the *tangi* part of the welcome. They were expressing sympathy for those who had lost loved ones during the past year. Following this, the leading man among the visitors, flourishing his cane, responded to the welcome, and told why they had come. He was followed by others, and then the group retired to give place for other groups to follow. Thus the home people welcome the visitors all through the day!

The next morning we received evidence, and each succeeding day confirmation, that the "Hui Tau" is a well disciplined organization. Every person on the grounds was expected to respond with promptness and dispatch to the following signals:

At 6:15 a.m. a clanging bell drove Morpheus to his sunless cave and bade his subjects get up!

At 7 a.m. it called to "Karakia" or morning service; at 8 a.m. to "Kai" (breakfast); at 10 a.m. to "Karakia" or first session of conference; 1 p.m. to "Kai" (lunch); 2 p.m. to "Karakia," second session of conference; 5 p.m. to "Kai" (dinner); 6:30 p.m. to "Karakia," evening service; 7 p.m. to the evening session of the conference.

Twice a day as intimated above, everybody excepting the women folk preparing the breakfast, assembled in the large tent and participated in devotional services consisting of (1) singing, (2) prayer, (3) repeating in concert passages of scripture; and (4) questions and discussion. The quotations were selected from the *Ready References*,[13] and chanted in unison. It was significant that only the older Maoris participated in this memory work, the younger ones who joined them read from the book. This is explained by the fact that when the gospel first came among the Maoris, very few could read, so they memorized what was taught them. The chant or song was given as an aid to memory. There were those present who can repeat every passage in the *Ready References*, under its appropriate subject. The meaning of the passages was made clear, and their applicability to the Latter-day work shown during the discussion that followed. It was plainly evident that the Maoris had assembled to learn more of the Gospel of Christ, and not merely to be entertained.

Following the service, as many as could be seated at the first tables, answered the call to "Kai." Under a canopy fully as large as that in which services were held, were arranged eight long tables each with a seating capacity of forty persons. Four girls furnished these tables and served the guests, each group taking charge of eighty persons at every sitting.

Each group, too, had its own boiler for cooking, its own tanks for dish washing and its own cupboards for the dishes, and every plate, cup and saucer, knife, fork and spoon was accounted for.

Boiled meat, potatoes, spinach, bread, butter, jam and cheese made the principal eatable; but cake, watermelons, and other fruits and delicacies were also served. Some of the meat and potatoes were prepared in the "Hangi," that is, cooked in a pit in the good old Maori fashion, except that chains were heated instead of rocks. And we must admit that meat thus cooked is far more tender and delicious than that boiled in the more modern manner.

As the women peeled the potatoes, it seemed by the ton, or washed dishes, literally by the hundred, they worked in unison to the rhythm of some song, hummed as gleefully as though they were having a Jubilee. Sometimes the young girls having "finished the dishes" would wind up with a touch of the "Kopi Kopi" or "Hula Hula."

How efficient this organization and how effectively it worked may be partly realized when I tell you that during the four and one half days of the "Hui Tau" approximately 10,000 meals were served! And that, too, without any apparent extraordinary effort!

Some of the best homes in the district were given over entirely to the accommodation of the visitors, Elder Cannon and I each having a room and a bed as comfortable as one could wish. The fifty Elders, however, did not fare so well. They slept on mats laid on straw on the floor of the church. It was truly a community bedroom!

While the religious purpose of the "Hui Tau" is evident on every hand, and Gospel conversations and discussions are carried on with almost every group between meetings, there is no dearth of amusement and legitimate entertainment. Chief among these I think I shall name the "Poi Dance" as given on two different occasions by fifteen young Maori maidens dressed in native costume. Combining as it does rhythm, beauty, grace and skill, the "Poi Dance" easily ranks among the most beautiful dances of the world. I have never seen any that excel it.

If the "Poi" is beautiful, the "Haka" is the most thrilling! After seeing this native war dance, one can readily understand how the ancient warriors, aroused to the highest pitch of enthusiasm, if not frenzy, rushed so madly into battle, or stormed with bare hands and naked bodies almost impregnable "pas!"

We were given a glimpse, too, of the "Koro Phio Pi" or "Hula Hulu"; but one of the native brethren suggested that they "go slow on that"; and "a hint to the wise" was in this case "sufficient."

Too much credit cannot be given to the "Hui Tau" committee, composed entirely of native men, who have so successfully managed these gatherings for many years. Brother William Duncan is chairman and a more able, loyal Church worker than he is seldom found anywhere in the world! He is a man among men, a worthy example of what "Mormonism" will do for those who will accept and live it! He has been ably assisted by four others, equally worthy of commendation and esteem.

Though each annual gathering costs between $2,500.00 and $3,000.00, the committee is free from debt and has a fair balance in the bank. Besides this, they have accumulated considerable property, such as tents, a dynamo, electrical appliances, stoves etc., etc.

But the things mentioned above are only adjuncts to the principal features of this notable gathering! The glory of the "Hui Tau" is seen and felt in the twelve or fourteen worshipping assemblies which culminated in a wonderfully inspirational priesthood meeting. The earnestness, faith, and devotion of the audience, the manifestation of the inspiration of the Lord upon the speakers, native as well as European, the excellent music, and the confidence, sympathy, and brotherly love that flowed from soul to soul, all combined to make every service a supreme joy.

Not the least remarkable feature of this memorable event was the skill, the intelligence, the accuracy, and the inspiration with which Elder Stewart Meha interpreted the addresses of the visiting brethren. His interpretation was simply marvelous! Truly he was remarkably blessed.

The spirit, intelligence, and earnestness of the three score elders and lady missionaries were distinct contributions to the success of each session. No more devoted self-sacrificing men and women can be found anywhere in the world. I could not help but think how proud and happy the parents and wives of those young men would be if they could have seen these missionaries in the glory of their work as we met them!

Success and long life to the "Hui Tau"! May each succeeding one be more successful than the last! May its influence extend until it becomes a power not only to cement the love and increase the faith of the Church members, as it does even now, but also to break down the barriers erected by the ignorant and vicious to impede the progress of the Church of Christ.[14]

The lady missionaries referred to by Brother McKay were: Ida A. Taylor, wife of President George S. Taylor, [Lillian] Austin Schwendiman,[15] wife of Mission Secretary Frederick W. Schwendiman,[16] [May] Ida F. Stott,[17] wife of Principal Franklin E. Stott[18] of the Church Agricultural College, Flora D. Fisher,[19] wife of Elder [Asael H.] Fisher,[20] a teacher in the college, and Sisters Miriam and Priscilla Taylor,[21] daughters of the mission president.

The district in which the "Hui Tau" is held furnishes the food, which is served without cost, and all on the grounds are welcome, regardless of whether or not they are affiliated with the church. On this occasion fourteen beeves and thirty sheep were contributed by prosperous farmers and much more meat was purchased from butchers. Potatoes and vegetables came in by the wagonload and large sums were contributed in cash. The efforts made by church members and nonmembers to secure this gathering for their district on the following year impress one with the thought that contributions are gladly given.

Before this chapter is closed credit should be given to Elders Gordon C. Young[22] and Roland C. Parry,[23] both of whom speak the Maori language fluently, for the assistance they gave the visitors in translating for their benefit the sermons and remarks of the native brethren.

Prayer prevents sin, and sin prevents prayer.
—Brigham Young[1]

Had doubt existed as to the wisdom of having one of the Twelve visit outlying missions, it would have been entirely dispelled during the "Hui Tau." Brother McKay preached the gospel with the power of his holy calling upon him, as indeed he had done in all lands previously visited. Missionaries and saints listened raptly to his inspired words. They had anticipated his coming with joy and were in nowise disappointed with message or messenger. Maoris and whites alike will always hold him in loving remembrance. His sermons were of a nature to awaken, not merely a temporary enthusiasm which would pass when farewell was said, but a deep and abiding love for the truth.

More than one was heard to express devout gratitude for the testimony, divinely given, that "He gave some apostles, and some prophets . . . for the perfecting of the Saints, for the work of the ministry, for the edifying of the body of Christ; till we all come in the unity of the faith, and of the knowledge of the Son of God, unto a perfect man, unto the measure of the Stature of the fulness of Christ."[2]

Even strangers who attended the meetings out of curiosity— for many came from Auckland[3] and other places drawn by the news that an apostle from Utah was among them—were deeply impressed. The words of St. Matthew might well be quoted to describe this visit: "The people were astonished at his doctrine; for he taught them as one having authority and not as the scribes."[4]

Many persons afflicted with disease were blessed during the conference, and before its completion testified that they were much improved in health. One woman who had been married for several years and had prayed for a child was promised that her prayers should be answered. Shortly after their return home the brethren learned that this prediction had been fulfilled.

In the missionary meeting many splendid testimonies were borne, all of which were worthy of being recorded. One alone must suffice. Elder Haloy E. Bachman[5] said his prayer had been that he might fill a mission, but nine years previous to this time he was afflicted with enlargement of the heart and his doctor had stated he would never be able to leave his bed. Brother Jonathan G. Kimball[6] promised him he would fill a mission and in a patriarchal blessing[7] this promise was repeated.

It might be added that these prophecies were literally fulfilled. He completed his labors in New Zealand, received an honorable release, and has since died.

The Maoris, with all other Polynesians who have accepted the Gospel, love it sincerely and furnish splendid evidence of its power to save. They understand that salvation comes through obedience to law, and these humble people manifest a childlike obedience. They naturally love to smoke, drink, and gamble, but in almost every case these weaknesses are laid aside when they begin seriously to investigate the principles of truth. They comprehend better than some highly civilized nations that the gospel redeems men from sin but cannot save them in sin.

The ability to sincerely repent is also a native characteristic. When a Maori falls into wrongdoing whether the offense be trivial or serious, he usually comes to the proper officers, makes confession, and humbly seeks forgiveness. Men who have been guilty of violating the Word of Wisdom often refuse to open a meeting with prayer or perform any other duty.

A typical example of this characteristic was called to the attention of the visitors. In a branch which during the world war had been left alone because of shortage of missionaries one of the native brethren had returned to his former habit of smoking. Elder Graham H. Doxey, now bishop of the Third Ward[8] in Salt Lake City, and a companion were sent to this branch to learn conditions. The brother was asked to open meeting with prayer, but to the surprise of the missionaries he declined to do so. They afterwards asked why, when he held the priesthood and at one time had been very active.

"I have been guilty of smoking," the man answered penitently. "The other members know it, and I could not face them if I addressed the Lord in their presence when I have not been keeping his law."

Mingling with the members of the church at the "Hui Tau" were two missionaries of the Reorganized Church[9] who did their utmost to attract attention.[10] More than one meeting was disturbed by the questions which they shouted at the speaker. Whenever they could find anyone who would listen, they followed their usual custom and berated the Utah Mormons in a shameful manner. Finally they became so abusive that Elder Benjamin Brown[11] and two local brethren told them they must conduct themselves as gentlemen or leave the place. Apparently they had no desire to do either, and at last the brethren decided that patience had ceased to be a virtue. A young Maori, a star player on the church school football team, lifted the more obstreperous of the two offenders over the fence, and the other undesirable visitor beat the athlete to the gate by a few inches. It is worthy of note that these two men had partaken of the food which was dispensed without charge in the dining tent.

Subsequently, the three brethren who had taken matters into their own hands were summoned before Brother McKay. They approached him with considerable trepidation, uncertain how he would view their action.

"Did you throw that man over the fence?" he sternly asked the young native.

"Yes, sir, but I—but he—"

There was no occasion to finish, for Brother McKay took him in his arms and gave him a hug which brought peace to his heart and a smile to his face which did not disappear as long as the conference lasted.

It is a delight to mingle with the Maoris. Men six feet [1.83 m] tall and over were greatly in evidence, and there was a dignity—something even king-like—about them which was most admirable.

Generosity appears to be a racial trait. To illustrate this: Elder Elmo F. Jacobs[12] had just received word of his father's death, and he was released to assume the responsibility of caring for his mother and six younger children. A purse containing $175 was raised for him in a few moments and at the same time $200 was collected to pay the balance on a meetinghouse which had been erected in one of the branches. Nor did it end there. Elder Rulon H. Manning[13] had the misfortune to lose his pocketbook with $25 in it. This amount, and a little more, was handed him.

The visiting brethren also have occasion to remember this generous spirit. While at the home of Brother William Duncan, already referred to in a former chapter, he presented each of them with a beautiful and costly traveling rug. These gifts were modestly given in the name of the "Hui Tau" committee. But when asked for the names and addresses of the members who had contributed, so that letters of thanks could be sent them, he hesitated. Brother McKay insisted.

"But they don't know the rugs are being given," Brother Duncan stammered.

Further questioning revealed the fact that he was presenting the rugs personally but was trying to give the committee credit for the kind act.

In the beautiful home of this faithful native brother there is a room which is kept exclusively for use of the mission president when he visits this part of his field, in addition to which there are always accommodations for all the elders who travel that way.

The difficulties encountered in the Orient in securing places on steamers were repeated here. Only after considerable difficulties were the brethren able to find anything on the *Tofua,* which was sailing for the Tongan[14] and Samoan Islands.[15] It was not necessary to say good-bye to New Zealand or to its interesting people, for they were to return and finish their work here after making a tour of the missions on the islands above mentioned.

In the first chapter of this work, reference was made to a cabin which was assigned to our missionaries and two priests. During the five days that the four were together many pleasant conversations were had, in which the Catholics, at least the one who was not bedfast from seasickness, asked many questions about church organization and policy. Particularly was he interested in our missionary system. He seemed fair-minded and was certainly courteous and highly educated.[16]

The entrance to the harbor of Suva,[17] principal city of the Fiji group,[18] is a devious one. The vessel winds in and out in order to avoid the dangerous but attractive reef. The water swarmed with sharks.

Here was another new world. No hats are worn either by native men or women, great bushy heads of hair protecting them from the intense tropical heat. Naturally, shoes and stockings are never worn and the dress of the men consists merely of a "lava lava," a cloth tied about the loins and hanging to the knees. The women are somewhat more modestly attired.

The Fijians seem to be inordinately fond of jewelry. Not alone the women, but men and boys also wear earrings and many of them nose rings. Frequently a button, apparently of gold, is fastened through the side of the nose and not infrequently there is one on each side as well as a pendant hanging from the nose over the upper lip. One woman was seen who had cut the lobes of her ears until they hung down in long and disgusting rings.

Though scarcely a generation has passed since these people were cannibals they appear to be good-natured and kindly. Unlike the Polynesians, they are of the Negroid race and closely resemble the Negroes of our own land in general type. They are like the American colored folks, too, in this, that when religion does strike them, they manifest it in a fervent and ostentatious manner. As yet, no missionary work has been done among them by this church.[19]

No human painter has ever been able to adequately reproduce the richness of coloring which one sees in sky and water of the South Seas. How could they when these colors were put together by the greatest of all Masters! Beautiful as is the harbor of Suva, that of Nukualofa,[20] capital of the Tongan or Friendly Islands, surpassed it. This is rated by globe-trotters as being one of the most scenic of the world. Here, too, a skillful navigator is required to direct the vessel's course so that she will avoid the numerous small islands and coral reefs among which she must wind, making an immense letter S before reaching the point of anchorage.

Our travelers had heard so much of the harbors of this group that they feared their expectations were too high to ever be realized, but after seeing them they felt "the half has never been told." First of all, as they drew near the reef there was the ghostly wreck of the steamer *Knight of St. George*, standing high on the rocks, a monument to the folly of a captain who thought he could run a ship and drink liquor at the same time. She had already been there ten years and was gradually succumbing to waves, storms, and rust.

One could look through the clear water whose hues were as variable as that of a chameleon, and often the bottom of the ocean could be seen, with the coral formation which is being built up, so that at some future period of time the land will extend much farther seaward than at present. A long, low island in the distance resembled a man of war, the tall, slender coconut palms being the masts.

The highest point on the main island, Tongatapu,[21] on which Nukualofa is situated, is ninety feet [27.43 m] so that the climate is even more equable than that of Samoa or Fiji.

Much to their disappointment, the special missionaries were not allowed to go beyond the wharf, as the ship, and consequently the passengers, were quarantined because of an epidemic of measles which had prevailed in Fiji. As this is a much dreaded and rather fatal disease among the natives the officials were determined to run no risks.

President Mark V. Coombs,[22] of the Tongan Mission,[23] and Elder J. Kenneth Rallison,[24] who was released to return home, came aboard the *Tofua* and proceeded with the brethren to Samoa, where President Coombs had labored as a missionary in former years.

Not a whit behind the harbor of Nukualofa in scenic beauty was that of Neiafu,[25] the chief city of the Vavau group,[26] a part of the Friendly Islands.[27]

Though they had little reason to expect visitors, Elder Stirling I. May[28] and Elder Reuben Wiberg[29] of the last named place were at the wharf, or at least as near it as quarantine regulations permitted them to come. In an incredibly short time they had their native brass band together and much to the delight of the ship's passengers played some stirring selections. The officials apparently thought that if the measles germs were strained through a picket fence, no serious danger would ensue and the visitors were able to speak to the assembled members through an interpreter—and through the fence. Incidentally, a number of their fellow voyagers, with whom the brethren shared the loads of fruit and coconuts which had been brought them, heard something of the gospel; and this resulted in many questions being asked subsequently.[30]

After a few hours spent here, the *Tofua* which had come winding into the harbor began the process of unwinding to reach the open sea. Before this was reached, however, the ship dropped anchor and in two immense lifeboats, holding about fifty people each, the passengers who cared to go were taken to the famed "Swallows' Cave." This is located in the tiny mountain island of Otea.[31] The cave is sufficiently large that it was possible to row both boats into the great opening at the same time and several others might have accompanied them without overcrowding. The water in the cavern is most changeable in color, inky blue, almost purple and every variety of green. Stalactites, with many colored surfaces and of varied and grotesque forms, hung from the roof. Crabs ran or crawled along the sides, sparrows flew about screaming protestations against this violation of their sanctuary.

No man can become a saint in his sleep.
—Drummond[1]

Anent the scant clothing worn by natives of the South Seas, Elder [Joshua K.] Rallison relates the story of a belated Tongan passenger who rushed frantically to the wharf just as the steamer was leaving. Not wishing to draw up to the pier again, the sailors who had been using the derrick to unload freight swung it around and told him to take hold of the rope with which they would bring him to the deck where a large number of passengers were congregated. With the man hanging high in the air and his "lava lava" fluttering in the stiff breeze the men, deciding to have a little amusement, began swinging him about. Clinging desperately to the rope he first dropped the bundle from under his arm, then a look of horror crept over his face for the "lava lava" had begun to loosen. He clutched at it convulsively with one hand, but his hold on the swinging rope was uncertain, and it became a question of losing his sole covering or falling himself to the deck or perhaps into the water. He chose the first alternative and hung grimly on with both hands and thus unadorned was lowered to the vessel to the great amusement of the male and the consternation and instant dispersion of female passengers.

The Samoan or Navigator Islands lie near that mythical line, the 180 meridian, where an eastbound ship "sails out of one day into the day before." Or if the direction be westward, it sails out of today into day after tomorrow. To illustrate: The *Tofua* anchored in Apia[2] roadstead, having come from the west, Wednesday evening. The special missionaries slept onboard all night and it was still Wednesday morning when they landed. After their visit was completed, they sailed away from Apia going toward the west on Monday evening; the next morning when they arose it was Wednesday.

Not only are South Sea scenes exquisitely beautiful, but there is about them a subtle power which makes one forget previous experiences and sincerely feel that the present excels in charm everything heretofore seen. So thought the brethren while steaming between the islands of Savaii[3] and Upolu[4] as they approached Apia. The sun had set, leaving behind it the usual gorgeous tropical tints. Not even a ripple disturbed the mirror-like surface of the sea. Above Savaii were heavy dark clouds casting shadows of nameless color over land and water, and the crescent moon gave a finishing touch to this scene of romance and beauty.

But why attempt to describe the indescribable! As Brother McKay said, "These scrubby words are so lifeless in comparison that they make a beautiful South Sea twilight look like an American sign board."

It is not possible for large vessels to draw up to the pier at Apia, owing to the shallowness of the water. The *Tofua*, therefore, anchored out in the crescent shaped harbor and was immediately surrounded by boats. In one of these President John Q. Adams[5] and Elders Gilbert R. Tingey,[6] George W. Robinson,[7] Walter J. Phillips,[8] Cleon J. Wilcox,[9] and Chauncey L. Witbeck[10] were seated. They reported that preparations had been made to welcome the visitors, but owing to the late hour their program could be carried out better in the morning. Brother McKay acquiesced and another night was spent onboard.

The welcome accorded the visitors is quite as indescribable as a tropical landscape or sunset. President Adams and his wife, Thurza T. Adams,[11] and Elder Frank D. Griffiths[12] and his wife, Retta M. Griffiths,[13] were early alongside the *Tofua*, each couple being in a long rowboat decorated with garlands of vines and flowers. Brother McKay was taken in one of these boats with twenty-two muscular and highly elated natives handling the usual long oars. Brother Cannon and President Coombs were taken in the other with Brother and Sister Griffiths and eighteen sturdy rowers who used short paddles instead of oars; and when they applied their strength in perfect unison to these paddles the boat almost jumped out from under its occupants. The boys had to be held in check as they were much inclined to beat the boat with the chief visitor to the pier.

Upon landing, the custom officials threw open the gates and courteously declined to make any examination of luggage. The streets were packed with people, and the church school band from Sauniatu,[14] composed of native boys with the exception of Elder Ray W. Berrett,[15] played stirring strains. After the greetings were over, a procession was formed headed by the band, and the visitors were taken to mission headquarters. Business in the town was at a standstill. Stores, banks, and offices were closed and everybody was on the streets. All had heard of apostles, but this was the first opportunity ever given most of these people to see one. Be it said to the credit of practically all the natives and a large percentage of whites, that regardless of their own religious beliefs they looked upon Brother McKay as a divinely called servant of the Lord.

As the procession passed the Catholic school, the children and their teachers were standing at attention in front of the building and among them were the priests who from Auckland to Fiji had occupied the same cabin with the brethren. The pleasant greeting which they extended as the procession passed indicated that the association had given them a better understanding of the church and its representatives.

It is estimated that at least fifteen hundred people were assembled on the spacious grounds of the mission home. Among them were the ex-king Malieatoa and his wife, U.S. Consul Quincy Roberts[16] and his wife, Dr. Roberts, the Chinese consul, and two score or more of high chiefs of the islands, many of them church members but also a number who were not. Under a large bowery erected especially for the occasion about three hundred people sat down, cross-legged, to partake of a feast, the excellence of which could hardly be surpassed in any land.

Chapters might be written on the details of this highly interesting welcome but to go into detail would prolong the narrative far beyond reasonable length. Reference must be made, however, to the visits made by tribes from surrounding villages who came scantily clad but in organized and well disciplined bodies. At the head of each group were two maids honored with this position because of their virtue. These groups looked very warlike, but there was nothing but kindness and a desire to show courtesy in their acts. All were loaded with presents of mats and beads, fans, and rings of shell and silver, for the guests. Before the ceremonies were concluded there were great piles of these gifts, many of which were very rare and precious.

Then came the highest honor which can be shown a visitor, the drinking of "Kava"[17] with the chiefs of the various tribes. No council, howsoever dignified its members nor how important the matters before it for consideration, could excel this august gathering in solemnity. No one who has been present on a similar occasion is likely to easily forget it. One could not withhold admiration for these kingly men, though their clothing consisted merely of the "lava lava" and shirt, and they were sitting on the floor cross-legged.

Here the virgin who has been specially chosen to occupy the most exalted position among her sex prepares the drink which is made from the root of the kava. The juice from this root is now extracted by beating it to a pulp. Formerly, the dusky maid chewed it and spit the juice into the wooden receptacle, but in the interest of sanitation that method has been abandoned, for which Brother McKay was duly thankful. During its preparation a discussion occurs among the chiefs as to who is to be honored with the presidency of the gathering. In this instance each deferred to the other, but finally that question was settled, and the chief selected for the place made the following speech which was translated and written by President Adams:

> This is a blessed day. It is as a fragrant and beauteous flower. The spirit of love prevails. No wonder, as has been said, a certain Gardener was highly pleased when he visited his garden and found it filled with fragrance from many different flowers. In delight, he ordered the wind to blow to all parts of the world bearing this sweetness. Such an instance is to be compared to this blessed day on which we meet. Our hearts are filled with joy and thankfulness to the Almighty King for permitting us to meet on this memorable occasion. Solomon said "Hope deferred maketh the heart sick; but when the desire cometh it is a Tree of Life."[18]
>
> We welcome you, Apostle McKay and President Cannon, and it is a pleasure to meet you in these Samoan Islands. Thankful are we to heaven that your trip was a pleasant one and that we who awaited your coming have been blessed. Let us love, not alone with words and lips, but with hearts and action.
>
> This is a little tribute, Brothers McKay and Cannon, we would like to give you so you may realize that we appreciate seeing you. May your Excellencies and this people whom you are visiting be blessed.[19]

After a suitable response from Brother McKay, other chiefs spoke, and then the question was put: "Who is the greatest chief among us and to whom shall we give the first cup of kava?" The answer was unanimous:

"Apostolo McKay," and one of the men received the cup from the maiden and with a sweeping bow presented it to their guest. After this the others, according to their rank, were served.

Sitting cross-legged for two hours is not a feat to be lightly undertaken and the only thing which detracted from the solemnity and interest of this occasion was the fact that the visitors' limbs became so cramped as to awaken a tormenting fear that these useful appendages would be useless ever afterwards.

Stopping over in Western Samoa

All Polynesians seem to be alike in the matter of generosity. It is said that all food for the feasts and $400 in cash were contributed by church members and friends, not an inconsiderable part coming from the latter class.

But it may be said here as it was said of the New Zealand gathering, that its main purpose was not to eat and sing and visit one with another. Very early the next morning, and without the use of a spade, shovel, hammer, nail, rope, or string a very excellent bowery was erected in which to hold meetings, it being evident the regular chapel was entirely too small for the occasion. The sides of the building were open and the roof was composed of banana and palm leaves laid upon a framework of poles. It was sufficient to keep out the scorching rays of the sun and also a moderate shower of rain.

Under this shelter a crowd of eager people gathered. Chairs were furnished for the visitors and for presiding brethren and sisters; all others sat Samoan fashion on mats which they had brought with them.

One of the interesting features of these and other meetings held in this land is that when the speaker refers to a passage of scripture, there is a keen race to see who among the congregation can find it first, the winner reading it aloud.

Here, as in other missions visited, Brother McKay preached Christ and him crucified and the restored gospel in a manner which will never be forgotten by his hearers.

In a meeting held with the missionaries, local brethren as well as elders from Utah, almost every man who reported said the people were anxious to have their children taught the Word of Wisdom, whether they themselves belonged to the church or observed this commandment or not, for they acknowledged it as the best doctrine ever brought to the islands.

Between meetings, chiefs from distant as well as nearby tribes visited the grounds, brought gifts, made speeches, bore testimony to the good the church is doing, and promised to assist with the commendable work. President Adams stated that the participation of outside chiefs in this welcome and the resultant removal of prejudice would justify the world trip, even had nothing else been accomplished.

During this conference an unusually impressive baptism service was held in a limpid stream near the mission home. Amid tropical foliage and surrounded by the white-clad figures, those present felt they were standing almost in the visible presence of angels. Elder Ralph A. Thacker[20] led twenty-one humble converts into the water; among them was Robert Reid, said to be the most influential half-caste in British Samoa. Brother Reid's father was a dear friend of Robert Louis Stevenson[21] who, as is well known, lived for a long time on these islands and whose body lies buried on a nearby hillside. This young man was named after the author.

Missionaries laboring in this field were equal in integrity to those found elsewhere in the world. From President Adams down there was not a man who would not willingly have given his life for the work if that had been required. Among these faithful workers were two young fellows, Gilbert R. Tingey and Clarence Henderson, both orphans, who were preaching the gospel on their own means.

And it is hardly necessary to say that the sisters were not one whit behind in the matter of devotion. Indeed, the visitors had occasion to marvel at the unselfish willingness to sacrifice themselves and their own comfort which was manifested by the good women in every field visited. Sister Adams is a gem of rare quality, and this might truly be said of all the wives of mission presidents and indeed, of all lady missionaries.

Nor are the heroines of Mormondom all in the mission field. Several of the elders had widowed mothers who were obliged to struggle exceedingly hard to support their sons. What a blessing to the church these women are! The writer of these lines is acquainted with a sister whose two sons were laboring in Europe. She and her husband received a letter from the mission president stating that the boys were doing excellent work. At the time this word was received the mother was tired, perhaps somewhat discouraged with the extra burden that was placed upon her through lack of their help, but she sat down and cried for pure joy. Yes, she cried out of sheer happiness, although the world would hardly understand how a woman could cry for joy just because she and her husband had to send $75 or $80 away each month for the boys' support and at the same time be deprived of their assistance and companionship.

Another devoted mother, also with two sons in the field, was called, after a painful and expensive sickness to her final reward. Her husband was in straitened financial circumstances and himself had very poor health, but the dying woman's last words were, "My boys must remain at their posts and finish their missions." The mother in this case belonged to the fourth generation in the church and her husband to the third.

[87]

Stopping over in Western Samoa

Resting in American Samoa

 When heaven sends trouble, there is always a means of sustaining it, but a man's own folly is a thing from which he rarely escapes.

—Tia-Kia, ancient Chinese king

All travelers who enter the harbor of Apia, capital of Western Samoa, soon hear of the disaster of March 15th and 16th, 1889. If unfamiliar with the story, they solicit a recital of it upon seeing the huge mass of rusting steel which has lain on the reef for nearly two score years, but which still bears the outlines of a ship.

A terse but graphic account of the frightful hurricane which caused this wreck is found in the Samoan Mission history written by Elder Joseph H. Dean,[1] at that time mission president. On the date mentioned, seven battleships were anchored in the roadstead some little distance out from the pier at Apia. They were the British *Calliope*; the American *Trenton*, *Vandalia*, and *Nipsic*; and the German *Olga*, *Adler*, and *Eber*.

President Dean and Elders A. [Adelbert] Beesley[2] and Edward J. Wood,[3] all well known to church people, had come in a small boat to Apia from the island of Tutuila[4] and were eyewitnesses to much of the disaster herein imperfectly described. On the way over, their little craft was capsized, the baggage had gone to the bottom, and they narrowly escaped drowning. Their lives were saved by natives who subsequently plunged into the water and recovered the lost satchels. While preparing to return to Tutuila they were strongly prompted not to do so. Had this warning been ignored they must inevitably have perished in the appalling storm which arose when they would have been well out at sea. Surely guardian angels watch over missionaries.

The storm began Friday, March 15th. Riding idly at anchor, the war vessels were unable to obtain a full head of steam before the hurricane in all its devastating fury broke upon them. Shortly thereafter, the *Eber* and the *Adler* were driven onto the coral reef with such force that they were torn almost to pieces, and one hundred of their men were drowned or beaten to death on the rocks.

Through the long night the officers and men aboard the vessels worked like demons in an effort to reach the open sea where there was at least a measure of safety, but in spite of their maneuvers, with bows pointed seaward, with full steam on and all anchors down they could not withstand the gale and were being slowly driven toward the rocks and certain destruction.

Trees were laid low, houses were demolished, and the roar of the breakers resembled the thunder of a thousand cannons.

Saturday morning came, and, convinced that his ship was doomed and hoping that the hundreds of natives might be able to save at least a part of his crew, the *Nipsic*'s captain deliberately drew up anchors, turned the bow landward, and with full steam ahead, and the hurricane helping him on, drove her as high onto the rocks as possible. His vessel was of course wrecked, but the natives responded most heroically. Repeatedly they dashed into the surf with a lifeline, only to be dragged back beaten into unconsciousness by the tremendous waves. Finally one of them succeeded in reaching the stricken ship and most of the men were saved.

Meanwhile, the British *Calliope*, the highest powered of all the seven vessels, found that with full steam on the anchors were holding her from being driven back. With newly awakened hope, her stokers redoubled their seemingly superhuman efforts. Slowly but surely she was gaining, her anchor chains slackened, the great "mud hooks" were hoisted, and though at first the gain was almost imperceptible it was real, and she was moving out to sea and comparative safety. With men and machines working at highest tension, she crept past the American ships, and the plucky lads trained under the Stars and Stripes, though they had reason to believe that they were facing death, stopped long enough to cheer sailors of another nation who were escaping the fate which awaited them, and as their applause arose above the tumult of roaring wind and water, the band played "Britannia Rules the Waves." Needless to say, the British sailors responded right lustily and their band played "Yankee Doodle." What voice could have failed to give the doomed men an encouraging cheer?

Instead of abating, the storm increased in intensity. Imagine a hurricane so fierce that powerful warships, with full steam on and three anchors down, cannot face it! It seems incredible. These vessels were as nearly invincible as human skill could make them, were manned by officers and crews trained for just such emergencies, but when actually pitted against omnipotent power they were as impotent as the frailest toy.

Resting in American Samoa

The watchers onshore saw the *Vandalia*, despite anchors and steam, drifting helplessly toward the coral reef which she finally struck stern first. Elder Dean's record says that each monster wave would pick her up and drop her onto the rocks until she was crushed, and settled down with decks just below the water. Hundreds of men were clinging to the rigging, many were swept overboard and some jumped, hoping they could swim ashore but the current carried most of them out to sea. The missionaries say that thirty or forty perished in this way before their eyes. They and the crowd lining the beach were as helpless as the ships themselves.

It is said that for more than thirty hours Rear Admiral [Lewis Ashfield] Kimberly[5] did not leave the bridge of his flagship *Trenton*. The storm played with her as a cat plays with a mouse. Time and again she made headway against the mountains of water which swept the decks; but each time when hope of reaching the open sea was highest, the hurricane with tantalizing fury drove her back. As the darkness of Saturday night came on, the watchers could see her drifting helplessly down on the *Vandalia*, and the dawn of Sabbath morning revealed that the *Trenton*, notwithstanding her gallant fight, was also a wreck. Fortunately, however, by this time the storm had abated somewhat and all the men were saved. Previous to this the captain of the *Olga*, following the example of the *Nipsic*, had voluntarily run his ship onto the reef. None of his crew was lost.

Though six of the seven vessels went to pieces, the special missionaries were told by the captain of the *Tofua* that officers and men emerged the disaster with stainless names. During the weeks which elapsed before the United States could send other vessels to take away the stranded marines, they were royally entertained, and many tender, and a few pathetic, farewells were whispered when parting time finally came. The tragic story is current of a native girl who had fallen hopelessly in love with one of the officers and who wrote Samoa's favorite farewell song, "Tofa mai Feleni" (Goodbye, my Friend). The tradition is that she swam after his vessel singing it as he sailed away, perhaps to another love, and to lands which to her were unknown. It is a beautiful song which quickly takes hold of one's heart, and if not equal to Hawaii's famous "Aloha Oe," it is a very close second.

Elder Dean concludes his interesting reference to the hurricane and the resultant loss of life with the laconic but significant sentence, "We brought home a cartload of wreckage."

The chief officer of the *Tofua* said that gales such as this are hurricanes in the South Seas, typhoons in the China Sea,[6] monsoons in the Indian Ocean,[7] cyclones in the Gulf of Mexico,[8] and hell in all waters. He added with apparent earnestness that he had no intention of being profane, but such a storm at sea, as Sherman's definition of war, can be adequately described by that one word only.

One evening with this story still ringing in their ears, the special missionaries in company with President and Sister Adams, Brother and Sister Griffiths, President Coombs, and Elders Leland H. Stott[9] and J. Kenneth Rallison passed these rusting hulks of warships and went aboard the diminutive gasoline launch, the *Marstal*, which had been engaged to carry them over to Pago Pago[10] on the island of Tutuila. The weather was threatening and as the *Marstal* was absolutely without accommodations for passengers the sixteen-hour ride was not viewed in the light of a pleasure excursion. But to preach the gospel was Brother McKay's mission; all else was subordinate to that divine obligation.

The little boat possessed one redeeming feature—though she was tossed about on the waves like a cork, literally stirring the passengers to their very depths, one step brought the afflicted voyager to the vessel's side, and as practically all of them had to reach the side pretty often and quickly, this was a distinct advantage. Oh, what a pitiably seasick lot they were! This malady came on insidiously, as temptation comes, and the party were like the man who could resist anything but temptation. Brother McKay usually does nothing by halves, but this occasion may have been an exception. Naturally, no measurements were taken, but as nearly as one might estimate he divided himself about equally and threw away the "worser part."

Sister Thurza T. Adams showed her heroic and unselfish disposition. Though the sickest of the party, her thoughts during the entire night were for the comfort of everybody but herself. When the recording angel makes up his list of world heroines, the women who have labored as missionaries in the South Seas will surely be placed in an enviable position.

Before leaving port, Brother McKay had done a generous thing, and richly were he and his companions repaid for this act. The *Marstal* had been chartered to convey the missionaries to Pago Pago, wait until their work was completed and then bring them back to Apia, but just as they were ready to set sail, the owner requested that the boat be permitted to return immediately with some freight and passengers. He promised to have it back in Pago Pago sufficiently early to meet Brother McKay's requirements. This consent was given. Among the passengers for whom this trip was made was Father Dennis O'Reilley, one of the Catholic priests to whom reference has heretofore been made. Subsequently, he gave the following account of their experiences:

Resting in American Samoa

We had hardly emerged from the harbor before we were soaked to the skin by rain and a few moments later by the waves which dashed completely over the tiny craft. During the night the engine balked and no amount of coaxing would induce it to go. There is only one thing worse in the world than sailing on the *Marstal* and that is being aboard her when she is not sailing, but is tossing wildly, but idly, in the rough open sea. Sunday morning found us still with a disabled engine, and completely out of sight of land. The captain, who travels about these islands with no other instrument than a compass, confessed complete ignorance as to our location. Though a sail was hoisted he had no idea as to the direction in which to steer. As evening approached, the boat was found to be leaking and the captain, abandoning hope said we should prepare for the worst.

The natives aboard began saying goodbye to one another. However, being urged by the white passengers, the captain continued working on the engine, while crew and passengers took turns pumping. Before daylight of Monday morning the captain had the engine shooting, but very irregularly. After several hours we sighted land, and in the afternoon the *Marstal* limped through the coral reef and into the quiet little bay on the opposite side of the island from Apia, to which point my companion and I walked the following day.[11]

An experience similar to this would doubtless have come to the brethren had the boat waited until they were ready to return. Instead she came, though two days late, with a repaired and properly working engine.

However, before this happened the missionary party chugged along the green coast of Tutuila en route to Pago Pago. The suggestion that it is wondrously beautiful made by one of the voyagers who, however, was not sufficiently enthusiastic to raise his head to behold the grandeur he described, had little effect, for the rest of the party neither knew nor cared whether or not it was beautiful.

A haggard, weary, and disconsolate-looking lot landed under the Stars and Stripes which somewhat revived their drooping spirits, and these were almost completely restored by the hearty welcome given them at the conference house by President William S. Muir[12] and his hospitable wife, Edna Walton Muir.[13]

The church owns a longtime lease on a large plantation, consisting principally of coconut trees, at Mapusaga[14] about twelve miles [19.31 km] from Pago Pago, and here one of the best church schools on the islands is maintained. The school band, under the leadership of Elder Lorenzo E. Peterson, and a multitude of members and friends headed by Elder William K. Brewer[15] and Harry S. Jacobs extended a welcome as hearty, if not so elaborate, as any extended the special missionaries. Many distant as well as nearby villages were represented by their chiefs and chosen "Taupos" (virgins).

The days spent here were full of delightful experiences. Meetings were held, instructions given, and testimonies borne. The joy manifested by these humble people at the privilege of shaking hands with one of the General Authorities cannot be described. The more phlegmatic whites of the church, both in Zion and abroad, might with profit have viewed this demonstration.

The need of more and better schools was apparent. Scarcely one of the elders was a trained teacher, and still it was really surprising how well they were doing. The following translated petition will perhaps be of interest:

> Tutuila, Samoa, May 23, 1921
> To His Excellency, the Prophet,
> Church of Jesus Christ of Latter-day Saints
> This will be presented to Apostle McKay and President Adams of the Samoan Mission.
> Your Highness:
> We petition you with respect and deference and due honor as follows:
>
> We respectfully and in love request you to kindly accede to our desires that you send us some school teachers for the school in Mapusaga. We know assuredly that this is the one way in which the inhabitants of this island can quickly obtain knowledge, and by this acquisition of knowledge men will be made acquainted with the Gospel.
>
> If it is in accordance with your will, please send some male teachers for the boys, and lady teachers for the girls.
>
> We have prepared this petition with sincerity in our hearts; we depend upon your great love to receive our request.
>
> Soifua, (May you be blessed)
> We are the High Chiefs and authorities of the church in Tutuila.[16]

This was presented by twenty-five chiefs.

At the conclusion of the conference and their inspection of the school and the plantation, the special missionaries left Mapusaga ahead of the main body of visitors. After their departure one of the native boys, who was to assist in carrying the satchels, said: "We must hurry, for the 'Apostolo' and Brother Cannon have gone. It has stopped raining now, but it will start again as soon as they reach Pago Pago. If we are not there by that time we will get wet." And Sister Adams added, "Do you hear that? I believe it, and I'm not going to wait for breakfast."

The boy's statement proved to be correct. No sooner were the missionaries in the conference house than the rain descended in floods.

Some readers of this narrative may not know that the United States controls American Samoa,[17] using it as a naval base. It consists of the islands of Tutuila, Manua,[18] Olosega,[19] Ofu,[20] Aunuu,[21] and the uninhabited coral atoll Rose Island,[22] with a total population of about 7,500. At the time of this visit Captain Waldo Evans[23] was governor, and a pleasant interview was had with him and with the Superintendent of Instruction and also the Minister of Native Affairs. The relation of church schools to the government, uniform text books, and other important matters were profitably discussed.

It was 9 p.m. when the *Marstal* with the tired party of missionaries reached Apia on the return voyage, and it was feared that they would have to spend another night on the uncomfortable boat, but thanks to the intervention of United States Consul Roberts and the consequent courtesy of the custom officials, the offices were kept open for their benefit and they were thus permitted to land. Another courteous thing was done. The captain of the mail boat *Ajax* delayed his departure from Apia for more than two hours, thinking perhaps the brethren might have some mail which they desired to send out.

This is moral perfection: to live each day as though it were the last; to be tranquil, yet not indifferent to our fate.

—Marcus Aurelius[1]

Among white races one often hears the statement that the gospel deprives men of liberty and makes slaves of them. The Samoans, even nonmembers of the church, view this differently and, in truth, more sensibly. They consider that man a slave who uses tobacco or liquor and cannot overcome the habit, accepting literally the Savior's words: "Whosoever committeth sin is the servant of sin. . . . If the Son therefore shall make you free, ye shall be free indeed."[2]

Because of the childlike and inspiring faith of the Islanders the Lord gives them unusual manifestations as He did the Lamanites, their ancestors, whenever they humbled themselves and came to him in faith. Almost every church member can tell of something supernatural through which he was made to understand the plan of salvation, and these stories are related with a sincerity which banishes doubt as to their genuineness.

Sauniatu is the principal branch of the church in Samoa. Here the best school on the islands is located, and the church owns a large plantation of coconut trees. Brothers McKay and Cannon and President [John] and Sister [Thurza] Adams rode on horseback to this place. The trail over which they traveled skirted the sea-coast, sometimes along sandy beaches, and occasionally over precipitous cliffs. The intense blueness of the sky, the still deeper blue of the water, the thundering surf on the coral reef, magnificent trees of every tropical variety, among which the stately coconut palms predominated, will never be forgotten by those who have had the good fortune to pass that way. Everywhere natives were gathering and breaking coconuts for the market. It would surprise a European to see how completely these nuts cover the ground. There were literally millions and millions of them, and preparing them for shipment is one of the chief occupations of the people. Reference has heretofore been made to the thirst-quenching liquid which these nuts contain. The natives are very proficient in selecting those of proper ripeness and are always ready to climb a tree to obtain for a stranger the very best drink which can be had. On a hot day, and there are no days in Samoa which are not hot, this beverage is very refreshing.

Word had evidently gone ahead that "Apostolo" McKay was coming, for in every village groups of curious and in most cases reverential people were gathered. Many of these were not affiliated with the church, but our members are held in high esteem, and it was easy for the natives to revere one of their leaders. In the village of Fusi,[3] in which place no Mormons were living, the men all stood at attention as the missionary party drew near. At a word of command, they saluted, many of them kneeling as they did so. It was a mark of courtesy which was the more appreciated because it was so spontaneous and unexpected.

The distance between Apia and Sauniatu is twenty long miles [32.19 km], and the luggage of the missionaries was carried on the shoulders of young natives who walked the entire distance barefooted and kept pace with those on horseback. The regrets which Brother McKay felt at seeing these sturdy fellows walking while he rode were dissipated during succeeding days, for those who had performed this arduous task were considered by all as having been especially favored. Among those who walked also were a number of elders, and as the visiting brethren looked at the hardy young chaps they saw ample justification for the pride the church feels in its missionaries. As a rule they are as pure minded and clean in thought and act as maidens; sturdy, virile, and physically fit as any men in the world; men who dare to do right and with a courage which enables them to face any difficulty, including the scorn of the thoughtless or ignorant; men who would go to the ends of the earth if they were asked; so self-sacrificing that they will walk miles to preach the gospel of Christ to an investigator or to administer to an unknown afflicted person; young men appreciative of the fact that their parents, or not infrequently widowed mothers, are working longer hours than they should, wearing shabby clothes, staying awake nights planning how to make ends meet and keep their sons in the field; men who would not only die for their faith, but who live for it—these are they whom the world stamps as wicked impostors who are laying snares to entangle the feet of their fellowmen. How incredibly blind!

From the village of Fusi, one of the high chiefs accompanied the party to its destination, and at his order some of his people brought presents of mats, many kinds of fruits and other food, among which was a whole roasted pig.

At the Sauniatu plantation, the party was met by a group of missionaries and church members headed by Elder Ray W. Berrett, president of the conference. Brother McKay's description of the welcome follows:

> As we walked slowly toward the conference house, the band struck up "The Star Spangled Banner."[4] To hear that old air away off here in Samoa, played so impressively by Samoan boys, to see the women of the village, all dressed in white and men well dressed standing in line opposite the women; to walk along a well-cleaned roadway strewn on each side with palm branches; to realize that every heart was beating a welcome, even though it was accompanied by a feeling of curiosity, made me feel that this simple unostentatious greeting from the little village of Sauniatu was one of the most impressive of our entire trip. My feelings were stirred and found expression in a tear or two that trickled over the eyelids.

The three days which followed were among the most memorable of this memorable journey. With feasts and concerts, with native dances and gifts of fruit, beads, and mats, the good people endeavored to show their appreciation of the visit. And these tokens of goodwill did not come solely from church members. Many delegations headed by their chiefs and made up entirely of non-members came with songs, speeches, dances, and gifts.

The spirit of the Lord was remarkably manifest in the meetings, and instructions were given which those in attendance will never forget. The Sunday school deserves special mention. While the organist played, the people of the village led by a little girl came marching in, graded in size from the baby up to the adult.

The people carried neatly folded mats under their arms and these when spread on the cement floor furnished seats for the congregation. This organization is impressing upon the hearts of old and young lessons of priceless value. In these gatherings taro, the root of a plant,[5] is used instead of bread for the sacrament.

Brother McKay and five other missionaries were guests at the home of Brother Sai Masina and family. This was the first individual Samoan family to entertain in real native fashion one of the General Authorities. The travelers had been in many Samoan huts and had participated in greater feasts, but this was purely a family affair and was typically characteristic of the South Seas.

As the party approached the hut with its open sides and its thatched roof, resembling that of a miniature tabernacle set on upright posts, the family arose and the children sang a song of welcome. Mats were spread upon the clean pebble floor and these were bounteously covered with taro, chicken, plates of soup, pork, cocoa, pudding, coconuts, bananas, and other fruits. Of course it was necessary to sit cross-legged on the ground while partaking of this repast.

Though inclined to postpone the hour of departure from this interesting village, the time for parting came at last. Speeches were made by the orators and chiefs of this and surrounding villages. Chief Fa'ifai, a non-member of the church, closed his remarks with tears in his eyes and with these words:

> Our hearts are broken to hear your parting words. . . . We request that when you return to Zion and meet the Prophet and the Quorum of the Twelve that you put Samoa in your hearts as a seal. May your Excellencies be blessed, also President Adams and Mrs. Adams as well as all the elders and saints.

The actual departure of the brethren was delayed for more than an hour while they administered to afflicted children and adults. This duty finally accomplished, Brother McKay and his party emerged from the back room of the conference house and were at once overwhelmed by crowds awaiting them in the front room. The Relief Society[6] sisters and others began a farewell song, accompanied by the band, but weeping soon took the place of singing. Many knelt and kissed the hands of the visitors and bathed them in tears.

A former statement may properly be repeated, that these people had looked forward with as much anticipation to Brother McKay's visit as a white race would display while awaiting one of the ancient apostles if they knew through prophecy that he would appear in his resurrected form at a given date. To illustrate this statement: Chief Sai Masina, eighty-four years old, at whose home the brethren had been entertained, as he knelt and kissed Brother McKay's hand said, with tears streaming down his furrowed cheeks, "My prayers have been answered; I have seen an Apostle of the Lord, and now I am ready to go." The first word the brethren received after they had finally left the islands was that this good man had passed on to his reward.

Their own feelings deeply stirred and with bedimmed eyes the visitors pressed through the crowds and mounted the horses which were in waiting. The people followed them across the bridge which spans the beautiful stream and the band played "Tofa mai Feleni." (Good-bye, my Friend). As Brother McKay looked back through the avenue of trees and saw the band and crowd following, he felt impressed to return and offer a prayer with them, and this inspiration was immediately followed.

As he prayed for and blessed the multitude, one was unconsciously reminded of that touching farewell which the Savior took of the people, as recorded in the Book of Mormon, Third Nephi, chapters 17 and 18. Though the Christ was not present in person, he was represented by a divinely chosen servant and his comforting spirit was felt by all. Later it was learned that the prayer had been written, as nearly as it could be remembered by Brother Sua Kippen and others, and was placed in the cornerstone of an impressive monument which was erected on the place.[7]

Here was seen a splendid example of the fact that the gospel of Jesus Christ makes one of all mankind. These people were strangers to the visitors. They had never met until a few days previously; they were of a different race, with different language, color, and customs. One thing only was held in common—their faith—and yet genuine tears of sorrow were shed on each side at parting. It was an affecting and unforgettable experience.

In Apia the day before departure of Brother McKay's party from Samoa, eighteen missionaries and a host of natives sat down in the commodious home of Brother Ah Ching,[8] a full-blooded Chinese and a faithful member of the church. He is a wealthy man and his auto was always at the disposal of the brethren. One of his sons has been educated in China with the thought that he may be needed later as a missionary to that land. The story of this man's life reads like a novel. He was cook for a long time on a ship, and with typical Chinese thrift had saved three thousand dollars. This was entrusted to a confidential friend, but the money was dishonestly used and lost to Brother Ching. At the time, he was not a member of the church and made up his mind to kill the man who had thus wronged him, and for this purpose he obtained a long knife "as sharp as a razor." Then something came over him which caused a complete change of heart. He decided to permit the man to live, though he felt sure the untrue friend would always be rich while he himself would always remain poor. However, the anticipated conditions were exactly reversed. He had become rich while the man who robbed him had come many times as a beggar to his door, and, be it said to the credit of this faithful Chinese brother, that his former enemy was always given clothing and food.

There were present at this feast, in addition to names mentioned elsewhere in this chronicle, Elders Ralph A. Knowlton,[9] Arthur Huntsman,[10] Lewis B. Parkin,[11] and Ralph Putnam.

During this same entertainment another church member who had been an officer on a small trading schooner told of a visit to the Phoenix group of islands,[12] where he had witnessed a dangerous method of fishing for sharks. These fish were very numerous in the harbor, but were shy and would not come near enough to the fishing boat to be speared. At last the natives tied a rope about the waist of one of their number who jumped into the water. The sharks darted for him, and as he was jerked violently into the boat a dozen hungry jaws snapped at the spot where a moment before his legs had been. By means of this human bait the natives were able to throw their spears into the backs of these fish.

Despite their frequency, the touching farewells which the visitors experienced in the South Seas never became commonplace. It was no easier to say good-bye to the friends in Apia than it had been in other places. These faithful souls acknowledged in Brother McKay's visit an answer to prayer; they had listened to inspired words and had received additional confirmation of their faith that the Almighty does have divinely chosen men to lead his people.

Boys comprising the school band had walked the twenty miles [32.87 km] from Sauniatu carrying their instruments, even the big bass drum, in order to cheer the travelers on their way.

It was dark when the brethren boarded the *Tofua*. Their cabin was filled with fruits and flowers. Many members and friends accompanied them on board and could hardly be induced to leave when the last bugle sounded warning that the vessel was about to sail. The band and crowds of members and friends were on the pier and strains of music from instruments and voices accompanied the ship as it sailed out into the night.

Your sole contribution to the sum of things is yourself.
—Crane[1]

Brother McKay entertained the hope that the quarantine which prevented his party while en route to Samoa from landing in Tonga would be raised and that they could land on the return journey, a hope encouraged by officers of the vessel. It proved, however, to be fallacious. The *Tofua* stopped at Vavau,[2] which had lost none of its romantic beauty since the previous visit, and meetings might have been held. But no one was permitted to land. This experience was repeated at Haapai,[3] another island of the Tongan group where there is a branch of the church. It became evident that the only way to visit these islands was to go into quarantine for two weeks at Nukualofa. This meant that passengers would be held literally as prisoners on a little island in the harbor. A native would be sent out from the mainland to cook and here they could "set and think," or when tired of that, could just "set."

It was interesting to watch the struggle through which Brother McKay passed. The work awaiting the brethren in New Zealand furnished ample excuse for his going on and leaving Brother Cannon to visit these islands. To his restless spirit the thought of remaining almost in complete idleness for two weeks was well nigh maddening. The reality of it, he feared, would be quite so. Naturally the desirable and comfortable thing to do was to proceed with the *Tofua*. But he knew these people, as those of the other islands, had been expecting to see one of the Twelve and would be bitterly disappointed with a substitute. Resisting his own personal inclinations, therefore, he decided to remain and have Brother Cannon go on to New Zealand to which point he would follow as soon as possible.[4]

President Mark V. Coombs, having been in Samoa, was also obliged to go into quarantine as were the newly arrived missionaries, Clarence Henderson,[5] Walter J. Phillips, Lewis B. Parkin, and George W. Robinson. Upon the arrival of the vessel at Nukualofa, they and about thirty other unfortunates were loaded into a barge which was towed across the bay to the quarantine island.[6]

Ordinarily such isolation would have furnished excellent opportunities for preaching the gospel to fellow prisoners and, even with a rather serious handicap, before they were finally released a number of lasting friendships had been made. Most readers of this narrative already know that Brother McKay is a "good mixer."[7] In this instance his task was a difficult one, for two of the passengers with him and his party were Wesleyan[8] ministers who were horrified when they learned that a fellow prisoner professed to be an apostle of the Lord Jesus Christ; and so strong was their prejudice that it was not easy for them to be decently civil. Naturally, they had considerable influence over a number of those present. Nevertheless the uniform courtesy of the missionaries, the spirit with which they sang the hymns of Zion, always a potent means of overcoming opposition, and the consistency of the doctrines were irresistible. At some of the services which were held many "who came to scoff, remained to pray."

Naturally, such ministers were not happy in Brother McKay's presence. When the counterfeit is placed side by side with the genuine the contrast is too marked, and the feelings of these men were probably similar to those they will have hereafter should they be permitted to come into the presence of apostles and prophets.

More deep-seated opposition to the restored gospel is met in Tonga than in other island groups of the South Seas.[9] Representatives of various denominations have done considerable work among the natives with the result that there is much disunion among them, but they fraternize in a manner worthy of a better cause whenever it is possible to do or say anything against the Mormons. If further evidence were needed of the divinity of this work, it could be found in the sudden unity which occurs among man-made systems whenever they come in contact with truths revealed anew in this dispensation. In Tonga all the leading men of the islands were invited to attend the meetings, but, unlike the Samoans, none of them responded.

Brother McKay was able, however, to have a profitable interview with the prince consort, Uiliamo Tugi, upon whom he made an excellent impression, according to the report of President Coombs who was present during the conversation. The prince said the sole objection to the preaching of Mormonism on the islands was that it took too many members from the Protestant churches.

The reception given to the visitor on these islands resembled those accorded him in Samoa. All wanted to press his hand and no one was denied the privilege. An old lady who had been sickly for some time reported that she felt entirely well after having grasped his hand.

The story is told of another lady, a non-member, who had been investigating the gospel and who desired to have Brother McKay administer to her. The elders knew her as an inveterate smoker, and one of them suggested that she should observe the Word of Wisdom before making such a request.

"But I do keep the Word of Wisdom," was her response.

"Indeed? When did you quit smoking?" asked the missionary.

"Last night," came the unabashed reply.

After holding conference in Nukualofa, it was decided to visit branches in Haapai and Vavau on the other islands, and a small two-mast schooner was chartered. There were in the party, besides Brother McKay, President Coombs and his wife and three small children, three missionaries, and several natives. The following is taken from President Coombs' account of the trip:

All the Saints were at the wharf to see us off, while some of the more venturesome boys came aboard the vessel and remained until we were nearly a mile [1.61 km] out to sea, when with a farewell wave of the hand they dove from the top of the mast and swam ashore.

We were no sooner outside the protecting reefs than a strong wind sprang up. How the boat did rock! We were nearly all sick. The writer was so sick that he could not help his wife. She was so sick that she would not look after the children. But the natives came to the rescue and tended the babies as though they were their own.

More than once during the night huge waves swept completely over us, wetting us through and through. Elders Clark and [Clement] Oborn[10] were nearly washed overboard, and would have been lost, but fortunately they became entangled in the rigging which held them on. A mountainous wave washed the only life boat loose, and it crushed a poor old woman's foot so badly that she was in the hospital for eight weeks.

During all this time the captain had tied the helm and was letting the boat drift with no hand to guide it. He had commenced to drink and thought more of his liquor than he did of the lives of his passengers. Seeing that something must be done, Brother McKay finally took the bottle from him by force, and though deathly seasick himself was compelled to watch the captain during the whole of that stormy night to prevent him from becoming too drunk to navigate the vessel.

So we sailed all that night and the next day. It was not until eight o'clock in the evening that we landed at Haapai. We held meeting with the Saints there and prepared to leave the next morning at daybreak for Vavau. When morning came, however, it was discovered that the heavy seas of the night before had split the rudder so that it had to be repaired.

It was two o'clock in the afternoon before we finally set out. Again as soon as we were outside the reef an extremely heavy wind arose. We expected to make Vavau that night, but the captain, again under the influence of liquor, set the course too far to the west, so that when evening came no Vavau was in sight, and we did not know where we were. We tacked back and forth all night and when morning came, instead of seeing Vavau we could see the island of Leyte[11] and realized that we were fifty miles [80.47 km] off our course. However, it was a consolation to know our whereabouts, and we were a very thankful party of people when we came alongside the Vavau wharf at three o'clock in the afternoon, nearly twenty-four hours after the expected time of arrival.

Traveling to and from these islands one hears even yet many heartrending stories of suffering and death which occurred during the years 1918 and 1919 when the "flu" spread over the earth with such devastating results.[12] The mortality among church members was notably less than among those not of our faith and many remarkable cases of healing are related. Nevertheless there were numerous fatalities even among the Latter-day Saints and one missionary, Elder [Charles J.] Langston,[13] succumbed to the malady. It seems necessary in fulfillment of the Lord's plan that some of his servants lay down their lives as evidence of their sincerity of purpose in every land where the gospel is being preached. Though Elder Langston's voice is stilled, his testimony will ever live. His parents have sent a fitting headstone for his grave, and he sleeps in that beautiful and restful place, among the people whose salvation was dearer to him and to his associates than were their own lives. This faithful missionary was properly buried, for his co-laborers performed that task, though they themselves were weak from disease.

A law in Tonga provides that every young man upon attaining his majority shall be given a piece of land of sufficient size, if it be properly cultivated, to maintain a family. This he cannot legally sell, though under some circumstances it may be leased. Thus every Tongan becomes a freeholder. The story was told to Brother McKay of a young native of high birth who had joined the church. He was offered large tracts of land, in addition to that which would naturally come to him, and a very desirable position in the government as well, if he would but relinquish his church membership; but he unhesitatingly replied that he would not exchange the joy which the gospel gave for the entire Tongan group and all their wealth. He was alike unmoved by the pleadings of former friends and offers of position and riches. He, as all who actually receive the testimony of the spirit, knew he had received something more priceless than wealth or the transitory honor of men.

While Brother McKay was passing through these stirring experiences in Tonga, Brother Cannon was having an uneventful voyage toward New Zealand. To one who has been promised that if he is seasick "it will be of very short duration," ocean travel is delightful. It would have been particularly so on this trip except that the brethren had been together so much it seemed unnatural to be traveling alone.

Only two things occurred which were out of the ordinary. When Brother McKay left the ship at Nukualofa, two young men were put in the cabin with Brother Cannon. One of these seemed from the first to be far from normal, and the other who was acquainted with him did not conceal his fear that something might happen. It did. The young man had been acting strangely all day and during the night he completely lost his mind and began to rave. The captain was called and the poor fellow was locked up in a padded cell and remained there until Auckland was reached.

While nearing Suva, the *Tofua* received word that the *Attua*, a sister ship belonging to the Burns-Philps line,[14] had run onto the beach at Naitonitoni,[15] about a hundred miles [160.93 km] distant. Her captain, endeavoring to save a few miles of travel, had cut so close to the reef that he struck it a glancing blow which tore a great hole in the side of his vessel. By closing the watertight doors and confining the water to one compartment the ship was able to sail four miles [6.44 km] and there they had been compelled to beach her. No lives were lost but many hundreds of tons of sugar were destroyed.

The *Tofua* made a hurried run to Naitonitoni and picked up the passengers as well as a large amount of uninjured sugar. In addition to this cargo at Suva, the *Tofua* took on eighteen thousand cases of bananas and an enormous number of bunches which were not cased, as well as several thousand cases of oranges.

President L. [Leonidas] H. Kennard, of the Tahitian Mission, had come to New Zealand in accordance with instructions from

Brother McKay, and he and Brother Cannon spent some little time in securing figures from shipbuilding firms for a schooner for use in the Tahitian islands.

In company with President George S. Taylor and his estimable wife,[16] Brother Cannon attended conferences in Thames, where the branch is made up of whites, and Omahu,[17] where the membership is almost wholly native. In the former place President Benjamin Brown and Elders James A. Thornton,[18] Francis L. Wilcox,[19] and Ray Nelson[20] were laboring and in the latter the visitors met President Alvin T. Maughan[21] and Elder William C. Warner.[22]

It is not always pleasant to sleep with comparative strangers, but Brother Cannon felt greatly blessed in having the privilege of sleeping with President Brown. All day long he had been almost devoured by fleas. He managed to rid himself of a few of these tormenting pests while preparing for bed but no sooner were the covers pulled up over him than he felt them in large and industrious numbers. Brother Brown soon came to bed, and these pests instantly left Brother Cannon, much to his relief. They had found someone more to their liking. The next morning when Brother Brown showed the marks of battle on his legs and body, Brother Cannon felt somewhat conscience smitten, but still declares he will never miss an opportunity of sleeping with Brother Brown if they are in a country where fleas abound.

Any native New Zealander will scoff at the suggestion that America's Yellowstone is comparable for a moment with their famed Rotorua.[23] The two places are not unlike. In each, one has the same feeling that the earth may suddenly open up or explode or perform some other unnatural and dangerous feat, but the true American is just as certain that there is no comparison between the two places as is the New Zealander. The visit to Rotorua was made on the first of July, almost midwinter in this hemisphere, and it was extremely cold, especially for one who had just come from the tropics.

The only sacrifice which Jesus asked of his people was the same sacrifice which the farmer makes when he throws his seed into the soil.

—Babson[1]

Much might be written about the famous thermal region of Rotorua, its geysers and hot pots, its villages where all the cooking, as well as the family washing, is done in the boiling springs, and where the natives warm themselves by sitting on hot rocks. The visitor hears of the wonderful pink and white terraces, destroyed more than two score years ago by a terrible volcano and series of earthquakes.

Space will not permit of even a passing reference to many of these things and fortunately it is unnecessary as better descriptions than one could hope to give here may be found elsewhere.

While awaiting Brother McKay's return to New Zealand, Brother Cannon was guest at the mission home in Auckland and was made welcome by President and Sister Taylor and their two daughters[2] as well as by Secretary Frederick W. Schwendiman and his wife,[3] Pres. Joseph Anderson,[4] Wallace L. Castleton,[5] Heber Dean Hall, and Abram M. McFarland[6] who were living there.

One evening he and some of these brethren were invited to have supper with Brother and Sister Kewene, a Maori family. Upon their arrival, they found the family greatly excited and learned that a few moments before, a fire had broken out in the home. A lighted candle had been left in an open window of the room where their baby was sleeping; the wind had blown the curtain into the flame and from this the blaze started. A neighbor across the way, seeing the trouble, sent his little boy over to tell the people their house was on fire. The little chap walked around the building to the back door and knocked timidly. His knock was answered by one of the boys of the family and the messenger asked to see the father, and when he finally came he was told the house was on fire. The little babe was almost suffocated when they rushed in, and it was revived with the utmost difficulty.

After Brother McKay's return from Tonga to New Zealand, conferences were held in Auckland and in the Ngapuhi,[7] Porirua,[8] Dannevirke,[9] and Hastings[10] Districts. Varied experiences were had in each of these places, many meetings were held, and the visitors were entertained in royal native style. Numberless noses were pressed, and the wild "Haka" and the graceful "Poi" dances were witnessed.

One of the meetings in Auckland was disturbed by a number of Re-organites who had come with their usual challenge to a public debate. Missionaries are accustomed to meeting a spirit of hatred, but it is seldom found in more virulent type than among these people. Satan knows full well that the more truth is mixed with his falsehoods the more dangerous it is, and he surely has prepared a poisonous mixture for those who listen to those people. Brother McKay handled the situation with a dignity which won the following remark from a gentleman as he shook hands cordially: "Good-bye, I wish you success. I like your style."

While in Auckland the special missionaries saw Elders Roland C. Parry[11] and Warren J. Stallings,[12] who had just been released, depart on their journey around the world. They also said good-bye to Elder Milton Halls[13] who, almost protesting, was leaving for home because of ill health.

They were also entertained by Mr. Walter E. Bush, city engineer of Auckland, who had been in Salt Lake and, while there, had formed the acquaintance of Bishop Sylvester Q. Cannon[14] who at that time was city engineer. The visitors listened to an address which he made before the Rotary Club of Auckland in which he showed some of New Zealand's latent possibilities, particularly in the line of undeveloped power projects. It was surprising to learn that Auckland has almost trebled in size in the fourteen years prior to this visit.

At Ngapuhi the travelers met Brother Joseph Hay. This man has a unique profession. He obtains a lease on a forest of the stately and useful kauri trees[15] and at a certain season climbs the trees and cuts into the bark in various places. A few months later he again climbs them and gathers the gum which has exuded from the wounds.[16] The man has a rope looped around the tree and encircling his waist. He has sharp hooks made for his hands and wears a clog on each foot with a spike in it and these enable him to walk up the side of a kauri tree, whose nearest branches are sometimes sixty feet [18.29 m] from the ground, with as much apparent ease as an ordinary person ascends a flight of stairs. New Zealanders are justifiably proud of the kauri. According to reports it is not uncommon for one of them to contain 15,000 feet [4,572 m] of lumber.

The thoughtful kindness manifested by the natives to strangers is often very touching. For instance, at one of the entertainments the visitors were sitting in the open air, listening to speeches which were being made in their honor, when a gray-haired, sweet-faced old lady, the mother of Brother Stewart Meha who had distinguished himself in translating for the brethren, came with a pot of burning charcoal and placed it at their feet. As the weather was really chilly the warmth from these coals was appreciated, but the loving solicitude of this gentle native sister will be remembered long after the physical warmth has been forgotten.

Apparently nothing gives the Maoris greater pleasure than to prepare a big banquet. The excellent quality of the food served is only surpassed by the quantity, and the visitor scarcely leaves the table at one meal before preparations are begun for the next. This was particularly true at the homes of Brothers Elliot Nopera and William Duncan, both full-blooded Maoris—and an honor to their race. Indeed, any white race might well be proud of them. Both have beautiful homes. At both places, Brother McKay and party were taken from the station in large, high-powered automobiles belonging to these brethren. The visitors were each given a room furnished so well as to cause Brother McKay to remark, "If these people should ever visit me I could not give them as good a room as this."

Brother Nopera's place is on the outskirts of Dannevirke. When asked how many acres he had in the farm, the good brother appeared to be a little puzzled, but at last he understood.

"Oh, this isn't my farm, this is my city place. I have only three hundred acres here."

"How many acres have you in your farm?" Brother McKay asked in surprise.

"I have nine hundred acres in the farm proper, but there are several thousands acres of grazing lands connected with it."

The home of Brother William Duncan is also a commodious one and it, and everything else he has in the world, is at the disposal of the church. From his house to the railway station the visitors had a thrilling ride. To *hongi* and say good-bye to those assembled had required so much time that the roar of the express train, with which they were scheduled to travel, was heard in the distance as they entered the waiting auto. The handsome young Maori, William Duncan, at the wheel promised to beat the train to the station which was about two miles [3.22 km] distant. And how he did drive! And what a picture he made with his curling hair, dark skin, flashing eyes, and beautiful teeth whenever he glanced back to see how near the train was! At last Brother McKay wisely suggested that he would watch the train if the driver would watch the road.

The principal church school in New Zealand is at Hastings[17] and is rated as an Agricultural College.[18] Good work was being done by this institution which had been under the direction of Principal Franklin E. Stott, though at the time of this visit Elder Leo B. Sharp[19] arrived to take over this position as Brother Stott was about to be released. Brother Sharp had declined an offer of a position with the Ames Agricultural College in order to fill this mission. His wife[20] accompanied him and during the very first day of her mission displayed qualities, as the other lady missionaries had already done, which stamped her as a real missionary. With Brother Sharp were Elders [Irvin S.] Merrill,[21] [Charles H.] Hollingworth,[22] and [Glenn A.] Jorgensen,[23] the last named brother being appointed to take the place of Elder [Asael H.] Fisher as teacher in the school. Other brethren who were engaged either in the school or on the mission paper were Elders Erwin W. Meser, Joseph M. Stephenson,[24] F. Anderson, Glen B. Cannon,[25] Paul R. Buttle,[26] Henry J. Armstrong,[27] Richard G. Andrew, and Amasa S. Holmes.[28]

A great celebration was held at the college in honor of the visitors. Oratory is a highly prized gift among the natives and apparently they begin early to develop it. The speeches and other program numbers furnished by native students were very creditable. At the conclusion of the regular exercises and at a signal from their class leader, a young Maori, not a church member but who only awaited his father's consent to be baptized, a group of stalwart boys seized Brother McKay and, hoisting him high in the air while another group carried Brother Cannon in the same perilous position, they galloped around the hall singing, "For He's a Jolly Good Fellow." Though appreciative of this high honor, the honored ones considered it too high and felt more comfortable when occupying a more lowly position.

Though feasts among the Maoris play an important role in all social events, they do not always think of eating. Sunday is almost invariably a fast day with them. Going without food is preferable to preparing it on the Sabbath day, and even in the evening when their fast is broken, they eat simple things which have been prepared previously.

Indeed, all through New Zealand, the people show a very commendable respect for the Lord's Day. Except on the trunk line between Wellington and Auckland, no trains run on that day. And, although commendable, it was very inconvenient for the visitors,

CHAPTER 18

for they had engaged passage on the *Ulimaroa* which was to leave Auckland Tuesday morning, and in order to make proper preparations for departure, it was necessary to take the night train. But there was no night train from Hastings to Palmerston North,[29] a distance of 112 miles [180.25 km]. Brother Duncan and others offered to hire an auto, as none of them had theirs along, but the price asked was exorbitant. However, Mr. Webb, a very courteous gentleman who was in the meeting at Dannevirke, had driven to Hastings again to attend the service and insisted on taking the brethren in his Hudson to Palmerston North where they could board the midnight train for Auckland. Many church members would balk at a drive of 224 miles [360.49 km] to accommodate strangers. Mr. Webb not only did this, but waited at the station until the train came shortly before one o'clock a.m. in order to have a few moments longer with Brother McKay.

During this visit to New Zealand, and in addition to those whose names are mentioned elsewhere in this volume, the special missionaries met the following elders: James A. Rawson,[30] Edward M. Stanger,[31] Peter M. Johnson,[32] Leon Willie,[33] Melvin C. Stewart,[34] William H. Clark, Russell Lane, Warren Tonks,[35] Jonathan R. Bennett,[36] Gerald F. Heaton,[37] Ralph V. Baird,[38] Ephraim R. Nelson,[39] Harold Hawkes,[40] Joseph E. Francom,[41] Donald L. Hunsaker,[42] Joseph R. Egbert,[43] Ernest A. Ottley,[44] Newel S. Brown,[45] Hyrum V. Bell,[46] Edgar W. Barber,[47] Jacob I. Smith,[48] George S. Winn,[49] Leo E. Coombs,[50] Earl A. Frederickson,[51] Lonell W. Miller,[52] Harold Jenkins,[53] Heber Hymas,[54] Frank L. Crockett,[55] Carlos W. Clark,[56] William Arley Cole[57] and Arthur W. Gudmundson.[58]

The farewells in New Zealand were perhaps not so demonstrative as were those of some other isles, but were quite as affecting. Here, too, tears were shed, and the sorrow which these good people felt in parting was as sincere as that manifested in any land.[59]

The journey to Sydney,[60] Australia, ordinarily requires four days. In this instance five were consumed because of a terrific storm which prevailed. At several meals not more than a dozen people appeared, though there were more than three hundred passengers aboard. During one entire day not more than seven passengers were in the dining room at one time, and at one meal only three were present. President [Anthon H.] Lund's promise still held, and Brother Cannon was one of the three.[61]

Courage and perseverance have a magical talisman, before which difficulties disappear and obstacles vanish into air.

—John Quincy Adams[1]

Sydney, Australia, formerly Port Jackson,[2] boasts of having one of the finest landlocked harbors in the world. It has nearly two hundred miles [321.87 km] of waterfront and is so deep that the largest steamers can draw up to piers within a very few moments' walking distance of the busiest business district.

As the storm-tossed *Ulimaroa* entered this peaceful haven on a smiling Sabbath day, the passengers felt they were emerging from a tempestuous world into a veritable Garden of Eden.[3] This comparison might well have occurred to them because of the change in weather conditions, but a contributing cause was found as their eyes searched the rapidly approaching shore and on their right they saw wandering about in apparently untrammeled freedom all manner of wild animals—lions, tigers, bears, and other things which go to make up a well-equipped Eden—or a modern zoo. As the steamer drew nearer, and even with the aid of binoculars, passengers failed to discern anything resembling a cage. A subsequent visit to the place, however, revealed deep and impassable cement trenches which kept the animals within bounds.

At the landing stage, the brethren were met by President Don C. Rushton[4] of the Australian Mission[5] and several other missionaries.

The church members in Australia are all white, practically no work having been done among the Aborigines.[6] The welcome extended the visitors at mission headquarters by Sister [Elizabeth J.] Rushton[7] and a number of assembled saints was no whit less sincere, even though less demonstrative, than those witnessed among the Polynesians. For the first time in this dispensation, or in any other as far as we have record, one of the

General Authorities had set foot on this land. Naturally, the Latter-day Saints rejoiced to meet Brother McKay, at first because of his exalted position, but afterwards because of his personality which instantly won their hearts.[8]

It was the first Sunday in August, consequently fast day, and Brother McKay expressed the desire to hear the members bear testimony. It was a source of joy to find here in the Antipodes the same positive knowledge of the divinity of this work that is so noticeable in other climes. Many people belonging to other churches believe, most of them in a rather superficial way, that their religion is true; but how rarely is one found who claims through prayer and study to have gained an absolute and personal testimony from the Almighty on this point? That vital and compelling conviction is usually absent. On the other hand, how seldom is a Latter-day Saint of mature age found who does not know that the Father and the Son appeared to Joseph Smith, that through them and their subsequent messengers the gospel, with all its saving graces, was restored to earth!

This special mission demonstrated that the knowledge of the Almighty and his divine plan has spread abroad, and Isaiah's words are gradually being fulfilled: "The earth shall be full of the knowledge of the Lord, as the waters cover the sea."[9]

Who has not heard of Port Jackson, Botany Bay,[10] Van Diemen's Land [Tasmania]?[11] As is generally well known, Australia was once England's convict settlement. To this country offenders were banished and naturally the early history abounds in tales of crime as well as in pathetic stories of people innately good but struggling hopelessly against an unkind fate. Years elapsed before England realized that she was turning over to her expatriated citizens one of the best of her colonial possessions. Since then, many of her worthiest sons and daughters have established homes there and today Australia is justly proud of her citizenry, her resources and culture. Two of the cities, Sydney and Melbourne,[12] are approaching the million mark in population and are as modern and interesting as any cities of their size in the world.

Brother McKay, with every right-thinking Latter-day Saint, believes the acquisition of knowledge and proper experience is a duty. With this thought in mind he, in company with Brothers Cannon and Robert K. Bischoff,[13] visited the famous Jenolan caves. No task could be more impossible of fulfillment than to adequately describe these wonderful formations, located far under the ground, the stalactites, the stalagmites, the dainty coloring, weird shapes, many of them seemingly the work of a master sculptor who had been called away before his task was completely finished.

The visitor is overwhelmed by the vastness, the uniqueness, and the sublime grandeur of countless chambers. There are exquisitely tinted curtains, transparent and looking as soft as the finest silk, delicately woven shawls, handkerchiefs, and draperies of fluffy lace which would win the ladies' hearts; there are flags and icicles and waterfalls; there are ferns and flowers, birds and animals, men and women. In one chamber the Madonna and Child are surrounded by glorified beings; in another are weird and grotesque figures which seem to belong to the nether regions. And all these are of stone made through forgotten ages by an omnipotent hand.

For untold centuries these marvels remained here, unknown, until an accident revealed the first of the caves to man. The thought comes to the visitor that all about are great and beautiful truths waiting for man's eyes to be opened so that they can be seen.

It required three hours to traverse the Orient cave, the most famous of the group, with its innumerable caverns. In doing so, one must climb and descend fourteen hundred steps. In the bottom of this cave is an underground river which is crossed in a boat. All about were strange forms which were reflected by electric lights in the clear water, and the visitor feels indeed that he is in an enchanted fairyland.[14]

Between the caves and the hotel, the travelers saw many rock wallabies, miniature kangaroos, somewhat larger than an ordinary rabbit, and which were almost as numerous and quite as tame as the sparrows in Utah.

Australia is typically English in at least one respect. Whether visiting famous caves, or traveling by auto or train, shopping or sightseeing, the traveler who does not have "Tea" every few hours is looked upon as a freak.

Several meetings were held in Sydney, after which a trip was made to Melbourne about six hundred miles [965.61 km] distant. There a missionary meeting was held with the elders. These brethren were working with energy and finding in their efforts that same spirit of sweet contentment so characteristic of faithful missionary work. There were present at these meetings President Milton Jensen[15] and Elders Sterling Johnson,[16] Thomas G. Smith,[17] Franklin D. Fronk,[18] Alvin Englestead,[19] and John E. Hipwell.[20]

From Melbourne, Brother McKay and his party took boat across Bass Strait[21] to Tasmania,[22] landing after an all-night ride at the little town of Burnie[23] and traveling 230 miles [370.15 km] from that place to Hobart.[24] On this island President Edward Eugene Gardner,[25] Wallace O. Walker,[26] Joseph R. Hunsaker,[27] and James E. Hendricks[28] were laboring. Hobart is one of the most southerly cities in the world, and one is forced to admire these young chaps who were working in this isolated field, seldom seeing missionaries other than their coworkers and, because of the great distances, not being favored with frequent visits from the mission president. One can easily understand, therefore, how much they appreciated Brother McKay's visit. He not only gave them excellent instruction but delivered a message in the town hall which, if obeyed, will lead those who heard it back into the presence of the redeemed. In this instance also "some who came to scoff, remained to pray."

As the brethren were leaving Tasmania they were greeted at the wharf at Launceston[29] by a number of members and friends. Among them was Brother Chidwick who celebrated his 81st birthday by seeing an apostle for the first time. His joyful face bore evidence that it was one of the eventful days of his life.

After returning to Melbourne from Hobart, the special missionaries and President Rushton traveled to Adelaide,[30] 483 miles [777.31 km] distant. The elders from the Melbourne district came down to the train to see the brethren off. They were a splendid looking lot physically, averaging better than six feet [1.83 m], and as they were standing by the train the conductor said in surprise, "My word! But it's unusual to see so many large men together." When Brother McKay told him they were all Mormon missionaries his astonishment was intensified.

The plan had been for the missionary party to go to Perth[31] in Western Australia, but it was found that the return to Sydney could not be made sufficiently early to catch the boat for Singapore,[32] and the plan had to be abandoned. The elders from Perth, therefore, came to Adelaide, a distance of 3,200 miles [5149.90 km] for the round trip, in order to receive the instructions which Brother McKay had to impart. There were in attendance at the missionary meeting, Presidents Austin S. Tolman,[33] George A. Christensen,[34] and Elders Herman E. Bayles,[35] Earl R. Hanson,[36] and Thomas W. Lutz,[37] Doris Baker,[38] William C. Warner, and Thomas G. Smith, besides the visitors.

Attending the meetings held in Adelaide were some members who had come 200 miles [321.87 km] to meet Brother McKay. They brought with them a hunger and thirst for the word of the Lord, and the promise made by the Savior to all such was completely fulfilled. All were unanimous in saying that a trip of many times the distance would have been small sacrifice for that which they received.

While looking for a suitable hotel at which to stay, the visitors had been thoroughly disgusted by the drinking and carousing in the public houses which were connected with every hotel.

Following the English custom, barmaids served the drinks in these places. However, when the Sabbath came, the brethren were forced to admit that our own fair state could in some respects profitably follow the example of this land. Trams did not run until late in the afternoon, and the picture shows and all places of business were closed.

At the time of this visit, the Sunday school in Sydney was presided over by Brother J. N. Hansen. Before he joined the church, he and his wife and little daughter went from Australia to Utah and located in the Thirty-first Ward, Salt Lake City. The wife was taken fatally ill and in his hour of greatest distress the family was visited by Relief Society sisters who aided him in every possible manner. His wife died, after telling him that the unexpected kindness had prompted her to ask the Lord whether Mormonism was divine or not. She bore solemn testimony just before she passed on that these principles were true and urged him to accept them. However, he was so disconsolate after her death that he returned to Australia, but later he sought and found the missionaries and he and his daughter became devoted members. Missionaries in foreign lands are not the only ones who preach the gospel.

Another missionary meeting was held in Sydney attended by President [Don] and Sister [Elizabeth] Rushton, Elders Robert K. Bischoff, Sterling Johnson, Marion G. Romney,[39] William W. Horne,[40] William L. Jones,[41] Robert H. Andrus,[42] Raymond P. Nelson,[43] Charles M. Bowen,[44] Lorenzo F. Hansen,[45] and the two visiting brethren.

Much has been said about the faithful services of the wives of mission presidents, and Sister Rushton was no whit behind her sisters in devotion. She had the love and confidence of elders and members and was a worthy mother to her flock. The missionaries, too, laboring in this land measure up to those of any field visited as do also the members. Though they assist the missionaries in their zealous efforts to convert, it cannot be said that the work, judging by the number of baptisms, is making great headway in Australia. If the sole purpose of the church in sending representatives abroad were to win a large membership, the prospects in the Antipodes would be rather disheartening. Inasmuch, however, as its mission is to preach the "gospel of the kingdom in all the world for a witness unto all nations,"[46] there is no cause for discouragement, and indeed those faithful ones, though few in number, who recognize the voice of a servant of the Lord are well worth all the effort expended in that land.

Before leaving Australia, indeed before steamship tickets could be purchased, it was necessary to have visas from the British officers to enter India and Egypt and from the Dutch officers to enter

Java. These were not easily obtained. Nations had not yet reached a state of normalcy after the war and officials acted with the most exasperating deliberation. Under no circumstances could they be hurried. It appeared after all that the *Marella* might leave before the necessary papers could be obtained. But Brother McKay's principle is to go as far as he can, trusting in the Almighty to open the way further. He and President Rushton, therefore, went to Brisbane[47] by rail, at which point the steamer was scheduled to call, leaving Brother Cannon to secure the papers and follow with the *Marella*.

Satan seemed determined to make this special mission as difficult as possible. Even more apparent, however, was the divine power, manifested so convincingly that the brethren knew they had but to proceed calmly and prayerfully with arrangements, no matter what apparently insurmountable obstacles might arise, and the way would be invariably opened. Had they hearkened to officials who assured them the papers could not possibly be prepared in time, their journey would have been seriously impeded.

Herein lies an important lesson which Brother McKay never failed to emphasize. "Even though a stone wall appears to cross your path," he was wont to say, "go as far as you can, and you will usually find an opening through which you can pass." To illustrate this point, he related the experience of the late James L. McMurrin, laboring as a missionary in Scotland, when a very young man. Brother McMurrin had been appointed to hold meeting in a neighboring town, to which he must travel by train. He was penniless. The distance could not be traversed on foot in the time at his disposal. "I cannot go," he thought, "because of lack of means," but this was supplanted by a better thought, "I have been given this appointment and will go as far as possible and will only stop when I cannot go a step farther." He walked to the station and to the gate where he must show his ticket. Suddenly he met a friend who asked if he had any money and, upon receiving a negative reply, gave him enough for his railroad fare.

In no field visited was a better spirit manifested than in Brisbane, a flourishing town in Queensland[48] in the northern part of Australia. The members, themselves joyful in their belief, are preaching the gospel by word and by example. The following elders were laboring in this field: [Niels W.] Oldroyd,[49] Gerald O. Billings.[50]

It was not easy for these good people to say good-bye to Brother McKay nor for the brethren to say good-bye to them. Many miles of land and water must be traversed before church members would again be met. This was the last of the missions to be visited in the western hemisphere.

Another stop of twenty-four hours was made at Townsville,[51] an industrious little town from which large quantities of meat are shipped. No missionary work was being done there. The brethren rode from the pier into the city in an old-fashioned carriage drawn by two spirited little horses. A few words of praise to the driver about his ponies prompted him to show what they could do; the result was that every horse-propelled vehicle on the road was passed. How pleasant are words of praise about something we love!

Naturally, there was a decided change in temperature as the voyagers sailed in a northwesterly direction along the north coast of Australia, for here they were nearer the equator than they were while in Samoa. The vessel stopped nearly forty hours at Port Darwin,[52] the most northerly of all Australian towns, and during this time the brethren witnessed a most interesting exhibition of native war dancing, put on for their special benefit. Having heard there was to be something of the kind given by the Aboriginals, they walked out on a beautiful moonlit night into the country where these natives live. Their village consists of many small white cottages which in the moonlight seemed to be neat and well kept. People as black as coal were sitting in the doorways but took no notice of the visitors who walked through the entire village until they came to a great cliff overlooking the ocean. There they found a group of men and children and a few women, but the dance was over.

A young boy who spoke a little English was asked by Brother McKay what they would charge to put on a special exhibition.

"How many people do you want to take part?" asked the lad.

"All there are here."

"Would a shilling be too much?"

As there were about fifty people present, Brother McKay first thought the lad meant a shilling apiece, which would have been rather expensive, but he soon discovered that it was a shilling for the lot. The coin was immediately produced and another was promised if they gave a good performance.

Most of the men were completely naked and the combined clothing of those who were "dressed" could have been tied up in a pocket handkerchief. The dance was quite unlike anything the brethren had seen before, though it is something after the order of the "Haka" in New Zealand. It commenced by all slapping their bare thighs in unison. This became faster and faster. Then one of the men came forward from the group and danced with terrific speed, while the others continued the chanting and slapping with a uniform movement of the body. When the dancer was completely exhausted he retired and another took his place. It should be added that the women took no part in the exhibition.[53]

The Commonwealth of Australia is made up of six states and one territory, which is under the control of the federal government much as our territories formerly were. They are: New South Wales,[54] which is two and a half times as large as Great Britain and Ireland; Queensland, Victoria,[55] Tasmania, the island lying to the south of the main continent; South Australia,[56] Western Australia,[57] and the Northern Territory.[58] Their combined area is three million square miles [4,828,032 sq. km], or about the same size as Europe. Australia has less than two inhabitants per square mile, while Java, which the brethren were to visit en route to Singapore, has six hundred.

One of the incomprehensible blunders of this enterprising nation is the condition of the railroads. Each state is the owner of its own system, and almost without exception it has a different gauge[59] from all others. The result is that the traveler is compelled to change cars frequently when traveling from place to place. This is inconvenient. But when one remembers that freight must also be transferred, one realizes what a needless cost is involved. It is said that freight from Perth in the extreme west to Sydney has to be transferred four times before finally reaching its destination. Otherwise, the train service is very tolerable and in some cases excellent.

Prophecy is best proved in the light of its [own] fulfillment.
—Dr. James E. Talmage[1]

Australia's annual liquor bill amounts to many million pounds sterling.[2] At the time of the visit herein described, the country was suffering from a shortage of water and officials were urging that it be used sparingly. One of the daily papers dryly remarked that this was not intended to mean Australians could not drink what water they needed; and one of the reporters concluded, after making a trip which took him into many of the saloons, that most Australians felt they could not be loyal citizens and waste water by drinking it.

The tobacco bill must also be enormous. The man who does not smoke is rather a rarity and the women seem to be taking on this obnoxious habit with appalling rapidity. With the boat on which the brethren were traveling were many young people off on an excursion to India. With one exception they all smoked, both men and women. The exception was a very beautiful young lady, just the kind of a girl a man of middle age would be proud to claim as his daughter. She steadfastly refused the cigarette offered her by insistent friends until the night before Singapore was reached. The missionaries felt like shedding tears when they saw her weaken at the last moment and accept and smoke the proffered "coffin tack." It was a sad example of the danger of bad associates.

Some modernists find some difficulty in believing that prayers can be heard and answered. Such people would limit the Creator of the universe in his powers, though all are willing to admit that man, his creation, is unlimited. Here is an illustration of what men can do: These brethren were almost on the opposite side of the earth from their homes in Utah. One evening as the ship plowed through the waters of the Indian Ocean, Brother Cannon mentioned that on the following day his mother would be eighty-two years old. Brother McKay ordered him to send her a wireless message of love and congratulation. This was done, and as the good woman was eating her breakfast on the morning of her birthday, the words which had traversed thousands of miles of land and water were delivered to her. In face of such wonders who will say the Almighty cannot hear the appeals of his children or even read the thoughts of their hearts?

The Dutch East Indies [Netherlands East Indies][3] forms the largest cluster of islands known to man and is one of the world's most densely populated spots. Java, the most important island of the group, is about two-thirds the size of Utah but has a population of between thirty and forty million people. Besides sustaining this great number it has a considerable amount of jungle in which the royal tiger, black panther, rhinoceros, wild boar, and other game are found.

There were people everywhere—bathing in rivers and canals, lying in the shade, squatting by the roadside, eating, drinking, smoking, a few pretending to work, but most of them doing nothing, everywhere as thick as ants. Indeed they would remind one of ants or bees in a hive, except that ants and bees are industrious.

Canals and rivers appear to play an important role in the country's daily life. From beds of streams much of the building sand is taken; they furnish a means for most of the transportation of the country, carry off the sewage, and supply bathing places for man and beast. One might have said for women also, but as President [Charles W.] Penrose used to say, man embraces the woman. The brethren saw a man scrubbing his oxen which had been driven into the stream. Not far away a woman was doing the family washing while nearby another woman was washing her hair.

A barbershop in Java is unique. The barber goes about the town with a small stool and a little box containing his tools. When a customer is found the "shop" is set up in the shade and the desired shave or haircut is given. Restaurants partake of the itinerant character of the barber shop. The stock in trade and diminutive heater are moved about on wheels or the entire lot is divided into two loads and balanced in a basket on each end of a pole and carried Chinese fashion on the proprietor's shoulders.

At Surabaya,[4] the town next in importance to Batavia [Jakarta][5] on the island of Java, the special missionaries were met by Frank W. Becraft,[6] of Ogden,[7] who at the time was holding a responsible position with the Krain Sugar Company. Brother Becraft was a former student of Brother McKay's, and far as known was the only Mormon among thirty million people. Though living in this isolated land and among a people with extremely low moral standards, his exemplary life did credit to parents, teacher,

*Traveling up the
Malay Peninsula*

and church. Having an auto at his disposal, he placed it and himself in the hands of his visitors and this kindness enabled them to see much that otherwise would have been missed. After driving about the city and surrounding country he took them out to the sugar mill. A part of the machinery in this factory was made in Provo,[8] and an invention of Albert Genther, of Salt Lake City, was being installed.

Among the foreign population few nations are without representatives and even among the natives many distinct races are seen. Principal among these, besides the Javanese themselves, are the Sudanese, the Madurese, from adjacent islands, and the Malays from the Malay Peninsula.[9] The Javanese homes are distinguishable from those of the other natives because they are built on the ground, whereas the others are built on poles in the air. There are no windows or chimneys, and when cooking is done in the house the smoke must get out as best it can. However, fires are never made for heating and, except in stormy weather, the cooking is done outside.

The native food consists almost solely of rice and dried fish. A very small plot of ground furnishes the one, and sea and river furnish the other. It is said that "to lack rice is to lack food." As for clothing, many of the men are "naked from the waist up and from the thighs down," though not infrequently trousers and even shirts are worn. The women with instinctive modesty are attired in "mother hubbards."

A stay of twelve hours in Batavia enabled the brethren to see Buitenzorg [Bogor],[10] the military and governmental headquarters of the Dutch East Indies. The Governor General's home is a veritable palace, as fine as that of any European king.

Scientists have said that in Java and Sumatra,[11] a neighboring island, there is a greater degree of volcanic activity than anywhere else on earth. History records that Mt. Thunder[12] in 1843 "during a slight eruption threw ten million tons of dust ten thousand feet [3,048 m] high." One wonders what a severe eruption would do. At Batavia, from the 26th to the 29th of August, 1883, the sky was obscured, caused by the eruption of the Krakatau[13] volcano on an adjoining island of this name. This has been described "as the greatest and loudest explosion ever recorded." It was distinctly heard in the Philippines[14] and Japan, and even in Europe, though not so distinctly there. Forty thousand people were swept from one island by a great tidal wave following the eruption.[15]

No organized missionary work has been done by this church in Java. The low moral standard of the natives would make it difficult to obtain a foothold there. The whites temporarily residing in that land have gone with the idea of quickly enriching themselves, and consequently would hardly be inclined to study the gospel seriously. Still there are doubtless many honest-hearted people in Java and at the proper time, the church authorities will be inspired to open that populous field.

Forty hours of sailing from Batavia brings the traveler to the city of Singapore at the point of the Malay Peninsula. Approaching the harbor, the *Marella* was met by a veritable flotilla of frail canoes whose occupants begged the passengers to throw money into the water. When this was done it was interesting to see the skill displayed not only in diving for the coins but in climbing back into the skiffs without upsetting them.

Singapore lies directly north of the equator, but seven and one half degrees to be exact. It is of course extremely hot, and visitors are warned that they must either remain indoors during the day, or carry sunshades. The special missionaries, having neither sunshades nor any time to waste, ignored this advice, and managed to pull through.

Illustrative of how hot it is, one might mention that in hotels no provision is made for covers on the beds. One sleeps on sheets but not under them. By lying thus with all doors and windows open, and with a powerful electric fan playing upon him, the guest is able to obtain a fair night's rest. Of course the beds here, as in all tropical countries, are enveloped in a canopy of mosquito netting—a most necessary protection against insect pests.

It was late in the afternoon when the missionaries arrived at the hotel, and shortly thereafter they received a call from a Chinese tailor who solicited orders for linen suits, which he promised to have ready the following morning. Naturally everybody wears white clothing in the tropics, and being rather travel-stained, the brethren were in the market for something of this kind. Four linen suits were therefore ordered. Two of these were delivered the following morning at six o'clock and the other two before evening of the same day, at a cost for the four of about fifteen dollars.

It is claimed that more nationalities are represented in Singapore than in any other city of the world. And a few hours' stroll about the crowded streets rather substantiates this statement. After an evening walk the visitor is inclined to wonder what the houses are used for, impressed as he is with the thought that most of the inhabitants live on the streets. Men, women, and children are asleep in doorways, on window ledges, and on the sidewalks, which are also used for the numerous itinerant merchants, hucksters, and beggars.[16]

Again difficulties were encountered in finding accommodations from Singapore on towards Calcutta.[17] Brother Cannon was told that this would be impossible under two weeks, but during the afternoon arrangements were made to sail the next day with the *Bharata*.[18]

The remarkable promise pronounced by President [Anthon H.] Lund upon the head of Brother Cannon that if he were ill it would be of very short duration had additional fulfillment here. En route from Singapore to Rangoon [Yangon][19] he was attacked by an excruciating pain. It was not a new experience, for several times in his life he had been similarly afflicted, and on all such occasions the pain had lasted for days. It was about two o'clock in the morning. He arose and went on deck. Naturally at that hour everything was quiet. Perspiration streamed from every pore, not because of the heat but due to intense suffering. When it seemed that this could not be longer endured, he called upon the Lord, and reminded him of the above-mentioned promise. Instantly the pain vanished and did not return.

This experience is not related boastfully, but solely with the hope that it will increase faith in the hearts of the readers and as a humble testimony that the Lord lives and fulfills his every promise. The unbeliever will close his eyes to the miraculous healing, which was the fulfillment of an inspired prediction. He fails to see God's goodness. While in Australia these travelers met a faithful member of the church, John Allen, who was completely blind. On one occasion this good man visited his brother-in-law, a pastor. Brother Allen bore testimony to the divinity of this work, to which the pastor replied, "John, you are blind; you cannot see." Brother Allen answered, "True I am physically blind, but your misfortune is greater than mine, for without eyes I can see the truth, while you are blind to that which is most precious in life."

Few cities in the world are more interesting than Rangoon in Burma.[20] An incongruous mixture of wealth and squalor greets the eye. One passes rapidly from disgustingly filthy streets to beautiful avenues lined with stately residences and artistic gardens. The difference in individuals, too, offers quite as violent a contrast as do the streets. There were esthetic and intelligent-looking fellows with long hair, others with hair closely shaven except for one lock, similar to the scalping lock of the old-time American Indians. Some men were gorgeously robed, while all about were those who wore nothing but ragged breechclouts. And, judged by their faces and some conversations which were held, there is among them as wide a range of intellectual poverty and wealth, as is noticeable in physical appearance and temporal surroundings. Some of the beggars were revoltingly mutilated. The statement is reliably made that they disfigure themselves the better to appeal to a sympathetic public. The missionaries saw many groups of both sexes industriously hunting something smaller than elephants in each other's heads. They were left to guess what these hunters were seeking, but their guess was that they had better keep a safe distance from the groups, not an easy thing to do in the crowded condition of the streets.

The Shwe Dagon is one of the noted buildings of the world.[21] It is the first thing one sees on approaching Rangoon and the last thing upon which the gaze of the traveler lingers as the vessel moves down the muddy Rangoon River [Yangon River],[22] a branch of the Irrawaddy,[23] toward the sea. It was built many centuries ago as a Buddhist temple, indeed its commencement dates back to 500 BC The great dome surmounting the building is covered with gold leaf, valued, according to the guide books, at about five million dollars. The pillars which support the various shrines are inlaid with glass mosaic which is not only beautiful but represents a vast amount of patient skill. In addition to the gold, there are 3,664 rubies, 541 emeralds, and 433 diamonds in this dome. The cost of other parts of the building is correspondingly great. Though the walks approaching and surrounding this impressive edifice were extremely dirty, the attention of the brethren was called to an illuminating sign, "Foot-wearing Prohibited." Before a curious crowd, therefore, they were obliged to turn up their trousers, unfasten garters and remove shoes and stockings. On either side of a long flight of steps leading to the court of this pagoda are open shops of all kinds. In one of these a man was trying to reach something from a high shelf. Not being tall enough and failing to see anything else on which to stand, he spoke to his wife, and she obediently lay down on her stomach, and by standing on her he was able to obtain the desired article. It was the first time the brethren had seen a woman used as a stepladder. Though the ground was too holy for the missionaries to walk on except with bare feet, men and women were smoking long black cigars of unusual thickness, and dogs and chickens added to the dirt.[24]

One of the peculiar things about this place was the numerous professional prayer makers. The visitor who desires a special blessing but who is too timid or ignorant to pray may, for a small gratuity, have one of these professionals do it for him.[25]

The brethren were "On the Road to Mandalay,"[26] made famous by Kipling's[27] verses, but they did not travel far thereon, as by good fortune they were able to exchange tickets on the *Bharata* for places on the *Arankola*, belonging to the same company, and which not only left Rangoon sooner, but was a much faster boat.[28]

Investigating India

 But dost thou know what I would tell thee? In the primitive church the chalices were of wood, and the prelates of gold; in these days the church hath chalices of gold and prelates of wood.

—Savonarola[1]

Think of approaching India! Is there a well-read person in the world who has not desired to visit this densely populated and mystical land, with its ancient and almost forgotten civilization, its master builders long since dead, and its bloody but absorbing history? To the westerner, eastern countries are full of incongruities, and no other land, Japan possibly excepted, has more surprises for the traveler than has India. One is inclined to think her primitive agricultural methods and her renowned buildings, which the most gifted pens have vainly attempted to describe, do not belong to the same race. Their farming methods awaken the thought in the visitor's mind that he is living in Adamic days; while white marble structures, surpassing anything else of the kind on earth, make him wonder if he has not been suddenly transplanted from this mundane to a celestial world, and is gazing on the palace of some heavenly king.

A globe-trotter, whom the brethren met in Japan, said that travelers should see India, and then write FINIS across the bottom of the page, as there was nothing more worth seeing. Though his statement was extravagant, it was not without foundation. From the moment the missionaries left the muddy Bay of Bengal,[2] discolored for many miles by the turbid water of the Ganges[3] and its numerous subdivisions, and entered the still muddier Hugli,[4] until they sailed from Bombay [Mumbai][5] into the Arabian Sea,[6] en route to Egypt, every hour is now a treasured memory. Their one regret was that a longer stay was impossible.

Who has not heard of the Ganges River, whose waters were formerly considered sacred, and still are to some extent? It has its source in the ice cave on the southern slope of the Himalayas[7] and has a total length of more than 1,500 miles [2,414.02 km]. Its most important branch, the Hugli, is navigable by large steamers as far as Calcutta, about 80 miles [128.75 km] from the seaboard.

Many great thinkers have been born among this race. A number of England's outstanding men spent years in India—Clive,[8] Hastings,[9] Thackeray[10] (who was born there), MaCaulay,[11] Roberts,[12] Kitchener,[13] and others. One can easily believe that their greatness is in considerable measure attributable to the habit of thought which was and, to an extent is, a predominating native characteristic.

Despite their vast numbers—almost a quarter of the earth's inhabitants—and the many splendid characters heretofore developed from this race, they are now considered incapable of self-government, and for years England has performed that duty for them.[14] It reminds one of a puny man commanding a massive elephant, which has the potential power to crush its master, but is held in check by superior intelligence. A casual observance of the men would indicate that they are effeminate and physically weak, but in this respect appearances seem to be deceptive. The missionaries saw slightly built youths carrying trunks, which weighed at least one hundred and fifty pounds, on their heads, and going up and down stairs with these burdens and with a satchel in each hand.

Few women are seen on the streets, and these usually have their faces covered. Indeed, it is hardly an exaggeration to say the women use nearly as much cloth to hide their faces as the men do for their entire covering, or as their European and American sisters do for a dress.

For ages the cow was looked upon in India as being sacred, and to this day more or less sanctity is attached to her.[15] But with the ox it is different. His lot and that of the Asiatic buffalo is so hard, all the heavy work being assigned to them, that were they capable of thought they might anticipate the butcher's block as a paradise. The brethren had occasion to go into the largest bank in Calcutta, located on the city's most prominent corner. This institution was large enough that 125 clerks were visible, but directly before the entrance a cow was lying and peacefully chewing her cud, while pedestrians walked in the street rather than disturb her. In a city of more than a million inhabitants, this seemed to be giving the cow a rather prominent place.

Missionaries working in lands where fleas abound are wont to complain if they have one or two of these disturbing insects on them. But what would they think of this statement, for the truthfulness of which both the brethren will vouch: In their room in a hotel in Calcutta, partly stripped, they sat under electric fans, each with a basin of water. Brother Cannon caught and counted 157 fleas. Brother McKay did not count his, but insists that he found even a larger number. The effectiveness of these pests was materially lessened because the bodies and clothing of the brethren were so moist from perspiration, otherwise the torment would have been unendurable.[16]

The traveler in India is obliged to carry his bedding with him. In a sleeping car he not only furnishes bedding but also makes his bed, unless he has a servant along, as of course most travelers have. However, missionaries do not have personal servants, so our brethren waited upon themselves, much to the surprise of fellow travelers and somewhat to their own embarrassment. When the train comes into a station a coolie asks for permission to sweep the car, for which service he expects a gratuity. No self-respecting servant in India would think of doing such work.

The motley throng of Arabs, Turks, Persians, Indians of many different tribes, and many other nationalities, all chattering like so many monkeys, made a scene at the Howrah[17] station in Calcutta not soon to be forgotten. These people discuss a trivial matter, such as the time of departure or arrival of a train, and the way they shout and gesticulate makes one think a new revolution has commenced.

Inadvertently the missionaries took places in a compartment reserved for a gentleman and his two sons. Instead of resenting the intrusion, as Americans or Europeans would have done, these dark-skinned people showed true courtesy to the strangers, even offering to go themselves into another car. As soon as their mistake was discovered, the missionaries prepared to find another place, but the proper owners of the compartment politely but firmly insisted that they remain, and had their servants bring refreshments to the intruders. Truly a person seeking suggestions for self-improvement will find them everywhere. These gentlemen were true noblemen. As the sun went down their servant spread a rug before the window on the floor of the car and the father offered his evening prayer. First he knelt with folded hands. Then he raised hands to face, after which he knelt and twice touched the floor with his forehead. This same thing was repeated many times. When the father had finished, the older son went through the same ceremony, but the younger man declined, though repeatedly urged by his father to do so. Whether this was due to bashfulness in the presence of strangers, or to lack of faith, the missionaries were not to discover. The men impressed the observers as being deeply sincere and one had to admire them

[128]

CHAPTER 21

for performing a duty even though it might attract unfavorable attention. When the praying was finished they produced a pack of cards and the young man joined his father and brother readily enough in a game.[18]

From the car windows the brethren saw many camels and occasionally an elephant feeding in the yards with domestic animals. Men and women were plowing with forked sticks, such as were used thousands of years ago, and with various contrivances were dipping water from the streams and pouring it into the thirsty soil.

Comparatively few people in Utah know anything about Agra,[19] but all have heard of the renowned Taj Mahal, "A Dream in Marble."[20] This structure is considered by travelers the most beautiful building in the world. Artists and poets have attempted to describe it, but these efforts fall so far short that no attempt will be made here, for the beauty of its architecture and the material of which it is composed, consisting of white marble adorned with precious stones, is indescribable.

The mature person, who has not stood before things so beautiful that he has not known whether to kneel down and pray or sit down and cry, is deserving of pity. Such feelings come over the visitor to the Taj Mahal. With uncovered head, one stands in awe before it. If a word passed between Brothers McKay and Cannon during this visit, it was spoken in a whisper. There are many larger buildings in the world, but a faint idea as to the fineness of workmanship can be had when one remembers that 20,000 men worked 17 years in constructing it. It was built three centuries ago by the emperor Jahan[21] as a mausoleum for his beloved wife, and his own body now reposes in a marble casket by the side of that in which she rests.[22]

Scarcely less beautiful and no less interesting is The Fort,[23] also located in Agra. One could see in imagination the gorgeously arrayed elephants carrying the royal party up the incline from the gates to the inner dwellings. The marble mosque was one of the finest things the brethren saw during all their travels. The queen's bedroom of marble, overlooking the Yamuna River[24] along the bank of which a caravan of camels moving in stately procession could be seen, must have gratified the taste of the most esthetic. Before the door of this bedroom is a marble basin, in which the queen took her rosewater bath. In another part was the harem, before which was a great marble bathing pool with seats around the sides for thirty-four ladies. Over each seat was a fountain, so if they preferred to sit and have the cool water pour over them instead of sporting in the basin, they could do so. Below was the prison where refractory members of the harem, who displeased their lord, were sent for punishment. Sometimes this was close confinement for hours, days, or even years. Not infrequently it was death, and the gallows is still there to which they were hanged by a silken rope.

The city of Agra is 792 miles [1,274.60 km] from Calcutta, and Delhi [New Delhi][25] is 115 miles [185.07 km] farther inland. Brother McKay's purpose in traveling so far was to meet Brother John W. Currie, who lives at Srinagar,[26] and other church members. From letters, however, which were awaiting him at Delhi, it was learned that all members in India with the exception of Brother Currie, had left the church and did not care to be visited.

From his correspondence one judged Brother Currie to be a faithful member, but he wrote that due to the expected visit to Srinagar of the Viceroy of India and an official party, it would be impossible to obtain the necessary conveyance from Rawalpindi,[27] the end of the railway line, to his home, 200 miles [321.87 km] distant. After a prayerful consideration of the subject it was decided that a delay of several weeks was not justifiable, in order to visit the one faithful church member. Long letters were written to him, and preparations were made to sail from Bombay with the steamship *Egypt*.

Comparatively little missionary work has been done in India, though a few faithful men and women have joined the church in that land. Many years ago two young sailors, members of the church, were in Calcutta and left a tract at the garden gate of a very beautiful home. A servant was about to throw it away when the master asked for it. He was a doctor in the British Army and through this tract became a convert.[28] Subsequently he went to Utah, and was a devoted church member during his remaining years. President George W. McCune[29] of the Los Angeles Stake is one of his grandsons.

Delhi is the present capital of India, and the government offices of the country have been recently moved to this city from Calcutta. Though interesting and historical, with a fair share of noted buildings, one wonders why it should be the capital instead of Calcutta, which is much larger and more accessible to the outside world. Large oceangoing vessels can come to the former city, while it requires 24 hours with a fast train from the seacoast to reach the latter.

From Delhi the brethren traveled to Bombay nearly nine hundred miles [1,448.41 km] and requiring 32 hours with a fast train. Bombay is beautiful and in many respects modern, though some of the sights it presents appear very strange to a westerner. For instance, a crowd of women were excavating a cellar. They carried the dirt out in baskets on their heads. It was slavish work, but every woman wore bracelets and earrings, most of them had nose rings, and a few had anklets and toe rings, and of course all were barefooted.[30]

There are in India alone 220 million Hindus[31]—more than the total number in the world belonging to the various Protestant religions. Christians are prone to look upon these people as heathens, but they often appear to be more devoted to their religion than are many who profess Christianity. And, while this statement may offend some professed followers of the Savior, the Hindu is frequently, though by no means always, a more potent factor for righteousness in the lives of its adherents, than is modern Christianity. And why? Certainly it is not because its principles have more saving power, but because many Hindus believe more devoutly in their religion than do some Christians. It is a well-known and lamentable fact that an alarmingly large number of so-called Christians do not believe that Jesus Christ was actually the Son of God. They do not believe in his atoning death, or in his literal resurrection.[32]

The special missionaries discussed this point as they, aboard the *Egypt*, sailed out of the picturesque harbor of Bombay into the Arabian Sea, and expressed sincere gratitude for their testimony of his divinity, that he died for mankind, and brought about the resurrection of the body. To them this testimony was priceless, more desirable than all the gold, silver, and precious stones of the earth.

On the ship was a pleasant and refined-looking lady traveling with her three-month-old baby. The little one was fretful and the mother tired. Brother McKay, in the kindness of his heart, offered to relieve her by taking the child for a time. The mother feared it would not be good, but when he told her how many of his own he had lulled to sleep, she accepted the offer. He walked about the deck with the babe and soon it was fast asleep. One who saw it could not easily forget the look on his face when he brought the sleeping infant back to its mother and found her smoking a cigarette. Subsequently this woman was seen to nurse her baby and smoke at the same time.

chapter 22   Wandering in Egypt

Fear ye not, stand still, and see the salvation of the Lord, which he will show to
you today.

—Exodus 14:13

Immediately after sailing from Bombay the brethren reached a
point in the Arabian Sea which is exactly on the other side of the
world from Utah. When it is six o'clock in the evening in Salt Lake
it is six o'clock in the morning there. The first stop after leaving
India was at Aden[1] on the Arabian Peninsula,[2] at the southerly end
of the Red Sea.[3] And of all the barren, desolate, and unattractive
places visited by these travelers, Aden was the most forbidding.
Records show that it is no rare occurrence for two years to pass
without a drop of rain falling, and the average rainfall is but a half
an inch annually. The hills surrounding the city are as void of vegetation as is a paved street.[4]

A stranger never lacks company in Aden. From the moment he
steps out of the rowboat which has brought him from the vessel,
anchored out in the harbor, until his departure, he is surrounded
by a train of mendicants and peddlers, which, while robbing the
trip of some of its pleasure, adds to its interest. These creatures
can devise countless reasons why one should give them money.
A young man about twenty years old deliberately put his bare foot
in the way of one of the travelers. This action was observed in time
to avoid stepping on it with full weight, but not soon enough to
turn aside entirely. The whimpering fellow demanded compensation for what he claimed was a permanent injury and was noisily
abetted by voluble sympathizers, though the ruse was so absurdly
palpable. Of course he was not paid, but for a few moments a riot
seemed inevitable.

From Aden our travelers entered the Red Sea, and sailed
1,200 miles [1,931.21 km] in traversing this body of water, which
played such an important role in Biblical and Book of Mormon

history.[5] Often Arabia[6] was visible on their right and Africa on their left. One of the peaks on the Arabian side was pointed out as Mount Sinai.[7] However, there is grave doubt as to whether or not this is the original Sinai, on which the ancient law was given.

In imagination one could see the intrepid Moses, so confident in the power of the Lord that the complaints of his followers were unnoticed, raising his staff with the command: "The Lord shall fight for you and you shall hold your peace."[8]

It was also easy to see in fancy the small colony led by Lehi,[9] whose trust in the Lord was as implicit as was that of Moses. He, too, remained as steadfast despite the grumblers, as did the other great leader.

[Ferdinand-Marie] de Lesseps,[10] the French engineer, achieved a lasting name for himself by building the Suez Canal.[11] As is generally known, it extends from the Mediterranean to the Red Sea and is 85 miles [136.79 km] long, and sufficiently wide for two large ocean liners by closely hugging the banks to pass each other. The country on either side is desolate, but its very barrenness is attractive. One feels the antiquity of the place. Not a blade of grass, not a tree or shrub or leaf was to be seen. One forms a slight idea of the barrenness of the country upon being told that when the 25,000 men engaged in building the canal had proceeded inland some distance, 1,500 camels were constantly required to carry drinking water to them.

The building of this canal was by no means a modern idea. In the fourteenth century BC, an effort was made by Rameses II[12] to construct such a water way, and this was repeated at subsequent times. History records that one of these attempts made in the 7th century BC was abandoned after it had cost the lives of 125,000 men.

Brother McKay and his companion disembarked at Port Said,[13] the point where the Suez joins the Mediterranean, and journeyed by rail to Cairo,[14] passing through Zagazig[15] on the way. Zagazig is said by students of Jewish history to be the place where the children of Israel maintained headquarters during the time of their captivity.[16] Date palms, tall and stately and with their fruit hanging in great red clusters, were everywhere to be seen. When taken from the trees the dates neither look nor taste like the prepared product which one purchases on foreign markets.

Cows, oxen, and men were turning cumbrous, old-fashioned, but still effective waterwheels, which raised water from the streams and poured it over the arid land.[17]

The Egyptians are fond of saying, "He who drinks from the Nile will come again." The thought is that water of this river, which exerts such a tremendous influence over their lives, has a subtle power of attraction. One might add without exaggeration, not the water alone but everything else in Egypt, the mosques, the pyramids, indeed the very atmosphere, and above all the history cast a fascinating spell over the visitor which makes him loath to leave the land, and the memory of which makes him long to return to it.

When the Nile behaves properly, Egypt has "fat years." Otherwise they are sure to be most tragically "lean." The difference between normal low and high water averages something more than eight yards [7.32 m]. Should it rise but slightly higher than this, great damage results; and if it fall but one yard [0.91 m] short of its usual high watermark, a famine of greater or less severity ensues.

Cairo is a modern city of three-quarters of a million inhabitants, among whom Mohammedans[18] largely predominate.[19] Women of the better class are veiled, but less heavily than those of India. The city is noted for its mosques and artistic gardens. One may worship in a different mosque every day of the year, for there are more than 365 of them. The Nile runs through the city, and visitors are shown the spot where the babe Moses was left in care of his sister that he might escape Pharaoh's cruel edict.[20]

One can travel the seven miles [11.27 km] by streetcar, or auto, or on a camel from Cairo to the stupendous pyramids of Giza,[21] which were built while the present race was still in swaddling clothes and which are rated even now as among the world's wonders. The road crosses the Nile and skirts the riverbank throughout this distance. It is a scenic and beautiful drive, lined on both sides for the greater part of the way with acacia trees.[22]

As Brother McKay and his companion traveled along this road one morning before sunrise, they passed hundreds of donkeys and camels loaded with vegetables, fruits, and other supplies for the city's markets. Indeed, almost everything—coal, brick, building stone, and lumber—is carried on the backs of these patient beasts. One camel, frightened at an approaching automobile, broke away from its master, and scattered its load as it went with surprising speed over the road.

To ride a camel is in itself a novel experience. The brethren engaged two of these animals to ride out to the pyramids. At a word of command from their driver they lie down while the riders mount; at another word they arise, cow-like, on their hind legs first, and unless the rider exercises care he will be precipitated over the animal's head.

And then came the pyramids and the Sphinx![23] The visitor desires to be alone, but with the tormenting beggars in endless numbers, solitude is something to be craved but not enjoyed. Just at sunrise the brethren mounted the top of one of the pyramids, an exhausting bit of work, as there are no steps and one must climb from one high block of stone to another. But the view from the summit well repays the effort. Looking eastward one gazes upon the fertile Nile Valley[24] with its fields of corn, its majestic date palms, its vegetable gardens. In the distance the picturesque spires and minarets[25] of Cairo glisten in the morning sun. To the north, west, and south is the Libyan Desert[26] as barren and devoid of vegetation as the Sahara.[27]

One may read of the pyramids and see pictures of them but to gain even a faint idea of their colossal proportions it is necessary to climb to the top of one of them. After doing so, one is prepared to believe that Cheops,[28] the largest of the group, contains 2,300,000 blocks of stone which average 3½ tons [3,175.15 kg] in weight, and that 100,000 men worked on its erection three months in each year for twenty years.

The ancient Egyptians believed in a literal resurrection, but the resurrection depended largely on the preservation of the body after death; hence the remarkable skill displayed in mummifying bodies and the sacredness with which these were viewed. For this reason, men of power and wealth built tombs in which their remains could be hidden. With what horror would they have looked into the future and seen these bodies dragged out of carefully prepared hiding places and exhibited in museums to the gaze of every curious visitor!

There are nine pyramids in this immediate vicinity, three large and six smaller ones. But they are not the only objects of interest. Indeed one is tempted to say they are less awe inspiring than the inscrutable but majestic Sphinx, which scientists say was no longer young when Abraham[29] visited Egypt thousands of years ago, because of famine in his own land.[30] It is hardly too much to say that more has been written about this figure than about any other one inanimate thing in the world. But it stands there silent and scornful, though part of its nose has been torn away by the bullets of vandals, incomparably greater than the sum total of all that has been said or written on the subject.

In the glory of a beautiful early morning, Cheops presents a majestic appearance. One approaches it with a feeling of deep solemnity. What does the mammoth thing mean and why was it erected? Was it built as an astronomical observatory, or that its sides should afford to posterity standards of measurement, or was it merely built as a tomb for one man, its builder? Is it a monumental prophecy foretelling the great events in the world's history but in a manner so obscure that only subsequent to its fulfillment is the prophecy recognized?

With camels and a guide the brethren rode from the pyramids of Giza to the ancient city of Memphis,[31] passing en route, the pyramids and tombs of Ti,[32] near Sakhara [Saqqâra].[33] One of these pyramids is said to be the oldest structure in the world. Among these tombs is one where the bulls of Apis[34] were buried, and with more pomp and ceremony than is usually accorded human beings, even of high rank, for these bulls were held sacred by the Egyptians. Not only were they buried in royal tombs, but their bodies were mummified as well.

How these monster sarcophagi,[35] each one carved out of a massive block of stone, and capable of holding the mummy of a bull, could be lowered into the underground grotto is one of the mysteries. At the time of this visit twenty-four had already been discovered, and it was expected that many more would be found.

On this trip the brethren passed a gay wedding party, conveying the bride to the bridegroom's house where the marriage ceremony would be performed. This procession reminded the guide of his own experience which he related. The details of an Egyptian match are arranged by other parties, the first meeting of bride and groom usually being at the place appointed for the ceremony. Abdul had paid one hundred pounds sterling to the father of his first bride, but the girl was so homely and otherwise unsuitable, in his opinion, that he sent her back to her parents, and lost his money. Subsequently, he decided to try again, and was told of a very beautiful girl, a real bargain at 150 pounds sterling. The recommendations appeared so genuine that he paid the required sum, and invited a number of English tourists to the wedding to see the jewel he had won. What was his chagrin when he found this bride-to-be worse even than the other! One of the English ladies exclaimed:

"My goodness, Abdul! Is that your wife?"

"No," was his answer. "That's my brother's wife. I decided to postpone my wedding." This girl therefore went the way of the other—to her parents—and he again lost his money. Brother McKay told him how such things were managed in America, and Abdul concluded by saying, "There's some sense to that. We're a lot of bloody fools over here."

A fast train carries one from Cairo to El Kantara,[36] where the traveler bound for Palestine crosses the Suez Canal on a pontoon bridge. From there an excellent train with sleeping and dining cars can be taken direct to Jerusalem.[37] The time consumed between the two capitals is about 15 hours.

On a world tour the traveler enters so many different countries that unconsciously he develops a marked degree of unconcern. But the "Holy City," the city of unnamable memories—no real

Christian can approach it without being overwhelmed by feelings of deep reverence. David O. McKay, himself an apostle and a special witness, and as sincere a believer in the divinity of Jesus Christ as any man who lives, was deeply moved, and his companion partook of the same spirit. To walk on ground once hallowed by the touch of the Savior's feet, to see the places where he lived and taught and suffered and finally performed the noblest act ever witnessed by mortal man is an inspiration to every true believer.

A gifted writer might perhaps describe imperfectly what one sees in Palestine. What one feels is wholly indescribable, and must be left to the imagination.

After traveling for miles over a level plain, the train puffed slowly through ravines and narrow valleys, terraced and planted with grapevines, up the somewhat steep grade to Jerusalem, which is 2,900 feet [883.92 m] above the Mediterranean. The surrounding hills are composed largely of white limestone and chalk formations and in the glaring sunlight of the east, these with the white buildings, make a sight that is decidedly dazzling. The city is a natural fortress being almost entirely surrounded by a valley three or four hundred feet [91.44 m to 121.92 m] deep. But despite its natural advantages, Jerusalem has been captured and recaptured oftener perhaps than any other city in the world.

Count Eberhardt,[38] a German writer, is credited with the saying:

> There are three acts in a man's life, which no one ought either to advise another to do or not to do; the first is to contract matrimony, the second is to go to the wars, and the third is to visit the Holy Sepulcher. I say that these acts are good in themselves, but they may easily turn out ill, and when this is so, he who gave the advice comes to be blamed as if he were the cause of its turning out ill.[39]

The significance of this statement can be appreciated after a visit to Bethlehem,[40] Calvary,[41] and the Holy Sepulcher.[42] Most Christians, regardless of church affiliations, who visit these places, join in the wish that they had been left as they were anciently, instead of having been ornamented by altars, crosses, and churches, all of which are profusely adorned with gold and silver. In the church now standing on Calvary is an immense cross, and over it the inscription in letters of diamonds, "Jesus, King of the Jews."[43] Nearby is a cabinet which contains, so our missionaries were told, treasures of gold, silver, and precious stones worth more than ten million pounds sterling. So interested are the guides and the average tourist in this gaudy display that nothing is said or thought of what the original cross cost in human suffering.

One hears much of perishable worldly treasures, but the value of imperishable Christianity is unmentioned.

This thought also comes to the visitor: Suppose an expert but dishonest jeweler should chip out the real gems and pure metals and replace them with glittering substitutes. Might not this counterfeit pass, undetected by the masses, until perchance the original builder came along? The spurious might closely resemble the genuine, yet his trained eye would at once note the deception, and he would expose the fraud. Then suppose the populace should exclaim indignantly: "There has been no substitution. These treasures as they are were accepted by our parents and they are good enough for us." Would not Calvary and its surroundings greatly resemble the present condition of Christianity?

CHAPTER 22

Or is it to be certain that my piece of bread belongs only to me when I know that everyone else has a share, and that no one starves while I eat?

—Tolstoy[1]

Sweet yet solemn thoughts enter the traveler's mind while journeying to Bethlehem, passing on the way from Jerusalem to the "fields of the shepherds," where these men "watched their flocks by night" and where they reverently and in awed wonderment listened to the heavenly choir as it sang, "Peace on earth, good will to men."[2]

Bethlehem has about eight thousand inhabitants, most of whom profess to be Christians. Over the spot where the holy manger stood, a church built by the Emperor Constantine[3] now stands. The Greek Catholics, Roman Catholics, and Armenians own the structure jointly, though each denomination must keep within its own boundaries. Under one roof, all worship (with their lips) the Prince of Peace, and hate each other so bitterly that a fight ensues if one of opposite faith dares cross the boundary line. A quarter of a century ago the Armenian Christians, who have but a small corner of the place for their altar, permitted a carpet to be moved beyond their rightful limits, while the floor was being swept. The consequence was a fight in which three men were killed. Pictures hang on the joint entrance hall so completely covered with dust that their outlines are not discernible, but no one dares touch them because of the jealousy of the other owners.

The silver and gold with which this sacred spot is decorated seem more of a desecration than an adornment. How could one think of beautifying the simple manger where the Son of God was born! Worldly treasures in this holy place are like the fantastic tales with which imaginative writers have attempted to color and make more beautiful the days of his babyhood.

Overwhelmed by a spirit of sadness, the visitor leaves, one by one, the Church of the Nativity,[4] the place of the Crucifixion, and the Holy Sepulcher, wondering whether Count Eberhardt was not right in saying one ought not to advise another to visit this place. A feeble and uncertain faith might easily be destroyed by an exhibition of the hatred which professed believers in the Nazarene have one for another.

Various denominational structures have been erected on the Mount of Olives,[5] and although many people were about, including groups of women engaged in picking the olives which were just ripening, it was possible for our missionaries to find a quiet spot where they could commune with the Lord. They had abundant reason to be thankful that their lives had been spared, that the prophetic promise made them had been fulfilled, and for the privilege of visiting this land. They thanked him for the work of redemption wrought by his Son and for the restoration of his saving plan. They invoked his blessing upon the church, and its members in their gathered and scattered condition, for all the honest in heart, and they besought the Almighty to remember the city and country lying at their feet, that the Jews might be returned to the land of their fathers in fulfillment of ancient and modern prophecies.[6]

It was an impressive occasion. The veil separating the brethren from the presence of the Lord seemed very thin. Below them was what is known as Stephen's Gate,[7] for here the first martyr, after the Savior, gave his life for his testimony.[8] These missionaries do not claim to have seen, as Stephen did, the heavens open and the Son sitting on the right hand of the Father, but they knew no less certainly of the existence of these beings.

It is about fifteen miles [24.14 km] in a straight line through the hills of Judea[9] from Jerusalem to the Jordan[10] and the Dead Sea.[11] It is twenty-one miles [33.80 km] by the road which, after passing Stephen's Gate, the Garden of Gethsemane,[12] the home of Mary, Martha, and Lazarus[13] in Bethany,[14] winds about the base of the Mount of Olives. Standing on the bank of the Dead Sea the visitor is on the lowest part of the earth's surface not covered by water. Engineers have figured that the surface of this "Sea of the Plain" is 1,308 feet [398.68 m] below sea level. The valley of the Jordan for the most part is uncultivated, but the high brush which covers it indicates fertility. Water and cultivation will make it once more blossom as the rose.[15]

The Jordan, Jericho,[16] Elisha's Fountain,[17] Mount Temptation,[18] and innumerable other historic points are deserving of mention but space will not permit.

Within the limits of Jerusalem are several hills. Next in point of interest perhaps to Calvary is Mount Moriah.[19] Its history dates back to the memorable occasion when Abraham came to it with his young son Isaac.[20] Later, the great temple of Solomon was erected here.[21] This was destroyed with the rest of the city as foretold by the Savior.[22] Since then, possession of the spot has passed to the Mohammedans, and now the great Mosque of Omar[23] stands on the sacred hill.

There are few streets in Jerusalem which will accommodate a vehicle of any kind. They are narrow and evil smelling, crowded with people and donkeys, and are ideal breeding places for all kinds of vermin.

The special missionaries were in Jerusalem on November 2, 1921. On that date every shop in the city was closed and the people indulged in such serious rioting that British soldiers were called into action and armored trucks carrying machine guns were stationed about the city. The trouble started as a protest against the declaration of Lord Balfour[24] of England that Palestine should be set apart for the Jews. By this declaration, the British statesman set in motion, to a far greater extent than he imagined, the fulfill-ment of prophecy, for not only do the Bible and the Book of Mor-mon foretell such a gathering of the Jews,[25] but a modern prophet, Orson Hyde,[26] one of the Twelve, predicted in [1841] that England would play a leading part in this gathering.[27]

Mohammedans and Christians, united in their hatred of the Jews, if on no other point, stoned these unfortunates in the streets, and naturally where their numbers warranted it, the Jews retali-ated. At one place Brother McKay, in righteous wrath, ordered a number of Christians to desist in the assault upon some helpless Jewish women and children, and with such sternness that the offenders were convinced he would, if necessary, follow his orders with physical force. The missionaries made an excursion into the Jewish district where they found frightened but sullen and defiant people. An hour or so later in that same street a bomb was thrown which killed a number of Jews and injured many more. At five o'clock in the afternoon everybody was ordered off the streets and heavily armed British soldiers and armored trucks with machine guns soon thereafter restored order.

The guide, professedly a devout Christian, who showed the brethren about, but only through the quiet streets, said that rivers of blood would flow before the Jews would be permitted to return to Jerusalem. However, they were convinced from the man's timidity that he will shed no blood; and if anyone sheds his, it will be because they can outrun him.

The following is a note taken from Brother McKay's journal:

> I have not been disappointed in my visit to old Jerusalem. Its picturesque site on the four historic and frequently

mentioned mounts, with its relative position to other Biblical centers, has been so clearly impressed upon my mind that this geographical significance itself is quite a sufficient reward for the journey. Besides this, the trip from Jerusalem to Jericho and the valley of the Jordan, with all their Biblical associations, was so full of interest and instruction that, were there nothing else, I should feel satisfied.

No, I am not disappointed but grieved—grieved to see the manger, the sacred cradle, profaned by the ostentatious spirit of the jarring selfish creeds—grieved to see the spot desecrated by lavish wealth—grieved to learn of the feuds and quarrels that have occurred upon the very spot where the Son of God was born—grieved to see the keys of the Holy Sepulcher kept by a follower of Mohammed because the professed Christians cannot trust one of their number with them! Grieved to witness the same so-called Christians uniting with Mohammedans in opposing the return of the Jews to the Holy Land!

How far, oh how far from the simple principles of the Gospel have they wandered who now profess to be the direct descendants of the primitive church! Greeks and Romans both are completely apostatized, and the very sects of Protestantism, of course, are ever wandering in darkness because they have no authority.

The reader may remember that Brother McKay's party returned to Utah after having been in China and Japan. Prior to leaving Salt Lake the second time, President [Heber J.] Grant suggested it might be advisable to have someone who had labored in Syria meet these special missionaries and assist in distributing the money which had been collected for the suffering Armenian saints.[28] This suggestion was welcomed by Brother McKay, but nothing definite was decided at the time of leaving.

In Cairo, word was received that Joseph Wilford Booth, who was the last missionary to labor in Syria and the surrounding country, had again been called to that land, and had already left for his mission. In the prayer offered on the Mount of Olives, already referred to, the Lord was asked so to direct the brethren that they might meet Brother Booth. He understood the language and the needs of the people, and it seemed imperative that they find and cooperate with him.

Brother McKay had planned to leave Jerusalem by auto, traveling through Samaria.[29] However, after descending from the Mount of Olives, the brethren were united in feeling they should go by rail to Haifa,[30] on the Mediterranean coast and immediately below

Mount Carmel,[31] which is remembered especially as the place of contest between Elijah and the prophets of Baal as recorded in 1 Kings 18, and which resulted so disastrously for those who had without warrant assumed divine authority.

It should be remembered that Brother McKay had left Salt Lake on the 26th of March traveling west, and Brother Booth on September 16th traveling east. Neither party was informed as to the whereabouts of the other. Indeed, Brother McKay had just learned that Brother Booth had been called and for all the latter knew, Brother McKay might still have been in Australia or India or might even have passed Palestine en route home.

Usually before these special missionaries entered a city, they made inquiries as to the name of a suitable hotel, but in this instance it was not done, though the brethren intended doing it, and spoke of it more than once. Ignorant of where they were to go, a delay of a few moments ensued in the station at Haifa, and as they were finally leaving, a man suddenly rushed up with an exclamation, "Isn't this Brother McKay?"

The inquirer was Brother Booth. Leaving Utah nearly six months later than the others and traveling in the opposite direction, he had met them exactly at the spot where it was absolutely necessary for them to meet in order properly to perform their work. Had they not met at Haifa, it is doubtful whether they would have done so at all, for Brother McKay's intention was to go to Damascus,[32] while Brother Booth planned to proceed to Beirut. His passport entitled him to go to this point and no further. This fortunate meeting, apparently the result of chance, and in which the skeptic would admit nothing but a remarkable coincidence, was due to divine intervention in answer to prayer; and the three missionaries gratefully acknowledged the omnipotent hand in it.

Because of letters which Brother McKay carried from the secretary of state in Washington, the consul in Beirut approved of Brother Booth's going further into Syria and, while he could not guarantee the protection of the United States, he did promise that if any trouble occurred with the officials or with lone bandits, he would use all the power of his office to give relief.

It was necessary to make the journey of about 80 miles [128.75 km] from Haifa to Beirut by auto. The road for almost the entire distance runs along the scenic coast of the Mediterranean and passed through the old and historic cities of Tyre [Sur][33] and Sidon.[34]

The route followed, after their business in Beirut was completed, led the brethren over the mountains of Lebanon[35] to the city of Baalbek.[36] From these mountains Solomon obtained cedars for the great temple at Jerusalem.[37] The hills are now entirely denuded, no trace of the trees for which they were once so famous being visible.

The origin of Baalbek is unknown, though ample evidence exists of its great antiquity. Ancient writers describe it as being one of the finest of Syrian cities, beautified with fountains, gardens, palaces, and monuments. These have passed with the years, but the ruins of a series of temples, among them the Circular Temple and the Temple of the Sun, which must have been one of the greatest of the world, still remain. In one of the walls, which is still standing intact, are three great blocks of stone of such extraordinary size that one wonders what methods of building the ancients had, which would enable them to raise such massive stones and mortise them so exactly in a wall. In viewing these timeworn structures, one concludes that the thousands of intervening years have brought but little progress in the builders' art.

Brother McKay's party, now augmented by President Booth, was not long in Aleppo before realizing how helpless they would have been without the last named brother; for the others did not understand the language, nor the conditions, and their visit would have been almost in vain. Being well acquainted in the city, and with many businessmen, Brother Booth soon located a member of the church and in a few hours was in touch with all of them.

On the ship between Bombay and Port Said the brethren became rather well acquainted with General Frazier of the British army, who had spent many years in the Holy Land and the surrounding country, and who was looked upon as an authority on conditions there. He said to Brother McKay: "Unless you are prepared to leave your head behind, you should not go to Aintab [Gaziantep]."[38]

This opinion was apparently shared by all consuls with whom the brethren talked. The most encouraging word they heard came from the British representative, who was met in the offices of the American consul in Aleppo. He said: "Oh, you may get through all right. The Turkish brigands are swooping down on the road every day or two, and robbing and in some cases murdering travelers, but if you happen to choose a lucky day you may have no trouble."

In describing dangers through which they passed, there is no desire to make heroes of these missionaries. Brother McKay is known as a fearless man, but his calmness and that of his companions was due not so much to courage as it was to faith, a faith which transcends courage. The prophet of the Lord had said to Brother McKay that he should be able to avoid dangers, seen and unseen, and in this promise the three brethren had sublime faith. All they had seen in recent days reminded them of that sermon— brevity and content considered, the most wonderful delivered since the beginning of time—"Fear not, only believe."[39] To have doubted would, they felt sure, have been an insult to God.

It is 80 miles [128.75 km] from Aleppo to Aintab, and with no railroad connection. This trip, therefore, had to be made by auto. It was arranged to leave one afternoon, but the spirit of the Lord indicated that they should not go, though their baggage was already in the car when Brother McKay decided to postpone the trip. Next morning it was different. All were eager for the journey, and, though their driver was manifestly nervous, he alone was thus affected. Other autos were on the road, and one noticed a disposition on the part of drivers to keep close together as a matter of mutual protection, but the trip was made without interruption. Many wrecked cars were seen whose occupants had been robbed and the cars burned.

So uneventful was this journey that the missionaries might easily have felt the reports of danger were greatly overdrawn, but if such feelings existed they were dispelled when it was learned that the very day they passed over this road a company of people traveling with carriages and wagons was held up and robbed of everything worth carrying away, including sixty horses. No lives were reported lost, but these unfortunates were left helpless, with vehicles but with no means of propelling them.[40]

One cannot conceive of more heartrending stories than those to which the brethren listened from the saints in Aintab. Having suffered for food and shelter, they clung to the visiting brethren as they would to angels from heaven. Not a person was present but had lost some relative at the hands of the merciless Turks. One mother, with tears streaming down her cheeks, told of having become separated from her husband and three-year-old daughter in one of the raids made upon them. Later she learned of her husband's violent death, but had never heard a word from her babe and did not know whether it was alive or dead.

The money being distributed by these missionaries was raised for this purpose by a special fast day held in all stakes of the church. It is not too much to say that every man or woman or child in Utah who fasted on that occasion would be willing to abstain from food for a week, or longer if necessary, could they have seen the good which their money was doing. Before Brother McKay left Syria, arrangements had been made to transplant all our members from the danger zone to Aleppo or Beirut where their lives at least would be safe, and where opportunities could be created for them to earn a livelihood. No man in the church is better qualified than is Brother Booth to carry out this work. Though these events occurred more than six years ago, he is still in that land laboring unselfishly and with zeal. This good man loves the Lord and his fellowmen with all his big generous heart and is willing to spend his mortal life in their service. It may be interesting to our readers to know that he is a brother of Sister May Booth Talmage, wife of Dr. James E. Talmage of the Quorum of the Twelve.

It was not easy to say good-bye to him and leave him alone in Aleppo. His family was in Utah and he had no missionary companions. And still he was not alone, for few men have more of the companionship of the Holy Spirit than does he. Since this visit was made his wife[41] has been called to labor with him.

CHAPTER 23

So it's home again, and home again, America for me!
My heart is turning home again, and there I long to be.
In the land of youth and freedom beyond the ocean bars,
Where the air is full of sunlight and the flag is full of stars!
—Van Dyke[1]

En route from Aleppo to Haifa the brethren visited Damascus. This city, according to many authorities, is the oldest in the world, and all concede that it is one of the oldest.[2] Towards this place Saul of Tarsus was journeying "yet breathing out threatenings and slaughter against the disciples of the Lord," when he saw the light which resulted in his complete conversion.[3] The street called "Straight" is still one of the most interesting thoroughfares in this ancient city. It is little more than four yards [3.66 m] wide and the pedestrian is jostled not only by fellowmen, but also by camels and donkeys.

Along this street Ananias came, responsive to the Lord's command, and found Saul, humble and blind since the wondrous vision. One might suppose that a "chosen vessel" who had talked with the Lord needed nothing more, but Paul, as the Savior, had to obey the law of God, so he was baptized. The house where this meeting occurred still stands as does also that of Ananias, where, tradition says, Paul lived for some time while he sought to undo the harm he had formerly done. In another building one may see the window from which friends of the zealous convert lowered him over the wall in a basket, that he might escape his watchful enemies.[4]

The Barada River[5] flows through Damascus, and is one of the really attractive things about the city. This river, the Abana of the Bible, is the stream of which the great Syrian captain spoke so boastfully when commanded by the prophet to dip seven times in the waters of Jordan, "Are not Abana and Pharpar, rivers of

Damascus, better than all the rivers of Israel?[6] May I not wash in them and be clean?"[7]

The brethren were in Damascus on the birthday of Mohammed,[8] and as most of the city's inhabitants belong to this faith, it was a great holiday. Buildings and even sidewalks were adorned with various draperies, among them being some very ornate and costly Turkish rugs. The people were all arrayed in festive attire. In Paul's day but few Christians were in Damascus, and if one may judge from a brief and superficial observation, there are even fewer today who really believe in and follow the teachings of the Savior.

Together with other travelers, the brethren took auto from Damascus over the mountains of Lebanon to Beirut and from there again through ancient Tyre and Sidon to Haifa. Tyre and Sidon themselves are old-fashioned, with narrow, crooked, and in most cases, dirty streets, but they occupy attractive sites on the shore of the Mediterranean, and in spite of dirt and beggars invite a longer stay.

In this day of high speed, it is not easy to realize how small the territory was to which the Savior's earthly ministry was limited. In two days, without undue loitering, one may drive by auto from Jerusalem to Bethany, Jericho, the Dead Sea, through the Jordan Valley,[9] around the Lake of Galilee [Lake Tiberias],[10] Tiberias,[11] Cana,[12] Nazareth,[13] and back to Jerusalem through Samaria, visiting practically every place honored by a mortal visit from our Lord.

And yet one feels after a few weeks' stay that many long years would be insufficient to absorb and properly digest all that should be learned in this land. Every spot has a history. Here is the cave near the brook Cherith in which the prophet Elijah lived when ravens brought him bread and flesh morning and evening.[14] There is the spot where he stood, in company with Elisha, and divided the water of Jordan by smiting it with his mantle.[15] Yonder is the field where the child which was given the Shunammite woman as a son of promise was stricken with illness, and farther on is the probable spot where the parents lived and where the little one was restored through divine favor.[16]

Yon somber towering peak is Mount Temptation where tradition says the Savior was tempted of Satan.[17] Over there John was preaching repentance when Christ came to him demanding baptism. Into this stream they went and the Son of God was buried in water by one having authority "to fulfil all righteousness." From the opened heavens the Father thus acknowledged this act of obedience, "This is my Beloved Son, in whom I am well pleased."[18]

To the north is Nazareth,[19] Christ's boyhood home.[20] The well, still known as the Virgin's well and from which, following the ancient custom, the boy and his mother doubtless carried water for the household use, is to be seen.[21] Nearby is the rocky promontory from which his angry townsmen proposed to throw him after his first sermon in their midst.[22] Between Nazareth and Tiberias stands the village of Cana, scene of the first miracle, the changing of water to wine.[23]

And Galilee! The very name is inspiring. Gazing upon its blue surface, one need not be strongly imaginative to see a picture of the living Christ, healing the sick, casting out unclean spirits, giving sight to the blind, stilling the storm, walking on the water, even raising the dead. One remembers how he, with perfect knowledge of nature's laws, created from surrounding elements sufficient food to satisfy the multitude.[24]

There is not complete agreement among Bible students as to the mountain on which the transfiguration occurred or on which the beatitudes were given; but undoubtedly both are in the vicinity.[25]

It is not easy to describe the contradictions which confront the traveler in the Holy Land. Uplifted by the sacred truths which have been taught, he feels his own life enriched by contemplating the lives of those inspired teachers. But he sorrows in the glaring evidences of apostasy wherein professed followers of the Nazarene "have a form of godliness but deny the power thereof."[26]

The last evening of their stay in Palestine was spent by the missionaries on Mount Carmel. It requires about one hour of good walking to reach the summit. Here a stone marks the supposed place where the prophet Elijah called down fire from heaven.[27] From this point the beauty of the surrounding scene is indescribable. The moon had just risen over the peaceful waters of the Mediterranean, and the lights from steamers and boats twinkled in the harbor. In the opposite direction one could look into the valley of the Esdraelon[28] and almost into that of the Jordan. At the foot of the mountain was the quaint city of Haifa. It was a fitting place and hour to bid farewell to the country toward which the hearts of all Christians naturally turn.

Long before daylight next morning the brethren left by rail for Egypt. They again crossed the Suez at El Kantara. Two days later aboard the *Ormonde* they were steaming across the Mediterranean toward Italy.[29]

In Utah one thinks of Europe as being far away, but now after all their journeyings it seemed that they were coming into the borders of their own land.

Between Port Said and Naples[30] they passed Fair Havens[31] on the small island of Crete[32] where the Apostle Paul, then a prophetic prisoner en route to Rome,[33] entreated the centurion to put up for the winter. "Nevertheless the centurion believed the master

Returning Home to Utah

and the owner of the ship, more than those things which were spoken by Paul."[34] Failing to heed the inspired words, the captain after severe buffeting by wind and wave, saw his vessel wrecked and its passengers cast upon the little island of Melita [Malta],[35] barely escaping with their lives.[36] Melita was also visible from the *Ormonde*'s deck.[37]

A short time after passing those islands the brethren sailed between the real, not metaphorical, Scylla and Charybdis,[38] so renowned in ancient story. Scylla[39] is a dangerous rock on the Italian coast, and Charybdis[40] a whirlpool on the coast of Sicily,[41] a short distance away. This narrow passage seems to have lost its terrors for mariners; the *Ormonde* entered it just after nightfall, when by hurrying it might have passed through by daylight.

The Bay of Naples[42] is considered the most beautiful in Europe. On the starboard side as the vessel steamed into harbor, dense clouds of smoke were issuing from temperamental Vesuvius,[43] and this was reddened from time to time by a fiery glare from seething lava within. On their port side was Naples, very attractive in the early morning light. All about were row boats whose occupants were out early in the hope of obtaining money. Many of them offered fruits and flowers; some were following the Pacific Islanders' custom of diving for coins; a quintet was furnishing music and of a better quality than is usually heard under such circumstances; not a few were unvarnished beggars who made no pretense of offering anything in return for what they received.

Vesuvius, though greater because of past achievements than for its present power, has by no means reached a condition of senility; and the constant rumbling reminds the spectator who peers over the side that it may again break out and bury under molten ashes all surrounding regions. Pompeii,[44] of course, is a stern reminder of what this volcano can do in a destructive mood. One cannot gaze into this molten pit without realizing what tremendous power lies in the forces of nature, and how utterly dependent man is upon the Almighty. Remove his controlling hand but for a moment and think what havoc would be wrought by wind, water, and fire!

The thoughtful Christian's heart is peculiarly stirred upon seeing Rome, with its numerous and costly churches, especially after visiting the Holy Land and being impressed with the manner in which the gospel was formerly taught.[45] On the one hand was simplicity, humility, self-sacrifice, where the greatest was "the servant of all." On the other, one sees pompous pride, men haughtily holding out hands to be kissed, mysterious ceremonies, and the poor and downtrodden of the earth shout out from the presence of the so-called representatives of the loving Christ. What has Rome done for Christianity? The answers would be as varied as the religious complexions of those giving them.

Now fallen into disuse and partially in ruins is the great Coliseum.[46] Here gladiators fought with each other or with animals, and here, too, defenseless Christians, men, women, and even little children, were torn to pieces by wild animals rather than abandon faith in their Redeemer, while more than fifty thousand spectators, no less cruel than the ferocious beasts, taunted victims and gloated over their deaths. It is interesting to know that this great structure was completed by Titus,[47] the Roman general who destroyed Jerusalem according to the predictions of the Savior, something less than four decades after the prophecy was uttered.[48]

It is supposed that both Peter and Paul met death in Rome, the former by crucifixion and the latter by being beheaded. Now two great churches stand on the supposed sites of the martyrdom and bear the names of the two apostles.[49] One wonders why, after centuries of teaching, the world still persists in deifying dead prophets and apostles and rejecting and, in some cases, killing the living ones.

Among the most interesting sights of Rome are the catacombs, great subterranean rooms and passageways where, during the cruel persecution of the early Christians, they held meetings and frequently lived in hiding to escape the searching soldiers. The careful observer can trace in these underground galleries signs of departure from the simple Christian faith and in its place the introduction of ceremonies which were so inseparable from the Roman worship of their idolatrous gods.[50]

Viewing these things, the Latter-day Saint is grateful for the simplicity of his faith, so free from ostentation and all that is mysterious, its sole adornment being the "beauty of Godliness."

Brother McKay's oldest son, David Lawrence [McKay],[51] was laboring as a missionary in Lausanne,[52] Switzerland, and, naturally, it was planned to visit him in his field of labor. The young man was anxiously waiting the train's arrival at midnight, though he had little reason to expect his father, as the telegram which was sent had not been delivered.

Young Brother McKay is a worthy son and loves his parents with a deep and sincere affection. If no other reward were ever to come to him for his devotion to this work, he would be repaid in the pride and joy written on his father's face as they sprang into each other's arms. It reminded one that someday we will all meet our Heavenly Father. Will he joyfully greet us with open arms, and will we be able to hold our heads erect and look fearlessly into his searching eyes?[53]

This may be an opportune place to mention a lesson which Brother Cannon learned during this trip. As was natural, Brother McKay always prayed for his missionary son in the joint petitions which he and his companion offered each day. Brother Cannon fell into the habit, when asked to be mouth, of mentioning Lawrence by name. He soon came to love the young man dearly, though prior to the meeting in Lausanne they were not acquainted. He learned that we love those for whom we sincerely pray. To follow Christ's example we must love our enemies; therefore we must pray for them. To be guided by the authorities of the church we must love them; therefore we must pray for them also. And for the same reason we should pray for all mankind.

An interesting conference was held at Lausanne under the direction of President Serge F. Ballif[54] of the Swiss and German Mission,[55] who translated the remarks of the visitors into French. The special missionaries had not met with saints for some many weeks and they rejoiced in the spirit which is so characteristic of such meetings. In addition to young Brother McKay, elders were met in Lausanne.

There is something sadly lacking in the man, who, after spending months in foreign lands and among strange peoples, can turn his face homeward without being thrilled to the depths of his soul. To think of one's native land, of home, of wife and children and other dear ones makes the thoughtful and appreciative man praise God. With the departure from Palestine, Brother McKay felt that the work for which he was especially called had been accomplished, and desired to return as soon as possible. Christmas was approaching and by hurrying, the brethren could spend this blessed day with their families. Merely the high points, therefore, in the journey from Port Said to Utah are touched.

A brief but very pleasant visit with President Serge F. Ballif and his wife[56] and daughter was made in the mission home in Basel,[57] and a crowded meeting was held there. Brother Max Zimmer translated for Brother McKay while Brother Cannon struggled through his address without help. And it was a struggle, for more than sixteen years had elapsed since he left the Swiss and German Mission, and during that period he had used the language but rarely.

At Frankfurt[58] a crowded meeting was held. Here Brother Jean Wunderlich, then a boy in high school, made his first attempt at public translating from English into German and acquitted himself most creditably. Since then he has translated for at least five of the Twelve.

Time did not permit a trip by boat down the historic Rhine[59] to Cologne,[60] but from the car windows a fleeting glimpse was had of the scenic hills and castles, as well as the renowned Mouse Tower[61] in the center of the stream.

At the time of this visit, President John P. Lillywhite[62] was presiding over the Netherlands Mission[63] which included Belgium,[64] and he and President Ballif, of the Swiss and German Mission, and David Lawrence McKay were in attendance at the Liege Conference.[65] At the present writing, President Lillywhite is again presiding in Holland [the Netherlands],[66] this being his third mission to that land. The special missionaries also met Elders Alvin Smith Nelson[67] and Karl M. Richards,[68] who were laboring in Liege. There is much to see in Brussels[69] and in Paris, but little time was had for these cities.

More than twenty years before this world trip was undertaken, Brother McKay labored[70] in Glasgow,[71] Scotland, and immediately upon setting foot on British soil he made a hurried trip to his old field while Brother Cannon visited the London Conference. The missionaries in England were laboring with fidelity but the people lacked the interest manifested in former years. A spirit of gloom and depression was apparent.

A royal welcome awaited the brethren at mission headquarters in Liverpool.[72] President Orson F. Whitney[73] and his hospitable wife[74] made the few hours spent with them most agreeable. They and Elders William A. Morton,[75] and [others] were on the pier to bid the two travelers "bon voyage" as the *Cedric* moved out to sea.[76]

Since leaving home, these brethren had spent many days on the water. They had traveled on a great variety of vessels and had encountered all kinds of weather. Outwardly, Brother McKay seemed to have become a really first-class sailor, but he admitted, as they neared port, that inwardly, though not actually overcome by seasickness, he had not been really comfortable during any waking hour of the final trip. A world tour, therefore, is not all sunshine and pleasure.

The brethren had been stirred by the sight of colorful Japan, of the mammoth Chinese wall, of historic pyramids, the chaste Taj Mahal. But surpassing all else is the thrill which comes to an American when, after a long absence he sees the inspiring Statue of Liberty[77] at the entrance to New York harbor,[78] and behind this his own native land.

Always interesting is the docking of a mammoth ocean liner at its pier. In close quarters, such as one finds in the Hudson,[79] a large vessel is most unwieldy and must be shoved into its place by numerous small but sturdy tugs.

It is a trying period for people on deck who see loved ones waiting for them, but no amount of impatience can hurry the tedious process of landing. Not having any loved ones or even friends, as far as they knew, waiting for them on the pier the special missionaries were able to give their entire attention to the interesting sights.

Although unknown to them, Elder George Ashton, Jr.,[80] was there to meet the travelers and conduct them to the mission home, presided over by Brother and Sister[81] George W. McCune. However, it was first necessary to pass the custom officials, a duty which, in the opinion of most Americans, robs homecoming of much of its sweetness. These troublesome but necessary officers are stricter in the United States than anywhere else in the world. It is not enough to open one's satchel or trunk and have the investigator look into it perfunctorily and close it again, as is usually done in European countries. First of all, the traveler must make a declaration of everything purchased abroad and with its price. With this paper before him the officer usually goes through everything, sometimes dumping the contents of a trunk onto the tables and carefully inspecting every article. Woe to him who has something which has not been declared. However, Brother McKay's party had no serious trouble and very little delay.

During a large part of this tour, the brethren had been completely out of reach of their families. Any of their loved ones might have been dead for several weeks before word could have reached them. This, in itself, was sufficient cause for gratitude that they were again within telegraphic reach of home.

In Chicago a short visit was had with President Winslow Farr Smith,[82] now president of the Ensign Stake, who then was in charge of the Northern States Mission.[83]

The welcome accorded the missionaries by President [Heber J.] Grant and his associates was at a nature to make their hearts rejoice.[84] They were given to understand that their mission had been completed to the satisfaction of those who had called them.

During this trip which required 366 days, the missionaries traveled on 24 oceangoing vessels. They spent the equal of 153 days on the water, traveled a total of 61,646 miles [99,209.62 km] not counting trips made by auto, streetcars, tugs, ferry boats, horseback, camels, etc. Of the miles traveled, 23,777 [38,265.37 km] were by land and 37,869 [60,944.25 km] were by water.

Who can utter the mighty acts of the Lord? Who can show forth all his praise?
—Psalms 106:2

Friends have frequently asked: "What was the most wonderful thing you saw on this journey around the world?" The brethren usually answer by inquiring, "What in your opinion is the most wonderful thing to be seen on such a trip?" Of course the answers are many and varied. The Chinese wall is often suggested. Stretching from the sea at Shanghaiguan inland for about fifteen hundred miles [2,414.02 km], equal to the distance from Salt Lake City to Chicago, it is indeed a structure which inspires wonder. As has been stated, an engineer once estimated that it contained enough material to build a wall six feet [1.83 m] high and two feet [0.61 m] wide which would encircle the globe at the equator. It has stood for more than two thousand years, and one wonders how the stupendous task of building it was ever completed. The purpose of the wall was to keep out the hordes of invading Tartar tribes and, in the days prior to heavy artillery, it must have been impregnable. But to it the credit of being the most wonderful thing cannot be given.

Perhaps then the greatest active volcano in the world, the mammoth Kilauea on the Hawaiian Islands, can be accorded the honor. One who has had the privilege of seeing this lake of fire, a veritable Hades of boiling and hissing lava, of hearing the sputtering and rumbling and roaring which it emits, can certainly imagine nothing of its kind which would be more impressive or unforgettable. But no, we must seek farther for the most wonderful thing.

One ventures to suggest the pyramids of Giza. These monster structures have stood for thousands of years and are rated by everybody as being among the world's wonders. How the 2,300,000 blocks of stone averaging 2½ tons [2,267.96 kg] each, which went into Cheops, the largest of the pyramids, could be assembled so early in the world's history still remains a mystifying problem. From the summit of one of these monstrous structures, a view may be had whose equal is not easily found. With the inscrutable Sphinx near its base, the fertile Nile Valley to the east and otherwise almost surrounded by the barren Libyan Desert, with the memory of interesting or tragic historical events which have occurred in the vicinity, this view alone would compensate for a world trip if nothing more were to be seen. To this land Abraham, father of the faithful, came. Here Joseph, interpreter of dreams, saved Egypt, and proved a savior also to his father's house.[1] Almost at one's feet, Moses, the great leader and lawgiver, was born and grew to manhood.[2] Here the children of Israel served until the Lord miraculously led them across the Red Sea.[3] To this land the prophet Jeremiah is said to have come and here met death.[4] In fancy one can see Joseph and Mary and the Holy Child toiling painfully over dusty plains to escape Herod's jealous wrath.[5] But the inquirer must be told that this is not the feature of the world trip which will remain longest in memory.

Perhaps it was the ruins of the Temple at Baalbek. High in these ruined walls are stones more than sixty feet [18.29 m] long and thirteen feet [3.96 m] wide and estimated as weighing not less than two hundred tons [181,436.95 kg], and these are mortised into the stone beneath, and the stones above are mortised into them with an astonishing skill.

Or it may have been the Taj Mahal, that wondrous dream in white marble erected in Agra, India, at such cost of time and treasure, by the Emperor Jahan something more than three centuries ago. When one looks upon this structure and thinks of what mortals can do, it is easy to believe in the omnipotence of God. If mansions in heaven are to exceed this in splendor, they are indeed worth all man's effort.

Or if none of these, then it must have been Bethlehem or Calvary.

Now the inquirer is approaching the answer, but has not yet reached it; for as man now attempts to measure the sanctity of the simple manger by the cost of the gold and silver which adorn it, and evaluates Calvary by the diamonds and other so-called precious stones which cover it, so also has man for a price bedecked Christianity, so beautiful in its simplicity, with glittering ceremonies originating in human minds until the precious teachings of our Lord are well nigh obliterated.

No, the most impressive thing these missionaries saw was not the Chinese wall, or pyramids, volcanoes, marble halls, storms at sea, or even, and one says it reverently, Bethlehem or Calvary.

It was the spirit of Christ manifested in the preparatory work being done by the church. He is coming to reign; and his coming as King of Kings, announced to the world by our elders, will be infinitely greater than his simple birth or his cruel death. This spirit prompts men to sacrifice their personal interests in order to help prepare the way. It causes a feeling of brotherhood among peoples of different color and language and custom. In other words, the most wonderful thing in the world is the gospel of the Lord Jesus Christ, unadorned and unadulterated. Perhaps some little space may be used in explanation. And as space is limited, reference can be made to but a few instances and with utmost brevity.

In Peking, with its million inhabitants, the special missionaries were divinely directed to the one suitable place in the city where the dedicatory prayer could be offered. On that day the Lord gave unmistakable testimony that he accepted what had been done and that this benighted people, comprising a quarter of the earth's inhabitants, would in due time hear the saving message. No less an authority than Ambassador Charles R. Crane stated that this church could make a wonderful contribution to that afflicted country. The assurance came forcefully to the brethren that China, land of floods, droughts, famines, of pestilence and of revolution, will emerge from chaos and the sun of truth will rise upon her.

Let the reader recall that when the brethren went to the Pacific Islands, they were total strangers to the Islanders. These were of a different race, color, and language and with strange habits of dress and manners. There was but one thing in common—the gospel, but that is destined to unite all mankind, regardless of all else. On this trip its power to do so was marvelously manifested, more even among the Polynesians where racial differences are the greatest, than among the whites, if such a thing is possible. The story has already been told of these dark-skinned, scantily clad people falling on their knees and kissing and bathing in tears the hands of the brethren at Sauniatu, on the Samoan Islands. And the visitors were no less moved. Their tears also were shed in bidding farewell to simple souls whom they had never met until a few days previously.

This same spirit of oneness was abundantly manifest with elders met in fifteen different missions, though in most cases missionaries and visitors had never met previously. Furthermore, is anything more remarkable than to find hundreds of young men foregoing the association of loved ones, paying their own way, remaining clean despite alluring temptations, and finding unspeakable joy in such service?

In connection with this trip many prophecies were made and all were literally fulfilled. That is an indisputable, not an imaginary, fact. One fulfilled prediction might be attributed to chance, but when the number grows into more than a dozen, what explanation can be offered?

Mention has been made and might be repeated of the way our travelers obtained passage on vessels which were already filled. So frequent were occurrences of this kind that none but ingrates would fail to give the Almighty credit for preparing the way. If there was nothing supernatural about it, why should these remarkable things occur to them times without number and not to other travelers whom they met?

When the angel Moroni visited the unknown youth in Palmyra,[6] he said that the name of Joseph Smith should be known for good and evil throughout the earth.[7] In eastern and western, northern and southern lands, the brethren saw the fulfillment of this prediction. Often the words "Mormon" or "Joseph Smith" brought a smile of derision to the lips of those who heard it; and occasionally it led to open and in some cases violent abuse. This occurred in the Antipodes and, indeed, in all parts of the world. On the other hand, people were met in all climes who gratefully acknowledged God's goodness in revealing to them that Mormon and Joseph Smith were holy prophets who, when every knee bows and every tongue confesses that Jesus is the Christ, will be recognized as having been chosen vessels.

In view of these and innumerable unmentioned things, the assertion is again made that the spirit of the Gospel of Jesus Christ and its effect upon mankind is the most wonderful thing in the world.

A word in conclusion: It was not intended in the beginning to extend this account into a book of such size. The work has been done hurriedly at odd moments and in the midst of numerous pressing duties. Many important incidents have been overlooked, while often others less important have been mentioned. Perhaps an apology is due for the prolixity of the narrative, but like the elusive word "Amen" in some sermons, it has been difficult for the author to write

FINIS.

Chronology of LDS Missions Visited by Elder David O. McKay and Hugh J. Cannon, 1920–1921

Mission Name	Acting President	Month of Arrival
Northwestern States[1]	Heber C. Iverson	December 1920
Japan[2]	Joseph H. Stimpson	December 1920
Hawaiian[3]	E. Wesley Smith	February 1921
California[4]	Joseph W. McMurrin	March 1921
Tahitian[5]	Leonidas H. Kennard	April 1921
New Zealand[6]	Frederick W. Schwendiman	April 1921
Samoan[7]	John Q. Adams	May 1921
Tongan[8]	Mark V. Coombs	June 1921
Australian[9]	Don C. Rushton	August 1921
Turkish[10]	Joseph W. Booth	November 1921
Swiss and German[11]	Serge F. Ballif	November 1921
Netherlands[12]	John P. Lillywhite	December 1921
British[13]	Orson F. Whitney	December 1921
Eastern States[14]	George W. McCune	December 1921
Northern States[15]	Winslow F. Smith	December 1921

1. The Northwestern States Mission was comprised of Oregon, Washington, Montana, northern Idaho, British Columbia, and Alaska. In 1890, Latter-day Saints created the Oregon Lumber Company near Baker City, Oregon. By 1893, the number of Latter-day Saints in the area had grown, and the church organized a branch in Baker City. The branch was included in the Oneida Stake. When President George C. Parkinson visited the Oregon branch, he informed the First Presidency that missionaries could successfully labor in the area. In 1896, the First Presidency sent Edward Stevenson and Matthias F. Cowley to begin proselyting, and on July 26, 1897, the church organized the Northwestern States Mission. George C. Parkinson was called as president, retaining his duties as president of the Oneida Stake. On June 12, 1898, the Montana Mission was dissolved and incorporated into the Northwestern States Mission, with Franklin S. Bramwell as its new president. Meeting with success, in 1901 the church organized the Union Stake and moved the mission headquarters to Portland, Oregon. (This and the following mission histories have been excerpted from Andrew Jenson, *Encyclopedic History of the Church of Jesus Christ of Latter-day Saints* [Salt Lake City: Deseret News Publishing Company, 1941], 594–96.)
2. The Japan Mission was located in the former Empire of Japan. The mission was opened in 1901 by Apostle Heber J. Grant and Elders Louis A. Kelsch, Horace S. Ensign, and Alma O. Taylor. These missionaries arrived on August 12, 1901. On September 1, President Grant dedicated Japan on a hill near Yokohama. On March 8, 1902, President Grant baptized the first Japanese convert, Hajime Nakazawa, who formerly was a Shinto priest. The second convert, Saburo Kikuchi, was baptized by President Grant on March 10. The first Sunday school in Japan began on November 29, 1903, in Tokyo. The Book of Mormon was translated into Japanese in 1904 by Alma O. Taylor. He was aided by Japanese

Latter-day Saints, two Japanese professors, and Elder Frederick A. Caine. Success was rare in the Japan Mission, with only 127 members in 1920. (Jenson, *Encyclopedic History of the Church*, 373–74.)

3. The Hawaiian Mission was comprised of the Hawaiian Islands. In 1850, Apostle Charles C. Rich called ten elders who were working in California to be missionaries in Hawaii, and they arrived in Honolulu on December 12, 1850. The missionaries soon dispersed to all of the islands. However, the language was difficult, and the missionaries struggled with the native foods and customs. The first baptism was performed by President Clark on February 10, 1851. On August 6, 1851, the first branch was organized on Maui, in the village of Kealakou. By the close of 1853, church membership in Hawaii totaled 4,000, with branches on every inhabited island. In 1854, Elder George Q. Cannon began to translate the Book of Mormon into Hawaiian, and finished in 1855. In 1858, the missionaries were recalled because of the Utah War, and native elders ran the mission. However, in 1860, Walter M. Gibson was called to serve in the South Pacific Islands, but instead stayed in Hawaii. After taking too many powers to himself and acting without authorization, Elder Gibson was excommunicated in 1864. Gibson had taken property from the saints' gathering place on Lanai, and the church purchased the Laie Plantation on Oahu instead. The mission office remained at the Laie Plantation until 1919, when it was moved to Honolulu. (Jenson, *Encyclopedic History of the Church*, 322–25.)

4. The California Mission included California and parts of Arizona and Nevada. It was organized in 1846 with Samuel Brannan as president. The mission did not remain open long, and was closed in 1858. From 1858 to 1892, there was no organized mission in California. The first missionary called to the area after it had been closed was Elder John L. Dalton. The church already had branches in San Francisco and Oakland, and in 1892 Elder Dalton was called to labor in those cities. In 1894, Karl G. Maeser ran the Utah exhibit of the Mid-Winter Fair. While living in San Francisco, he also presided over the mission and is believed to have reorganized it. The mission's success led to the creation of the Los Angeles Branch on August 20, 1895. (Jenson, *Encyclopedic History of the Church*, 109–10.)

5. The Tahitian Mission included the Windward Islands, Leeward Islands, Tuamotu Archipelago, and Tubuai Archipelago. The first missionaries to the South Pacific, Noah Rogers, Addison Pratt, Benjamin F. Grouard, and Knowlton F. Hanks, were originally called to serve in the Sandwich Islands. However, upon arrival in Tubuai on May 4, 1844, the missionaries decided to stay and labor there on account of the warm reception by the natives. The first branch was organized on July 29, 1844, on Tubuai. By March 28, 1847, when Elder Pratt left for America to report on the mission's status, over 2,000 converts had been baptized. Elder Grouard continued to serve on Tubuai, and soon he became a confidant of the king. Soon afterwards, nearly the entire island of Tubuai had joined the church. In May 1850, Elder Pratt was sent by President Brigham Young to preside over the mission. In 1853, a new local government took power and expelled the missionaries. Nearly forty years later, on September 20, 1892, the first missionaries returned to the islands. In the absence of missionaries, the church in the mission fell into disarray. Miraculously, despite the long absence, one hundred members in one branch on Takaroa remained true to the church. The church sent Elder James S. Brown, who had previously served in the mission before its closure in 1853, to preside. The Book of Mormon was translated and printed in Tahitian in 1904. (Jenson, *Encyclopedic History of the Church*, 804–7.)

6. The New Zealand Mission included the islands of New Zealand—North Island and South Island—and the surrounding small islands. The mission began as part of the Australian Mission, and in 1854 preaching in New Zealand was commenced by Augustus Farnham. After two months, he returned to the Australian Mission where he presided, and left an Elder Cooke to preside in New Zealand. By March 1855, he created the first branch near Wellington with ten converts. Missionary work in New Zealand continued to be sporadic, but on December 30, 1871, eleven Latter-day Saints emigrated to Utah. By 1878, New Zealand was included in the Australasian Mission, and President Elijah F. Pearce moved the mission headquarters from Sydney, Australia, to Auckland, New Zealand.

In 1881, missionaries were sent to the native Maoris, and on February 25, 1883, the first Maori branch was organized. By 1887, 2,243 of the 2,573 members of the church in New Zealand were Maoris. In 1889, Ezra F. Richards and Sonda Sanders Jr. completed the translation of the Book of Mormon into Maori. In 1897, the Australasian Mission split to form the Australian Mission and the New Zealand Mission. Ezra F. Richards was called as the new president of the New Zealand Mission. (Jenson, *Encyclopedic History of the Church*, 580–82.)

7. The Samoan Mission included the Samoan or Navigator Islands. The first missionaries were native Hawaiians who were sent without authorization by Walter M. Gibson, who had appointed himself as president of the Hawaiian Mission. Although Gibson was excommunicated by apostles in 1864, the two natives, Kimo Belio and Samuela Manoa, continued to labor in Samoa. Their endeavors were not known to the church until they sent a letter to the missionaries in Hawaii in 1871. They informed the church that they had converted nearly 200 Samoans and had built churches. However, one of the missionaries died and the other was injured and confined to a home for fifteen months. During this time, most of the converts apostatized, and no more missionary work was done until June 1888, when Joseph H. Dean was sent from the Hawaiian Mission to preach in Samoa. His first baptism was on June 25, 1888, and soon after he rebaptized Samuela Manoa and ordained him an elder. Three more missionaries, William O. Lee, Adelbert Beesley, and Edward J. Wood, arrived on October 11, 1888. (Jenson, *Encyclopedic History of the Church*, 764–66.)

8. The Tongan Mission was made up of the Tongan, or Friendly, Islands in the South Pacific. Elders Brigham Smoot and Alva J. Butler were sent from the Samoan Mission in 1891 to begin missionary work in Tonga. On July 15, 1891, they met with King Tubou, and he allowed them to preach despite the misgivings of his advisors. The first mission home was built in the city of Mua and President Smoot dedicated the building on May 15, 1892. Unfortunately, the missionaries met with little success and the mission was closed in 1897. However, the mission was reopened in 1917 under President Willard L. Smith. Tonga had become a British protectorate in 1899, and as a result the missionaries no longer were impeded by the native leaders. The church established the headquarters of the mission in Mua and built a new building. Later, Nukualofa became the mission headquarters. The missionaries were very successful in their labors following the reopening of the mission in 1917. (Jenson, *Encyclopedic History of the Church*, 878–79.)

9. The Australian Mission was comprised of Australia, Tasmania, and other islands, including those of New Zealand for a time. The first missionary to Australia, William Barrett, was called by Apostle George A. Smith in 1840. In 1842, Andrew Anderson was sent by Apostle Orson Pratt, and he had more success, opening a branch of eleven members in Sydney. The mission was officially opened in Sydney on October 30, 1851. John Murdock and Charles W. Wandell soon had a few converts and were able to publish thousands of copies of pamphlets. A new branch was opened later in Melbourne. On April 6, 1853, a number of Latter-day Saints emigrated to Utah, and Elder Wandell traveled with them. Soon after, Elder Augustus Farnham arrived in Australia with ten elders to take charge of the mission. The mission began publishing the *Zion's Watchman* periodical to deal with anti-church sentiment by local journalists on August 13, 1853. In 1854, New Zealand was included in the mission and it was renamed the Australasian Mission until 1897, when it again became the Australian Mission. From 1880 to 1897, the headquarters of the mission was located in Auckland, New Zealand. (Jenson, *Encyclopedic History of the Church*, 35–37.)

10. The Turkish Mission included the countries of Turkey, Armenia, Syria, and Palestine in Asia Minor. Elder Jacob Spori was called in 1884 to labor in Constantinople, Turkey, in response to a letter from a Mr. Vartooguian requesting to meet with Latter-day Saint elders. Shortly after his arrival, Elder Spori baptized Mr. Vartooguian and his family. Elders Joseph M. Tanner and Francis M. Lyman Jr. arrived a short time later. The LDS Church was not officially recognized by the Turkish government, and the missionaries were not allowed to hold public meetings. As a result, they traveled to preach to a German community in Haifa, Palestine. The missionaries were successful in Haifa and also at Jaffa, Palestine. Two native converts helped the recently arrived Elder Ferdinand F.

Chronology of LDS Missions Visited by Elder David O. McKay and Hugh J. Cannon, 1920–1921

Hintze translate and publish *The Articles of Faith* and another tract in Turkish. The first known Arab converts were baptized on September 22, 1889, by Elder Janne M. Sjodahl. The missionaries were successful and soon opened branches in the cities of Aintab and Sivas in Turkey, and also Aleppo, Syria. However, custom did not allow for men and women to worship together, resulting in separate meetings for them. Due to political circumstances, missionaries were recalled from Turkey in 1895, but returned in September 1897. The members of the church opened a cloth factory in Aleppo in 1899. Elder Hintze completed the translation of the Book of Mormon into Turkish in Boston in 1906. In 1909, more political strife caused the missionaries to be recalled until 1921, when the fighting between Armenia and Turkey ceased. (Jenson, *Encyclopedic History of the Church*, 888–90.)

11. The Swiss and German Mission included Switzerland and the western half of Germany. The mission was originally opened as the Swiss and Italian Mission in 1850 by Apostle Lorenzo Snow. The name later changed to the Swiss, Italian, and German Mission, and in 1868 became the Swiss and German Mission because of limited success in Italy. By 1868, the mission consisted of 13 branches, 538 members, and only four missionaries. The mission began publishing a monthly periodical, *Der Stern*, in German in January 1869. In 1883, the mission sent Elders Thomas Biesinger to Vienna and Paul E. B. Hammer to Prague where they met with some success. Later in 1883, Elder Hammer was arrested in Prague and banished from the country for preaching. By 1887, there were 26 branches and 717 members in the mission. However, as the Latter-day Saints continued to emigrate some branches were dissolved. The mission split into the German Mission and the Swiss Mission in 1897, but the two were rejoined on May 22, 1904. (Jenson, *Encyclopedic History of the Church*, 853–54.)

12. The Netherlands Mission was comprised of the Netherlands. Apostle Orson Hyde was the first missionary to preach in the Netherlands as he passed through while traveling to the Holy Land in 1841. The next missionaries to labor in the Netherlands were Elders Paul Augustus Schettler and A. Wiegers Van der Woude in 1861. They operated under the Swiss and German Mission. The first converts were baptized by Elder Van der Woude on October 1, 1861, and included two of his own relatives living in the Netherlands. Elder Schettler also baptized a few converts in Amsterdam on December 23, 1861. The elders created the first branch in the Netherlands in Amsterdam in 1862. Elder Schettler was transferred to Switzerland in September of 1862, and Elder Van der Woude left the Netherlands in 1863. The next missionary sent to the Netherlands was Elder Joseph Weiler, who arrived in October of 1864. Shortly before his arrival, sixty-one converts emigrated to Utah. On November 1, 1864, the Netherlands Mission was created from the Swiss and German Mission. In 1891, Belgium was added to the Netherlands Mission. The mission began publishing the periodical *De Ster* in 1896. (Jenson, *Encyclopedic History of the Church*, 569–71.)

13. The British Mission was comprised of Great Britain and Ireland. The first missionaries to England, Apostles Heber C. Kimball and Orson Hyde, along with Willard Richards, Joseph Fielding, John Goodson, Isaac Russell, and John Snider, arrived in Liverpool on July 20, 1837. The elders were soon successful, and the first branch was opened in Preston on August 6, 1837. By the end of 1837, eight more branches had been organized in England. Apostles Kimball and Hyde returned to the United States in 1838 and placed Elder Fielding in charge of the mission. The first branch in Scotland was later opened in Paisley, and afterwards missionaries were sent to Wales, Ireland, the Isle of Man, and the Channel Islands. In 1840, the mission began publishing the *Millennial Star* periodical. The headquarters of the mission was originally in Manchester, but in 1842 was relocated to Liverpool along with the publication of the *Millennial Star*. Between 1840 and 1868, around 89,500 Latter-day Saints emigrated to America on 150 ships. (Jenson, *Encyclopedic History of the Church*, 92–94.)

14. The Eastern States Mission was comprised of New York, New Jersey, Pennsylvania, Maryland, Connecticut, Massachusetts, Rhode Island, Delaware, and the District of Columbia. the church was organized in Fayette, New York, on April 6, 1830. The first missionaries sent to preach in the eastern states were Elders Orson Hyde, Samuel H. Smith, Orson Pratt, and Lyman E. Johnson. The missionaries were very successful and organized branches in many of the

eastern states. In May 1835, the church sent the Twelve Apostles to the eastern states on their first mission. Apostle Parley P. Pratt arrived in New York City in July of 1837, and soon organized a branch and published the tract *Voice of Warning*. In 1843, Apostle Pratt began weekly publication of *The Prophet*. In 1853, Apostle Orson Pratt began publication of *The Seer*. In 1857, almost all missionaries were recalled due to the threat of the Utah War. Hardly any missionary work was done in the eastern states during the Civil War, which then were divided between other missions. The mission was reopened in 1893, but in 1897 Pennsylvania, Maryland, and West Virginia were placed under the jurisdiction of the Northern States Mission. (Jenson, *Encyclopedic History of the Church*, 211–14.)

15. The Northern States Mission included the states of Illinois, Indiana, Iowa, Michigan, Ohio, and Wisconsin. The Civil War prevented most missionary work from being done in the United States as many as ten years after its conclusion in 1865. However, Elder Bengt P. Wulffenstein labored in Minnesota from 1875 to 1877, and Elder William H. Palmer served in Michigan in 1876. The elders met with great success among Scandinavians, and in 1878 the Northwestern States Mission was created. Cyrus H. Wheelock was called as the mission's first president. In 1889, with the United States expanding, the name was changed to the Northern States Mission. In 1887, the headquarters of the mission moved to Council Bluffs, Iowa, and in 1896 moved to Chicago, Illinois. By 1919, all of the states, except for the original six, had been divided into other missions. (Jenson, *Encyclopedic History of the Church*, 593–94.)

"Around the World with Elders McKay and Cannon: One of a Series of Letters Recounting the Experiences, Grave and Gay, of Elders David O. McKay and Hugh J. Cannon, in their Trip to the Pacific Islands, the Orient and Perhaps Around the Globe," No. 1, *Deseret News*, January 15, 1921 (written December 18, 1920)

No. 2, *Deseret News*, February 19, 1921 (written January 17, 1921)

No. 3, *Deseret News*, March 12, 1921 (written February 3, 1921)

No. 4, *Deseret News*, March 19, 1921 (written February 25, 1921)

No. 5, *Deseret News*, April 2, 1921 (written March 28, 1921)

No. 6, *Deseret News*, April 30, 1921 (written April 7, 1921)

No. 7, *Deseret News*, June 25, 1921 (written April 16, 1921)

No. 8, *Deseret News*, June 25, 1921 (written April 27, 1921)

No. 9, *Deseret News*, July 2, 1921 (written May 6, 1921)

No. 10, *Deseret News*, August 13, 1921 (written June 6, 1921)

No. 11, *Deseret News*, September 3, 1921 (written June 12, 1921)

No. 12, *Deseret News*, September 3, 1921 (written June 15, 1921)

No. 13, *Deseret News*, September 10, 1921 (written June 17, 1921)

No. 14, *Deseret News*, September 17, 1921 (written July 4, 1921)

No. 15, *Deseret News*, September, 24, 1921 (written July 12, 1921)

No. 16, *Deseret News*, October 1, 1921 (written August 5, 1921)

No. 17, *Deseret News*, November 12, 1921 (written August 18, 1921)

No. 18, *Deseret News*, November 19, 1921 (written September 18, 1921)

No. 19, *Deseret News*, December 31, 1921 (written October 19, 1921)

No. 20, *Deseret News*, January 7, 1922 (written October 23, 1921)

No. 21, *Deseret News*, January 14, 1922 (written December 14, 1921)

No. 22, *Deseret News*, January 21, 1922

No. 23, *Deseret News*, January 28, 1922

No. 24, *Deseret News*, February 4, 1922

No. 25, *Deseret News*, February 11, 1922
No. 26, *Deseret News*, February 18, 1922
No. 27, *Deseret News*, February 25, 1922
No. 28, *Deseret News*, March 4, 1922
No. 29, *Deseret News*, March 11, 1922
No. 30, *Deseret News*, March 18, 1922
No. 31, *Deseret News*, March 25, 1922

List of Hugh J. Cannon's
Deseret News *"Around the*
World" Articles, 1920–1922

List of Elder David O. McKay's Diaries, Conference Notebooks, and Family Correspondence, 1920–1921

Diaries

Diary, holograph, December 1920 (David O. McKay Papers [DOMP], MS 668, Box 6, Folder 1, Manuscripts Division, J. Willard Marriott Library, University of Utah, Salt Lake City)

Diary, holograph, December 1920–January 1921 (DOMP, Box 6, Folder 2)

Diary, holograph, February 1921 (DOMP, Box 6, Folder 3)

Diary, holograph, February–April 1921 (DOMP, Box 6, Folder 4)

Diary, holograph, April–May 1921 (DOMP, Box 6, Folder 5)

Diary, holograph, May 1921 (DOMP, Box 6, Folder 6)

Diary, holograph, May–June 1921 (DOMP, Box 6, Folder 7)

Diary, holograph, June–July 1921 (DOMP, Box 6, Folder 8)

Diary, holograph, July 1921 (DOMP, Box 6, Folder 9)

Diary, holograph, October–December 1921 (DOMP, Box 6, Folder 10)

Diary, typescript, December 1920 (DOMP, Box 6, Folder 11)

Diary, typescript, December 1920–August 1921 (DOMP, Box 6, Folders 12–20)

Diary, typescript, March–September 1921 (DOMP, Box 7, Folders 1–7)

Conference Notebooks

Notebook, holograph, February 1920–May 1921 (DOMP, Box 12, Folder 1)

Notebook, holograph, January and May 1921 (DOMP, Box 12, Folder 2)

Family Correspondence

David O. McKay to David L. McKay (son), October 22, 1920
   (DOMP, Box 2, Folder 1)

David O. McKay to David L. McKay, October 29, 1920 (DOMP,
   Box 2, Folder 1)

David O. McKay to Emma Ray McKay (wife), December 7, 1920
   (DOMP, Box 1, Folder 4)

David O. McKay to David L. McKay, December 20, 1920 (DOMP,
   Box 2, Folder 1)

David O. McKay to Emma Ray McKay, December 24, 1920
   (DOMP, Box 1, Folder 4)

David O. McKay to Emma Ray McKay, December 27, 1920
   (DOMP, Box 1, Folder 4)

David O. McKay to Emma Ray McKay, January 2, 1921 (DOMP,
   Box 1, Folder 4)

David O. McKay to Emma Ray McKay, April 24, 1921 (DOMP,
   Box 1, Folder 4)

David O. McKay to Emma Ray McKay, May 4, 1921 (DOMP,
   Box 1, Folder 4)

David O. McKay to Lou Jean McKay (daughter), May 5, 1921
   (DOMP, Box 1, Folder 5)

David O. McKay to Emma Ray McKay, June 2, 1921 (DOMP,
   Box 1, Folder 5)

David O. McKay to Emma Ray McKay, July 4, 1921 (DOMP,
   Box 1, Folder 5)

David O. McKay to Emma Ray McKay, August 8, 1921 (DOMP,
   Box 1, Folder 5)

David O. McKay to Emma Ray McKay, September 13, 1921
   (DOMP, Box 1, Folder 6)

David O. McKay to Emma Ray McKay, September 15, 1921
   (DOMP, Box 1, Folder 6)

David O. McKay to Emma Ray McKay, October 24, 1921
   (DOMP, Box 1, Folder 6)

David O. McKay to Emma Ray McKay, November 8, 1921
   (DOMP, Box 1, Folder 6)

David O. McKay to Emma Ray McKay, November 9, 1921
   (DOMP, Box 1, Folder 6)

David O. McKay to David L. McKay, December 10, 1921 (DOMP,
   Box 2, Folder 4)

*List of Elder David O.
McKay's Diaries, Conference
Notebooks, and Family
Correspondence, 1920–1921*

Editor's Preface

1. For an expanded definition of the Pacific, see Matt K. Matsuda, "AHR Forum: The Pacific," *American Historical Review* 111 (June 2006): 770. See also Arrell Morgan Gibson and John S. Whitehead, *Yankees in Paradise: The Pacific Basin Frontier* (Albuquerque: University of New Mexico Press, 1993).
2. For a historical and bibliographical survey of early Mormonism in the Pacific basin frontier, see Reid L. Neilson and Laurie F. Maffly-Kipp, "Nineteenth-century Mormonism and the Pacific Basin Frontier: An Introduction," in *Proclamation to the People: Nineteenth-century Mormonism and the Pacific Basin Frontier*, ed. Laurie F. Maffly-Kipp and Reid L. Neilson (Salt Lake City: University of Utah Press, 2008), 3–20.
3. Hugh J. Cannon, "Around-the-World Travels of David O. McKay and Hugh J. Cannon," ca. 1925, typescript, 1, microfilm, Church History Library, The Church of Jesus Christ of Latter-day Saints, Salt Lake City, Utah.
4. Gregory A. Prince and William Robert Wright, *David O. McKay and the Rise of Modern Mormonism* (Salt Lake City: University of Utah Press, 2005), 358–59.
5. Mary Jane Woodger, "David O. McKay," in *Encyclopedia of Latter-day Saint History*, ed. Arnold K. Garr, Donald Q. Cannon, and Richard O. Cowan (Salt Lake City: Deseret Book, 2000), 726–27; and Prince and Wright, *David O. McKay and the Rise of Modern Mormonism*, 358–59.
6. Andrew Jenson, *Latter-day Saint Biographical Encyclopedia: A Compilation of Biographical Sketches of Prominent Men and Women in The Church of Jesus Christ of Latter-day Saints*, 4 vols. (Salt Lake City: Andrew Jenson History, 1901–36), 4:233, 507. See also Eleanor Knowles, *Deseret Book Company: 125 Years of Inspiration, Information, and Ideas* (Salt Lake City: Deseret Book, 1991), 1–10, 45.
7. Cannon, "Around-the-World Travels," 213.
8. Hugh J. Cannon, *David O. McKay Around the World: An Apostolic Mission, Prelude to Church Globalization* (Provo, Utah: Spring Creek, 2005), 236.
9. "The Death of Hugh J. Cannon," *Deseret News*, October 6, 1931, 1–2; and "Church Heads Pay Tribute to Hugh J. Cannon," *Deseret News*, October 9, 1931, 2; and Cannon, *David O. McKay Around the World*, xiii.

10. George Richards Cannon, "A Son's Tribute to the Author," in Cannon, *David O. McKay Around the World*, 227–32.

11. Knowles, *Deseret Book Company*, 79–80.

12. For an overview of post–World War II LDS expansion in Asia, see Donald Q. Cannon and Richard O. Cowan, *Unto Every Nation: Gospel Light Reaches Every Land* (Salt Lake City: Deseret Book, 2003), 322–91.

13. A. Hamer Reiser to David O. McKay, November 6, 1951, copy in editor's possession. See also A. Hamer Reiser to George Richards Cannon, November 6, 1951, copy in editor's possession.

14. George R. Cannon to A. Hamer Reiser, November 14, 1951, copy in editor's possession.

15. George R. Cannon to David O. McKay, November 16, 1951, copy in editor's possession.

16. David O. McKay to George R. Cannon, December 3, 1951, copy in editor's possession, emphasis added.

17. George R. Cannon to A. Hamer Reiser, December 13, 1951, copy in editor's possession.

18. George R. Cannon to A. Hamer Reiser, February 9, 1952, copy in editor's possession.

19. A. Hamer Reiser to George R. Cannon, February 15, 1952, copy in editor's possession.

20. The typescript microfilm is currently cataloged as MS 7351, Church History Library.

21. I checked the published indexes for the *Instructor, Improvement Era*, and the *Church News*.

22. Cannon, *David O. McKay Around the World*. See *Teachings of Presidents of the Church: David O. McKay* (Salt Lake City: The Church of Jesus Christ of Latter-day Saints, 2003).

23. Prince and Wright, *David O. McKay and the Rise of Modern Mormonism*; and Mary Jane Woodger, ed., *Heart Petals: The Personal Correspondence of David Oman McKay to Emma Ray McKay* (Salt Lake City: University of Utah Press, 2005).

24. In his editorial procedures for the posthumous publication of Brigham H. Roberts's typescript opus *The Truth, The Way, The Life*, editor John W. Welch writes: "Insignificant differences that Roberts would surely have wanted the printer and proofreader to catch have been corrected in this edition without any special notation. . . . We trust that if any other such errors had been called to his attention, Roberts would have wanted them noted and corrected." Because Cannon also died, leaving a largely polished book manuscript for publication, I likewise assume that he would have felt the same way. See B. H. Roberts, *The Truth, The Way, The Life: An Elementary Treatise on Theology*, ed. John W. Welch (Provo, Utah: Brigham Young University Studies, 1994), cc–ccv.

25. I have benefited greatly from the editorial guidelines in Dean C. Jessee, ed. and comp., *The Personal Writings of Joseph Smith* (1984; reprint, Salt Lake City: Deseret Book, 2002), xix–xxi; and Jan Shipps and John W. Welch, eds., *The Journals of William E. McLellin, 1831–1836* (Urbana: University of Illinois Press, 1994), xv–xx.

26. See Shipps and Welch, *The Journals of William E. McLellin*, 415.

27. David O. McKay, Diaries (DOMD), 1920–21, David O. McKay Papers (DOMP), MS 668, Manuscripts Division, J. Willard Marriott Library, University of Utah, Salt Lake City.

28. David O. McKay, Correspondence (DOMC), 1920–21, David O. McKay Papers (DOMP), MS 668, Manuscripts Division, J. Willard Marriott Library, University of Utah, Salt Lake City.
29. David O. McKay, Scrapbooks (DOMS), 215 volumes with assorted contents and no pagination, MS 4640, Church History Library.
30. Each of McKay's three oldest children produced a volume of their father's history. See David Lawrence McKay, *My Father, David O. McKay*, ed. Lavina Fielding Anderson (Salt Lake City: Deseret Book, 1989); Llewelyn R. McKay, comp., *Home Memories of President David O. McKay* (Salt Lake City: Deseret Book, 1959); and Jeanette McKay Morrell, *Highlights in the Life of President David O. McKay* (Salt Lake City: Deseret Book, 1966). McKay's longtime personal secretary (1935–1970) also compiled a collection of his writings. See Clare Middlemiss, comp., *Cherished Experiences from the Writings of President David O. McKay* (Salt Lake City: Deseret Book, 1955). A more recent McKay biographer collected the church president's teachings on a variety of gospel subjects. See Mary Jane Woodger, comp., *The Teachings of David O. McKay* (Salt Lake City: Deseret Book, 2004). See also Mary Jane Woodger, *David O. McKay: Beloved Prophet* (American Fork, Utah: Covenant Communications, 2004).
31. A. Hamer Reiser to David O. McKay, November 6, 1951, copy in editor's possession.

Introduction

1. "Plan Visit to Island Missions," *Deseret News*, October 23, 1920.
2. Hugh J. Cannon, "Around-the-World Travels of David O. McKay and Hugh J. Cannon," ca. 1925, typescript, 213, microfilm, Church History Library, The Church of Jesus Christ of Latter-day Saints, Salt Lake City, Utah.
3. Cannon, "Around-the-World Travels," 4.
4. See Jan Shipps, *Mormonism: The Story of a New Religious Tradition* (Urbana: University of Illinois Press, 1985), 53–65; and John W. Welch, "The Acts of the Apostle William E. McLellin," in *The Journals of William E. McLellin, 1831–1836*, ed. Jan Shipps and John W. Welch (Urbana: University of Illinois Press, 1994), 13–26.
5. See Richard O. Cowan, "An Apostle in Oceania: Elder David O. McKay's 1921 Trip around the Pacific," in *Pioneers in the Pacific: Memory, History, and Cultural Identity among the Latter-day Saints*, ed. Grant Underwood (Provo, Utah: Religious Studies Center, Brigham Young University, 2005), 189–200; Mary Jane Woodger, *David O. McKay: Beloved Prophet* (American Fork, Utah: Covenant Communications, 2004), chapter 6; David Lawrence McKay, *My Father, David O. McKay*, ed. Lavina Fielding Anderson (Salt Lake City: Deseret Book, 1989), chapter 7; and Francis M. Gibbons, *David O. McKay: Apostle to the World, Prophet of God* (Salt Lake City: Deseret Book, 1986), chapter 7.
6. Joseph H. Stimpson to Lafayette C. Lee, February 18, 1919, Japan Mission Outgoing Letters, Church History Library.
7. Joseph H. Stimpson to Harold G. Reynolds, January 31, 1919, Japan Mission Outgoing Letters, Church History Library.

8. Understaffed mission presidents in Japan begged church leaders in Utah for more elders and sisters, especially during the last decade of the mission's existence. Some have suggested that World War I explains why church leaders sent so few elders and sisters to Japan during the second decade of the twentieth century. However, even before World War I, General Authorities allocated Japan the fewest resources of any mission in the world. In the five years (1910–1914) leading up to World War I, church leaders called 4,354 missionaries to serve throughout the world. Of these missionaries, 2,312 (53 percent) served in the United States and Canada, 1,599 (37 percent) labored in Europe, 372 (9 percent) evangelized in Pacific-Asia (excluding Japan), 30 (0.7 percent) missionized in South Africa, 20 (0.5 percent) made their way to Latin America, while only 21 (0.5 percent) worked in Japan. Even during World War I, when missionaries were recalled from Europe, the numbers in Japan did not improve significantly. Nearly three thousand LDS elders and sisters served during the Great War (1914–1918). This was a decrease of only 32 percent globally compared to the previous period (1910–1914). From 1915 to 1919, 2,252 (76 percent) men and women evangelized in the United States and Canada, 389 (13 percent) served in Europe, 294 (10 percent) labored in the Pacific basin (excluding Japan), 6 (0.2 percent) missionized in Latin America, and 20 (0.7 percent) worked in South Africa. This left only 18 (0.6 percent) to evangelize in Japan. See Gordon Irving, *Numerical Strength and Geographical Distribution of the LDS Missionary Force, 1830–1974* (Salt Lake City: Historical Department of The Church of Jesus Christ of Latter-day Saints, 1975), 16–18. Clearly missionaries were available for assignment in Japan, but LDS officials sent them elsewhere, despite the fact they had pulled out missionaries from Europe by October 1914. Moreover, by 1917 the British government was withholding travel visas from Americans, including LDS missionaries, trying to enter Australia and New Zealand, as well as making it additionally hard for elders and sisters to enter Great Britain after April 1917. In contrast, Japan never closed its borders or limited its entry visas to LDS missionaries: there was no need. See Thomas G. Alexander, *Mormonism in Transition: A History of the Latter-day Saints, 1890–1930* (Urbana: University of Illinois Press, 1986), 232.

9. Years earlier Stimpson had invited Heber J. Grant, then president of the Quorum of the Twelve Apostles, to visit Japan following their attendance at the dedication of the Hawaii Temple. "We understand that there will be a number of the Authorities of the church coming to Hawaii in the near future to attend the dedication of the new temple there. I do not know the convenience of yourself or any of the other Brethren but if it is possible we would appreciate a visit, preferable from you, and if it be impossible for you from some other one of the Apostles or General Authorities. We are so far away from headquarters that we almost feel that we are forgotten." Joseph H. Stimpson to Heber J. Grant, February 22, 1917, Japan Mission Outgoing Letters, Church History Library.

10. Joseph H. Stimpson to Presiding Bishopric, January 29, 1920, Japan Mission Outgoing Letters, Church History Library.

11. Joseph H. Stimpson to David O. McKay, March 18, 1920, Japan Mission Outgoing Letters, Church History Library.

12. Ibid.

13. Joseph H. Stimpson to Heber J. Grant, June 10, 1920, Japan Mission Outgoing Letters, Church History Library.

14. First Presidency to Joseph H. Stimpson, July 20, 1920, Japan Mission Incoming Letters, Church History Library.

15. Although many observers of Mormon history are aware of the tremendous evangelistic outreach of the LDS Church, few are alert to the historical variety of missionary assignments, including similar fact-finding expeditions. During the second half of the nineteenth century, for instance, President Brigham Young and other church leaders living in the Great Basin Desert called hundreds of families and individuals on colonizing missions throughout Utah, Idaho, Wyoming, Nevada, Arizona, and California, and even north to Canada and south to Mexico. Notable settlement assignments included the Carson Valley (Nevada), Cotton Mission (southern Utah), Elk Mountain (Moab, Utah), Iron Mission (Cedar City, Utah), Las Vegas (Nevada), Muddy (Nevada), Salmon River (Idaho), San Juan (Utah), and Santa Clara (Indian). General authorities also called men and women as genealogical missionaries to gather family and temple records, lumber missionaries to harvest wood, mining missionaries to search for gold in northern California and iron in southern Utah, rag missionaries to aid in paper production, and even art missionaries to study European painting techniques in preparation for temple mural painting. Furthermore, during the twentieth century, church leaders called elders and sisters as humanitarian, healthcare, educational, and building missionaries to serve primarily beyond the borders of North America. See David J. Whittaker, "Mormon Missiology: An Introduction and Guide to the Sources," in *Disciple as Witness: Essays on Latter-day Saint History and Doctrine in Honor of Richard Lloyd Anderson*, ed. Stephen D. Ricks, Donald W. Parry, and Andrew H. Hedges (Provo, Utah: Foundation for Ancient Research and Mormon Studies, Brigham Young University, 2000) 459–538.

16. Andrew Jenson, *Autobiography of Andrew Jenson* (Salt Lake City: Deseret News Press, 1938), 386–87. The South Africa and India missions were closed at this point and the Japan Mission would not be opened until 1901.

17. Minutes of the Quorum of the Twelve Apostles, April 1, 1896, Anthon H. Lund Collection, typescript in D. Michael Quinn Papers, Yale University Library. I am grateful to Jed Woodworth for bringing this source to my attention.

18. Ronald W. Walker, "Strangers in a Strange Land: Heber J. Grant and the Opening of the Japanese Mission," in *Taking the Gospel to the Japanese, 1901–1924*, ed. Reid L. Neilson and Van C. Gessel (Provo, Utah: Brigham Young University Press, 2006), 148; and Gregory A. Prince and William Robert Wright, *David O. McKay and the Rise of Modern Mormonism* (Salt Lake City: University of Utah Press, 2005), 358.

19. See Reid L. Neilson, "Alma O. Taylor's Fact-Finding Mission to China," *BYU Studies* 40, no. 1 (2001): 177–203.

20. "Two Church Workers will Tour Missions of Pacific Islands," *Deseret News*, October 15, 1920, 5.

21. First Presidency to Joseph H. Stimpson, October 15, 1920, Japan Mission Incoming Letters, Church History Library.

22. Stimpson informed his missionaries of McKay's forthcoming visit. "This letter confirms the reports that have been coming this way for some time," he exclaimed. "It means the beginning of a new era of prosperity for the mission. The visit of the brethren of the general authorities is something I have been asking for and praying for for some time." Joseph H. Stimpson to the Missionaries Laboring in Japan, November 23, 1920, Japan Mission Outgoing Letters, Church History Library.

23. Cannon, "Around-the-World Travels," 1.

24. Thomas A. Tweed, *Crossings and Dwellings: A Theory of Religion* (Cambridge, Mass.: Harvard University Press, 2006), 124, 127.

25. See James B. Allen, "Technology and the Church: A Steady Revolution," in *2007 Church Almanac* (Salt Lake City: Deseret Morning News, 2006), 118–58.

26. Cannon, "Around-the-World Travels," 3.

27. Tweed, *Crossings and Dwellings*, 125.

28. Cannon, "Around-the-World Travels," 213.

29. Tweed, *Crossings and Dwellings*, 125.

30. Cannon, "Around-the-World Travels," 12–13.

31. Ibid., 26.

32. Ibid., 20–21.

33. Ibid., 33.

34. Ibid., 35.

35. Ibid., 45.

36. Ibid., 46.

37. Ibid., 132.

38. Ibid., 133.

39. Ibid., 167.

40. Ibid., 187.

41. Ibid.

42. Cannon, "Around-the-World Travels," 83–84.

43. Tweed, *Crossing and Dwelling*, 125–27.

44. Cannon, "Around-the-World Travels," 79.

45. Ibid., 79–80.

46. Ibid., 168–69.

47. Ibid., 213.

48. See Prince and Wright, "An International Church," in *David O. McKay and the Rise of Modern Mormonism*, 358–79.

49. Cannon, "Around-the-World Travels," 1.

Chapter 1

1. Henry Drummond, *The Greatest Thing in the World* (New York: Thomas Y. Crowell, 1888), 7. Drummond (1851–1897) was a Scottish clergyman and writer.

2. Samuel Taylor Coleridge (1772–1834), English poet and romanticist.

3. *The Works of Samuel Taylor Coleridge, Prose and Verse. Complete in One Volume* (Philadelphia, Pa.: Thomas, Cowperthwait, 1840), 216.

4. An island of Indonesia located southeast of Sumatra.

5. A high-ranking priesthood leader ordained by the laying on of hands by the First Presidency and Quorum of the Twelve Apostles.

NOTES TO PAGES XXIV–2

6. A priesthood ordinance sanctioning a church member to serve in a specific ecclesiastical responsibility.

7. See Hebrews 5:4.

8. In 1820 Joseph Smith prayed and experienced a theophany in a grove of trees in the vicinity of Palmyra, New York. See Joseph Smith— History 1:7–20.

9. Second-highest governing body in the church.

10. Heber Jeddy Grant (1856–1945), born on November 22, 1856, at Salt Lake City, Utah. Seventh president of the church, apostle, business- man, and mission president. Died on May 14, 1945, at Salt Lake City, Utah.

11. Highest governing body in the church.

12. David Oman McKay (1873–1970), born on September 8, 1873, at Huntsville, Utah. Ninth president of the church, apostle, educator, church commissioner of education, and missionary. Died on Janu- ary 18, 1970, at Salt Lake City, Utah.

13. Hugh Jenne Cannon (1870–1931), born on January 19, 1870, at Salt Lake City, Utah. Missionary, publisher, stake president, member of the General Board of the Sunday Schools and Young Men's Mutual Improvement Association. Died on October 6, 1931, at Salt Lake City, Utah.

14. One of Jesus Christ's original twelve apostles in Palestine.

15. Port city on New Zealand's North Island.

16. Joseph Wilford Booth (1866–1928), born on August 14, 1866, at Alpine, Utah. Set apart as president of the Armenian Mission on Septem- ber 14, 1921. Died on September 5, 1928, at Aleppo, Syria.

17. Port capital of Lebanon.

18. Town in eastern Lebanon located north of Damascus.

19. City in northern Syria.

20. Temple of Baalshamin originally constructed in AD 17.

21. Biblical area of Palestine.

22. Philemon C. Merrill (1820–1904), born on November 12, 1820, at Byron, New York. Missionary and member of the Mormon Battalion. Died on September 15, 1904, at Thatcher, Arizona.

23. Joseph Smith Jr. (1805–1844), born on December 23, 1805, at Sharon, Vermont. Founding prophet of the church, translator of the Book of Mormon, and builder of cities. Died on June 27, 1844, at Carthage, Illinois.

24. See George Q. Cannon, *The Life of Joseph Smith, the Prophet* (Salt Lake City: Juvenile Instructor Office, 1888), 449–51.

25. Prophet-leader and founder of the Nephite civilization in the Book of Mormon.

26. See 1 Nephi 3:7; and 1 Nephi 17:3.

27. See Doctrine and Covenants 1:14.

28. Title given to all members of the First Presidency and Quorum of the Twelve Apostles.

Chapter 2

1. Thomas Carlyle, *The Works of Thomas Carlyle (Complete): Critical and Miscellaneous Essays Collected and Republished*, volume 15 (New York:

Peter Fenelon Collier, 1897), 323. Carlyle (1795–1881) was a Scottish essayist.

2. Sacred structure where sacred rituals are performed for both the living and dead in the heart of Salt Lake City.
3. Anthon Hendrik Lund (1844–1921), born on May 15, 1844, at Aalborg, Denmark. Member of the First Presidency, apostle, mission president, and missionary. Died on March 2, 1921, at Salt Lake City, Utah.
4. Emma Ray McKay (1877–1970), born on January 23, 1877, at Salt Lake City, Utah. Her husband, David O. McKay, was called on a fact-finding mission around the world in 1920. Died on November 14, 1970, at Salt Lake City, Utah.
5. Robert Riggs McKay (1920–living).
6. Sarah Richards Cannon (1889–1988), born on July 13, 1889, at Tooele, Utah. Her husband, Hugh Jenne Cannon, was called to accompany David O. McKay on a fact-finding missionary mission around the world in 1920. Died on March 27, 1988, at Bountiful, Utah.
7. Alice Richards (1920–living).
8. Port city in northwestern Oregon, United States.
9. City in southeastern Idaho, United States.
10. Frederick Augustus Caine (1884–1929), born on March 24, 1884, at Coalville, Utah. Set apart as a missionary to Japan on June 26, 1902, and returned on April 26, 1910. Died on August 14, 1929, at Idaho Falls, Idaho.
11. Ecclesiastical unit similar to a Catholic diocese in southeastern Idaho, United States.
12. Ecclesiastical unit similar to a Catholic parish.
13. Heber Charles Iverson (1868–1948), born on July 1, 1868, at Salt Lake City, Utah. Set apart as a missionary to Northwestern States on April 6, 1919, and returned on June 29, 1922. Died on October 17, 1948, at Salt Lake City, Utah.
14. Anna Bertha Erickson Iverson (1868–1954).
15. Port city in western Washington, United States.
16. William Stephen Maxwell (1899–1974), born on July 14, 1899, at Salt Lake City, Utah. Set apart as a missionary to Northwestern States on June 10, 1919, and returned on July 18, 1921. Died on June 16, 1974, at Salt Lake City, Utah.
17. Port city in northwestern Washington, United States.
18. Port city in southwestern British Columbia, Canada.
19. Stephen Markham Dudley (1900–1973), born on July 20, 1900, at Jensen, Utah. Set apart as a missionary to Washington on August 14, 1918, and returned on August 26, 1920. Died on September 18, 1973, at Provo, Utah.
20. Stephen Markham (1800–1878), born on February 9, 1800, at Avon, New York. Early Latter-day Saint convert and Utah pioneer. Died on March 10, 1878, at Spanish Fork, Utah.
21. City on Mississippi River in western Illinois, United States.
22. City where Joseph Smith was murdered near Quincy, Illinois, United States.
23. The June 1844 assassinations of Joseph and Hyman Smith in the Liberty Jail, Carthage, Illinois.
24. Annie Elizabeth Bingham Dudley (1879–1961).
25. General priesthood leaders of the church.
26. Confucius (551–479 BC), Chinese philosopher.

27. Book of ancient American Christian scripture translated and published by Joseph Smith.
28. See Alma 39:5.
29. Collection of revelations received by Joseph Smith and his prophetic successors accepted as scripture by Latter-day Saints.
30. See Doctrine and Covenants 121:45–46.
31. Serious church disciplinary action that results in loss of church membership.
32. Port city in southeastern Honshu, Japan.
33. Port city in western California, United States.
34. Islands in southwestern Alaska, United States.
35. See Jonah 1–2.
36. Thomas Jefferson (1743–1826), American statesman, third president of the United States.
37. The left side of a ship looking frontward.
38. The right side of a ship looking frontward.
39. David O. McKay to Stephen, George, and Adam Bennion as transcribed in McKay, Diary, December 17, 1920.

Chapter 3

1. Horace Gregory and Marya Zaturenska, eds., *A History of American Poetry, 1900–1940* (New York: Harcourt, Brace, 1946), 53. Edwin Markham (1852–1940) was an American poet.
2. The line of longitude on the opposite side of the globe from the Prime Meridian.
3. Highest mountain in Japan (Mount Fuji).
4. Mountain system in south central Europe.
5. The countries of Asia generally.
6. A two-wheeled vehicle pulled by one person.
7. A traditional long robe worn as an outer garment.
8. Wooden clogs worn outside.
9. Japanese money.
10. Weekly church classes designed to teach church doctrine. McKay was called as church commissioner of education in 1919.
11. Capital city in southeastern Honshu, Japan.

Chapter 4

1. *The Dialogues of Plato*, trans. B. Jowett (Oxford: Clarendon Press, 1875), 195.
2. See appendix 1.
3. Joseph Henry Stimpson (1885–1964), born on June 12, 1885, at Riverdale, Utah. Set apart as mission president to Japan on February 15, 1915, and returned on March 10, 1921. Died on April 22, 1964, at Salt Lake City, Utah.
4. Joseph Allen (b. August 13, 1915), William Eldon (b. November 6, 1917), and Inez Ei (b. June 11, 1919).
5. Mary Emmeline Stimpson (1894–1971), born on March 11, 1894, at Riverdale, Utah. Set apart as a missionary to Japan on February 15,

1915, and returned on March 10, 1921. Died on May 4, 1971, at Salt Lake City, Utah.

6. For a detailed account of the holiday festivities, see David O. McKay, "Christmas in Tokyo," *Juvenile Instructor* 56 (March 1921): 112–15.

7. City in south central Honshu, Japan.

8. Port city in southern Honshu, Japan.

9. Island in northern Japan.

10. Smallest LDS ecclesiastical unit.

11. City in central Honshu, Japan.

12. McKay, Diary, December 27, 1920:

"Until you have seen Nikko, never say splendid!" is the interpretation of a common Japanese expression regarding this beautiful place; and I accept it as being most applicable.

I have never seen a more beautifully interesting spot, nor can I imagine any other where may be combined in such an array of resplendent beauty the grandeur and sublimity of mountain scenery, the skill of exquisite art in carving and painting, and the mystic worship of past ages!

13. Evergreen tree of the pine family.

14. McKay, Diary, December 29, 1920:

Courtesy and politeness are inborn in the Japanese people. It is my opinion that they are excelled in these qualities by no other people on earth. Their politeness is not a veneer, either; it is a spontaneous expression of the desire to serve as well as to please. Time and again we have been astonished at the unexpected regard for our comfort and convenience shown by these people.

15. Christian Daniel Fjeldsted (1829–1905), born on February 20, 1829, at Copenhagen, Denmark. One of the first seven presidents of the Quorum of the Seventy. Died on December 23, 1905, at Salt Lake City, Utah.

16. Priesthood leaders called to support the First Presidency and Quorum of the Twelve Apostles.

17. Prestigious private university in Tokyo, Japan.

18. McKay, Diary, January 5, 1921:

We have observed, however, that no man ever gives up his seat in a street car to a woman, unless it be an old woman, or a woman with a baby on her back or carrying bundles. No aged person is ever permitted to stand.

The first time Bro. Cannon and I were given seats, we were carrying satchels, and the kindness of the gentlemen who stood up for us made us deeply grateful. The next time, we concluded it was because we were foreigners, and we were even more grateful; but about the fifth or sixth time, it suddenly dawned on me that these people were giving us seats because they thought us two old men! It seems that Bro. Cannon had surmised as much before, because when I said,

"Do you know, I believe I understand why these men give us their seats in the car?" Bro. Cannon smiled and said,

"Has it just dawned on you?" And then for his personal comfort only, he added:

"And I've noticed that you've always been the first to be given consideration."

Well, though this realization somewhat lowered my appreciation of the kindness, I still maintain that the Japanese are second to none in true courtesy and hospitality.

19. McKay, Diary, January 5, 1921:

Perhaps the first deep impression I received about Japan as a nation was the strength and virility of men, women, and children on every hand. Among the laboring class, men work like animals. They pull jinrikishas, and run for several miles, some even running forty miles a day. They are sturdy, husky fellows, enured to exposure, and capable of strong endurance.

Then there are the laborers who pull heavily loaded carts, exerting sometimes a strength that seems entirely beyond them. But on they toil, either pulling or pushing hour after hour, and day after day; and through it all keeping up a vigor that attests a strong vitality.

Among this class, too, the women work side by side with the men, and bear their babies meanwhile. These women look pretty haggard to me and yet they must possess a wonderful virility to endure such hardships.

The soldiers and policemen are nearly all fine specimens of physical manhood—short in stature, it is true, but well-proportioned, alert, keen well-disciplined.

The jui jitsu men are world famed.

And finally the babies! Heavens, what they can endure! Cuddled on their mother's backs, they seem comfortable enough, but when they begin to run around, they are bare-legged and bare-footed in the coldest weather. Indeed, they object to having their feet covered. I have heard a two-year-old youngster yell until his mother removed his slipper-like stockings and let him down bare-footed on the cold oilcloth covering the floor, and I was none too warm with my overcoat on! I saw one baby's bare feet sticking out behind his mother's back during a winter blizzard in Aomori! Kiddies were barefooted, excepting the sandal, when snow covered the ground!

That Japan is a growing nation, and a nation of men and women capable of physical endurance, and withal possessing a keenness of intellect and sturdiness of character that puts them at least on an equality with other civilized peoples, there can be no doubt in the minds of those who visit among them.

20. Myrl Leroy Bodily (1898–1988), born on October 27, 1898, at Fairview, Idaho. Set apart as a missionary to Japan on May 13, 1917, and returned on May 21, 1921. Died on May 12, 1988, at Preston, Idaho.

21. Louring Arthur Whittaker (1897–1944), born on May 17, 1897, at Circleville, Utah. Set apart as a missionary to Japan on November 28, 1917, and returned on February 24, 1922. Died on January 21, 1944, at Richfield, Utah.

22. Owen McGary (1896–1989), born on July 26, 1896, at Taylorsville, Utah. Set apart as a missionary to Japan on March 13, 1917, and returned on May 31, 1921. Died on August 26, 1989, at Shelley, Idaho.

23. Irwin Todd Hicken (1898–1992), born on November 8, 1898, at Heber City, Utah. Set apart as a missionary to Japan on April 23, 1920, and returned on April 21, 1924. Died on November 28, 1992, at Heber City, Utah.

24. Joseph Sterling Pyne (1895–1972), born on December 23, 1895, at Provo, Utah. Set apart as a missionary to Japan on November 28, 1917, and returned on March 1, 1922. Died in October 1972, at Carmel, California.
25. Deloss Watson Holley (1898–1985), born on November 3, 1898, at Slaterville, Utah. Set apart as a missionary to Japan on April 23, 1920, and returned on January 1, 1924. Died on November 16, 1985, at Ogden, Utah.
26. Alma Howard Jensen (1898–1988), born on April 3, 1898, at Brigham City, Utah. Set apart as a missionary to Japan on April 23, 1920, and returned on April 21, 1924. Died on April 13, 1988.
27. City in Honshu east of Osaka, Japan.
28. A range horse.
29. Port city in southwestern Honshu, Japan.
30. Port city in southeastern Korea (Pusan).
31. "Lead, Kindly Light," *Hymns of The Church of Jesus Christ of Latter-day Saints* (Salt Lake City: The Church of Jesus Christ of Latter-day Saints, 1985), no. 97.

Chapter 5

1. Formal consecration of something through prayer.
2. For a history of the 1853 LDS mission to Hong Kong, see R. Lanier Britsch, "Church Beginnings in China," *BYU Studies* 10, No. 2 (Winter 1970): 169.
3. Region in northeastern China.
4. McKay, Diary, January 6, 1921:

   Our first impression is that the Japanese are a far superior people to the Koreans, and that it is fortunate for the country that the former have control. The first thing I did was to hunt a barber shop and succeeded in finding what appeared to be a fairly respectable one. The Jap running it seemed to be exceptionally short of stature, and their lamps and other appliances attached to the ceiling were hung for their convenience. I created surprise when I entered, but when my head came in contact with a globe, the chatter, laughter, and exclamations were vociferous! The chair I occupied could not be raised and lowered, so I had to screw myself down in it so the little fellow could cut my hair conveniently. True to the Japanese custom of doing everything backward, he started to cut on the top first, but on the whole made a very good job of it. He then gave me a shampoo. Evidently that operation is his forte! Shaving came next. I could only indicate what I wanted and then trust to fate for the outcome. His shaving of the face was about the same as that of any other barber, except that several times he pushed the razor instead of pulling it; but when he started to shave my ears, I began to get interested. I submitted, being determined to accept everything he had to offer. But, having finished my ears, when he lathered my nose and shaved it, I concluded he had gone far enough! What if he took my eyebrows, as I saw another barber take off a Japanese maiden's! I had permitted him to shave below my eyes but was prepared to jump if he started above. But he was satisfied with having shaved my face, my neck, my nose, my ears, and so was I!

The whole operation took nearly one hour and a half and cost one yen (50 cents) which I concluded from the first price he indicated with his fingers was just 33⅓ percent more than he charged his fellow-countrymen! I had been given full value for my yen!

5. Town on Gulf of Liaodong, China.

6. A defensive wall constructed between China and Mongolia.

7. Capital city of China.

8. McKay, Diary, January 8, 1921:

Having had no opportunity to secure accommodations ahead, we found ourselves in, what appeared to be in the darkness, and what undoubtedly it is, the strangest city in the world. Relying upon the hope that the ticket agent could understand a little English, we followed the crowd along the platform to the station. In vain we sought for some officials who could tell us where to go, or at least could tell where to check our luggage. Despairing in this, we walked from one side to the other, and from the other side back, all the while followed by a pack of jabbering Coolies.

I had proposed that one of us stay in the waiting room while the other secured rooms in a reasonably priced hotel. We knew the names of two, but preferred not to go to either with our luggage until we knew the price of each.

But Bro. Cannon thought we had better check the baggage, and both stay together. And he was right!

Finding no check room, I said, "Come on, let's get out of this; maybe we can find a hotel near here!"

What we met and saw, and heard in front of that station, I shall never forget! Human beings swarming and squirming, horns blowing, gongs ringing, and human voices yelling! As soon as we moved from the station, it seemed to me that this whole human avalanche moved toward us! Jinrikisha men came on the walk directly across our path. We wabbled along for perhaps a hundred yards, and then realizing how hopeless it would be for us to think of finding a hotel amidst such a bedlam, we sat in a rikisha each and said "hotel."

9. See Matthew 7:6.

10. Walled enclosure containing the Imperial Palace in Beijing, China.

11. Charles William Penrose (1832–1925), born on February 4, 1832, at London, England. Member of the First Presidency, apostle, mission president, and missionary. Died on May 16, 1925, at Salt Lake City, Utah.

12. Priesthood office that oversees all church patriarchs. Now defunct.

13. A presiding council largely in charge of temporal affairs of the LDS Church.

14. For a history of the 1921 apostolic dedication of China, see Hugh J. Cannon, "The Land of China Dedicated," *Juvenile Instructor* 56 (March 1921): 115–17.

15. McKay, Diary, January 16, 1921:

I. *China is a disintegrating nation*. Faded is the glory of her past, impotent, the power of her once mighty government!

The art and splendor of her picturesque temples, like the old Wall, are permitted to go to decay; so is the manhood and the womanhood of the nation.

China needs another Confucius, another Kubla Khan, or a Roosevelt to lead and inspire the young Chinese who are glimpsing the light.

II. *China is a mercenary nation.* Everybody's sole aim, seemingly, is to get money; and the system of "squeezing," operating from the central government to the provinces, and then from the Mandarins down through the various castes and classes until the poor wretched producer who cannot squeeze is crushed hopelessly and sometimes lifelessly to the ground.

Before China can redeem herself, this mercenary spirit must be supplanted by the spirit of Loyalty and Unity. Several provinces, but *One* China and one *Language.*

III. *China is a land of Beggars and Parasites!* If there are more hideous, loathsome creatures to be found on the globe than we have seen in Peking, in Tien Tsin, or even in Shanghai, I hope I may avoid the sight of them.

Beggars here are organized, with a King of Beggars at their head. Individuals even resort to self-mutilation in order to prey more successfully on the sympathies of the public.

How indifferent and careless and impotent that government which permits such human parasites to ply their trade on every street, and near every public space.

IV. *China appears to be made up of not a religious but a superstitious people.* Their so-called religion is a mixture of Taoism, Confucianism, and Buddhism. This will not be an insurmountable obstacle in their way of accepting the Gospel, once their superstition regarding evil spirits can be overcome.

V. *The Chinese are a polite, courteous people.* This admirable trait is almost as evident among the better classes as it is among the Japanese. Nice distinctions and considerations in deportment show a sense of true refinement. . . .

VI. *The Chinese nation needs the friendship and protection of the United States*; and I hope Old Glory may ever be seen waving in the breeze at every principal port, and in all the principal cities of the Celestial Empire, now the struggling young Republic of China.

16. For a history of the LDS evangelization of the Chinese diaspora in the Pacific, see Russell T. Clement and Sheng-Luen Tsai, "East Wind to Hawai'i: Contributions and History of Chinese and Japanese Mormons in Hawaii," in *Voyages of Faith: Explorations in Mormon Pacific History*, ed. Grant Underwood (Provo, Utah: Brigham Young University Press, 2000), 89–106.

Chapter 6

1. Ralph Waldo Emerson, *Ralph Waldo Emerson*, ed. Oliver Wendell Holmes (Cambridge: Riverside Press, 1884), 122. The epigraph taken from Emerson's famous Harvard Divinity School address should read: "The stationariness of religion; the assumption that the age of inspiration is past, that the Bible is closed; the fear of degrading the character of Jesus by representing him as a man; indicate with sufficient clearness the falsehood of our theology." Emerson (1803–1882) was an American essayist and leading transcendentalist.

2. Charles Richard Crane (1858–1929), American Arabist and U.S. ambassador to China.

3. For a similar comment by an American diplomat in Japan, see Sandra T. Caruthers, "Anodyne for Expansion: Meiji Japan, the Mormons, and Charles LeGendre," *Pacific Historical Review* 38 (May 1969): 129–39.
4. See Isaiah 55:9.
5. Ivy League university in New York City, United States.
6. City in northeastern China.
7. City in northern Utah, United States.
8. Port city in northeastern Illinois, United States.
9. Port city in eastern China.
10. Port city in northeastern China.
11. Coastal province in northeast China.
12. Port on north bank of the Chang River, China.
13. River in central China.
14. City on the Chang River in eastern China.
15. Wilford Woodruff (1807–1898), born on March 1, 1807, at Farmington, Connecticut. Fourth president of the church, apostle, outdoorsman, and missionary. Died on September 2, 1898, at San Francisco, California.
16. Port city in southern Honshu, Japan.
17. River in northern China.
18. Port city in western Kyushu, Japan.
19. Countries of East Asia and the Malay Archipelago.
20. Inlet of the Pacific in southwestern Japan.
21. City in west-central Honshu, Japan.
22. Lloyd Oscar Ivie (1890–1967), born on October 9, 1890, at Salina, Utah. Set apart as a mission president to Japan on January 18, 1921, and returned on February 9, 1924. Died on May 7, 1967, at Salt Lake City, Utah.
23. McKay, Diary, January 24, 1921:

In the afternoon, Bro. Cannon when alone in the heart of Tokyo, had one of the most striking demonstrations of the many so far experienced of the genuine and courteous treatment the Japanese people seem delighted to render visitors. By signs and language combined, we had made a policeman standing at a busy street intersection understand where we wanted to go, and had received direction accordingly. Mistaking his instructions, we passed the street down which we should have turned and continued straight on toward the next. The policeman, who evidently had kept his eye on us, left his duty and ran three quarters of a block, halted us, and led us back to the right street. He did it too in such a dignified, gentlemanly manner that we bowed our acknowledgments as graciously as we could and then simply exclaimed to each other in astonishment.

These people are certainly winning my admiration and true esteem. The refinement and courtesy so manifest at nearly every turn, the taste in dress and the beauty of many of the better class of women, the charm and beauty of young maidenhood and sweet young girlhood, the luxuriance of foliage and the graceful well-preserved trees in the groves and forests that abound everywhere, the splendor of Nature in gorges and waterfalls, and everything else, all combine to attune a man's sense of appreciation to the highest pitch!

Certainly it is that thirty days in Japan and China have completely changed my views hitherto entertained of the Orient and Oriental people.

24. Group of islands in Central Pacific, United States.

25. McKay, Diary, January 27, 1921:

> It was very evident from the pitching and rolling of this big boat that we encountered, some time in the night, a pretty rough sea. If we need for further proof, the dashing of the waves against our porthole, and the swishing of the water out on deck would have been sufficient.
>
> Although I was not feeling quite 100 percent in physical alertness, and desire for breakfast, I arose with a pretty fixed determination to pay no attention to the rolling boat nor the heaving sea. I went on deck, took a brisk walk, and wrapped myself up in my deck robe. When the breakfast call came, I responded, though very reluctantly, Bro. Cannon assuring me that he always felt better when "he had something on his stomach."
>
> I felt quite proud of myself when, upon entering the dining room, I saw so many vacant seats. Ordering a cup of hot water and some milk toast, I sat in misery until the waiter returned. I was impatient to get that "something on my stomach."
>
> With one swallow of hot water and one bite of toast, I excused myself with as much dignity and leisure as I could command and walked out. My deck chair and I met each other just in time; though for the next few minutes it was very doubtful whether I or the fishes would have that one bite of toast! Though I won out, I felt pretty miserable, and sat for an hour or two wondering what good an ocean is anyhow! Why couldn't the Lord have made just beautiful lakes, rivers, and dry land?

Chapter 7

1. George Quayle Cannon (1827–1901), born on January 11, 1827, at Liverpool, England. Member of the First Presidency, apostle, Utah statesman, publisher, evangelist, and business tycoon. Died on April 12, 1901, at Monterey, California.

2. Port city of Oahu, Hawaii, United States.

3. Elias Wesley Smith (1886–1970), born on April 21, 1886, at Laie, Hawaii. Set apart as president of the Hawaiian Mission on May 8, 1919. Died on December 28, 1970, at Salt Lake City, Utah.

4. Mary Huskinson Smith (1884–1973), born on December 18, 1884, at Salt Lake City, Utah. Set apart as a missionary to Hawaii on May 8, 1919. Died on May 5, 1973, at Salt Lake City, Utah.

5. Roland Spencer Browning (1901–1983), born on June 25, 1901, at Ogden, Utah. Set apart as a missionary to Hawaii on November 23, 1920, and returned on April 23, 1921. Died on June 10, 1983, at Sunset Beach, California.

6. Wealthy Clark (1895–1923), born on October 31, 1895, at Farmington, Utah. Set apart as a missionary to Hawaii on April 20, 1920, and returned on June 7, 1922. Died on August 13, 1923, at Farmington, Utah.

7. Ivy May Frazier (1897–?), born on July 12, 1897. Set apart as a missionary to Hawaii on June 8, 1920, and returned on August 18, 1921.

8. Joseph Fielding Smith (1838–1918), born on November 13, 1838, at Far West, Missouri. Sixth president of the church, apostle, missionary, and historian. Died on November 19, 1918, at Salt Lake City, Utah.

9. For detailed descriptions of this event, see Lavina Fielding Anderson, "Prayer Under a Pepper Tree: Sixteen Accounts of a Spiritual Manifestation," *BYU Studies* 33, No. 1 (1993): 55–78.

10. Town on Oahu, Hawaii, United States.

11. Mary Saphrona Christensen (1889–1978), born on August 17, 1889, at Bear River, Utah. Set apart as a missionary to Hawaii on July 1, 1920, and returned on April 12, 1921. Died on April 17, 1978.

12. Evelyn Olson (1889–1977), born on September 25, 1889, at Bear River, Utah. Set apart as a missionary to Hawaii on July 1, 1920, and returned on June 30, 1922. Died on April 8, 1977.

13. Edith Lenore Bell (1895–¿), born on January 30, 1895. Set apart as a missionary to Hawaii on July 1, 1920, and returned on June 30, 1922.

14. Jane Jenkins (1895–1936), born on October 22, 1895, at Samaria, Idaho. Set apart as a missionary to Hawaii on July 1, 1920, and returned on August 31, 1922. Died on December 18, 1936, at Preston, Idaho.

15. Genevieve Hammond (1900–1980), born on October 23, 1900, at Mancos, Colorado. Set apart as a missionary to Hawaii on March 23, 1920, and returned on August 11, 1921. Died on March 17, 1980, at Moreland, Idaho.

16. Elizabeth Howe Hyde (1896–¿), born on May 15, 1896, at Logan, Utah. Living in Logan, Utah, when called on a mission to Hawaii. Set apart as a missionary on August 22, 1920, and returned on June 30, 1922.

17. Thomas Marr Waddoups (1910–1982), born on September 24, 1910, at Bountiful, Utah. Lived in Hawaii as son of the mission president. Died on May 27, 1982, at Honolulu, Hawaii.

18. This multicultural experience later prompted McKay to establish the Church College of Hawaii, the forerunner to Brigham Young University–Hawaii, as a place where different nationalities could come and learn together in harmony.

19. William Mark Waddoups (1878–1956), born on February 8, 1878, at Bountiful, Utah. Set apart as a mission president to Hawaii on July 3, 1918, and returned on July 1, 1924. Died on September 2, 1956, at Bountiful, Utah.

20. Olevia Sessions Waddoups (1883–1969), born on September 21, 1883, at Bountiful, Utah. Set apart as a missionary to Hawaii on July 3, 1918, and returned on July 1, 1924. Died on December 17, 1969, at Mission, Texas.

21. Steep cliffs in Oahu, Hawaii, United States.

22. Mountain in Kauai, Hawaii, United States (Mount Waialeale).

23. Byron Daniel Jones (1897–1990), born on October 27, 1897, at Provo, Utah. Set apart as a missionary to Hawaii on April 10, 1918, and returned on June 24, 1921. Died on October 5, 1990, at Salt Lake City, Utah.

24. Chester Hart Nelson (1899–1966), born on May 16, 1899, at Ogden, Utah. Set apart as a missionary to Hawaii on June 3, 1920, and returned on April 4, 1922. Died on August 19, 1966, at Ogden, Utah.

25. Lester Williams (1899–1990), born on December 24, 1899, at Salina, Utah. Set apart as a missionary to Hawaii on February 5, 1920, and returned on May 17, 1921. Died on August 25, 1990.

26. David Keola Kailimai (1873–1940), born on March 6, 1873, at Kahuwa, Hawaii. Served a mission to Hawaii. Died on June 26, 1940, at Hilo, Hawaii.

27. See Davis Bitton, *George Q. Cannon: A Biography* (Salt Lake City: Deseret Book, 1999), 1–32.

28. Ibid., 441–44.

29. Samuel Edwin Woolley (1859–1925), born on October 22, 1859, at Salt Lake City, Utah. Served as president of the Hawaiian Mission from 1895 to 1919. Died on April 3, 1925, at Salt Lake City, Utah.

30. Louis Robert Sullivan (1892–1925), American anthropologist.

31. The Bernice Pauahi Bishop Museum, founded in 1889.

32. City in Maui, Hawaii, United States.

33. Jonathan Hawaii Napela (1813–1879), born on September 11, 1813, on Maui, Hawaii. Early convert to Mormonism in Sandwich Islands, assisted in translation of the Book of Mormon into Hawaiian. Died on August 6, 1879, on Molokai, Hawaii.

34. George Q. Cannon, *My First Mission* (Salt Lake City: Juvenile Instructor, 1879).

35. Crater of dormant volcano on Maui, Hawaii, United States (Haleakala Crater).

36. City in Maui, Hawaii, United States.

37. Historian Richard O. Cowan questions this account: "No such episode is recorded either in George Q. Cannon's missionary diary or in his later summary of his experiences in Hawaii, entitled *My First Mission*, nor is it corroborated in any other contemporary source. Moreover, Napela was not baptized until months after this episode was said to have taken place." See Richard O. Cowan, "An Apostle in Oceania: Elder David O. McKay's 1921 Trip around the Pacific," in *Pioneers in the Pacific: Memory, History, and Cultural Identity among the Latter-day Saints*, ed. Grant Underwood (Provo, Utah: Religious Studies Center, Brigham Young University, 2005), 191, n. 14.

38. See Anderson, "Prayer Under a Pepper Tree."

39. Port city in Hawaii, Hawaii, United States.

Chapter 8

1. City on northwest coast of Maui, Hawaii, United States.

2. Volcano in Hawaii, Hawaii, United States.

3. Edwin Kent Winder (1894–1985), born on August 19, 1894, at Salt Lake City, Utah. Set apart as a missionary to Hawaii on July 1, 1919, and returned on January 30, 1922. Died on February 17, 1985, at Salt Lake City, Utah.

4. John Rex Winder (1821–1910), born on December 11, 1821, in London, England. Counselor in the First Presidency, apostle, member of the presiding bishopric. Died on March 27, 1910, in Salt Lake City, Utah.

5. Alma Eliza Cannon Winder (1896–1966), born on May 29, 1896, at Philadelphia, Pennsylvania. Set apart as a missionary to Hawaii on July 1, 1919, and returned on January 30, 1922. Died on June 16, 1966, at Salt Lake City, Utah.

6. Edith Virginia Budd (1900–1994), born on July 12, 1900, at Salt Lake City, Utah. Set apart as a missionary to Hawaii on November 23, 1920, and returned on October 13, 1922. Died on September 29, 1994, at Salt Lake City, Utah.

7. Roscoe Cleon Cox (1898–1972), born on July 8, 1898, at Fairview, Utah. Set apart as a missionary to Hawaii on February 5, 1920, and returned on July 27, 1923. Died on March 1, 1972, at Salt Lake City, Utah.

8. Boyd Charles Davis (1899–1983), born on March 14, 1899, at Provo, Utah. Set apart as a missionary to Hawaii on January 13, 1920, and returned on April 27, 1922. Died on October 22, 1983, in Utah.

9. Milo Franklin Kirkham (1901–1929), born on June 17, 1901, at Lehi, Utah. Set apart as a missionary to Hawaii on December 9, 1919, and returned on March 2, 1923. Died on April 21, 1929, at Salt Lake City, Utah.

10. Leland Naylor Goff (1898–1978), born on February 6, 1898, at West Jordan, Utah. Set apart as a missionary to Hawaii on January 3, 1920, and returned on August 29, 1923. Died on March 15, 1978, in Utah.

11. Leslie F. Stone (1898–1990), born on April 24, 1898, at Ogden, Utah. Served as a missionary in Hawaii. Died on February 18, 1990, at San Francisco, California.

12. George Mortimer Bronson (1887–1972), born on October 26, 1887, at Fairview, Idaho. Set apart as a missionary to Hawaii on April 29, 1919, and returned on April 27, 1922. Died on August 26, 1972, in Utah.

13. See 2 Nephi 2:25.

14. Volcanic crater in Hawaii, Hawaii, United States.

15. The blessed hereafter in Greek mythology.

16. George Bowles (1866–1942), born on December 28, 1866, at Red Hill, England. Set apart as a missionary to Hawaii on April 21, 1920, and returned on April 5, 1923. Died on June 30, 1942, at Salt Lake City, Utah.

17. Ecclesiastical unit similar to a Catholic parish in Salt Lake City, Utah, United States.

18. Christine Andrew Bowles (1866–1937), born on September 14, 1866, at Salt Lake City, Utah. Set apart as a missionary to Hawaii on April 21, 1920, and returned on April 5, 1923. Died on November 13, 1937, at Los Angeles, California.

19. George Alfred Bowles Jr. (1900–1985), born on May 22, 1900, at Salt Lake City, Utah. Set apart as a missionary to Hawaii on April 21, 1920, and returned on April 5, 1923. Died on May 7, 1985, at Kanab, Utah.

20. Wilford Jenkins Cole (1867–1951), born on November 25, 1867, at Nephi, Utah. Living in Nephi when called on a mission to Hawaii. Set apart as a missionary on April 20, 1908. Died on January 23, 1951, at Nephi, Utah.

21. John Lavon Larsen (1896–1977), born on August 25, 1896, at Preston, Idaho. Set apart as a missionary to Hawaii on January 13, 1920, and returned on April 21, 1923. Died on December 23, 1977, at Preston, Idaho.

22. Arnold Barratt Crystal (1901–1954), born on December 10, 1901, at American Fork, Utah. Set apart as a missionary to Hawaii on March 23, 1920, and returned on July 21, 1921. Died on February 23, 1954.

23. Arnold Benjamin Bangerter (1894–1985), born on October 26, 1894, at Bountiful, Utah. Set apart as a missionary to Hawaii on June 27, 1916, and returned on August 18, 1921. Died on May 19, 1985, at Fairview, Utah.

24. Hazel Pearl Meads Bangerter (1893–1978), born on February 27, 1893, at Salt Lake City, Utah. Set apart as a missionary to Hawaii on January 11, 1919, and returned on August 18, 1921. Died on August 1, 1978, at Fairview, Utah.

25. David Jenkins Smith (1901–1947), born on November 10, 1901, at Salt Lake City, Utah. Set apart as a missionary to Hawaii on May 25, 1920, and returned on May 18, 1923. Died on December 23, 1947, at Salt Lake City, Utah.

26. James Clair Anderson (1900–1971), born on May 14, 1900, at Spring City, Utah. Set apart as a missionary to Hawaii on September 28, 1920, and returned on November 2, 1922. Died on December 2, 1971.

27. Bay on southeast coast of Kauai Island, Hawaii, United States (Nawiliwili Bay).

28. The underworld river according to Greek mythology.

29. A punctual and predictable geyser in Yellowstone National Park.

30. Natural reservation in western United States (Yellowstone National Park).

31. Ora Haven Barlow (1896–1986), born on October 19, 1896, at Syracuse, Utah. Set apart as a missionary to Hawaii on January 13, 1920, and returned on July 5, 1923. Died on November 21, 1986, at Salt Lake City, Utah.

32. Kenneth Conray Weaver (1900–1986), born on March 15, 1900, at Ogden, Utah. Set apart as a missionary to Hawaii on January 3, 1920, and returned on July 27, 1923. Died on April 16, 1986, at St. George, Utah.

33. Ferrin Robert Harris (1900–1937), born on August 30, 1900, at Portage, Utah. Set apart as a missionary to Hawaii on February 5, 1920, and returned on April 4, 1923. Died on December 4, 1937, at Bountiful, Utah.

34. Douglas Farnes Budd (1902–1992), born on May 1, 1902, at Logan, Utah. Set apart as a missionary to Hawaii on November 23, 1920, and returned on February 2, 1924. Died on March 16, 1992, at Cambria, California.

35. John Henry Parker (1895–1943), born on April 9, 1895, at Payson, Utah. Set apart as a missionary to Hawaii on February 5, 1920, and returned on June 9, 1923. Died on June 1, 1943.

36. Joseph Fielding Smith (1899–1964), born on January 30, 1899, at Salt Lake City, Utah. Set apart as a missionary to Hawaii on April 20, 1920, and returned on September 23, 1922. Died on August 20, 1964, at Salt Lake City, Utah.

37. Hyrum Mack Smith (1872–1918), born on March 21, 1872, at Salt Lake City, Utah. Apostle and mission president. Died on January 23, 1918, at Salt lake City, Utah.

38. Asa Harris Chase Jr. (1901–1929), born on December 16, 1901, at Salt Lake City, Utah. Set apart as a missionary to Hawaii on November 23, 1920, and returned on April 12, 1921. Died on July 20, 1929, at Ogden, Utah.

39. Adelbert Barnett (1888–1957), born on November 10, 1888, at Hooper, Utah. Set apart as a missionary to Hawaii on March 23, 1920, and returned on May 2, 1923. Died on April 24, 1957, at Salt Lake City, Utah.

40. Wallace Herbert Penrose (1899–1982), born on July 15, 1899, at Salt Lake City, Utah. Set apart as a missionary to Hawaii on February 5, 1920, and returned on May 29, 1923. Died on March 11, 1982, at Bennion, Utah.

41. Robert Plunkett (1893–⸮), born on April 8, 1893. Set apart as a missionary to Hawaii on May 9, 1919.

42. Heber Smith Amussen (1886–1955), born on November 29, 1886, at Victoria, British Columbia, Canada. Set apart as a missionary to Hawaii on November 9, 1920, and returned on August 23, 1923. Died on May 14, 1955, at Logan, Utah.

43. Charles John Lehuakonoa Broad (1859–1933), born on December 6, 1859, at Honolulu, Hawaii. Served as a missionary in Hawaii. Died on March 13, 1933, at Honolulu, Hawaii.

44. King Kamehameha III founded this musical group in 1836.

45. Mekia Kealakai (1867–1944), composer and Royal Hawaiian Bandleader.

46. Islands of the central and South Pacific (Polynesia).

47. See Alma 56–58.

48. For an excellent overview on the subject of Pacific colonization, see K. R. Howe, *The Quest for Origins: Who First Discovered and Settled the Pacific Islands* (Honolulu: University of Hawaii Press, 2003).

49. McKay, Diary, February 21, 1921:

Today, Brother Wesley took us over to Dr. Louis R. Sullivan's office in the Bishop Estate Museum, and introduced us to this gentleman, who is associate director in the Department of Anthropology. He has been engaged several years with the American Museum of New York, which has made a special study of the American Indians, especially the Sioux. Dr. Sullivan is now studying the natives of the Polynesian Islands, and may be accepted as an authority.

"Dr.," I asked, "is there any relation between the Hawaiians and the American Indians⸮"

"Undoubtedly," he promptly answered. "There can be no doubt but they have come from the same source."

"How about the Japanese⸮" I asked.

"They, too, are of the same blood, but the Japanese are a mixed race; but all the natives of Polynesia have undoubtedly sprung from the same ancestry. But whether these Hawaiians, and Samoans, and Maoris came to America from Asia, and from America to these Islands as you people believe, or whether they have drifted direct from Asia is a question yet to be determined. Anthropology, however, has demonstrated the close relationship between the American Indians and the natives of these Pacific Islands. They are the same people."

Chapter 9

1. John A. Widtsoe, *Joseph Smith as Scientist: A Contribution to Mormon Philosophy* (Salt Lake City: Bookcraft, 1964), 33. Norwegian-born Widtsoe (1872–1952) was an apostle, educator, and president of the University of Utah.

2. Strait connecting San Francisco Bay with the Pacific Ocean, California, United States.

3. Areas of the Atlantic, Indian, and Pacific oceans in the southern hemisphere.
4. For a study of the Laie Temple, see Paul L. Anderson, "A Jewel in the Gardens of Paradise: The Art and Architecture of the Hawai'i Temple," in *Voyages of Faith: Explorations in Mormon Pacific History*, ed. Grant Underwood (Provo, Utah: Brigham Young University Press, 2000), 146–63.
5. Levi Edgar Young (1874–1963), born on February 2, 1874, at Salt Lake City, Utah. One of the first seven presidents of the Seventy, mission president, and professional historian. Died on December 13, 1963, at Salt Lake City, Utah.
6. Capital city of the United States (Washington, D.C.).
7. City in southwestern California, United States.
8. Joseph William McMurrin (1858–1932), born on September 5, 1858, at Tooele, Utah. One of the first seven presidents of the Seventy and president of the California Mission. Died on October 24, 1932, at Los Angeles, California.
9. Roman god of the sea, also known as Poseidon.
10. McKay, Diary, April 6, 1921:

    The following letter written to little Emma Ray will give an idea of what took place this morning:

    This morning we crossed the Equator, an imaginary line that passes around the middle of the globe, and separates the north half of the world from the south half. You are now in the northern hemisphere, but I am now in the southern hemisphere.

    Last night it was told among the passengers that when the ship crossed the line Old Neptune, the ancient god of the sea, would rise out of the ocean, and perhaps, come aboard. Of course, I didn't believe what was said, because I knew that Neptune was only an imaginary god, so I went to bed and slept and didn't even dream about him.

    When I awoke this morning, we had crossed the Equator, and I heard someone say that Old Neptune had come aboard. Still, I didn't believe it, because I knew Neptune did not exist.

    Pretty soon, a man came to me and said,

    "Mr. McKay, you are wanted."

    "By whom?" I asked.

    "By Neptune," he answered.

    And then he suggested that I take off my collar and tie, and coat and other things I did not want to get wet.

    This began to sound as though Old Neptune was really aboard, because I had heard that he ducked everybody who came across the Equator for the first time.

    Though I determined not to be thrown in the water, I walked aft along the deck, when suddenly I saw coming toward me Old Neptune himself, and who, do you think, was by his side? Mrs. Neptune! He had long white, rusty-like hair, that hung down to his shoulders, a long beard, same color as his hair, that was so thick and long that it covered half his naked breast. On his head he wore a crown with pointed tips all around it, and in his hand he held a three-pronged sceptre that looked like a short stubby pitchfork. His arms and legs were bare and looked for all the world as if he had been living in the sea for ages and ages.

Mrs. Neptune was a big, fat, jolly looking creature, with very red cheeks and lips, and a white tip on the end of her nose. She wore a blouse-like skirt, and had a lei around her neck.

There were some nymphs with them who looked like policemen with big clubs in their hands.

Well, we all wondered what these strange people would do to us!!

Pretty soon, after they had walked around the deck and ordered everybody to follow them, Old Neptune and Mrs. Neptune sat on a high place on the deck, and began to pick out the passengers who had entered his dominion for the first time.

One man was called up, and when he refused to go, the gnome-like policemen grabbed him, hit him over the head, and dragged him before Neptune, who now sat as a judge.

The man was quickly found guilty, sentenced to be shaved, and thrown into the "Bath."

With a large whitewash brush, the gnomes besmeared his face with a paste-like lather in a large bucket and then with a wooden razor about the size of a turkey's wing they shaved him, and then dragged him to a tunnel made of benches, and forced him to crawl through it.

As he did so, they turned a stream of water on him all the way through, completely sousing him from head to foot. When he came out, bedraggled, Old Neptune and Mrs. Neptune and all the others laughed, and said, "That's what you get when you cross the 'line' into our sea!"

Next, they accused a young lady. The old sea rascal sentenced her to be shaved, and "thrown into the bath." She fought and wouldn't be shaved, but she had to crawl through the tunnel-like bath and be doused with water.

"Mr. Cannon," he called out. Instantly the gnomes caught Brother Cannon, and dragged him to the feet of Old Neptune.

"You're charged with not having crossed this line thirty-five years ago; guilty or not guilty?"

"Guilty," said Brother Cannon. So old Neptune sentenced him to have his face shaved with the big wooden razor, his feet and legs also, and to crawl through the bath and be ducked, all of which was duly administered to him.

"Mr. McKay," cried Old Neptune. I didn't answer, but remained quiet in the crowd.

"Find Mr. McKay," he said to his old policemen.

"Mr. McKay is in his room, perhaps," I said; but the old ancient sea rascal was not to be fooled.

"You're Mr. McKay," he cried. "Seize him!"

Then as I stood a prisoner before him, he said:

"You are charged with crossing the line to go to New Zealand to win the hearts of the fair Maori maidens; are you guilty or not guilty?"

"Guilty," I answered. This rather surprised him, and seeing that I had my coat on, my collar and tie, white trousers and white shoes, and my kodak in my hand, he concluded not to duck me, but asked:

NOTES TO PAGE 58

"Do you smoke?" "No."

"Do you drink?" "No."

"Well, I sentence you to come into dinner with your hair parted in the middle."

I thanked him for his leniency and stepped back into the crowd, and watched about ten others get sentences, most of whom had to get ducked until they were as wet as Neptune himself is supposed to be.

I took a picture of him and his wife and court attendants. If it turns out well, I will send it to you so that you may see what this *make-believe* god of the sea really looks like.

11. Hugh Cannon.
12. The earth's axis points to this bright star in the northern hemisphere.
13. The seven major stars comprising the Ursa Major constellation.
14. Four brilliant stars in the southern hemisphere.
15. Port city of Society Islands, Tahiti.
16. Island in Windward group of the Society Islands.
17. Islands in South Pacific.

Chapter 10

1. Leonidas Hamlin Kennard, Jr. (1869–1948), born on October 26, 1869, at Farmington, Utah. Set apart as mission president to Tahiti on January 9, 1920, and returned on September 7, 1922. Died on November 28, 1948, at Logan, Utah.

2. Grant Lee Benson (1896–1960), born on October 28, 1896, at Grantsville, Utah. Set apart as a missionary to Tahiti on November 20, 1917, and returned on May 1, 1921. Died on December 3, 1960, at Sacramento, California.

3. George Clyde Nelson (1899–1954), born on November 9, 1899, at Safford, Arizona. Set apart as a missionary to Tahiti on June 29, 1920, and returned on December 9, 1923. Died on August 28, 1954.

4. Wallace Lester Martin (1901–1975), born on February 8, 1901, at Murray, Utah. Set apart as a missionary to Tahiti on November 3, 1920, and returned on June 10, 1923. Died on June 18, 1975, at Salt Lake City, Utah.

5. Leonard John McCullough (1897–1993), born on May 8, 1897, at Salt Lake City, Utah. Set apart as a missionary to Tahiti on November 20, 1917, and returned on May 25, 1921. Died on November 22, 1993, at Salt Lake City, Utah.

6. Viao Mohi.

7. Revealed health code of the Latter-day Saints (Doctrine and Covenants 89).

8. John 10:4, 5.

9. Venus Robinson Rossiter (1891–1963), born on February 10, 1891, at Salt Lake City, Utah. Set apart as a missionary to Tahiti on February 16, 1915, and returned on August 9, 1919. Died on May 20, 1963.

10. Ernest Crabtree Rossiter (1882–1965), born on October 16, 1882, at Salt Lake City, Utah. Set apart as mission president to Tahiti on February 16, 1915, and returned on August 9, 1919. Died on July 8, 1965, at Salt Lake City, Utah.

11. See appendix 1.

Chapter 11

1. Roger W. Babson, *Fundamentals of Prosperity: What They Are and Whence They Came* (New York: Fleming H. Revell, 1920), 34. Babson (1875–1967) was a business entrepreneur and philosopher.
2. Island in South Pacific in southwestern part of The Cook Islands.
3. Islands in South Pacific located southwest of The Society Islands (Cook Islands).
4. McKay, Diary, April 13, 1921:

   About 8:30 a.m., passengers heard the cry, "A Shark! They've caught a shark!" Brother Cannon yelled to me to "come see this shark." Nobody needed a second invitation. I saw him just as the sailors had pulled him over the deck railing. A hook the size of a bailing hook was in his jaw, a lasso rope around his tail, and he was flopping and writhing in a last, futile effort to free himself. They tied both ropes, stretched the monster out and struck him a blow on the nose which was supposed to kill him instantly; however, it failed, and so the shark was hammered on the head and stabbed in the brain.

   Thinking he was dead, I began to examine him, and took hold of his fins. He gave a sudden lurch that loosed his tail with which he gave me a blow on the legs that gave me a sensation I shall not soon forget. It's rather an unusual experience to come in contact with a live shark!
5. A cloth wraparound skirt.
6. See Helaman 3:7, 9, 11.
7. Part of the earth that lies south of the equator.
8. Constellation observable in the southern hemisphere at night (Crux Australis).
9. Constellation observable in the northern hemisphere at night (Ursa Major).

Chapter 12

1. Stephen L. Richards (1879–1959), born on June 18, 1879, at Mendon, Utah. Counselor in the First Presidency, apostle, and missionary. Died on May 19, 1959, in Salt Lake City, Utah.
2. McKay, Diary, April 22, 1921:

   Soon followed my first introduction to the *hongi*, the Maori mode of salutation. It consists in grasping the right hands, which are held down, and a gentle pressure of noses with a gradual increase of pressure, the intensity and prolongation of which express the intensity of feeling of persons greeting each other. I soon noticed that it is more convenient to *hongi* with some than with others; and the thought occurred to me that it is not unlikely that this queer custom might prove helpful to natives choosing their mates—on the principle that "opposites attract." I found that the point of my nose slipped off some, but stayed on others! When I looked at those whose noses mine fit, I had no inclination to be guided wholly by the possible rule mentioned above!
3. George Shepherd Taylor (1860–1924), born on July 16, 1860, at Salt Lake City, Utah. Set apart as mission president to New Zealand on

NOTES TO PAGES 64–68

November 3, 1920, and returned on August 1, 1923. Died on January 16, 1924, at Provo, Utah.

4. Graham Hayes Doxey (1900–1969), born on January 5, 1900, at Salt Lake City, Utah. Served a mission to New Zealand. Died on November 20, 1969, at Salt Lake City, Utah.

5. Julius Viggo Madsen (1899–1981), born on May 16, 1899, at Salem, Idaho. Set apart as a missionary to New Zealand on September 23, 1919, and returned on September 9, 1922. Died on June 15, 1981, at Springdale, Utah.

6. McKay, Diary, April 21, 1921:

After disposing of our satchels and suit cases and having secured the custom official's check upon them, President Taylor and I began to make a search for my trunk. To tell the truth, I had very little hope of finding it and had in my pocket a cablegram written to send to Brother Richards in San Francisco requesting him to collect $300.00 or institute legal proceedings.

The result of our first inquiry was to be directed to the Union Steamship Company's office in Warehouse "I." A walk of about a quarter of a mile took us to an upstairs office where the clerk had a list of "luggage" which evidently was to be called for.

"There is nothing listed here for Mr. McKay. Perhaps it is over in the 'Lost Luggage' department."

We retraced our steps and went about an eighth of a mile farther on, and after a little inquiry, found the clerk who had a list of the lost luggage. Thinking that a definite, tactful statement would insure more, I said, "You have a trunk here belonging to David O. McKay. It came on the 'S. S. Tahiti' which sailed from San Francisco, March 3rd."

While he and President Taylor scanned the lists, I looked amongst the piles of trunks and valises. But neither search revealed the trunk.

"Have you inquired at the custom's examination office?"

"No," we replied, "we have gone only where we have been told to go."

"The custom's examination office is in Warehouse 'A' in yon building undergoing repair."

Finding no trace of it in Warehouse "A," we received instructions to go to "H." I am sure the clerk did not have in mind the sulphurous place usually designated by "H—," but I thought of it when he said, "Go to H!" And, really, I was about ready to conclude that hunting a trunk in Wellington Warehouses was very much akin to the torment of that notorious lower region.

At "H" another quarter of a mile in the direction of "I," and then to the right, along the wharf "where the Tahiti docked," with the last spark of hope flickering if not entirely out, I walked up to the office window, and asked for a trunk belonging to David O. McKay.

While he was looking among his lists, Elder Madsen, who had joined us, cried from a corner in the warehouse—

"Here it is!"

Sure enough, there it was; and the sight of it after six weeks' inconvenience and despair of seeing it again made me pretty happy. We extricated it with the view of sending it up to the office, when we were told by the clerk that he could not let it go until we had given him a written order from the Union Steamship Co. We retraced our steps a half a mile, and after a little explaining, and a short, useless tilt in words, as to who should pay the storage, we secured the order, and returned to "H."

Then we were told that we should have to go to the "Harbor Office and obtain a receipt for the storage." This consumed another half hour, and necessitated another walk of three quarters of a mile.

Returning to "H," and handing the receipt for storage, the clerk said, "Did you call at the customs office?"

"No, we thought the customs office was here."

"There is none here, and, of course, you should get him; but I'll call him for you," and he turned to the telephone, thus saving us one more trip along the docks, for which we tendered him our sincere "thank you."

After a fifteen minute wait, that official appeared to examine the trunk. Not until we began to pull back the clasps on the trunk did I remember the fact that my keys were in my satchel. The trunk could not be opened.

It was then seven minutes to twelve. Brother Madsen said, "I can get those keys and be back here in seven minutes."

He did it; but we had to wait another ten minutes for the government officer, who had "just stepped into the office."

I have recorded this merely as an example of how warehouse efficiency, and government and official "red tape" may delay and inconvenience a "stranger in a strange land."

7. Maui Wiremu Pita Naera Pomare (1875–1930), New Zealand doctor and politician.

8. See James N. Lambert, in *Ninety-First Semi-Annual Conference of The Church of Jesus Christ of Latter-day Saints* (Salt Lake City: The Church of Jesus Christ of Latter-day Saints, 1920), 158–60.

9. David O. McKay, "'Hui Tau,'" *Improvement Era* 24, no. 9 (July 1921): 774.

10. City in North Island, New Zealand.

11. Ida Ann Taylor (1872–1965), born on March 18, 1872, at Springville, Utah. Set apart as a missionary to New Zealand on November 3, 1920, and returned on August 1, 1923. Died on June 16, 1965, at Salt Lake City, Utah.

12. Miriam Mae Taylor (1898–1978), born on May 27, 1898, at Provo, Utah. Lived in New Zealand as daughter of Mission President George Taylor. Died in February 1978.

13. *Ready References: A Compilation of Scripture Texts, Arranged in a Subjective Order, with Numerous Annotations from Eminent Writers* (Salt Lake City: George Q. Cannon and Sons, 1899).

14. McKay, "'Hui Tau,'" 770–77.

15. Lillian A. Schwendiman (1899–1998), born on May 5, 1899, at Lehi, Utah. Set apart as a missionary to New Zealand on June 28, 1918, and returned on October 10, 1921. Died on July 15, 1998, at Salt Lake City, Utah.

16. Frederick William Schwendiman (1898–1988), born on February 15, 1898, at Teton City, Idaho. Set apart as a missionary to New Zealand on June 28, 1918, and returned on October 10, 1921. Died on January 30, 1988, at Salt Lake City, Utah.

17. May Ida Fisher Stott (1885–1964), born on December 4, 1885, at Meadow, Utah. Set apart as a missionary to New Zealand on December 2, 1917,

and returned on September 24, 1921. Died on March 3, 1964, at Alhambra, California.

18. Franklin Earl Stott (1883–1965), born on February 19, 1883, at Meadow, Utah. Set apart as a missionary to New Zealand on December 2, 1917, and returned on September 24, 1921. Died on September 25, 1965, at Provo, Utah.

19. Flora Davis Fisher (1891–1984), born on July 29, 1891, at Provo, Utah. Set apart as a missionary to New Zealand on October 23, 1919, and returned on September 24, 1921. Died on June 10, 1984.

20. Asael Henry Fisher (1888–1976), born on July 1, 1888, at Meadow, Utah. Set apart as a missionary to New Zealand on September 23, 1919, and returned on September 24, 1921. Died on March 17, 1976, in Utah.

21. Priscilla Taylor (1907–1983), born on September 19, 1907, at Provo, Utah. Lived in New Zealand as daughter of Mission President George Taylor. Died on June 2, 1983.

22. Gordon Claridge Young (1898–1989), born on October 26, 1898, at Salt Lake City, Utah. Set apart as a missionary to New Zealand on March 15, 1919, and returned on January 14, 1923. Died on September 5, 1989, at Salt Lake City, Utah.

23. Roland Chauncey Parry (1897–1977), born on May 7, 1897, at Ogden, Utah. Set apart as a missionary to New Zealand on February 19, 1918, and returned on November 14, 1921. Died on October 18, 1977, at Ogden, Utah.

Chapter 13

1. Brigham Young (1801–1877), born on June 1, 1801, at Whitingham, Vermont. Second president of the church, apostle, western pioneer and colonizer, and businessman. Died on August 29, 1877, at Salt Lake City, Utah.

2. See Ephesians 4:11–13.

3. Port city on North Island, New Zealand.

4. See Matthew 7:28–29.

5. Haloy Elias Bachman (1898–?), born on April 21, 1898. Set apart as a missionary to New Zealand on September 23, 1919, and returned on June 25, 1923.

6. Jonathan Golden Kimball (1853–1938), born on June 9, 1853, at Salt Lake City, Utah. One of the first seven presidents of the Seventy and president of the Southern States Mission. Died on September 2, 1938, at Reno, Nevada.

7. An inspired declaration of Abrahamic lineage and personal direction offered by a church patriarch.

8. Ecclesiastical unit similar to a Catholic parish in Salt Lake City, Utah, United States.

9. Presently known as the Community of Christ, the historic Reorganized Church of Jesus Christ of Latter-Day Saints was formed in the years following the 1844 assassination of Joseph Smith and was initially led by his son Joseph Smith III.

10. For a history of the conflicts between the two main restoration groups Down Under, see Ross Geddes, "'A Storm in the Camp of Brighamism': LDS-RLDS Relations in Brisbane, Australia, 1901–1918," *John Whitmer Historical Association Journal* 11 (1991): 47–59.

11. Benjamin Brown (1876–1955), born on October 13, 1876, at Centerville, Utah. Set apart as a missionary to New Zealand on July 7, 1919, and returned on April 2, 1922. Died on January 7, 1955, at Salt Lake City, Utah.

12. Elmo Franklin Jacobs (1897–1934), born on October 31, 1897, at Lehi, Utah. Set apart as a missionary to New Zealand on June 24, 1919, and returned on July 8, 1921. Died on September 11, 1934, at Idaho Falls, Idaho.

13. Rulon Hollist Manning (1898–1980), born on December 9, 1898, at Garland, Utah. Set apart as a missionary to New Zealand on March 27, 1919, and returned on January 28, 1922. Died on January 16, 1980, at San Jose, California.

14. Islands in southwest Pacific.

15. Islands in southwestern central Pacific, north of Tonga Islands; divided into American, or Eastern, Samoa and independent Samoa.

16. Likely Father Dennis O'Reilly.

17. Capital of Fiji.

18. Islands in southwestern Pacific.

19. For a history of LDS interpretations of race and lineage, see Norman Douglas, "The Sons of Lehi and the Seed of Cain: Racial Myths in Mormon Scripture and Their Relevance to the Pacific Islands," *Journal of Religious History* 8, No. 1 (June 1974): 90–104. See also Armand L. Mauss, *All Abraham's Children: Changing Mormon Conceptions of Race and Lineage* (Urbana: University of Illinois Press, 2003), 1–2.

20. Capital city of Tonga (Nuku'alofa).

21. Island in southern Tonga.

22. Mark Vernon Coombs (1891–1979), born on February 5, 1891, at Nephi, Utah. Set apart as mission president to Tonga on July 13, 1920, and returned on July 30, 1926. Died on February 10, 1979, at Salt Lake City, Utah.

23. See appendix 1.

24. Joshua Kenneth Rallison (1898–1958), born on April 28, 1898, at Fairview, Idaho. Set apart as a missionary to Tonga on December 13, 1916, and returned on April 30, 1921. Died on March 25, 1958, at Los Angeles, California.

25. Port town on Vava'u Island, Tonga.

26. Island group in northern Tonga (Vava'u).

27. McKay, Diary, May 10, 1921:

> The quiet movement of the boat and the low, playful splash of the water told me as soon as I awoke that we were in a harbor. I arose immediately, and stepped out on deck where a number of passengers had preceded me.
>
> Many small conical-shaped verdure-clad islands rose abruptly out of the ocean on both sides of us, and stretching far ahead, with its bays and inlets and projecting capes, was an arm of the sea leading up to Vavau. The sun was sufficiently near the horizon to tinge the floating clouds with crimson and pink. The islands in the near distance seemed still to be sleeping under their mantle of green, while around some of them, lapped by the gentle waves of a rippling sea, nestled white sand beaches that looked like a long stretch of pongee silk. As we drew closer to the islands, we could discern first the coconut palms, struggling boldly and successfully to raise

themselves above the dense forest of vine-covered trees that battled for soil and sunshine. Among these lower trees were some laden with luscious, yellow and green oranges, growing large though rank and wild. That tree laden with white blossoms is the male "pawpaw," or "mummy fruit" tree, and the unadorned leafy ones standing near are the "mama" "pawpaw" trees which produce the delicious fruit.

Others in that dense, verdure clad wood, are the "candle-nut," the "Foa" and a common, willow-like shrub the name of which I could not learn. Undoubtedly a score or more trees of different varieties grew in the tangled verdure that contributed so much to the beauty of this island-dotted harbor, and all of them, by the overclimbing, overhanging, convolvus vine were united in stronger bonds of wedlock than those which often bind the natives who live contentedly and happily on the fruit of the ever-producing trees.

The little villages, which look like summer cottages set in the garden of Eden, are peeking out from palm trees, and hedges of the blooming red hibiscus and other less pretentious flowers. An old brown brindled cow, with horns threatening to grow back into her head as Nellie's, standing in the foreground lazily chewing her cud, and some chickens following a strutting rooster, boasting he will find food for the whole flock, and then making every hen scratch for herself and him, too—some pigs munching coconuts, and a horse tied or staked to a palm tree—all give signs of a domestic life that seems absolutely disturbance-proof.

28. Stirling Ibey May (1896–1963), born on May 6, 1896, at Cardston, Alberta, Canada. Set apart as a missionary to Tonga on February 7, 1917, and returned on October 3, 1921. Died on March 19, 1963, at Lethbridge, Canada.

29. Reuben Magnus Wiberg (1899–1964), born on October 27, 1899, at Sandy, Utah. Set apart as a missionary to Tonga on November 16, 1920, and returned on February 19, 1925. Died on April 15, 1964, at Roy, Utah.

30. McKay, Diary, May 9, 1921:

Met Professors Gifford and McKern, of the ethnological and anthropological expedition under the immediate supervision of the Bishop Museum, Honolulu. They are studying the Polynesians with the view of ascertaining their origin.

Professor McKern told me that he discovered a kind of feathered cloth woven by a tribe of Indians in California, which seemed to be identical with the same kind made by the Hawaiians. He knows of no other people who make it. However, he desires to make further investigations before being quoted.

31. Island near Vava'u, Tonga.

Chapter 14

1. Henry Drummond, *Addresses* (Philadelphia, Pa.: Henry Altemus, 1891), 72.
2. Port capital of independent Samoa.
3. Island of Samoa.
4. Island in independent Samoa.

5. John Quincy Adams (1882–1971), born on May 19, 1882, at Centerville, Utah. Set apart as a missionary to Samoa on December 10, 1919, and returned on November 25, 1923. Died on March 20, 1971, at Centerville, Utah.

6. Gilbert Randall Tingey (1901–1966), born on August 21, 1901, at Centerville, Utah. Set apart as a missionary to Samoa on December 10, 1919, and returned on May 18, 1923. Died on October 24, 1966, at Salt Lake City, Utah.

7. George Wilford Robinson (1899–1971), born on April 25, 1899, at Ucon, Idaho. Set apart as a missionary to Tonga on February 24, 1921, and returned on July 5, 1922. Died on April 8, 1971, at Idaho Falls, Idaho.

8. Walter Joseph Phillips (1902–1950), born on July 26, 1902, at Tooele, Utah. Set apart as a missionary to Tonga on March 24, 1921, and returned on October 11, 1924. Died on May 7, 1950, at Salt Lake City, Utah.

9. Cleon James Wilcox (1900–1998), born on May 1, 1900, at Garland, Utah. Set apart as a missionary to Samoa on March 11, 1920, and returned on July 22, 1923. Died on May 29, 1998, at Lebanon, Kentucky.

10. Chauncey L. Witbeck (1899–1960), born on February 14, 1899, at Aniani, Samoa. Set apart as a missionary to Samoa on November 16, 1920, and returned on December 8, 1922. Died on August 24, 1960.

11. Thurza Amelia Tingey Adams (1888–1960), born on February 13, 1888, at Centerville, Utah. Set apart as a missionary to Samoa on December 10, 1919, and returned on November 25, 1923. Died on September 14, 1960, at Centerville, Utah.

12. Frank D. Griffiths (1888–¿), born on April 28, 1888. Living in Minersville, Utah, when called on a mission to Samoa. Set apart as a missionary on September 3, 1919, and returned on July 23, 1921.

13. Retta Myers Griffiths (1891–¿), born on April 23, 1891. Living in Minersville, Utah, when called on a mission to Samoa. Set apart as a missionary on September 3, 1919, and returned on July 23, 1921.

14. City in Samoa.

15. Ray William Berrett (1899–1945), born on August 27, 1899, at North Ogden, Utah. Living in Ogden, Utah, when called on a mission to Samoa. Set apart as a missionary to Samoa on December 10, 1919, and returned on March 19, 1923. Died on January 12, 1945.

16. Quincy Franklin Roberts, career politician, U.S. vice consul to Samoa.

17. An intoxicating drink made from the root of an Australasian pepper.

18. See Proverbs 13:12.

19. McKay, Diary, May 11, 1921.

20. Ralph Alonzo Thacker (1895–1981), born on October 30, 1895, at Buysville, Utah. Set apart as a missionary to Samoa on September 3, 1919, and returned on May 18, 1923. Died on September 11, 1981, at Provo, Utah.

21. Robert Louis Stevenson (1850–1894), a Scottish novelist.

Chapter 15

1. Joseph Henry Dean (1855–1947), born on October 16, 1855, at Taunton, England. Set apart as a missionary to Samoa on February 2,

1916, and returned on July 19, 1918. Died on November 2, 1947, at Vernal, Utah.

2. Adelbert Beesley (1866–1948), born on January 3, 1866, at Salt Lake City, Utah. Set apart as a missionary to Samoa on September 11, 1888. Died on May 18, 1948, at Butte, Montana.

3. Edward James Wood (1866–1956), born on October 27, 1866, at Salt Lake City, Utah. Served three missions to Samoa. Died on April 24, 1956, at Cardston, Canada.

4. Chief island of American Samoa.

5. Lewis Ashfield Kimberly (1830–1902), commander in chief of the Pacific station of the U.S. Navy.

6. Sea in the Pacific Ocean between China, South Korea, Japan, and Taiwan.

7. Ocean east of Africa, south of Asia, and west of Australia.

8. Inlet of the Atlantic Ocean on the southeastern coast of North America.

9. Leland Hyrum Stott (1897–1981), born on February 17, 1897, at Meadow, Utah. Set apart as a missionary to Samoa on September 3, 1919, and returned on August 20, 1922. Died on November 28, 1981, at Detroit, Michigan.

10. Capital of American Samoa.

11. See also McKay, Diary, May 21, 1921.

12. William Smith Muir (1890–1966), born on September 15, 1890, at Hatch, Idaho. Set apart as mission president to Samoa on August 9, 1919, and returned on September 23, 1921. Died on September 3, 1966, at American Falls, Idaho.

13. Edna Walton Muir (1891–1980), born on February 13, 1891, at Coalville, Utah. Set apart as a missionary to Samoa on August 9, 1919, and returned on September 23, 1921. Died on October 25, 1980, at Pocatello, Idaho.

14. City in American Samoa.

15. William Karl Brewer (1899–1986), born on March 25, 1899, at Pinedale, Arizona. Set apart as a missionary to Samoa on November 16, 1920, and returned on June 15, 1923. Died on January 28, 1986, at Mesa, Arizona.

16. Cited in McKay diary, May 24, 1921.

17. Island group of eastern Samoa.

18. Islands in southwestern Pacific in American Samoa (Manua Islands).

19. One of the Manua Islands, American Samoa.

20. Westernmost island of the Manua Islands, American Samoa.

21. Atoll in American Samoa (Aunu'u).

22. Coral atoll in Samoa.

23. Waldo A. Evans (1869–1936), military governor of American Samoa and the U.S. Virgin Islands.

Chapter 16

1. Marcus Aurelius (AD 121–180), Roman emperor and philosopher, quoted in Harry Thurston Peck, Frank Richard Stockton, and Caroline Ticknor, eds., *The World's Great Masterpieces: History, Biography, Science, Philosophy, Poetry, the Drama* (New York: American Literary Society, 1901), 686.

2. See John 8:34, 36.

3. Village in Samoa.

4. The national anthem of the United States of America.

5. A plant of the Arum family.

6. The service-oriented women's organization of the LDS Church.

7. See R. Lanier Britsch, *Unto the Islands of the Sea: A History of the Latter-day Saints in the Pacific* (Salt Lake City: Deseret Book, 1986), 389–91.

8. See David O. McKay, "Ah Ching," *Improvement Era* 24 (September 1921): 992–97.

9. Ralph Ashford Knowlton (1897–1965), born on December 24, 1897, at Farmington, Utah. Set apart as a missionary to Samoa on March 11, 1920, and returned on July 22, 1923. Died on July 23, 1965, at Seattle, Washington.

10. Arthur Leland Huntsman (1898–1975), born on January 12, 1898, at Canesville, Utah. Set apart as a missionary to Samoa on December 9, 1919, and returned on March 17, 1923. Died on April 24, 1975, at Castledale, Utah.

11. Lewis Betts Parkin (1897–1945), born on March 16, 1897, at South Bountiful, Utah. Set apart as a missionary to Samoa on February 24, 1921, and returned on October 15, 1924. Died on January 15, 1945.

12. Islands in central Pacific, Kiribati (Phoenix Islands).

Chapter 17

1. Presbyterian minister Frank Crane (1861–1928), quoted in James Miller, *Voices from Earth* (Victoria, British Columbia: Trafford Publishing, 2004), 26.

2. Chief island of the Vava'u group, Tonga (Vava'u).

3. Island group in central Tonga (Ha'apai).

4. McKay, Diary, June 11, 1921:

   About 12:30 noon, we bade good-bye to our fellow-passengers; including Brother Hugh J., in whose agreeable company I have been almost constantly during the last six months. I felt pretty lonesome at parting from him, and gloomy at the prospects ahead. However, we decided to make the best of a bad business, and huddled amidst trunks, satchels, suit cases, bundles, and all other kinds of luggage in the "Cargo Lighter" that lay bobbing up and down at the wharf awaiting to be towed out to quarantine island.

5. Clarence Henderson (1901–1947), born on February 3, 1901, at Salt Lake City, Utah. Set apart as a missionary to Tonga on March 24, 1921, and returned on December 20, 1924. Died on October 11, 1947, at Salt Lake City, Utah.

6. McKay, Diary, June 13, 1921:

   It is truly surprising how many interesting things one can find around this little island! At first, I thought that all I could do would be to write articles and letters and read; but now I find interest in searching for beautiful shells when the tide has gone out. Then Brother Coombs and I began to examine the various forms of life hiding or crawling around the coral, some evidently in their native habitat, but others left stranded by the ebbing tide. I have never before realized with what myriads of forms of life the old ocean must teem! Crab-like things of all sizes, shell fish, jelly-like creatures, some beautifully colored like poppies, and others black, snakelike, and loathsome, star fish, some with a center smaller than a one cent piece, and thread-like tentacles, two or three feet long! Little fish stranded in pools among the coral reef, some gasping on the sand. How gratefully they swam when I helped them back into the ocean!

Men sometimes get stranded, and the current of human life flows on without them!

7. McKay, Diary, June 19, 1921:

I'm really homesick this morning. This monotonous life in the month of June is beginning to tell on my nerves. Last night and this morning I've thought almost continuously about the folks at home—wondering if they have moved to old Huntsville and whether Llewelyn has made his venture with the dairy investment. I can even now see the kiddies playing on the lawn, Mama and Lou Jean on the summer porch, and Llewelyn on his way to the Dry Hollow farm. June 15th I imagined him coming home with feet soaked and trousers wet to the hips, but happy because he had caught four fish. June is the most delightful month in the year in Ogden Valley; and truly, it seems more delightful than ever as I picture it in mind as I count the lagging hours here in quarantine on old Makahaa.

8. Protestant adherents of Arminian Methodism.

9. See R. Lanier Britsch, "Mormon Intruders in Tonga: The Passport Act of 1922," in *Mormons, Scripture, and the Ancient World: Studies in Honor of John L. Sorenson*, ed. Davis Bitton (Provo, Utah: Foundation for Ancient Research and Mormon Studies, 1998), 121–48.

10. Clement A. Oborn (1900–1922), born on May 15, 1900, at Ogden, Utah. Set apart as a missionary to Tonga on November 16, 1920, until May 11, 1922. Died on May 11, 1922, in Tonga of typhoid fever as a missionary.

11. Volcanic island in Tonga.

12. For a history of this pandemic, see John M. Barry, *The Great Influenza: The Epic Story of the Deadliest Plague in History* (New York: Penguin, 2004).

13. Charles J. Langston (1895–1918), born on March 24, 1895, at Rockville, Utah. Set apart as a missionary to Tonga on December 13, 1916, until November 26, 1918. Died on November 26, 1918, in Tonga.

14. Key Australian maritime shipping and tourism company that serviced the islands of the South Pacific.

15. City in Fiji.

16. Ida Ann Taylor.

17. City in North Island, New Zealand.

18. James Albert Thornton (1891–1948), born on September 18, 1891, at Neeley, Idaho. Set apart as a missionary to New Zealand on November 4, 1920, and returned on March 29, 1923. Died on September 1, 1948, at Pocatello, Idaho.

19. Francis L. Wilcox (1900–1977), born on September 13, 1900, at Preston, Idaho. Set apart as a missionary to Tonga on November 3, 1920, and returned on April 9, 1923. Died on March 30, 1977, at Salt Lake City, Utah.

20. Raymond Pool Nelson (1895–1968), born on July 8, 1895, at Ogden, Utah. Set apart as a missionary to Australia on December 22, 1920,

and returned on March 25, 1923. Died on October 28, 1968, at Goulburn, Australia.

21. Alvin Thomas Maughan (1892–1986), born on March 5, 1892, at Weston, Idaho. Set apart as mission president to New Zealand on February 11, 1920, and returned on September 14, 1923. Died on February 21, 1986, at Bountiful, Utah.

22. William Carlson Warner (1898–1982), born on February 12, 1898, at Benjamin, Utah. Set apart as a missionary to Australia on December 22, 1920, and returned on April 13, 1923. Died on March 15, 1982, at Rigby, Idaho.

23. City in north central North Island, New Zealand.

Chapter 18

1. Babson, *Fundamentals of Prosperity*, 47.
2. Miriam Mae and Priscilla Taylor.
3. Lillian A. Schwendiman.
4. Joseph Anderson (1872–1933), born on February 25, 1872, at Mantua, Utah. Set apart as a missionary to New Zealand on February 11, 1920, and returned on June 1, 1922. Died on May 16, 1933, at Ammon, Idaho.
5. Wallace Lowell Castleton (1900–1986), born on March 24, 1900, at Salt Lake City, Utah. Set apart as a missionary to New Zealand on October 5, 1920, and returned on August 9, 1923. Died on December 10, 1986, at Salt Lake City, Utah.
6. Abram Mattson McFarland (1896–1983), born on November 22, 1896, at West Weber, Utah. Set apart as a missionary to New Zealand on January 7, 1921, and returned on June 14, 1923. Died on March 6, 1983, at Ogden, Utah.
7. Region in North Island, New Zealand.
8. Region in North Island, New Zealand.
9. Region in southeast North Island, New Zealand.
10. Region in eastern North Island, New Zealand.
11. Roland Chauncey Parry (1897–1977), born on May 7, 1897, at Ogden, Utah. Set apart as a missionary to New Zealand on February 19, 1918, and returned on November 14, 1921. Died on October 18, 1977, at Ogden, Utah.
12. Warren Joseph Stallings (1896–1963), born on October 9, 1896, at Eden, Utah. Set apart as a missionary to New Zealand on February 19, 1918, and returned on November 14, 1921. Died on July 23, 1963, in Arizona.
13. Milton Enderby Halls (1901–1975), born on February 4, 1901, at Huntsville, Utah. Set apart as a missionary to New Zealand on July 7, 1919, and returned on June 28, 1921. Died on July 3, 1975, at Sacramento, California.
14. Sylvester Quayle Cannon (1877–1943), born on June 10, 1877, at Salt Lake City, Utah. Apostle, Salt Lake City engineer, and presiding bishop. Died on May 29, 1943, at Salt Lake City, Utah.
15. A tall, straight-grained wood tree.
16. A resin used in varnishes and linoleum.
17. City in eastern North Island, New Zealand.

18. Maori Agricultural College.

19. Leo Bennion Sharp (1894–1941), born on June 18, 1894, at Salt Lake City, Utah. Set apart as a missionary to New Zealand on June 28, 1921, and returned on August 26, 1924. Died on September 25, 1941, at Salt Lake City, Utah.

20. Marcella Turner Sharp.

21. Irvin S. Merrill (1900–?), born on January 15, 1900. Set apart as a missionary to New Zealand on May 31, 1921, and returned on August 20, 1924.

22. Charles Hanson Hollingworth (1901–1971), born on December 29, 1901, at Salt Lake City, Utah. Set apart as a missionary to New Zealand on May 31, 1921, and returned on June 2, 1924. Died on August 19, 1971, at Salt Lake City, Utah.

23. Glenn Arnold Jorgensen (1890–1966), born on August 6, 1890, at Logan, Utah. Set apart as a missionary to New Zealand on May 31, 1921, and returned on November 22, 1923. Died on September 20, 1966, at Ogden, Utah.

24. Joseph Maiben Stephenson (1897–1954), born on October 18, 1897, at Holden, Utah. Set apart as a missionary to New Zealand on January 7, 1921, and returned on March 24, 1924. Died on January 16, 1954, at Salt Lake City, Utah.

25. Glen Bennion Cannon (1897–1979), born on July 6, 1897, at Taylorsville, Utah. Set apart as a missionary to New Zealand on June 28, 1918, and returned on June 29, 1921. Died on April 22, 1979, at Salt Lake City, Utah.

26. Paul Rushton Buttle (1900–1961), born on July 16, 1900, at Salt Lake City, Utah. Set apart as a missionary to New Zealand on September 23, 1919, and returned on September 9, 1922. Died on July 20, 1961, at Salt Lake City, Utah.

27. Henry John Armstrong (1894–1984), born on January 23, 1894, at Palmerston North, New Zealand. Set apart as a missionary to New Zealand on October 12, 1920, and returned on February 23, 1923. Died on January 12, 1984, at Salt Lake City, Utah.

28. Amasa Stetson Holmes (1897–1969), born on March 24, 1897, at North Ogden, Utah. Set apart as a missionary to New Zealand on March 24, 1921, and returned on November 15, 1923. Died on May 14, 1969, at Ogden, Utah.

29. City in southern North Island, New Zealand.

30. James Arthur Rawson (1900–1981), born on November 16, 1900, at Nibley, Oregon. Set apart as a missionary to New Zealand on November 3, 1920, and returned on August 9, 1922. Died on December 31, 1981.

31. Edward Marion Stanger (1890–1965), born on October 6, 1890, at Neeley, Idaho. Set apart as a missionary to New Zealand on November 9, 1920, and returned on November 10, 1922. Died on December 15, 1965, at American Falls, Idaho.

32. Peter Moroni Johnson (1897–1973), born on May 1, 1897, at Logan, Utah. Set apart as a missionary to New Zealand on November 4, 1920, and returned on September 17, 1923. Died on April 9, 1973, at Bountiful, Utah.

33. Leon Grey Willie (1892–1981), born on August 3, 1892, at Mendon, Utah. Set apart as a missionary to New Zealand on July 7, 1919, and returned on August 4, 1921. Died on March 5, 1981, at Ogden, Utah.

34. Melvin Cormi Stewart (1899–1998), born on November 5, 1899, at Rockland, Idaho. Set apart as a missionary to New Zealand on January 7, 1921, and returned on August 1, 1923. Died on August 1, 1998, at Scottsdale, Arizona.

35. Warren Tonks (1897–1975), born on September 24, 1897, at Morgan, Utah. Set apart as a missionary to New Zealand on January 7, 1921, and returned on August 12, 1924. Died on April 5, 1975, at Provo, Utah.

36. Jonathan Royal Bennett (1898–1976), born on August 2, 1898, at Holden, Utah. Set apart as a missionary to New Zealand on January 7, 1921, and returned on June 2, 1924. Died on November 21, 1976, at Fillmore, Utah.

37. Gerald Frederick Heaton (1899–1971), born on September 16, 1899, at Orderville, Utah. Set apart as a missionary to New Zealand on November 3, 1920, and returned on August 2, 1923. Died on February 19, 1971, at El Cajon, California.

38. Ralph Vernon Baird (1901–1977), born on March 25, 1901, at Lewiston, Utah. Set apart as a missionary to New Zealand on March 24, 1921, and returned on November 1, 1923. Died on November 13, 1977, at Logan, Utah.

39. Ephraim Raymond Nelson (1887–1973), born on November 13, 1887, at Moroni, Utah. Set apart as a missionary to New Zealand on March 24, 1921, and returned on August 14, 1923. Died on September 27, 1973, at Payson, Utah.

40. Harold Lamb Hawkes (1899–1974), born on November 21, 1899, at Preston, Idaho. Set apart as a missionary to New Zealand on February 19, 1918, and returned on June 25, 1921. Died on March 21, 1974, at Boise, Idaho.

41. Joseph Edgar Francom (1899–1935), born on October 10, 1899, at Levan, Utah. Set apart as a missionary to New Zealand on March 27, 1919, and returned on April 13, 1922. Died on July 1, 1935.

42. Donald Lewis Hunsaker (1900–1990), born on June 17, 1900, at Elwood, Utah. Set apart as a missionary to New Zealand on March 27, 1919, and returned on February 1, 1922. Died on November 20, 1990, at American Fork, Utah.

43. Joseph Robert Egbert (1897–1965), born on July 23, 1897, at Lewiston, Utah. Set apart as a missionary to New Zealand on July 7, 1919, and returned July 1921. Died on January 31, 1965, at Pocatello, Idaho.

44. Ernest Arthur Ottley (1888–1968), born on April 20, 1888, at South Cottonwood, Utah. Set apart as a missionary to New Zealand July 7, 1919, and returned on January 30, 1923. Died on April 10, 1968, at Midvale, Utah.

45. Newel Sidney Brown (1893–1991), born on September 16, 1893, at Taylorsville, Utah. Set apart as a missionary to New Zealand on September 23, 1919, and returned on January 31, 1922. Died on December 3, 1991, in Utah.

46. Hyrum Victor Bell (1896–1979), born on December 4, 1896, at Pleasant Grove, Utah. Set apart as a missionary to New Zealand on September 23, 1919, and returned on February 9, 1923. Died on August 17, 1979, at Burley, Idaho.

47. Edgar Whitaker Barber (1898–1994), born on September 11, 1898, at Centerville, Utah. Set apart as a missionary to New Zealand on

August 23, 1919, and returned on January 22, 1922. Died on January 24, 1994, at Denver, Colorado.

48. Jacob Isaac Smith (1895–1965), born on September 18, 1895, at Weston, Idaho. Set apart as a missionary to New Zealand on July 7, 1919, and returned on August 18, 1922. Died on July 14, 1965, at Mesa, Arizona.

49. George Samuel Winn (1884–1959), born on April 12, 1884, at Nephi, Utah. Set apart as a missionary to New Zealand on February 11, 1920, and returned on May 20, 1922. Died on June 26, 1959, at Preston, Idaho.

50. Leo Edward Coombs (1894–1967), born on June 26, 1894, at Fielding, Utah. Set apart as a missionary to New Zealand on February 13, 1920, and returned on July 23, 1923. Died on November 23, 1967, at Garland, Utah.

51. Earl Abraham Frederickson (1896–1972), born on July 18, 1896, at Avon, Utah. Set apart as a missionary to New Zealand on February 11, 1920, and returned on November 12, 1922. Died on December 31, 1972.

52. Lonell Woodruff Miller (1898–1985), born on February 11, 1898, at Preston, Idaho. Set apart as a missionary to New Zealand on February 11, 1920, and returned on October 18, 1922. Died on February 12, 1985, in Utah.

53. Harold Jenkins (1897–1958), born on July 8, 1897, at Murray, Utah. Set apart as a missionary to New Zealand on February 13, 1920, and returned on November 2, 1923. Died on February 14, 1958.

54. Heber Hymas (1898–1924), born on February 16, 1898, at Liberty, Idaho. Set apart as a missionary to New Zealand on February 11, 1920, and returned on February 7, 1922. Died on June 18, 1924, at Rupert, Idaho.

55. Frank Lee Crockett (1898–1980), born on September 7, 1898, at Whitney, Idaho. Set apart as a missionary to New Zealand on February 11, 1920, and returned on April 19, 1923. Died on July 30, 1980, at Logan, Utah.

56. Carlos Waldron Clark (1899–1997), born on July 27, 1899, at Morgan, Utah. Set apart as a missionary to New Zealand on February 13, 1920, and returned on April 9, 1923. Died on June 30, 1997.

57. William Arley Cole (1900–1984), born on August 23, 1900, at Ogden, Utah. Set apart as a missionary to New Zealand on February 11, 1920, and returned on March 5, 1924. Died on March 24, 1984, at Salt Lake City, Utah.

58. Arthur Wasilius Gudmundson (1894–1949), born on October 20, 1894, at Salt Lake City, Utah. Set apart as a missionary to New Zealand on May 18, 1920, and returned on March 5, 1924. Died on August 31, 1949.

59. David O. McKay to the Elders and Saints in the New Zealand Mission, August 2, 1921, transcribed in McKay, Diary, August 2, 1921:
In a few hours the boat on which we sail to Australia will heave anchor. As it sails from New Zealand, the distance each succeeding day will widen between us. But no matter how far apart we may be, as measured in miles, we hope we shall always be near each other in spirit and cherished memory.

Our visit has been made enjoyable by your courtesy, thoughtful consideration, and many loving acts of service. Our hearts have been made to rejoice by expressions we have heard and manifestations we have seen of your devotion to the Church. We have met men and women in this mission, as well as in others, whose integrity, faith, and nobility of spirit are unexcelled by any other people in the world. This assurance, with a sincere appreciation of having associated with you in Hui Taus, socials, feasts, and home devotions, we shall treasure as long as memory lasts.

And now as we say farewell, may we express the more earnest desire and prayer of our hearts that *we all remain true to the Faith*. Difficulties may come, and clouds of discouragement may often hover over us; misunderstandings may sometime spring up, and enemies to the Truth may heap upon us scorn and ridicule; but if our hearts are truly anchored in a firm testimony of the divinity of the Restored Gospel of Jesus Christ, all difficulties will be overcome, clouds of discouragement will be dissipated by the sunshine of the Holy Spirit, misunderstandings will be supplanted by confidence and love, and enemies who scoff will be led to pray.

Perform regularly and constantly your various duties in the Church.

Pray continually—in secret and with your household. Pay your tithes and your offerings to the Lord.

Speak well of each other.

Sustain the priesthood.

Be honest in your dealings with your fellow men, and be kind even to your enemies.

Observe the Word of Wisdom, and keep yourselves "unspotted from the sins of the world."

If you will all observe these things, no power on earth can deprive you of your membership in the Church, and of your fellowship with Christ our Redeemer.

There is a great work yet to be done in this mission. May the Lord speedily open the way for its accomplishment! Under the able leadership of President Taylor the work is in excellent hands, and he is most ably assisted by his estimable wife and companion. May the blessings of heaven attend them and their daughters as compensation for their devoted and unselfish labors.

"Let virtue garnish thy thoughts unceasingly, then shall thy confidence wax strong in the presence of God, and the doctrine of the Priesthood shall distill upon thy soul as the dews from heaven.

"The Holy Ghost shall be thy constant companion, and thy sceptre an unchanging sceptre of righteousness and truth, and thy dominion shall be an everlasting dominion, and without compulsory means, it shall flow unto thee forever and ever." (Doc. & Cov. 121:45–46)

The memory of our associations with you, of our inspirational assemblies, kind friends whose hearts are pure as gold will ever be cherished among the glorious experiences of our lives.

God bless you, one and all, until we meet again.

60. Capital of New South Wales, Australia.

61. McKay, Diary, August 6, 1921:

About 4:00 p.m., the gale from the southwest increased in intensity and lashed the sea into a frenzy! As darkness approached, we were in the midst of the worst storm of the voyage. It became impossible even to sit on deck, let alone walk on it. As I sat in the music room, a steward came in swaying and staggering with a four month old baby in his arms. He came directly toward me and said, "Please hold this baby while I get the mother!"

Returning to the deck, he soon came in again leading the mother, who was thrown, however, on a sofa before she could cross the room.

Although the railing was on the table at dinner, some plates and the vegetable dish with contents were thrown pellmell to the floor. As I came out of the dining room, I was thrown against the door which swung open, and I dashed against a young man, pinning him to the staircase. It's with difficulty that one walks along the passage ways! The old vessel reels and rocks as though she were drunken; she squeaks and creaks and trembles but battles bravely forward! Now her prow is toward the sky as she grapples with an oncoming wave! Now she plunges toward the bottom of the sea, throwing the propeller completely out of the water. Now she reels to starboard, then balances again to port!

Though my stomach is growling, I'm not sick. I'm neither tired nor worried, but I'll be glad when we reach Sydney. We shall be at least twenty hours late arriving there!

Chapter 19

1. President John Quincy Adams, quoted in Frank Moore, ed., *American Eloquence: A Collection of Speeches and Addresses by the Most Eminent Orators of America* (New York: D. Appleton, 1857), 252.
2. Inlet of South Pacific in southern Australia.
3. Where Adam and Eve first lived, according to Genesis.
4. Don Carlos Rushton (1864–1950), born on March 8, 1864, at Salt Lake City, Utah. Set apart as mission president to Australia on October 19, 1920, and returned on September 21, 1924. Died on June 16, 1950.
5. See appendix 1.
6. For a short history of LDS evangelism among the Aborigines of Australia, see Marjorie Newton, *Southern Cross Saints: The Mormons in Australia* (Laie, Hawaii: The Institute for Polynesian Studies, Brigham Young University–Hawaii, 1991), 209–11.
7. Elizabeth Jane Rushton (1864–1944), born on April 1, 1864, at Watford, England. Set apart as a missionary to Australia on October 19, 1920, and returned on September 21, 1924. Died on January 18, 1944.
8. McKay, Diary, August 7, 1921:

One young man accosted me later by saying, "Well, Brother McKay, you're just a man after all, aren't you?"

"Why, I hope so," I replied. "What did you think I am?"

"Well, you know, we think of the old Apostles as being different."

9. See Isaiah 11:9.
10. Inlet of the South Pacific located in New South Wales, Australia.
11. Island in southeastern Australia.

12. Capital city of Victoria, Australia.

13. Robert Kenneth Bischoff (1898–1980), born on March 31, 1898, at Fountain Green, Utah. Set apart as a missionary to Australia on July 1, 1919, and returned on September 24, 1921. Died on June 4, 1980, at Idaho Falls, Idaho.

14. McKay, Diary, September 16, 1921:

I was very greatly interested in the Rock Wallabies, diminutive kangaroos, that were hopping around at the entrance to the Grand Arch.

The Cookaburra, or Laughing Jackass, was also an attractive feature, as indeed are all the other birds in these trees. They are so different, especially in their whistling—even the magpie is different from ours, has a blacker and a wider tail, flies about the same and seems to be just as cheeky and inquisitive as magpies at home.

Visited the Left Imperial, not so picturesque in general outline as the Arch but abounding in beautiful and wonderful chambers, grottoes, and charming details, chief among which are the Shawls and the Mystery.

During our tour of two hours, I heard everything described by two overworked adjectives. Women would look in admiration at a mass of amber-colored crystals and say, "Aren't they pretty?" They would look at the Madonna with its daintily festooned recess named Minnie's Grotto as a background, and exclaim, "Oh, isn't it pretty?"

In admiration of a cavern extensive and majestic in outline and abounding in grotesque shapes and spooky formations, they would say, "Isn't it pretty?" One girl said, "Isn't it dear?" The men would express their exultation by saying, "That's fine!"

Since no words can picture the wonders and beauties of these labyrinthian, subterranean passages, grottoes and jewel-bound statues and draperies, pretty, dear and fine will perhaps serve as well as any other words. No one can emerge from one of them, such as the Left Imperial, without being overwhelmed with the exquisite beauty and sublime grandeur!

But the crowning glory of all seems to have been centered in the Orient Cave, to see which 1400 steps must be trodden, through tunnels and low caverns, across yawning chasms, over underground waters, and up precipitous flights of stairs!

But it's worth it all and more. I came out of it this afternoon feeling that I had seen one of the most gloriously decorated, most lavishly draped, most artistically jeweled caves in the world.

15. Milton B. Jensen (1898–1976), born on July 19, 1898, at Mendon, Utah. Set apart as mission president to Australia July 1, 1919, and returned on February 12, 1921. Died on February 17, 1976, in Florida.

16. Sterling Johnson (1897–1987), born on April 21, 1897, at Provo, Utah. Set apart as a missionary to Australia on April 2, 1919, and returned on September 24, 1921. Died on March 3, 1987, at Lovell, Wyoming.

17. Thomas Gordon Smith (1899–1983), born on April 19, 1899, at Glendale, Utah. Set apart as a missionary to Australia on November 16, 1920, and returned on May 23, 1923. Died on October 30, 1983, at Parowan, Utah.

18. Franklin Dewey Fronk (1898–1964), born on July 17, 1898, at West Weber, Utah. Set apart as a missionary to Australia on May 25, 1921, and returned on October 3, 1923. Died on September 17, 1964, at Ogden, Utah.

19. Alvin Englestead (1892–1980), born on November 1, 1892, at Asay Ranch, Utah. Set apart as a missionary to Australia on October 19, 1920, and returned on March 17, 1923. Died on May 5, 1980, at Kanosh, Utah.

20. John Ernest Hipwell (1893–1961), born on April 24, 1893, at West Weber, Utah. Set apart as a missionary to Australia on January 18, 1921, and returned on May 18, 1923. Died on September 22, 1961, at Ogden, Utah.

21. Strait separating Tasmania and the continent of Australia.

22. Island in southeastern Australia.

23. Town on the north coast of Tasmania, Australia.

24. Capital city and port of Tasmania, Australia.

25. Edward Eugene Gardner (1888–1975), born on July 18, 1888, at Salem, Utah. Set apart as mission president to Australia on January 18, 1921, and returned on May 18, 1923. Died on August 12, 1975, at Delta, Utah.

26. Wallace Otis Walker (1897–1987), born on June 15, 1897, at Eden, Utah. Set apart as a missionary to Australia on December 22, 1920, and returned on September 8, 1922. Died on March 24, 1987, at Ogden, Utah.

27. Joseph Ross Hunsaker (1899–1989), born on March 18, 1899, at Honeyville, Utah. Set apart as a missionary to Australia on July 1, 1919, and returned on November 23, 1921. Died on November 17, 1989, at Salt Lake City, Utah.

28. James Elmer Hendricks (1898–1989), born on December 3, 1898, at Huntsville, Utah. Set apart as a missionary to Australia on December 22, 1920, and returned on March 18, 1923. Died on March 29, 1989.

29. Port city of Tasmania, Australia.

30. Capital city of South Australia.

31. City capital of Western Australia.

32. Island off Malay Archipelago in South China Sea.

33. Austin Smith Tolman (1893–1975), born on July 30, 1893, at Honeyville, Utah. Set apart as a missionary to Australia on July 11, 1919, and returned on November 23, 1921. Died on August 13, 1975, at Malad City, Idaho.

34. George Aaron Christensen (1890–1970), born on January 18, 1890, at Bear River, Utah. Set apart as a missionary to Australia on January 18, 1921, and returned on May 18, 1923. Died on August 27, 1970, at Salt Lake City, Utah.

35. Herman Evans Bayles (1896–1970), born on April 30, 1896, at Parowan, Utah. Set apart as a missionary to Australia on October 19, 1920, and returned on March 17, 1923. Died on April 19, 1970, at Parowan, Utah.

36. Earl Roland Hanson (1897–1979), born on November 21, 1897, at American Fork, Utah. Set apart as a missionary to Australia on December 22, 1920, and returned on May 18, 1923. Died on July 19, 1979, at Salt Lake City, Utah.

37. Thomas William Lutz (1896–1926), born on October 24, 1896, at Rexburg, Idaho. Set apart as a missionary to Australia on December 22, 1920, and returned on March 21, 1923. Died on October 20, 1926, at Rexburg, Idaho.

38. Doris Baker (1899–?), born on April 5, 1899. Set apart as a missionary to Australia on November 16, 1920, and returned on April 17, 1923.

39. Marion George Romney (1897–1988), born on September 19, 1897, at Colonia Juarez, Mexico. Set apart as a missionary to Australia on November 16, 1920, and returned on May 30, 1923. Apostle and member of the First Presidency. Died on May 20, 1988, at Salt Lake City, Utah.

40. William Wallace Horne (1897–1969), born on June 24, 1897, at Salt Lake City, Utah. Set apart as a missionary to Australia on October 20, 1920, and returned on March 16, 1923. Died on March 6, 1969, at Salt Lake City, Utah.

41. William Lunt Jones (1897–1976), born on September 14, 1897, at Cedar City, Utah. Set apart as a missionary to Australia on October 19, 1920, and returned on March 19, 1923. Died on April 1, 1976, at Cedar City, Utah.

42. Robert Howard Andrus (1896–1986), born on July 31, 1896, at Mill Creek, Utah. Set apart as a missionary to Australia on December 22, 1920, and returned on April 16, 1923. Died on August 25, 1986, at Idaho Falls, Idaho.

43. Raymond Pool Nelson (1895–1968), born on July 8, 1895, at Ogden, Utah. Set apart as a missionary to Australia on December 22, 1920, and returned on March 25, 1923. Died on October 28, 1968, at Goulburn, Australia.

44. Charles Mac Bowen (1889–1974), born on September 7, 1889, at Brigham City, Utah. Set apart as a missionary to Australia on January 18, 1921, and returned on March 31, 1922. Died on September 9, 1974, at Ogden, Utah.

45. Lorenzo Fredrick Hansen (1885–1924), born on December 20, 1885, at Brigham City, Utah. Set apart as a missionary to Australia on May 25, 1921, and returned on August 16, 1923. Died on February 17, 1924, at Brigham City, Utah.

46. See Matthew 28:19.

47. Port capital of Queensland, Australia.

48. State in northeastern Australia.

49. Niels William Oldroyd (1877–1954), born on January 25, 1877, at Glenwood, Utah. Living in Glenwood, Utah, when called on a mission. Set apart as a missionary to Australia on January 18, 1921, and returned on May 19, 1923. Died on March 1, 1954, at Manti, Utah.

50. Gerald Oraian Billings (1899–1982), born on February 12, 1899, at Fremont, Utah. Set apart as a missionary to Australia on December 22, 1920, and returned on April 13, 1923. Died on February 25, 1982, at Delta, Utah.

51. Port city in northeastern Australia.

52. Capital of Northern Territory, Australia.

53. McKay, Diary, September 16, 1921:

In the evening Brother Cannon and I walked out to the compound, where the aborigines are quartered. We had heard that the natives were giving a corroboree, or native dance, so inquiring our route, we walked out there alone.

The night was perfect. The full moon shone in the northeastern sky in all her silvery beauty, making the stars look few indeed in the blue southern sky. The air was balmy and the woods on each side of the road quiet and peaceful.

Arriving at the village, we saw groups of natives lying around enjoying the pleasant atmosphere. Approaching one of them, we inquired about the corroboree, a word which they understood; we were disappointed to learn that it was over.

However, a group of men were still lying around the open space in which it had been given, so we walked over to them. But the Corroboree was over.

We had come out two miles to see it, and I disliked very much to return without doing so. To a young fellow who could understand English, I said, "How much money do you want to show us the Corroboree?"

"You want us to Corroboree?"

"Yes, how much will you take to Corroboree?"

Then followed a "Goo-bul-oo-good-bul-oo-oo" such as I've never heard—all the twenty men talking at once.

"Three of us dance the Corroboree for three bob."

"You mean one bob each?"

"Yes, one bob for each."

"All right," I quickly answered, "go ahead."

Then the twenty began a rhythmic clapping and a chanting and a typical old aborigine—as naked as a monkey in a tree—worse, because the monkey has hair—began a contortive dance that was as interesting as it was grotesque. Two others followed when he had finished, we clapped our hands, cried "bravo," paid them their three shillings and two extra besides, and left them in fine spirits as they cried, "Goo-nit-goonit!"

Thus on this our last night in Australia, we had seen not only the real aborigines, but the Corroboree as well!

54. State in southeastern Australia.

55. State in southeastern Australia.

56. State in southern Australia.

57. State in western Australia.

58. Territory in central and northern Australia.

59. The gap between the rails.

Chapter 20

1. James E. Talmage, *"The Book of Mormon," An Account of its Origin, with Evidences of its Genuineness and Authenticity: Two Lectures* (Kansas City, Mo.: Southwestern States Mission, The Church of Jesus Christ of Latter-Day Saints, 1899), 23. Talmage (1862–1933) was an apostle, theologian, and geologist.

2. British money.

3. Country in Southeast Asia in Malay Archipelago.

4. Port city in northeastern Java, Indonesia.

5. Port capital in northwestern Java, Indonesia.

6. Frank William Becraft (1888–1972), born on March 12, 1888, at Ogden, Utah. Served as a missionary in Java, Singapore. Died on May 18, 1972, at Denver, Colorado.

7. City in northern Utah, United States.

8. City in northern Utah, United States.

9. Peninsula in southeastern Asia divided among Thailand, Malaysia, and Burma.

10. City south of Jakarta in Java, Indonesia.
11. Island in western Indonesia.
12. Mount Guntur, Java, Indonesia.
13. Island and volcano in Indonesia.
14. Country in East Asia.
15. For a description of this natural disaster, see Ian Thornton, *Krakatau: The Destruction and Reassembly of an Island Ecosystem* (Cambridge, Mass.: Harvard University Press, 1996).
16. McKay described:

Arrived at Singapore at 4:00 p.m., our vessel being only one among hundreds of sailing craft of all kinds and sizes, lying in the harbor.

There was no delay by haughty officials. As soon as an officer put his stamp upon our passports, we were ready to go ashore, no customs regulations or requirements in this open port.

[213]

NOTES TO PAGES 122–124

The town itself ranks in interest second only to Peking, not that there is anything of very great historical interest, nor that the city has anything very extraordinary about it architecturally or otherwise, but the motley tribe of human beings representing as they do so many different nationalities heightened my enthusiasm to a degree it hasn't attained since we left the islands. There are Chinese, Japanese, Mananese, Indians, Javanese, and Europeans, all retaining native dress and customs, jostling and trading and scheming among one another in this seaport town of the Orient. Jinrikishas, oxcarts, dogcarts, and automobiles crowd the streets during the business hours, and natives offering their wares for sale line the sidewalks at night. Life is really more like China than Japan, and one can purchase almost anything here which he can either in China or Japan.

A significant feature was the entire absence of women from the streets. Men there are by thousands and of all kinds and classes—including those with long black hair, sometimes hanging loosely over their shoulders, and sometimes done up in braids on top of their heads, but women were conspicuous by their absence. (McKay, *Home Memories of President David O. McKay*, 88–89)

17. Port city on the Hugli River in East India.
18. McKay described:

My most interesting experience here [Penang] was a short visit to the Chinese temple at Ayer Itam four miles from town. The auto drive was most delightful. Every turn of the road presents some beautiful view of large, spacious houses, in the midst of beautiful lawns and gardens.

The temple itself is only of passing interest to one who has seen more magnificent ones in China; but the scores, perhaps hundreds, of tortoises here add an interest not experienced at other temples. The large goldfish and other varieties contribute to the interest.

The Chinese temple is really a series of temples, built upon the sides of a hill. Looking up the hill one sees, stretching up and up continually, the ramping roofs, the raking gables of Chinese temple architecture. On the walls are lettered tablets in royal blue. The boulders of the hill are incised with Chinese characters in red. On every hand are shrines. Brass blazes in sunlight, or warms the shadows, in urns and jars and gongs and vessels of all shapes. Temple surpasses temple. In one a solemn figure broods and compels reverence. In another laughs a jolly god. Side by side sit hideous and gigantic demons crushing the wicked under foot. Everywhere is BUDDHA. Each race of Buddhists has here its own temple, Siamese, Japanese, Chinese, Burmese, Singhalese.

Returning from the temple by a different drive, I was soon again on board the *Bharata*. (McKay, *Home Memories of President David O. McKay*, 89)

19. Port capital of Myanmar.

20. Country in Southeast Asia on the Bay of Bengal (Myanmar).

21. A large cone-shaped Buddhist pagoda.

22. River in southern Myanmar.

23. River in Myanmar flowing into the Bay of Bengal.

24. McKay described:

Landing at Rangoon at 8:00 a.m. Brother Cannon and I went ashore before breakfast in order to visit the famous pagoda at this place, the golden dome of which we had seen as our boat came up the Rangoon River.

Securing a jinrikisha, both of us in one, with the assistance of a kind policeman, we directed the rikisha man to take us to the pagoda.

I endured watching the little wiry man pulling us two large fellows, until we were within half a mile of the pagoda, then I jumped out and walked.

The Shwe Dagon Pagoda is built on an eminence, the summit of which has been leveled to a sort of platform 900 feet long, 685 feet wide, and 166 feet above the city. No wonder the jinrikisha man had more than he could do to pull us up the incline.

At the southern entrance, which is one of four facing the cardinal points of the compass, we removed our shoes and stockings, and began our ascent of the stone steps leading 800 yards up to the pagoda. The steps were lined with sellers of flowers, trinkets, candles, food, pictures, etc., with little children whose parents are teaching them to beg, and with old decrepit and deformed professional beggars. The limit was reached, I thought, when we saw dogs and chickens running around! Why we should go barefooted amongst dogs and chickens was more than I could comprehend.

Images of Buddha greet the visitor or the devout worshipers at every turn. In some niches, he is sitting, in some reclining, and in others standing. Exquisite carvings and colored glass colonades abound. Resonant Burma bells are sounding, almost continually, and occasionally one of the large bells sends forth an appeal. The Great Bell, the third largest in the world, is 14 feet high, 7½ feet in diameter, 22½ feet in circumference, 15 inches thick, and over 42 tons in weight.

The perimeter of the base of the pagoda is 1,355 feet, its height, 370 feet above the platform. It is covered with gold leaf from top to bottom. It is supposed to have been founded 585 BC This is an error undoubtedly; for Buddha was not born until about 557 BC. (McKay, *Home Memories of President David O. McKay*, 90–91)

25. McKay described:

About 9:30 p.m. we were strolling leisurely through the crowded streets, swallowed up, so to speak, in the populace, when we came upon a multitude of people, most of whom, if not all, men, sitting on benches placed along the sidewalk, or standing on the edge of the street. A band concert, we thought at first, but there was no band. Convinced that something extraordinary was going on, and determined to find out, if possible, what that something was, we approached a group of young men and ventured in English this question, "What is this?"

As they began to edge away from us, we were made to understand that they understood no English, and were about to despair, when a stately young fellow came forward, and, answering our question said, "This is a death service."

Thinking he said *debt* service, I asked if these people were assembled for the purpose of contributing to pay the bankrupt's debts.

"No," explained our friend, "the man not in debt; he has expired."

Relieved to learn that the unfortunate man was better off than we first surmised, we ventured to ask about the nature of the service.

"The gentleman was buried last Wednesday," continued our informant, "and his friends have assembled to pay their respects to him. He has left a wife and three children. We read the Koran, that is our Bible, for one hour. They are doing that up in the room now."

We looked up, and saw a well-lighted room—a group of men, some of whom held manuscripts in their hands, either reading intently or listening attentively.

"We then pray for the departed soul, that he may be at peace."

"Do you all pray?" I asked, "every one of you here on the street?"

"Yes," he replied, "everyone of us."

"And then what do you do?"

"Then all the poor are fed," he said.

"Do you all contribute to defray the expense?"

"Oh, no, the widow bear all the expense," he informed us.

"Why, I exclaimed, there must be a thousand people here!"

"Yes, she feed a thousand people. She very wealthy. That building," pointing to a three-story business block, "is his mother-in-law's!"

He explained that all assembled were Mohammedans, and that Mohammedans worship, not Buddha, but God. (McKay, *Home Memories of President David O. McKay*, 91–92)

26. Central Myanmar. See Rudyard Kipling, *Works* (New York: Doubleday, 1914), 193.

27. Rudyard Kipling (1865–1936), English author.

28. McKay described:

We slept last night aboard the S.S. *Arankola*, and steamed down the river across the bar at about 5:00 a.m.

Mr. Cyril Gore, a fellow passenger, who has spent twenty years among the Hindus as a tea gardener and who employs over 1,000 of them continually, told me this morning that the Christian religion has made practically no headway among the Hindus. Generally only the outcasts accept it. He knew a minister, a German Lutheran, who had spent thirty-four years in missionary work who told him that he, the minister, did not believe he had made one genuine convert. (McKay, *Home Memories of President David O. McKay*, 92–93)

Chapter 21

1. Pasquale Villari, *Life and Times of Girolamo Savonarola* (London: T. Fisher Unwin, 1888), 184. Savonarola (1452–1498) was an Italian reformer.

2. Arm of the Indian Ocean between India and Sri Lanka on the west and Myanmar and the Malay Peninsula on the east.
3. River in northern India flowing from the Himalayas.
4. River in eastern India flowing into Bay of Bengal.
5. Port city in western India.
6. Sea in northwestern Indian Ocean.
7. Mountains in southern Asia.
8. Robert Clive (1725–1774), British general and creator of the British empire in India.
9. Warren Hastings (1732–1818), English statesman.
10. William Makepeace Thackeray (1811–1863), English author.
11. Thomas Babington MaCaulay (1800–1859), English historian.
12. Frederick Sleigh Roberts (1832–1914), British field marshal.
13. Horatio Herbert Kitchener (1850–1916), British field marshal.

14. See Denis Judd, *The Lion and the Tiger: The Rise and Fall of the British Raj, 1600–1947* (New York: Oxford University Press, 2004).
15. Hindu reverence of the cow.
16. McKay described:

When I entered the bathroom this morning, I noticed some little black things around my right ankle, which I thought to be cinders, but as I started to brush them off, they began hopping and crawling! I stripped and found my clothes alive. The things seemed smaller than fleas, and yet related to them. I called Brother Cannon who said they were the genuine breed. I asked him if he had been troubled through the night, but he had not. I caught thirty on my body and clothes, and lost about eight or ten for everyone I caught. Brother Cannon came in from his room with the report that he had undressed and caught 120. About noon he had captured 157!

In the afternoon we had secured a room at the Great Eastern Hotel, where we hope to be free from bedfellows! (McKay, *Home Memories of President David O. McKay*, 93)

17. City in eastern India.
18. McKay described:

At the station, we and a European were ushered into a first-class compartment. But no sooner were our satchels and parcels placed, and we comfortably seated than we were informed by the conductor that, "This compartment is reserved for another party."

We answered, "The guard unlocked the door and let us in."

"It doesn't matter, the names are written on the car for whom this has been reserved."

"Well, find us another compartment, and we'll leave this one."

He left, but before he returned the "party" for whom the reservation had been made entered. They were a Persian gentleman (merchant), his two grown sons, their servant, and baggage galore.

Before they had arranged their luggage, tipped the coolies, and tried to get seats, the train had started. In the meantime the merchant had begun addressing us in his native tongue, telling us, as we thought, that this was his compartment, and we should get out. Our European companion had called a guard, who had come to our rescue just as the train pulled out of the station; so we were seven besides the servant who had withdrawn to the washroom.

Imagine our surprise when the guard, interpreting, told us that the Persian gentleman was not asking us to leave but hoped that we would not be too much inconvenienced by the crowded condition of the compartment, that he was glad to have us share it with them, and wished us to choose the most comfortable seats and so forth. Talk about a gentleman! Although we were where we had been led by one who we thought knew what he was doing, and, therefore, were really not intruders, yet I began to feel like one.

We thanked him graciously, and bade him and his sons be seated. A few moments later he asked if his servants making coffee in the wash room would offend us in any way.

"Certainly not."

When it was prepared, the merchant offered it to us first. When we thanked him and told him we did not drink coffee, he served orange.

About this time, the European took out his pipe and began to fill it with tobacco. In striking contrast to the gentlemanly consideration of the Persian in regard to the making of coffee, the European did not deign to ask whether his smoking would be offensive!

And worse than that. When at the first station, this "refined" European gentleman ordered lemonade, he ordered three. Anticipating an embarrassment, I quickly said, "This is my treat," and ordered six.

We and Europeans assume a haughty, dignified air towards the Orientals, but, by goodness, the Orientals are far ahead of us in courtesy and good manners! (McKay, *Home Memories of President David O. McKay*, 93–95)

19. City in northern India.
20. Marble mausoleum completed in 1648. Perhaps the best example of Mughal architecture.
21. Shah Jahan (1592–1666), Mughal emperor of India.
22. McKay described:

One of our most interesting visits was to the Jama Masjid or Great Mosque, from the top of the tower of which, just at sunset of the 11th, we obtained a magnificent view of the city and surrounding country. This is another monument to the famous Shah Jahan's ability as a builder for the centuries.

Another was to the Ivory Palace where we saw the most exquisite workmanship in ivory carving and skilful [sic] woodwork—tables of all sizes, screens of various designs and uses, lacquer ware, ivory tusks carved artistically—in fact, everything in ivory and woodwork that one might desire we saw in this wonderful place.

We felt that we were in the heart of India here as we were in the heart of China at Peking. (McKay, *Home Memories of President David O. McKay*, 95)

23. Sixteenth-century Mughal monument also known as the Red Fort.
24. River in northern India.
25. Capital city of India.
26. City in India.
27. City in northeastern Pakistan.
28. See R. Lanier Britsch, *Nothing More Heroic: The Compelling Story of the First Latter-day Saint Missionaries in India* (Salt Lake City: Deseret

Book, 1999); and R. Lanier Britsch, "The East India Mission of 1851–56: Crossing the Boundaries of Culture, Religion, and Law," *Journal of Mormon History* 27 (Fall 2001): 150–76.

29. George William McCune (1872–1963), born on May 24, 1872, at Nephi, Utah. Set apart as president of the Eastern States Mission on April 24, 1919, and returned on July 11, 1922. Died in 1963.

30. McKay described:

Bombay is Europeanized and a very thriving city. But I saw more abject poverty and squalor here than I have seen in any other city since we left Peking and Tientsin—women half-naked sitting on the stone pavement with naked infants lying by their sides—others with two or three children with them begging on the street—little boys with the left arm cut off just above the elbow, who would hold out the withered stump of naked arms to awaken the sympathy of passers-by from whom they solicited alms—blind men—crippled men—miserable women, little children of all ages, begging, begging, begging!

At ten o'clock in the morning, I passed one man lying on the sidewalk, whose foot had either been crushed or was being eaten away with disease. There he lay exposed, with the flies covering the festering sore. At 6:00 p.m., I chanced to pass the same place and saw him still there. He had turned on his left side and seemed to be unconscious. The further I walked away from him, the more I began to wonder whether he might not have died during the day. After dinner, I walked back to make sure, but before I arrived at the spot at 10:00 p.m., he had been removed—but whether to the pyre or the river for the crocodiles I do not know. (McKay, *Home Memories of President David O. McKay*, 95–96)

31. Followers of the chief religion of India.

32. McKay described:

One cannot travel far or remain long in India without becoming intensely aware of the iron-bound system of caste that enslaves all classes.

"How oppressive and iniquitous this has been and still is," says the Hindu writer, "can easily be appreciated if, for the purpose of my explaining the matter, our social organizations were regarded as a huge, colossal, upright pillar of human atoms, encased by iron tubes placed tier upon tier from the bottom till the topmost cornice was reached.

"At the very bottom of the pillar you have the 'untouchable Sudras.' On their heads place a well-fitting, ventilation-proof, thick iron sheet on which put the (1) 'touchable Sudras,' and on their heads again place a similar sheet. On this sheet put the 'Vaisyas,' on whose heads a similar iron sheet being placed, let the 'Kshatryas' stand on it, and likewise let another sheet rest on the heads of the 'Kshatryas' and on that let the 'Brahmans' stand.

"Let there be a flag flying from the topmost cornice of the pillar with this inscription on it: 'Hindu Sumaj.' Now you have a complete picture of our caste system." (McKay, *Home Memories of President David O. McKay*, 96)

Chapter 22

1. Port city in southern Yemen.
2. Peninsula in southwestern Asia.
3. Sea between Arabia and northeastern Africa.
4. McKay described:

   When I came on deck this morning, we were approaching the seaport town of Aden, situated in the southwestern corner of the Arabian Peninsula, near the mouth of the Red Sea. The rugged islands on our left and the mainland on our right were equally barren. Dry and sand-swept, the landscape stretched a parched and naked waste as far as the field glasses could carry our vision. In this practically rainless region, not a tree or blade of grass grows. However, we thought we observed one exception—a clump of scrubby shrubs in the midst of a sand drift on a hillside at the foot of a sort of a ravine. Perhaps a little water seeping out made that spot an oasis.

   We anchored outside the wharf and took on coal.

   A dozen sampans soon ranged alongside, filled with baskets, ostrich plumes, shells, cigars, sharks' jaws, leopard skins, etc., which the garrulous owners, amidst loud hallooing and wild gesticulations, sold to the passengers. The articles were passed up for inspection by means of a basket attached to the middle of a long rope, one end of which was thrown up to the purchaser and the other held by the Adenite. If a sale was made, the money went down in the basket.

   Brother Cannon and I went ashore, but, owing to insufficient time, we did not drive out to the tanks, ancient reservoirs which are now and have been for years entirely dry.

   The camels with ropes and traces hitched to their shoulders and humps, pulling heavily-laden wagons through the streets were the most interesting of all things in this out-of-existence place.

   Aden is the most cheerless, the most barren, the most forsaken looking spot we have seen in our world tour! (McKay, *Home Memories of President David O. McKay*, 96–97)
5. See Exodus 13–14; and 1 Nephi 2.
6. The Arabian Peninsula.
7. Mountain where, according to the Bible, the Law was given to Moses; thought to be in the Gebel Musa on the Sinai Peninsula (Mount Horeb).
8. See Exodus 14:14.
9. Patriarch who fled from Jerusalem to the New World with his family in the opening chapters of the Book of Mormon.
10. Ferdinand-Marie de Lesseps (1805–94), French promoter of canals.
11. Inland waterway in northeastern Egypt.
12. Rameses II (reigned 1304–1237 BC), Egyptian pharaoh and builder.
13. Port city in northeastern Egypt on the Mediterranean.
14. Capital city of Egypt.
15. City in northern Egypt.
16. See Exodus 12:37.
17. McKay described:

    On our right through the glasses we can see camels lying lazily in the sun, some of them still carrying their loads on their backs. It may be that they are just getting ready to start out as a caravan because in the distance I can see three camels and a man starting across the sandy waste.

During the forenoon, we passed hundreds of men, mules, and camels working along the bank, evidently with the purpose of widening the canal. It was an interesting sight to see the camels, the faithful old beasts, lie down while the men shoveled the sand into the boxes attached to the backs of these ships of the desert, and then rise and wobble out of the pit, climb the hill, and go deposit their burden by again lying down. (McKay, *Home Memories of President David O. McKay*, 98)

18. Followers of Islam; Muslims.

19. McKay described:

We arrived at Cairo at 1:00 p.m. and secured rooms at the Continental. Cairo is said to be the largest city in Egypt, containing about 750,000 inhabitants. The oldest town, there are really four of them, was built on the eastern bank of the Nile and was known as Babylon. This was captured AD 641 by Amr, the general of Caliph Omar who built the part now known as Old Cairo.

Modern Cairo was founded AD 969 following the conquest of Egypt by Gohar, the general of the Moslem Army. Heliopolis, the new, is just a wealthy suburb founded in 1906.

Napoleon Bonaparte established headquarters here in 1798, following the battle of the pyramids.

Mohammed Ali Pasha, the man who massacred the Mamluk Beys, was the founder of the latest ruling family, and the man who instituted modern institutions, which being improved upon by his successors, have made Cairo what it is today.

Cairo is a city of mosques, there being 366 scattered throughout the town, the citadel and the dome and minarets of the Sultan Hassan Mosque, the finest Arabian monument in Egypt, towering above them all. (McKay, *Home Memories of President David O. McKay*, 98–99)

20. See Exodus 2.

21. City in northern Egypt. The ancient pyramids of Khufu, Khafre, and Menkaure comprise this Egyptian necropolis.

22. McKay described:

With "Abdul" as our dragoman, at 5:30 a.m. we stepped into an auto which he had waiting for us in front of the hotel and started our seven mile drive to the Pyramids. It was just breaking day. The air was cool and delightful except for the abominable smell arising from the refuse on the streets.

As we reached the outskirts of the city, scores and scores of camels, donkeys and men, walking in line one after another, were strolling into market. Occasionally, we saw a woman with a heavy load on her head, but these were more common later in the day.

We crossed the historic old Nile, and saw the flooded plain from which in three weeks all the water will be drawn, absorbed or evaporated, and the farmers will begin to prepare the soil for crops. Our drive through the long beautiful vista of acacia trees was glorious, and it was through these just as the eastern sky was tinged in rosy hue that we caught our first glimpse of the pyramid of Cheops.

As we approached nearer, and saw half-covered in mist the pyramid of Cheops standing near, I felt much the same sensation that

I had when I first glimpsed the Grand Canyon of the Colorado—a realization that I was not comprehending its magnitude. But as we climbed up the sandy incline and listened to Abdul and stood beside the massive stone in this wonder of wonderful tombs, its massiveness began to dawn upon me.

It was built by Kheops of Khufu about 3733 BC. In its construction, 100,000 men worked three months each year for twenty years.

It is 450 feet high. Each of its sloping sides is 568 feet long and 764 feet wide. Our guide Abdul said it originally covered thirteen acres. Eight feet of marble blocks, covering this entire pyramid, have been removed.

The pyramid of Khephren stands near Cheops, and the third largest of the group of nine stands just beyond.

This pyramid is 204 feet high, and may be ascended without much difficulty. From its summit we obtained a magnificent view of the surrounding country, just beginning to stir with life on this peaceful October morning.

The Sphinx, or Aboul-Houll (The Father of Terror) was built about 3,000 BC It represents a lion in body and has a man's face and a woman's head. It is 60 feet high, and 187 feet long. The paws of this animal are now covered with sand.

East of the pyramid of Cheops and fifty yards southeast of the Sphinx stand the ruins of an interesting old temple which was originally connected with the Sphinx.

In this we were shown a granite block 16 feet long, 5 feet thick, and 4 feet high, and other blocks, tongued and grooved, of almost equal size lie perfectly in place in the original wall. Its six chambers occupy 147 square feet, and its walls rise 46 feet.

Camels were placed at our disposal, and we rode from one structure to another.

We spent several hours visiting these huge monuments to the tyranny as well as to the greatness of the ancient Pharaohs. (McKay, *Home Memories of President David O. McKay*, 99–101)

23. A massive Egyptian monument in the form of a reclining lion with a human head.
24. Basin carved by Nile River in northern Egypt.
25. A lofty slender tower of a mosque.
26. Desert in northern Africa.
27. Desert region in northern Africa.
28. Cheops (twenty-sixth century BC), ruler of Egypt and pyramid builder.
29. An Old Testament patriarch.
30. See Genesis 12:10–20.
31. Ancient city on the Nile in northern Egypt.
32. Overseer of the pyramids and sun temples during Dynasty V.
33. Village in northern Egypt.
34. A bull venerated by the Egyptians.
35. Stone coffins.
36. Oasis in Algeria.
37. Capital city of Israel.
38. Eberhard II (circa 1315–1392), Count of Württemberg.
39. See *The Book of Wanderings of Brother Felix Fabri (Circa 1480–1483 A.D.)*, trans. Aubrey Stewart (London: Palestine Pilgrims' Text Society, 1896).

40. City in Palestine located southwest of Jerusalem, Israel.

41. Hill where Jesus was crucified near Jerusalem, Israel.

42. A church commemorating the traditional location of Jesus's crucifixion and burial.

43. See Matthew 27:37 and Mark 15:26.

Chapter 23

1. Russian novelist Leo Tolstoy (1828–1910), quoted in Upton Sinclair, ed., *The Cry for Justice: An Anthology of the Literature of Social Protest* (Philadelphia: John C. Winston, 1915), 110.

2. See Luke 2:13–14.

3. Constantine I (AD 306–337), Roman emperor who embraced Christianity.

4. A church in Bethlehem built over the traditional site of Jesus's birthplace.

5. Mountain ridge running north and south on the eastern side of Jerusalem, Israel.

6. For more details about the dedicatory prayer, see LaMar C. Berrett and Blair G. Van Dyke, *Holy Lands: A History of the Latter-day Saints in the Near East* (American Fork, Utah: Covenant Communications, 2005), 209–10.

7. Named after the first Christian martyr who was stoned here, also known as Lion's Gate. See Acts 7:54–60.

8. See Acts 7:58–60.

9. Ancient region of Palestine.

10. River in northeastern Israel.

11. Salt lake on boundary between Israel and Jordan.

12. The location where Jesus agonized over the sins of the world and was arrested. See Mark 14.

13. See John 11:1–18.

14. Village in Palestine located east of Jerusalem, Israel.

15. McKay described:

The Dead Sea is 129 feet [*sic*] below the level of the sea, and 3786 feet lower than Jerusalem. Its shore line is the lowest part of the earth's surface not covered with water.

I was not disappointed in the Jordan Valley, although it is dry and barren of all vegetation except a shrub that resembles our greasewood and rabbitbrush.

The Dead Sea is a beautiful body of water, and this day exceptionally so because the surface was sufficiently stirred to make the waves high and boisterous as they splashed against the pebbly shore.

We tried to secure a boat to row on it, but a man at a little station on the northern shore said it was too rough. I hired a native to swim out and secure two bottles of the clean water as specimens. It contains twenty-five percent mineral salt.

Across the sea to the east and running north and south are the Mountains of Moab. There stands Mt. Nebo from which Moses viewed the Promised Land. (Deut. 34.) It was near Mt. Nebo where Elijah was taken up to heaven.

Leaving the Dead Sea, we drove north through high dense weeds or shrubs, the name of which we did not ascertain, to the traditional place on the Jordan River where the children of Israel crossed into the Promised Land. Perhaps in that same vicinity the Savior of the world was baptized "to fulfil all righteousness."

Between the Jordan and Jericho, we were shown the place where at Gilgal, Joshua erected the pillar of twelve stones. (Joshua 4.)

As we stood near the tree which marks the spot, our guide pointed out the site of the ancient Sodom from which Lot and his family fled (Genesis 19); also where Lot's wife was turned into a pillar of salt.

Jericho

Jericho of today is a fertile spot standing near the site of the ancient city. Soudan Bedouins are the principal inhabitants of the small, dirty town. Orange and banana trees flourish here. Here we were shown the beautiful pools known as "Elisha's Fountain." (2 Kings, 2:19–22.) They are just below the excavated ruins of the old Jericho, down the walls of which Rahab assisted Joshua's spies to escape. (Joshua 19.) A portion of the walls of her house may still be seen. Jericho was the home of little Zaccheus and of the blind Bartimaeus.

The lofty mountain in the southwest is known as Mt. Temptation. Here is the supposed scene of the Savior's fasting and temptation.

Tomb of Lazarus

Upon our return in the afternoon, we visited the tomb of Lazarus at Bethany and the ruins of the two rooms in which Mary and Martha so often entertained their Lord. Mohammedans now own the place, and a dirty, dingy place it is, too, but I was all the while picturing in my mind the happy scenes that occurred here 2,000 years ago, so did not mind the debris and filth. I recognized no Marys nor Marthas in any of the women we passed in this much visited place by the Master.

Garden of Gethsemane

We visited the Garden of Gethsemane, now the property of Franciscan Fathers. As at every other sacred spot in Jerusalem there are too many modern things around here to realize at first that this is the garden to which Jesus and his disciples repaired so frequently for prayer; but the rock—thank heaven they can't change that—on which the three disciples sat and "watched," is sufficiently natural to make one partly picture the scene as it was on the fatal night when Judas betrayed his Lord.

Church of the Virgin

Although it was nearly 3:30 o'clock, we concluded that we still had time to drive to Bethlehem, six miles south of Jerusalem. Before starting, however, we visited the Church of the Virgin, which marks the spot where the mother of the Savior was buried. An auto was waiting for us near the place where Stephen was martyred, so before taking my seat, I stood a moment on what might have been the very spot from which, just before he died, he saw the heavens open.

NOTES TO PAGE 140

We passed the hotel on our way to Bethlehem, drove by the Jaffa Gate, and entered the Valley of Hinnim, a deep ravine which bounds Jerusalem on the south. This was the ancient boundary between Judah and Benjamin. On the south side of this is the Hill of Evil Counsel where the Jews counseled how to put Jesus to death, and where Solomon had built an altar to Moloch. (McKay, *Home Memories of President David O. McKay*, 110–12)

16. Town in western Jordan.
17. See 2 Kings 2:19–22.
18. See Matthew 4:1–11.
19. Hill in central Israel.
20. See Gen. 22:1–14.
21. See 1 Kings 6; 7:13–51.
22. See Luke 21:20, 24
23. The Dome of the Rock, erected by Abd el-Malik.
24. Arthur James Balfour (1848–1930), British statesman.

25. LDS belief that the children of Israel will be gathered back to their lands of biblical inheritance in the last days.
26. Orson Hyde (1805–1878), born on January 8, 1805, at Oxford, Connecticut. LDS apostle, missionary remembered for his dedication of the Holy Land, civic leader. Died on November 28, 1878, at Spring City, Utah.
27. See Berrett and Van Dyke, *Holy Lands*, 19–27.
28. See Berrett and Van Dyke, *Holy Lands*, 211–14.
29. District of ancient Palestine west of the Jordan River between Galilee and Judaea, Israel.
30. Port city in northwestern Israel.
31. Mountain ridge in northwestern Israel.
32. Capital city of Syria.
33. Town in southern Lebanon.
34. Port city in southwestern Lebanon.
35. Country in southwestern Asia.
36. Town in eastern Lebanon located north of Damascus.
37. See 1 Kings 5:1–10.
38. City in southern Turkey.
39. See Luke 8:50.
40. McKay described:

We arrived at Aleppo at 6:00 p.m. and at once realized how helpless we should have been in this Turkish Arabian–Armenian town without the aid of Brother Booth.

The three of us called on the U.S. Consul. We thought the road between here and Aintab not so dangerous now because of Turkish brigands as it has been, although frequent depredations are still reported. The British Consul, who came in while we were still there, said he thought we could get through to Aintab all right, "because while the Turks make raids every three or four days, we might strike the lucky day when they didn't come out!"

We visited one of the fourteen orphanages in the city. One girl with tattoo marks on her sweet young face had been taken by the Arabs after the death of her parents. The Arabs tattooed her. Several others showed by the same indications that they had shared a similar experience.

We met about forty fine members of the Church and friends, with whom we held a very impressive service. They are all poor and have suffered bitter experiences during the last few years. They have been sheep without a shepherd for twelve years, but their interest in and integrity to the church seem genuine and sincere.

At nine o'clock this morning (November 8), in a Ford car, we left Aleppo for Aintab. We had no trouble and encountered no brigands. A skeleton of an automobile which had been burned on the side of the road in the brigands' district and the presence of mounted soldiers (French) patroling the dangerous part of the highway were the only reminders of the fact that we were traveling through a danger zone. We had arrived (at Aintab) at 2:30 and the news spread literally like wildfire. At 5:15 p.m. there were assembled in a room prepared for the purpose seventy persons who had gathered for the meeting.

Never were people more delighted than these to meet again their old friend and missionary, Brother Booth! Their joy was unbounded. One kind woman with her face aglow and her eyes filled with appreciation, held my hand in both hers and said: "We have been in hell for seven years, now we are in heaven."

We were more than amply repaid for our effort to meet them and for any risk that we might have run in coming thus far on our own responsibility.

The French this day gave official notice by placards on the streets of their intention to withdraw from Aintab! This means that the Armenians must leave also or run the risk of being massacred. Having fought with the French against the Moslems, they will expect no mercy from their Turkish enemies who have already threatened that "four hours after the French evacuate the town, not an Armenian will be alive."

Out of 25,000 Armenians who came here ten years ago, there are now only 5,000. All the others have died, been killed, or died of starvation and exposure during the terrible exodus of December.

We concluded to remove our people from here within the next ten days. The few who have homes will just abandon them. The Turks will not purchase them because they know they will possess them anyway. (McKay, *Home Memories of President David O. McKay*, 113–14)

41. Mary Rebecca Moyle Booth.

Chapter 24

1. American author Henry van Dyke (1852–1933), quoted in *101 Patriotic Poems, Songs and Speeches* (New York: McGraw-Hill, 2003), 41.

2. McKay described:

Damascus, said to be the oldest town still in existence known to history, was this day in holiday attire. It is the birthday of Mohammed. Cannonading awoke us at 4:00 a.m., and bands began to play at seven. Streets are all decorated with French flags and Syrian colors and, what is unique, with costly rugs and rich plush cloth. Beautiful Turkish rugs adorn sidewalks, hang from houses, and form canopies in the streets.

In the afternoon, we turned our attention from the populace acclaiming Mohammed as Allah's prophet, to the persecuted Saul of Tarsus. We visited the old house in which Saul, blind and humbled, met Ananias, and in which by repentance and faith, Saul regained his sight.

From this little underground house of two rooms, now used as a church, we walked through the Eastern Gate, and saw the window or opening in the old wall through which the persecuted and enthusiastic Saul escaped in a basket from his enemies. These are two mean, unadorned spots, but they seemed far more sacred to me than the great, spacious, richly embellished mosque, which stands but fifteen minutes distant.

There were only a few Christians in Damascus in Paul's day, and, if we may judge from appearances and actions, there are fewer today, after a lapse of nearly 2,000 years. (McKay, *Home Memories of President David O. McKay*, 115)

3. See Acts 9:1–22.

4. See Acts 9:10–25.

5. A chief river of Damascus, Syria.

6. Ancient kingdom Palestine.

7. See 2 Kings 5:12.

8. Muhammad (*circa* 570–632), Arab prophet and founder of Islam.

9. Basin cut by Jordan River in Israel.

10. Lake in northern Israel.

11. City in northern Israel.

12. Village in Galilee region, Israel.

13. City in northern Israel.

14. See 1 Kings 17:1–7.

15. See 2 Kings 2:12–15.

16. See 2 Kings 4:18–37.

17. See Matthew 4:1–11.

18. See Matthew 3.

19. McKay described:

The drive to Nazareth was very pleasant. On the way we passed through Kafr Hattin; the mount of the Beatitudes was on our right, and Mount Hermon, the Mount of Transfiguration, away over the lake to the north.

When we reached the brow of the hill at a point east of the Jabel es-sikh, we obtained a fine view of the boyhood town of our Savior. Its white houses, nestling closely together on the south slope of the hill named above, stood out in charming contrast to the green olive trees and fig trees that dotted the scene in many places.

After lunch, we visited:

(1) Mary's Well, one of the most interesting spots in Palestine, because undoubtedly Mary and her son Jesus often came to this well with other inhabitants of the village to draw water. It is the only well or spring in the town. It is one of the few spots unprofaned by a gloomy old church.

(2) The Church of Annunciation, built upon the supposed spot where the angel visited Mary and promised her that she should become the mother of the Son of God.

(3) The Workshop of Joseph, where he "became subject to them." A carpenter shop nearby interested me more than the church, for it was undoubtedly just such a shop in which Joseph worked when Jesus was growing to manhood.

NOTES TO PAGES 147–148

(4) The synagogue in which Jesus preached his first sermon.

(5) We did not ascend the rocky promontory from which his angry townsmen intended to thrust Jesus, but we had it pointed out to us, not quite but nearly in the direction and position I had pictured it in my mind.

Though our visit to Nazareth was brief, I think I enjoyed being in the home town of the Savior more than having been in any other town in Palestine. The people seem to be just the same as I think they were 2,000 years ago. The old carpenter shops are probably little changed from Joseph's day. The well or spring is gushing forth the same pure water that filled Mary's jug every morning, and, as a mere coincidence, as we approached this well, we met three women, one of whom was the most beautiful woman we have seen on our tour. I pictured her as the madonna. The little children playing and prattling in the street reminded me of the words,

> He played as little children play
> The pleasant games of youth;
> But he never got vexed if the game went wrong,
> And he always spoke the truth. (McKay, *Home Memories of President David O. McKay*, 115–17)

20. See Matthew 2:23.
21. Known today as Mary's Well and is marked by a Greek Orthodox Church.
22. See Luke 4:16–30.
23. See John 2:1–11.
24. See Matthew 14:15–21.
25. See Matthew 17:1–9.
26. See 2 Timothy 3:5.
27. See 2 Kings 1:9–14.
28. Plain in northern Israel.
29. Country in southern Europe.
30. Port city in southern Italy.
31. Harbor in southern Crete, Greece.
32. Island of Greece in the Mediterranean Sea.
33. Capital city of Italy.
34. See Acts 27:11.
35. Group of islands in the Mediterranean south of Sicily.
36. See Acts 27:14–44.
37. McKay described:

    We were sailing on the Mediterranean Sea—fair weather—excellent voyage. Sunday the 20th, we passed Fair Havens, Crete, where Paul nearly two millenia ago advised the commander of his vessel to remain for the winter. But the skipper thought he knew more than the little, unattractive missionary-prisoner, and put out to sea.

    This island Melita (Malta), on which they were wrecked after battling many days in a storm-tossed sea, is on our left near Sicily.

    Inspiration is always superior to man's judgment. Fortunate and blessed is he who knows the voice of inspiration! (McKay, *Home Memories of President David O. McKay*, 117)

38. Suggesting one is between two dangerous alternatives.
39. According to Greek mythology, a nymph morphed into a monster dwelling in the Strait of Messina.

40. According to Greek mythology, a female monster in the form of a Sicilian-coast whirlpool.

41. Island in southern Italy in the Mediterranean.

42. Port city in southern Italy.

43. Volcano on Gulf of Naples, Italy.

44. A city in southern Italy.

45. McKay described:

With all the fascination of a historic past, with the accumulated art treasures in sculpture and painting, with the attraction of its own present beauty and progress, Rome is an intensely interesting city.

Our time being limited, we took occasion to visit with a guide only the following historic places:

(1) The Coliseum where gladiators of old fought to the death either with each other or with animals, where Christians suffered mutilation and martyrdom, while blood-thirsty, voluptuous spectators gloated and yelled in fiendish approbation. Forty-five thousand people could be seated in this vast arena at the same time, and ten thousand others could stand.

(2) The Pantheon, built as a pagan shrine by Hadrian, on the side of Agrippa's threefold temple. It is now known as the Santa Maria ad Martyres. Originally the building was covered with marble and the dome of the roof with gold and silver, but this has all been removed. It now contains the tomb of Raphael.

(3) Part of the Circus Maximus, formerly lying between the two hills.

(4) Several triumphal arches. (McKay, *Home Memories of President David O. McKay*, 117–18)

46. A first century AD amphitheater in Rome.

47. Titus Flavius Vespasianus (AD 39–81), Roman emperor.

48. See Matthew 24:1–2.

49. St. Peter's Basilica and St. Paul's Outside the Walls Basilica.

50. McKay described:

We drove out to the catacombs, visiting which was wonderfully interesting. These underground passageways impressed me most forceably with the tremendous difficulties under which the early Christians lived and worshiped. There were two stories of tombs below the one which we visited. The tombs of the third and fourth centuries bear the marks of the introduction of pagan superstition into the simple religion of the early followers of the Redeemer.

From here we drove to St. Peter's, thence to the Vatican where we spent several hours in the picture gallery, and the Sistine Chapel with the wonderful paintings.

Late in the afternoon, I visited the Forum, where the Roman orators swayed the populace, and where beautiful temples were erected to pagan gods. (McKay, *Home Memories of President David O. McKay*, 118)

51. David Lawrence McKay (1901–1993), born on September 30, 1901, at Ogden, Utah. Set apart as a missionary to Europe on October 19, 1920, and returned on October 19, 1924. Died on October 27, 1993, at Salt Lake City, Utah.

52. City in western Switzerland on Lake Geneva.

53. McKay described:

David L. (missionary son), President Ballif, and others had been at the station to meet the 8:15 train, but were disappointed at not meeting us. They were also informed that the next train from Milan would not arrive before 4:50 a.m. tomorrow. Consequently when we stepped off the train, there was no one to meet us. However, David L. had felt impressed to come down to the station to ascertain whether there might be a train some hour earlier than reported.

The result was that just as we stepped out onto the sidewalk and began to wonder where we should go, I saw a straight, dignified, young man walking down the hill about a block away, whom I recognized as my boy! In a moment or two we were in each other's embrace!

Seldom, if ever, have I felt purer joy than that which I experienced in my son's company that evening and succeeding days.

The happiness of parenthood, indeed, success in life depends upon the honor, integrity of our sons and daughters. (McKay, *Home Memories of President David O. McKay*, 118–19)

54. Serge Frederick Ballif (1859–1942), born on September 23, 1859, at Ogden, Utah. Set apart as president of the Swiss and German Mission on October 19, 1920, and returned on May 1, 1923. Died on November 17, 1942, at Oakland, California.

55. See appendix 1.

56. Zelnora Eliza Angell Ballif.

57. City in northwestern Switzerland.

58. City in eastern Germany.

59. River in Western Europe.

60. City in western Germany.

61. Landmark tower built as a tollhouse for river commerce.

62. John Philip Lillywhite (1882–1962), born on December 23, 1882, at Greenville, Utah. Set apart as president of the Netherlands Mission on July 13, 1920, and returned on April 23, 1923. Died on January 24, 1962.

63. See appendix 1.

64. Country in Western Europe.

65. Ecclesiastical unit similar to a Catholic diocese, comprised of mission branches, in eastern Belgium (district).

66. Country in northwestern Europe.

67. Alvin Smith Nelson (1900–1975), born on August 7, 1900, at Salt Lake City, Utah. Set apart as a missionary to the Netherlands on November 9, 1920, and returned on April 23, 1923. Died on April 4, 1975.

68. Karl Morgan Richards (1900–1980), born on December 22, 1900, at Salt Lake City, Utah. Set apart as a missionary to the Netherlands on December 31, 1920, and returned on November 1, 1923. Died on March 28, 1980, at Provo, Utah.

69. Capital city of Belgium.

70. See David O. McKay, *What E'er Thou Art Act Well Thy Part: The Missionary Diaries of David O. McKay*, ed. Stan Larson and Patricia Larson (Salt Lake City: Blue Ribbon Books, 1999).

71. Port city in south central Scotland.

72. Port city in northwestern England.

73. Orson Ferguson Whitney (1855–1931), born on July 1, 1855, at Salt Lake City, Utah. LDS apostle, speaker, educator, and writer. Died on May 16, 1931, at Salt Lake City, Utah.

74. May Wells Whitney.

75. William Albert Morton (1866–1930), born on January 10, 1866, at Bambridge, Ireland. Set apart as a missionary to Great Britain on May 26, 1921, and returned on April 6, 1923. Died on June 18, 1930, at Salt Lake City, Utah.

76. McKay described:

After dictating a few letters, and partaking of our last meal on foreign shores, we were driven to the wharf where lay at anchor the SS *Cedric*, on which we have secured passage.

President Whitney, Sister Whitney, President Wetherspoon, Brother Morton, and all the elders accompanied us, and came aboard to see us comfortably situated.

At 2:30 p.m., we bade them good-bye, they to go to Sheffield to attend conference, we to sail for home, home!! Blessed place always, but especially after twelve months' absence!

Since leaving Bombay, I have traveled 5,928 miles by land and 3,180 by water, making a total since leaving home of 21,277 miles by land and 34,619 miles by water. A grand total of 55,896 miles! (McKay, *Home Memories of President David O. McKay*, 120)

77. Statue of a woman gripping a torch of liberty located on Liberty Island.

78. Inlet of the Atlantic at the mouth of Hudson River (New York Bay).

79. River in eastern New York, United States.

80. George William Ashton, Jr. (1896–1949), born on November 1, 1896, at Salt Lake City, Utah. Set apart as a missionary to the Eastern States on October 26, 1920, and returned on April 25, 1923. Died on November 21, 1949, at Cardston, Alberta, Canada.

81. Sarah Alice Scowcroft McCune.

82. Winslow Farr Smith (1881–1966), born on January 19, 1881, at Salt Lake City, Utah. Set apart as president of the Northern States Mission on June 8, 1919, and returned on February 1, 1923. Died on December 25, 1966, at Salt Lake City, Utah.

83. See appendix 1.

84. McKay described:

It's good to be back home again;
It's great to come back West,
Where sun and snow make flowers grow
In the choicest land and best.

It's good to be back home again
Where men are what they seem,
Who give their hands in loving grasp,
Whose eyes true friendship beam.

O it's joy to sail through Norway's fjords
And on Mediterranean blue;
To stroll along the Sieges Allee,
The Champs Elysees, too.

But their grandeur yields to mountain peaks
As moonbeams, to the sun
Statues show the skill of man,
The peaks, what God has done.

We've met keen minds and sincere souls,
Formed ties that will outlast time;
But the dearest friends in all the world
Are in Zion's favored clime.

It's good to be back home again
It's great to come back West;
To enjoy the glorious sunshine
With hearts we love the best.
(McKay, *Home Memories of President
David O. McKay*, 120–21)

Chapter 25

1. See Genesis 42–46.
2. See Exodus 2–3.
3. See Exodus 3–14.
4. See Jeremiah 43:6.
5. See Matthew 2:13–18.
6. City in western New York, United States.
7. See Joseph Smith—History 1:29–47.

101 Patriotic Poems, Songs and Speeches. New York: McGraw-Hill, 2003.

Alexander, Thomas G. *Mormonism in Transition: A History of the Latter-day Saints, 1890–1930*. Urbana: University of Illinois Press, 1986.

Allen, James B. "Technology and the Church: A Steady Revolution." In *2007 Church Almanac*, 118–58. Salt Lake City: Deseret Morning News, 2006.

Anderson, Lavina Fielding. "Prayer Under a Pepper Tree: Sixteen Accounts of a Spiritual Manifestation." *BYU Studies* 33, No. 1 (1993): 55–78.

Anderson, Paul L. "A Jewel in the Gardens of Paradise: The Art and Architecture of the Hawai'i Temple." In *Voyages of Faith: Explorations in Mormon Pacific History*, ed. Grant Underwood. Provo, Utah: Brigham Young University Press, 2000.

Anthon H. Lund Collection, typescript in D. Michael Quinn Papers, Yale University Library.

Babson, Roger W. *Fundamentals of Prosperity: What They Are and Whence They Came*. New York: Fleming H. Revell, 1920.

Barry, John M. *The Great Influenza: The Epic Story of the Deadliest Plague in History*. New York: Penguin, 2004.

Berrett, LaMar C., and Blair G. Van Dyke. *Holy Lands: A History of the Latter-day Saints in the Near East*. American Fork, Utah: Covenant Communications, 2005.

Bitton, Davis. *George Q. Cannon: A Biography*. Salt Lake City: Deseret Book, 1999.

Book of Wanderings of Brother Felix Fabri (Circa 1480–1483 A.D.). Trans. Aubrey Stewart. London: Palestine Pilgrims' Text Society, 1896.

Britsch, R. Lanier. "Church Beginnings in China." *BYU Studies* 10 (Winter 1970): 161–72.

———. "The East India Mission of 1851–56: Crossing the Boundaries of Culture, Religion, and Law." *Journal of Mormon History* 27 (Fall 2001): 150–76.

———. "Mormon Intruders in Tonga: The Passport Act of 1922." In *Mormons, Scripture, and the Ancient World: Studies in Honor of John L. Sorenson*, ed. Davis Bitton. Provo, Utah: Foundation for Ancient Research and Mormon Studies, 1998.

———. *Nothing More Heroic: The Compelling Story of the First Latter-day Saint Missionaries in India* (Salt Lake City: Deseret Book, 1999).

———. *Unto the Islands of the Sea: A History of the Latter-day Saints in the Pacific* (Salt Lake City: Deseret Book, 1986).

Cannon, Donald Q., and Richard O. Cowan. *Unto Every Nation: Gospel Light Reaches Every Land*. Salt Lake City: Deseret Book, 2003.

Cannon, George Q. *The Life of Joseph Smith, the Prophet*. Salt Lake City: Juvenile Instructor Office, 1888.

———. *My First Mission*. Salt Lake City: Juvenile Instructor, 1879.

Cannon, Hugh J. "Around-the-World Travels of David O. McKay and Hugh J. Cannon," ca. 1925, typescript, microfilm, Church History Library, The Church of Jesus Christ of Latter-day Saints, Salt Lake City, Utah.

———. *David O. McKay Around the World: An Apostolic Mission, Prelude to Church Globalization*. Provo, Utah: Spring Creek, 2005.

———. "The Land of China Dedicated." *Juvenile Instructor* 56 (March 1921): 115–17.

Carlyle, Thomas. *The Works of Thomas Carlyle (Complete): Critical and Miscellaneous Essays Collected and Republished*, volume 15. New York: Peter Fenelon Collier, 1897.

Caruthers, Sandra T. "Anodyne for Expansion: Meiji Japan, the Mormons, and Charles LeGendre." *Pacific Historical Review* 38, No. 2 (May 1969): 129–39.

"Church Heads Pay Tribute to Hugh J. Cannon." *Deseret News*, October 9, 1931, 2.

Clement, Russell T., and Sheng-Luen Tsai. "East Wind to Hawai'i: Contributions and History of Chinese and Japanese Mormons in Hawaii." In *Voyages of Faith: Explorations in Mormon Pacific History*, ed. Grant Underwood. Provo, Utah: Brigham Young University Press, 2000.

Cowan, Richard O. "An Apostle in Oceania: Elder David O. McKay's 1921 Trip around the Pacific." In *Pioneers in the Pacific: Memory, History, and Cultural Identity among the Latter-day Saints*, ed. Grant Underwood. Provo, Utah: Religious Studies Center, Brigham Young University, 2005.

"Death of Hugh J. Cannon." *Deseret News*, October 6, 1931, 1–2.

Dialogues of Plato. Trans. B. Jowett. Oxford: Clarendon Press, 1875.

Douglas, Norman. "The Sons of Lehi and the Seed of Cain: Racial Myths in Mormon Scripture and Their Relevance to the Pacific Islands." *Journal of Religious History* 8 (June 1974): 90–104.

Drummond, Henry. *Addresses*. Philadelphia, Pa.: Henry Altemus, 1891.

———. *The Greatest Thing in the World*. New York: Thomas Y. Crowell, 1888.

Emerson, Ralph Waldo. *Ralph Waldo Emerson*, ed. Oliver Wendell Holmes. Cambridge, Riverside Press, 1884.

Geddes, Ross. "'A Storm in the Camp of Brighamism': LDS-RLDS Relations in Brisbane, Australia, 1901–1918." *John Whitmer Historical Association Journal* 11 (1991): 47–59.

Gibbons, Francis M. *David O. McKay: Apostle to the World, Prophet of God*. Salt Lake City: Deseret Book, 1986.

Gibson, Arrell Morgan, and John S. Whitehead. *Yankees in Paradise: The Pacific Basin Frontier*. Albuquerque: University of New Mexico Press, 1993.

Gregory, Horace, and Marya Zaturenska, eds. *A History of American Poetry, 1900–1940*. New York: Harcourt, Brace, 1946.

Howe, K. R. *The Quest for Origins: Who First Discovered and Settled the Pacific Islands*. Honolulu: University of Hawaii Press, 2003.

Hymns of The Church of Jesus Christ of Latter-day Saints. Salt Lake City: The Church of Jesus Christ of Latter-day Saints, 1985.

Irving, Gordon. *Numerical Strength and Geographical Distribution of the LDS Missionary Force, 1830–1974*. Salt Lake City: Historical Department of The Church of Jesus Christ of Latter-day Saints, 1975.

Japan Mission Incoming Letters. Church History Library.

Japan Mission Outgoing Letters. Church History Library.

Jenson, Andrew. *Autobiography of Andrew Jenson*. Salt Lake City: Deseret News Press, 1938.

———. *Encyclopedic History of the Church of Jesus Christ of Latter-day Saints*. Salt Lake City: Deseret News Publishing Company, 1941.

———. *Latter-day Saint Biographical Encyclopedia: A Compilation of Biographical Sketches of Prominent Men and Women in The Church of Jesus Christ of Latter-day Saints*, 4 vols. Salt Lake City: Andrew Jenson History, 1901–36.

Jessee, Dean C., ed. and comp. *The Personal Writings of Joseph Smith*. 1984; reprint, Salt Lake City: Deseret Book, 2002.

Judd, Denis. *The Lion and the Tiger: The Rise and Fall of the British Raj, 1600–1947*. New York: Oxford University Press, 2004.

Kipling, Rudyard. *Works*. New York: Doubleday, 1914.

Knowles, Eleanor. *Deseret Book Company: 125 Years of Inspiration, Information, and Ideas*. Salt Lake City: Deseret Book, 1991.

Lambert, James N. In *Ninety-First Semi-Annual Conference of The Church of Jesus Christ of Latter-day Saints*. Salt Lake City: The Church of Jesus Christ of Latter-day Saints, 1920.

Maffly-Kipp, Laurie F., and Reid L. Neilson. *Proclamation to the People: Nineteenth-century Mormonism and the Pacific Basin Frontier*. Salt Lake City: University of Utah Press, 2008.

Matsuda, Matt K. "AHR Forum: The Pacific." *American Historical Review* 111, No. 2 (June 2006): 758–80.

Mauss, Armand L. *All Abraham's Children: Changing Mormon Conceptions of Race and Lineage*. Urbana: University of Illinois Press, 2003.

McKay, David Lawrence. *My Father, David O. McKay*, ed. Lavina Fielding Anderson. Salt Lake City: Deseret Book, 1989.

McKay, David O. Correspondence (DOMC), 1920–21, David O. McKay Papers (DOMP), MS 668, Manuscripts Division, J. Willard Marriott Library, University of Utah, Salt Lake City.

———. Diaries (DOMD), 1920–21, David O. McKay Papers (DOMP), MS 668, Manuscripts Division, J. Willard Marriott Library, University of Utah, Salt Lake City.

———. Scrapbooks (DOMS), 215 volumes with assorted contents and no pagination, MS 4640, Church History Library.

———. "Ah Ching." *Improvement Era* 24 (September 1921): 992–97.

———. "Christmas in Tokyo." *Juvenile Instructor* 56 (March 1921): 112–15.

———. "'Hui Tau.'" *Improvement Era* 24 (July 1921): 774.

———. *What E'er Thou Art Act Well Thy Part: The Missionary Diaries of David O. McKay*, ed. Stan Larson and Patricia Larson. Salt Lake City: Blue Ribbon Books, 1999.

McKay, Llewelyn R., comp. *Home Memories of President David O. McKay*. Salt Lake City: Deseret Book, 1959.

Middlemiss, Clare, comp. *Cherished Experiences from the Writings of President David O. McKay*. Salt Lake City: Deseret Book, 1955.

Miller, James. *Voices from Earth*. Victoria, British Columbia: Trafford Publishing, 2004.

Moore, Frank, ed. *American Eloquence: A Collection of Speeches and Addresses by the Most Eminent Orators of America*. New York: D. Appleton, 1857.

Morrell, Jeanette McKay. *Highlights in the Life of President David O. McKay*. Salt Lake City: Deseret Book, 1966.

Neilson, Reid L. "Alma O. Taylor's Fact-Finding Mission to China." *BYU Studies* 40, no. 1 (2001): 177–203.

Newton, Marjorie. *Southern Cross Saints: The Mormons in Australia.* Laie: The Institute for Polynesian Studies, Brigham Young University–Hawaii, 1991.

Peck, Harry Thurston, Frank Richard Stockton, and Caroline Ticknor, eds. *The World's Great Masterpieces: History, Biography, Science, Philosophy, Poetry, the Drama.* New York: American Literary Society, 1901.

"Plan Visit to Island Missions." *Deseret News*, October 23, 1920.

Prince, Gregory A., and William Robert Wright. *David O. McKay and the Rise of Modern Mormonism.* Salt Lake City: University of Utah Press, 2005.

Ready References: A Compilation of Scripture Texts, Arranged in a Subjective Order, with Numerous Annotations from Eminent Writers. Salt Lake City: George Q. Cannon and Sons, 1899.

Reiser, A. Hamer. Correspondence. Copy in editor's possession.

Roberts, B. H. *The Truth, The Way, The Life: An Elementary Treatise on Theology*, ed. John W. Welch. Provo, Utah: Brigham Young University Studies, 1994.

Shipps, Jan. *Mormonism: The Story of a New Religious Tradition.* Urbana: University of Illinois Press, 1985.

Shipps, Jan, and John W. Welch, eds. *The Journals of William E. McLellin, 1831–1836.* Urbana: University of Illinois Press, 1994.

Sinclair, Upton, ed. *The Cry for Justice: An Anthology of the Literature of Social Protest.* Philadelphia: John C. Winston, 1915.

Talmage, James E. *"The Book of Mormon," An Account of its Origin, with Evidences of Its Genuineness and Authenticity: Two Lectures.* Kansas City, Mo.: Southwestern States Mission, The Church of Jesus Christ of Latter-Day Saints, 1899.

Teachings of Presidents of the Church: David O. McKay. Salt Lake City: The Church of Jesus Christ of Latter-day Saints, 2003.

Thornton, Ian. *Krakatau: The Destruction and Reassembly of an Island Ecosystem.* Cambridge, Mass.: Harvard University Press, 1996.

Tweed, Thomas A. *Crossings and Dwellings: A Theory of Religion.* Cambridge, Mass.: Harvard University Press, 2006.

"Two Church Workers Will Tour Missions of Pacific Islands." *Deseret News*, October 15, 1920, 5.

Villari, Pasquale. *Life and Times of Girolamo Savonarola.* London: T. Fisher Unwin, 1888.

Walker, Ronald W. "Strangers in a Strange Land: Heber J. Grant and the Opening of the Japanese Mission." In *Taking the Gospel to the Japanese, 1901–1924*, ed. Reid L. Neilson and Van C. Gessel. Provo, Utah: Brigham Young University Press, 2006.

Whittaker, David J. "Mormon Missiology: An Introduction and Guide to the Sources." In *Disciple as Witness: Essays on Latter-day Saint History and Doctrine in Honor of Richard Lloyd Anderson*, ed. Stephen D. Ricks, Donald W. Parry, and Andrew H. Hedges. Provo, Utah: Foundation for Ancient Research and Mormon Studies, Brigham Young University, 2000.

Widtsoe, John A. *Joseph Smith as Scientist: A Contribution to Mormon Philosophy.* Salt Lake City: Bookcraft, 1964.

Woodger, Mary Jane. "David O. McKay." In *Encyclopedia of Latter-day Saint History*, ed. Arnold K. Garr, Donald Q. Cannon, and Richard O. Cowan. Salt Lake City: Deseret Book, 2000.

———. *David O. McKay: Beloved Prophet.* American Fork, Utah: Covenant Communications, 2004.

———, ed. *Heart Petals: The Personal Correspondence of David Oman McKay to Emma Ray McKay.* Salt Lake City: University of Utah Press, 2005.

———, comp. *The Teachings of David O. McKay.* Salt Lake City: Deseret Book, 2004.

Works of Samuel Taylor Coleridge, Prose and Verse. Complete in One Volume. Philadelphia, Pa.: Thomas Cowperthwait, 1840.

Adams, John Q., *plate 33*, *plate 41*, 83, 85, 91, 95, 159, 199n5
Adams, Thurza T., *plate 33*, *plate 41*, 83, 87, 91, 95, 199n11
Aden, 132, 219n4
Agra, India, 129–30
Aintab, Turkey, 145, 161n10
Aleppo, Syria, 4, 144, 145, 161n10, 224n40
Allen, John, 124
American Samoa, 88–98; culture, 96–98
Amussen, Heber S., 49, 189n42
Anderson, Andrew, 161n9
Anderson, F., 110
Anderson, J. Clair, 48, 188n26
Anderson, Joseph, 107, 203n4
Andrew, Richard G., 110
Andrus, Robert H., 116, 211n42
Apia, Western Samoa, *plates 33–35*, 82–85; hurricane of 1889, 88–90
Armenian Mission, xxxi
Armstrong, Henry J., 110, 204n27
Ashton, George, Jr., 154, 230n80
Australasian Mission, 160n6, 161n9
Australia, 112–19; culture of, 114, 116, 118, 120, 211n53; geography, 119, 209n14; missionaries to, 120–21
Australian Mission, 112, 160n6, 161n9

Baal, Temple of, 4, 175n20
Baalbek, Syria, 4, 156
Bachman, Haloy E., 77, 196n5
Baird, Ralph V., 111, 205n38
Baker, Doris, 115, 210n38
Ballif, Serge F., 152, 153, 159, 229n53, n54
Bangerter, Arnold B., 48, 187n23
Bangerter, Hazel M., 48, 188n24
baptism, *plate 37*, *plate 44*, 86, 159n2, 160n3, 161n7, n10, 162n12
Barber, Edgar W., 111, 205n47
Barlow, Ora H., 49, 188n31
Barnett, Adelbert, 49, 188n39

Barrett, William, 161n9
Bayles, Herman E., 115, 210n35
Becraft, Frank W., 121–22, 212n6
Beesley, Adelbert, 88, 161n7, 200n2
Belio, Kimo, 161n7
Bell, Edith Lenore, 185n13
Bell, Hyrum V., 111, 205n46
Bennett, Jonathan R., 111, 205n36
Benson, Grant L., 59, 192n2
Berrett, Ray W., *plate 35*, 83, 97, 199n15
Bethlehem, *plate 54*, 137, 139, 156, 222n4, n15
Biesinger, Thomas, 162n11
Billings, Gerald O., 117, 211n50
Bischoff, Robert K., 113, 116, 209n13
Bodily, Myrl L., 23, 179n20
Book of Mormon, *plate 43*, *plate 53*, 9, 51, 65, 99, 132, 141, 177n27; translated, 44, 159n2, 160n3, n5, n6, 161n10
Booth, Joseph Wilford, xxxi, 4, 159, 175n16
Bowen, Charles M., 116, 211n44
Bowles, Christine A., 187n18
Bowles, George A., Jr., 187n19
Bowles, George, 48, 187n16
Bramwell, Franklin S., 159n1
Brannan, Samuel, 160n4
Brewer, William K., 93, 200n15
Brigham Young University–Hawaii, xxxi, 185n18
British Mission, 162n13
Broad, Charles J., 50, 189n43
Bronson, George M., 47, 187n12
Brown, Benjamin, 78, 106, 197n11
Brown, James S., 160n5
Brown, Newel S., 111, 205n45
Browning, Roland, 39, 184n5
Budd, Douglas F., 49, 188n34
Budd, Edith Virginia, 47, 186n6
Buddhism, *plate 10*, *plate 14*, 125, 182, 213n18, 214n21
Butler, Alva J., 161n8
Buttle, Paul R., 110, 204n26

Caine, Frederick A., 7, 159n2, 176n10
California Mission, 160n4
Cannon, George Q., 39, 42–44, 46, 160n3; 184n1, 186n37
Cannon, George, xi, xii
Cannon, Glen B., 110, 204n25
Cannon, Hugh J., ix–xi, xv, xxix, *plates 2, 3, 5, 10–11, 13, 15, 17, 20, 26, 28, 30–32, 36–37, 40–41, 44, 47, 52*, 3, 44–45, 57, 60, 106, 113, 117, 120, 152, 153, 175n13, 193n4, 214n24; in China, xxvii; death of, xxxi; in India, xxviii, 128–29; in Japan, xxvii, 183n23; life after the journey, xxx–xxxi; in New Zealand, 101, 105–6; in Samoa, xxviii
Cannon, Sarah Jane Jenne, x
Cannon, Sarah Richards, xi, xxiv, 7, 56, 176n6
Cannon, Sylvester Q., 108, 203n14
Cannon, William T., Jr., 40
Carroll, Leroy E., 49
Castleton, Wallace L., 107, 203n5
Chase, A. Harris, 49, 188n38
Cheops, *plate 51*, 135, 155, 220n22, 221n28
China: contrast with Japan, *plate 16*, 36; culture, *plate 13*, 31, 181n15; dedication of, xxxi, 25, 27–28, 157; interior, 32–34; missionary efforts in, *plate 14*, 25–28; sites, *plate 14*, 26, 213n18
Ching, Ah, 99
Christensen, George A., 115, 210n34
Christensen, Mary S., 185n11
Christy, Sidney, *plate 32*, 70
Church History Library, xiii, xiv, xvi
Church of the Nativity, *plate 54*, 139, 222n4
Church of the Virgin, 222n15
Clark, Hiram, 160n3
Clark, Carlos W., 111
Clark, Wealthy, 39, 184n6
Clark, William H., 111, 206n56
Cole, Wilford J., 48, 187n20
Cole, William Arley, 111, 206n57
communication, 3, 59; technologies, xxiv–xxv, xxix–xxx, 121
Confucius, 8–9, 176n26
Coombs, Leo E., 111, 206n50
Coombs, Mark V., *plate 33*, 80, 83, 91, 102, 159, 197n22
Council of the Twelve. *See* Quorum of the Twelve Apostles
Cowley, Matthias F., 159n1
Cox, Roscoe C., 47, 187n7
Crane, Charles R., 32, 157, 182n2
Crockett, Frank L., 111, 206n55
Crystal, Arnold B., 48, 187n22

Dalton, John L., 160n4
Damascus, 143, 147–48, 225n2

Davis, Boyd C., 47, 187n8
Davis, Lloyd D., 49
Dead Sea, 140, 148, 222n15
Dean, Joseph H., 88, 90, 161n7, 199n1
Deseret News, xv, xxiii, Appendix 2
Diamond Head, *plate 24*
divine hand apparent in journey, 54–55, 84, 102, 113, 117, 124, 143, 152, 157–58
Doctrine and Covenants, 9, 177n29
Doxey, Graham H., 69, 77, 194n4
Dudley, Annie Elizabeth Bingham, 176n24
Dudley, Stephen Markham, 7, 176n19
Duncan, Chapman, 25
Duncan, William, 78, 109, 111
Dunn, Leslie, 42
Dutch East Indies, 121–22

Eastern States Mission, 162n14
Egbert, Joseph R., 111, 205n43
Egypt, *plate 50*, 133–36; sites in, *plates 51–52*, 134–36, 155, 219n17, 220n19, n22
Empress of Japan, *plate 3*, 10, 15
Englestead, Alvin, 114, 210n19
Ensign, Horace S., 159n2
European Mission, x
evangelists, modern-day, xix–xx
evangelization, xx
Evans, Waldo, 94, 200n23

famine: in China, 30, 32, 34; in Egypt, 134–35
Farnham, Augustus, 160n6, 161n9
Fielding, Joseph, 162n13
Fiji Islands, 79; customs of, 79–80
First Presidency, ix, xvi, xxii–xxv, xxix, xxxi, 6, 30, 39, 159, 174n5, 175n28, 178n16
Fisher, Asael H., 74, 196n20
Fisher, Flora D., 74, 196n19
Fjeldsted, Christian D., 22, 178n15
Folland, Richard E., xiii
Forbidden City, *plate 14*, 28
Francom, Joseph E., 111, 205n41
Frazier, Ivy May, 39, 184n7
Frederickson, Earl A., 111, 206n51
Friendly Islands, 80, 81
Fronk, Franklin D., 114, 209n18
Fujiyama, 15

Garden of Gethsemane, 222n15
Gardner, Edward Eugene, 114, 210n25
General Authorities, ix, xx–xxiii, xxxii, *plate 19*, 8, 42, 53, 93, 113, 172n8, n9, 173n15, 174n22
general conference, xxi
Genther, Albert, 122
German Mission, 162n11
Gibson, Walter M., 160n3, 161n7
Giza, pyramids at, 136, 154

globalization of the church, ix, x
Goff, Leland N., 47, 187n10
Goodson, John, 162n13
Grant, Heber J., xx, xxii, 3, 6, 54, 55, 142, 154, 159n2, 172n9, 175n10
Great Wall of China, *plate 15*, 26, 181n6
Griffiths, Frank D., *plate 33*, 83, 91, 199n12
Griffiths, Retta M., *plate 33*, 83, 91, 199n13
Grouard, Benjamin F., 160n5
Gudmundson, Arthur W., 111, 206n58

Haifa, Palestine, 142, 143, 147, 148, 149, 161n10
haka, *plate 31*, 73, 108, 118
Hall, Heber Dean, 107
Halls, Milton, 108, 203n13
Hammer, Paul E. B., 162n11
Hammond, Genevieve, 185n15
Hanks, Knowlton F., 160n5
Hansen, J. N., 116
Hansen, Lorenzo F., 116, 211n45
Hanson, Earl R., 115, 210n36
Harris, Ferrin R., 49, 188n33
Hawaii, *plates 18–19, 21–24*, 39–52; dedication of mission home, 51; missionary efforts in, *plates 19–20*, 39–40, 47, 49–52
Hawaiian Mission, 47, 51, 160n3, 172n9
Hawkes, Harold, 111, 205n40
Heaton, Gerald F., 111, 205n37
Henderson, Clarence, 87, 102, 201n5
Hendricks, James E., 114, 210n28
Hicken, Irwin T., 23, 179n23
Hintze, Ferdinand F., 161n10
Hipwell, John E., 114, 210n20
Hokkaido, Japan, 20
Holley, Deloss W., 23, 180n25
Hollingworth, Charles H., 110, 204n22
Holmes, Amasa S., 110, 204n28
Holy Land, 137–38, 139–152, 156; contradictions in, 149–50; desecration in, *plate 54*. See also Jerusalem
hongi, *plate 32*, 69, 71, 109, 193n2
Horne, William W., 116, 211n40
Hui Tau, *plates 28–32*, 69–74, 76
Hunsaker, Donald L., 111, 205n42
Hunsaker, Joseph R., 114, 210n27
Huntsman, Arthur, 99, 200n10
Hurst, Samuel H., 42
Hyde, Elizabeth Howe, 185n16
Hyde, Orson, *plate 53*, 141, 162n12, n13, n14
Hymas, Heber, 111, 206n54

Improvement Era, x
India, *plate 48*, 126–29; culture of, 127, 128, 129, 218n30, n32; missionary efforts in, 128

Instructor, xii, xiii
Italy, 149–51. *See also* Rome
Iverson, Anna Bertha Erickson, 176n14
Iverson, Heber C., 7, 10, 159, 176n13
Ivie, Lloyd O., 37, 183n22

Jacob, Elmo F., 78, 197n12
Jacobs, Harry S., 93
Japan Mission, xx, xxiii, 19–20, 159n2
Japan, *plates 5–9*; contrast with China, *plate 16*, 36; culture of, *plate 6*, *plate 12*, 16–17, 19, 21–22, 36, 37, 179n19, 180n4, 183n23; missionaries to, xxi, *plates 4, 12, 17*, 172n8; religious climate, 17–18; sacred places, *plates 10–11*, 20, 23
Java, 117, 121–22, 211n16
Jenkins, Harold, 111, 206n53
Jenkins, Jane, 185n14
Jenolan Caves, 113–14
Jensen, Alma Howard, 23, 180n26
Jensen, Milton, 114, 209n15
Jenson, Andrew, xxii
Jericho, *plate 54*, 140, 142, 148, 222n15
Jerusalem, *plate 53*, 137, 140–41
jinrikisha. *See* rikisha
Johnson, Lyman E., 162n14
Johnson, Peter M., 111, 204n32
Johnson, Sterling, 114, 116, 209n16
Jones, Byron D., 42, 185n23
Jones, William L., 116, 211n41
Jorgensen, Glenn A., 110, 204n23

Kailimai, David Keola, 42, 185n26
Kalani, David, 42
kauri tree, 108–9
kava, 84–85
Kealakai, Mekia, 50, 189n45
Kelsch, Louis A., 159n2
Kennard, Leonidas H., xxix, 59, 105–6, 159, 192n1
Kikuchi, Saburo, 159n2
Kimball, Heber, 162n13
Kimball, Jonathan G., 77, 196n6
Kimberly, Lewis Ashfield, 90, 200n5
Kirkham, Milo F., 47, 187n9
Knowlton, Ralph A., 99, 201n9
Korea, xxvii, xxviii, 23, 25, 40, 180n4

Laie, Hawaii, temple at, 40, 56
Lamanites, 51, 95
Lane, Russell, 111
Langston, Charles J., 104, 202n13
Larsen, John L., 48, 187n21
Lazarus, Tomb of, 222n15
Lebanon, mountains of, 4, 143, 148
Lee, Lafayette C., xx
Lee, William O., 161n7
Lewis, James, 25
Leyte, 104
Liberty Stake, xxiv

Lillywhite, John P., 153, 159, 229n62
Los Angeles Branch, 160n4
Lund, Anthon H., 6, 54, 56, 111, 124, 176n3
Lutz, Thomas W., 115, 210n37
Lyman, Francis M., xxiii
Lyman, Francis M., Jr., 161n10

Madsen, Julius V., 69, 194n5
Maeser, Karl G., 160n4
Malay Peninsula, xxviii, 122–23; culture of, 123
Manning, Rulon H., 78, 197n13
Manoa, Samuela, 161n7
Maoris: customs of, *plate 28–29*, 69–74, 109, 110; faith of, 77; missionary work among, 69, 160n6
Marama, 57–58, 59, 60, 64
Markham, Stephen, 7, 176n20
Marstal, 91–92, 94
Martin, Wallace, 59, 192n4
Maughan, Alvin T., 106, 203n21
Maxwell, William S., 7, 176n16
May, Stirling I., 81, 198n28
McCullough, Leonard J., 59, 192n5
McCune, George W., 154, 159, 218n29
McFarland, Abram M., 107, 203n6
McGary, Owen, 23, 179n22
McKay, David Lawrence, 151, 153, 229n53
McKay, David O., *plates 1, 2, 5, 10–11, 17, 20, 25–28, 30–32, 34–37, 39–41, 44–45, 47, 52*, 175n12; character of, 3–4, 8, 102, 108; as church commissioner of education, xxxi, xxxii, 177n10; as church president, xxxi; divinely called, *plate 35, plate 43*, 3, 8, 84, 152; church commissioner of education, xxxi, xxxii, 177n10; church president, xxxi; life after the journey, xxxi; prayers of, 28–31, 99, 140, 157, 206n59; sermons of, 76–77, 115, 144, 149
McKay, Emma Ray, xv, 7, 56, 176n4. *See also* Riggs, Emma Ray
McKay, Robert Riggs, 176n5
McMurrin, James L., 117
McMurrin, Joseph W., 159, 190n8
Melanesia, 76
Merrill, Irvin S., 110, 204n21
Merrill, Philemon C., 5, 175n22
Meser, Erwin W. 110
Michelson, Reed, 7
Millennial Star, 162n13
Miller, James W., 47
Miller, Lonell W., 111, 206n52
missionaries, xxx, 1, 7–10, 14–20, 31, 36, 39, 49–50, 59, 116, 128, 145, 160n3, 173n15; demographics, 172n8; interaction with those of

differing faiths, 102, 108, 214n28; varieties of, 173n15; zeal of, 49–50, 145
Montana Mission, 159n1
Mormonism, ix, xix, xxxi; effect in other countries of, xxxi, 1, 69, 98–99; message of, 8, 86, 102, 113, 116
Moroni, 158
Morton, William A., 153, 230n75
Moses, 133, 134, 156, 219n7, 222n15
Mount Carmel, 143, 149
Mount of Olives, 140, 142
Muir, Edna Walton, 92, 200n13
Muir, William S., 92, 200n12
Mukden (Shenyang), Manchuria, 25
Murdock, John, 161n9

Nagasaki, Japan, 35
Nakazawa, Hajime, 159n2
Nanking (Nanjing), China, 34
Napela, Jonathan H., 44–45, 186n33, n34
Nara, Japan, 23
Nazareth, 148–49, 226n19
Nelson, Alvin Smith, 153, 229n67
Nelson, Chester H., 42, 185n24
Nelson, Ephraim R., 111, 205n39
Nelson, George C., 59, 192n3
Nelson, Raymond P., 106, 116, 202n20, 211n43
Nephi, 5, 175n25
Netherlands Mission, 162n12
New Zealand Mission, 160n6
New Zealand, 4, 68, 107–111; church school in, 110. *See also* Maoris
Nikko, Japan, 20, 23
Nopera, Elliot, 109
Northern States Mission, 162n14, 163n15
Northwestern States Mission, 159n1, 163n15

O'Reilley, Dennis, 91–92, 197n16
Oborn, Clement A., 103, 202n10
"Occidental" civilization, xxvii, 15, 34–35, 126
ocean travel, *plate 3*; 14, 57, 197n27, 201n6, 208n61
Oldroyd, Niels W., 117, 211n49
Olson, Evelyn, 185n12
180th meridian, 14, 32, 82, 177n2
Oneida Stake, 159n1
"Oriental" civilization, xxvii, 15, 34–35, 126, 216n18
Osaka, Japan, 20, 23
Ottley, Ernest A., 111, 205n44

Pacific Islanders, xxxi, 16, 150
Palestine, *plates 53–54*, 1, 137–49
Palmer, William H., 163n15

Papeete, Society Islands: missionaries in, 61, 62
Parata, Rawhate, *plate 32*
Parker, John, 49, 188n35
Parker, Titus, 44
Parkin, Lewis B., 99, 102, 200n11
Parkinson, George C., 159n1
Parry, Alvary H., xi
Parry, Roland C., 75, 108, 196n23, 203n11
Pearce, Elijah F., 160n6
Peking (Beijing), China, 27
Penrose, Charles W., 121, 181n11
Penrose, Wallace H., 49, 189n40
Peterson, Lorenzo E., 93
Phillips, Walter J., 83, 102, 199n8
Plunkett, Robert, 49, 189n41
poi, 73, 108
Pomare, Maui, 69, 195n7
Pratt, Addison, 160n5
Pratt, Orson, 161n9, 162n14
Pratt, Parley P., 162n14
prophecies fulfilled, *plate 53*, 77, 140–41, 158
The Prophet, 162n14
prophets, 5, 8, 23, 76, 102, 151, 158; false, 50, 143
Putnam, Ralph, 99
Pyne, Joseph S., 23, 180n24
pyramids, xxviii, *plate 51, plate 52,* 134–36, 155, 220n21, n22

Quorum of the Twelve Apostles, ix, xix, xx, xxii–xxiv, *plate 2,* 3, 6, 39, 98, 162n14

Rallison, Joshua K., 82, 197n24
Rangoon, Burma, 124–26, 214n24
Raratonga, *plate 27,* 64–67
Rawson, James A., 111, 204n30
Red Sea, 132–33
Reid, Robert, *plate 37,* 86–87
Reiser, A. Hamer, xi–xii
Reorganized Church, 77, 108, 196n9, n10
Reynolds, Harold G., xx
Rich, Charles C., 160n3
Richards, Alice, 176n7
Richards, Ezra F., 160n6
Richards, Karl M., 153, 229n68
Richards, Stephen L., 68, 193n1
Richards, Willard, 162n13
Riggs, Emma Ray, ix, xxiv
rikisha, *plate 5,* xxvii, 15, 177n6
Robinson, George W., 83, 102, 199n7
Rogers, Noah, 160n5
Rome, 150–52, 228n45; catacombs of, 151, 228m50
Romney, Marion G., 116, 211n39
Rossiter, Ernest C., 62, 192n9
Rossiter, Venus R., 62, 192n8

Rotorua, New Zealand, 106
Royal Hawaiian Band, 50, 189n44
Rushton, Don C., 112, 115, 116, 159, 208n4
Rushton, Elizabeth J., 112, 116, 208n7
Russell, Isaac, 162n13

Samoa, xxviii, *plate 33, plates 37–39,* 4, 31, 79–80, 100; culture of, 95–99. *See also* American Samoa, Western Samoa
Samoan Mission, 88, 99, 161n7, n8
Sanders, Sonda, Jr., 161n6
Sauniatu, *plate 35, plates 41–43,* 83, 95–100; band, *plate 42*
Sauniatu Latter-day Saint Band, *plates 35, 42*
Schettler, Paul Augustus, 162n12
Schwendiman, Frederick W., 74, 107, 159, 195n16
Schwendiman, Lillian Austin, 74, 107, 195n15
Scott, Franklin E., 110
The Seer, 162n14
Shandong Province, China, 34
Shanghai, China, 33
Shanghaiguan, 25–26
Sharp, Leo B., 110, 204n19
Shintoism, *plate 10*
sickness on the journey, 6, 9–12, 54, 91, 104, 184n25
Singapore, Philippines, 120, 123, 213n16
Sjodahl, Janne M., 161n10
Smith, David J., 48, 188n25
Smith, E. Wesley, 39, 42, 159, 184n3
Smith, George Albert, xi, 161n9
Smith, Hyrum M., 188n37
Smith, Jacob I., 111, 206n48
Smith, Joseph F., 39, 49, 184n8
Smith, Joseph Fielding, 188n36
Smith, Joseph, Jr., 3, 5, 7, 113, 158, 175n8, 175n23
Smith, Mary H., 39, 184n4
Smith, Thomas G., 114, 115, 209n17
Smith, Willard L., 161n8
Smith, Winslow Farr, 154, 159, 230n82
Smoot, Brigham, 161n8
Snider, John, 162n13
Snow, Lorenzo, 162n11
Society Islands, 58, 59–63. *See also* Tahitian Islands
South Sea Islands, 3, 14, 83, 102
Spence, William C., xxiii
Sphinx, xxviii, *plate 52,* 134–35, 156, 220n22
Spori, Jacob, 161n10
Stallings, Warren J., 108, 203n12
Stanger, Edward M., 111, 204n31
Stephenson, Joseph M., 110, 204n24
Stevenson, Edward, 159n1

Stevenson, Robert Louis, *plate 45*, *plate 46*, 87, 199n21
Stewart, Melvin C., 111, 205n34
Stimpson, Joseph H., xx, *plate 4*, 19–21, 23, 37, 159, 174n22, 177n3
Stimpson, Mary E., 19, 20, 177n5
Stone, Leslie F., 47, 187n11
Stott, Franklin E., 74, 196n18
Stott, Leland H., 200n9
Stott, May Ida F., 74, 195n17
Stout, Hosea, 25
Strong, Melvin, 59
Suez Canal, 133, 149
Sullivan, Louis R., 43, 52, 186n30, 189n49
Swan, Ben E., 47
Swiss and German Mission, x, xxxi, 162n11, n12
Syria, 143–44

Tahitian Islands, 58, 106. *See also* Society Islands
Tahitian Mission, xxix, 62, 160n5
Taj Mahal, *plate 49*, 129, 156
Talmage, James E., 146
Talmage, May Booth, 146
Tanner, Joseph M., 161n10
Tasmania, 114–15, 161n9
Taylor, Alma O., 159n2
Taylor, George S., 68, 74, 106, 107, 193n3
Taylor, Ida A., 74, 195n11
Taylor, Miriam, 74, 195n12
Taylor, Priscilla, 74, 197n21
Tenyo Maru, *plate 16*, 37
Thacker, Ralph A., *plate 37*, 86, 199n20
Thornton, James A., 106, 202n18
Tianjin, China, 33
Tingey, Gilbert R., 83, 87, 199n6
Tofua, 4, 79, 80, 81, 82, 100, 105
Tokyo, Japan, 20
Tolman, Austin S., 115, 210n33
Tonga, 101, 102; culture, 104–5. *See also* Friendly Islands
Tongan Mission, 80, 161n8
Tonks, Warren, 111, 205n35
transportation, xix, *plate 7*, 7, 26, 27, 119, 121, 134, 136, 145, 154; technologies, xxiv–xxviii, xxx–xxxi, 34

Tugi, Uiliamo, 102
Turkish Mission, 161n10
Tutuila, Samoa, 91–93
Tweed, Thomas A., xxv, xxix

Ulimaroa, 111, 112
Union Stake, 159n1

Van der Woude, A. Wiegers, 162n12
Vavau, 81, 101, 104, 197n27
A Voice of Warning, 162n14

Waddoups, Olevia S., 41, 185n20
Waddoups, Thomas M., 185n17
Waddoups, William M., 41, 48, 185n19
Wagoner, Lee Van, 39
Walker, Wallace O., 114, 210n26
Wandell, Charles W., 161n9
Warner, William C., 106, 115, 203n22
Weaver, Kenneth C., 49, 188n32
Weiler, Joseph, 162n12
Western Samoa, 82–87
Wheelock, Cyrus H., 163n15
Whitney, Orson F., 153, 159, 230n73
Whittaker, Louring A., 23, 179n21
Wiberg, Reuben, 81, 198n29
Wilcox, Cleon J., 83, 199n9
Wilcox, Francis L., 106, 202n19
Williams, Lester, 42, 185n25
Willie, Leon, 111, 204n33
Winder, Alma Cannon, 47, 186n5
Winder, Edwin K., 46, 186n3
Winder, John R., 46, 186n4
Winn, George S., 111, 206n49
Witbeck, Chauncey L., 83, 199n10
Wood, Edward J., 88, 161n7, 200n3
Woodruff, Wilford, 34, 183n15
Woolley, Samuel E., 43, 186n29
Wulffenstein, Bengt P., 163n15
Wunderlich, Jean, 152

Yangtze River, 34
Yokohama, 9, 15
Young, Brigham, 160n5, 196n1
Young, Gordon C., 75, 196n22
Young, Levi Edgar, 56, 190n5

Zimmer, Max, 152
Zion's Watchman, 161n9